STAR BRAND
CLASSIC

STAR BRAND CLASSIC

Writers: Jim Shooter with Roy Thomas
Pencilers: John Romita Jr. & Alex Saviuk
Inkers: Al Williamson, Vince Colletta,
Rick Bryant, Al Milgrom & Art Nichols

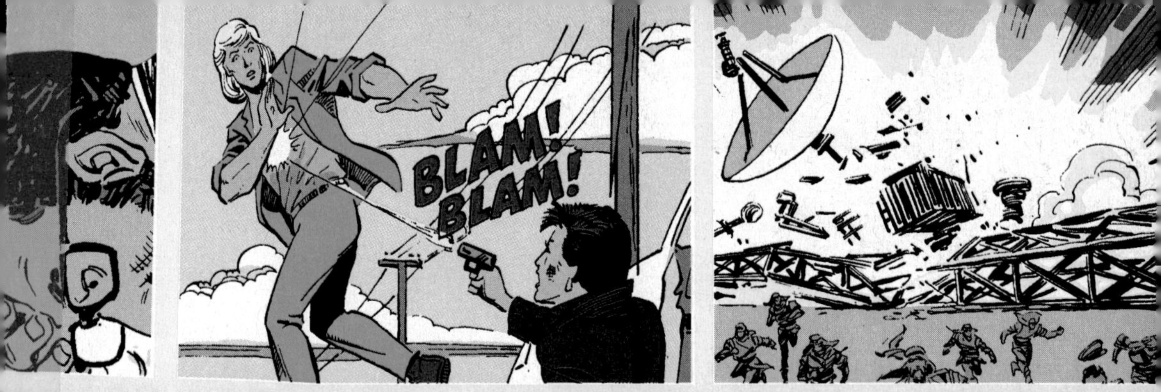
BLAM! BLAM!

Colorists: Christie Scheele, George Roussos,
Bob Sharen & Janet Jackson
Letterers: Joe Rosen & Rick Parker
Editor: Michael Higgins

Cover Art: John Romita Jr.
Cover Colors: Tom Smith
Select Color Reconstruction: Gotham

Collection Editor: Mark D. Beazley
Assistant Editor: Michael Short
Associate Editor: Jennifer Grünwald
Senior Editor, Special Projects: Jeff Youngquist
Vice President of Sales: David Gabriel
Book Designer: Dayle Chesler
Vice President of Creative: Tom Marvelli

Editor in Chief: Joe Quesada
Publisher: Dan Buckley

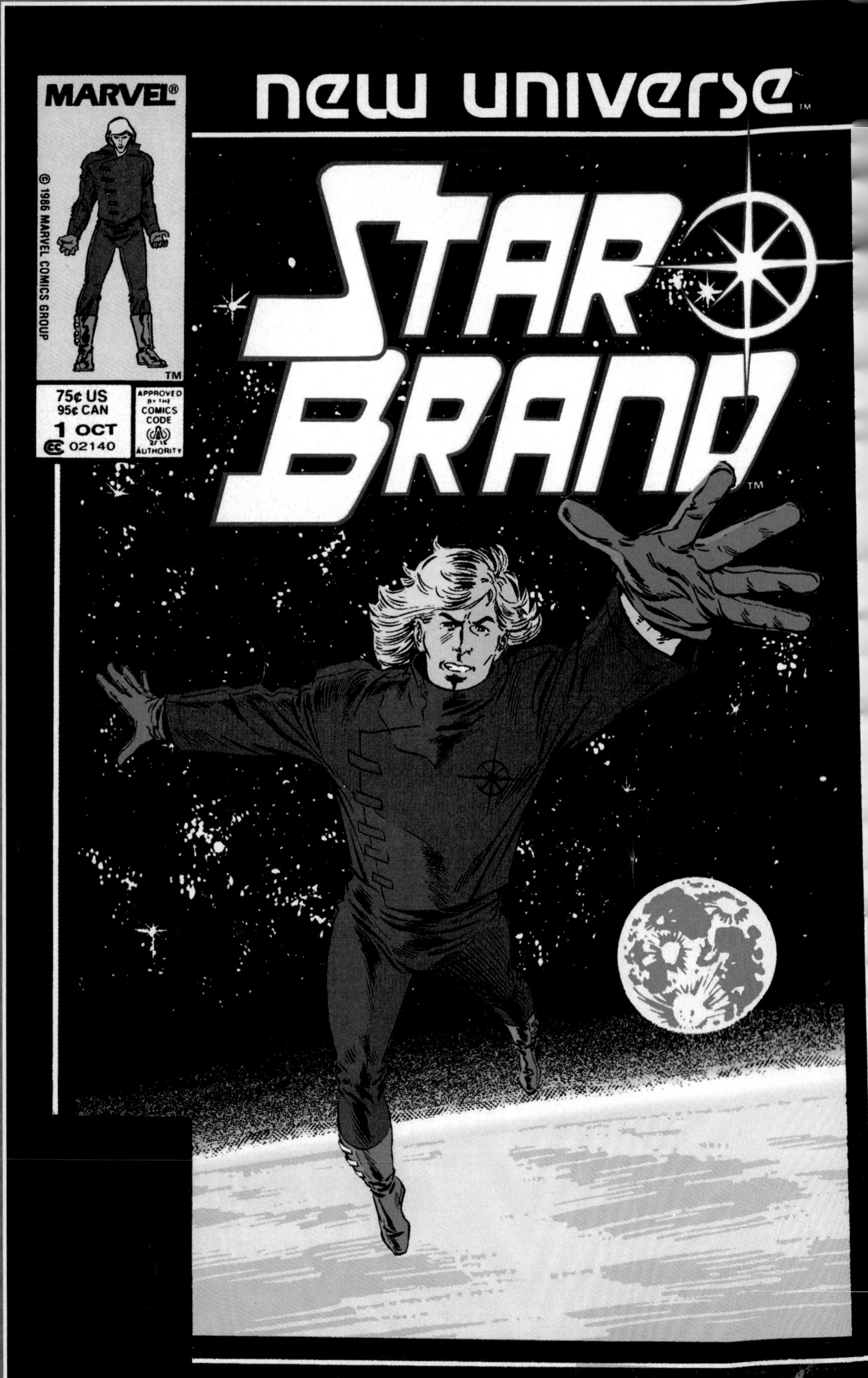

MARVEL®
© 1986 MARVEL COMICS GROUP
TM
75¢ US
95¢ CAN
1 OCT
02140
APPROVED BY THE COMICS CODE AUTHORITY
new universe™
STAR BRAND™

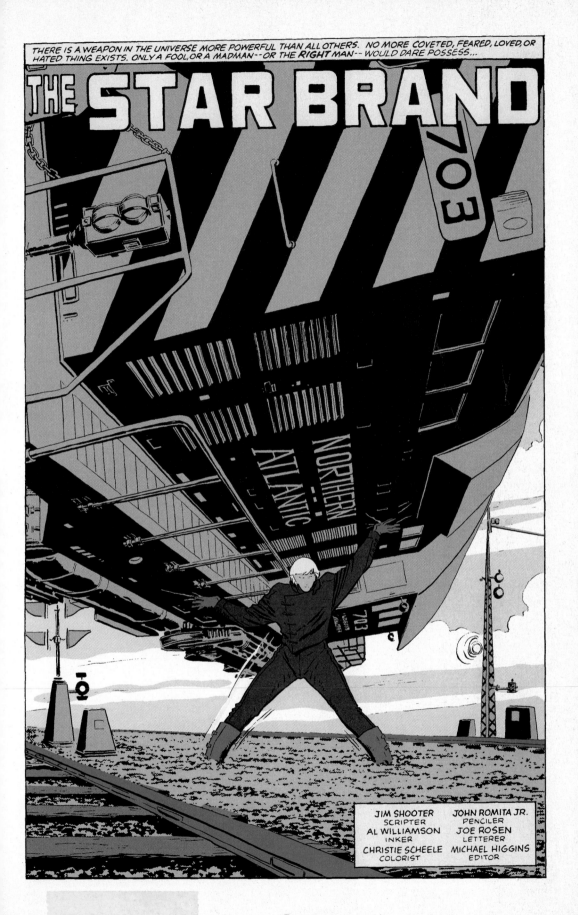

THERE IS A WEAPON IN THE UNIVERSE MORE POWERFUL THAN ALL OTHERS. NO MORE COVETED, FEARED, LOVED, OR HATED THING EXISTS. ONLY A FOOL, OR A MADMAN--OR THE *RIGHT* MAN--WOULD DARE POSSESS...

THE STAR BRAND

JIM SHOOTER SCRIPTER	JOHN ROMITA JR. PENCILER
AL WILLIAMSON INKER	JOE ROSEN LETTERER
CHRISTIE SCHEELE COLORIST	MICHAEL HIGGINS EDITOR

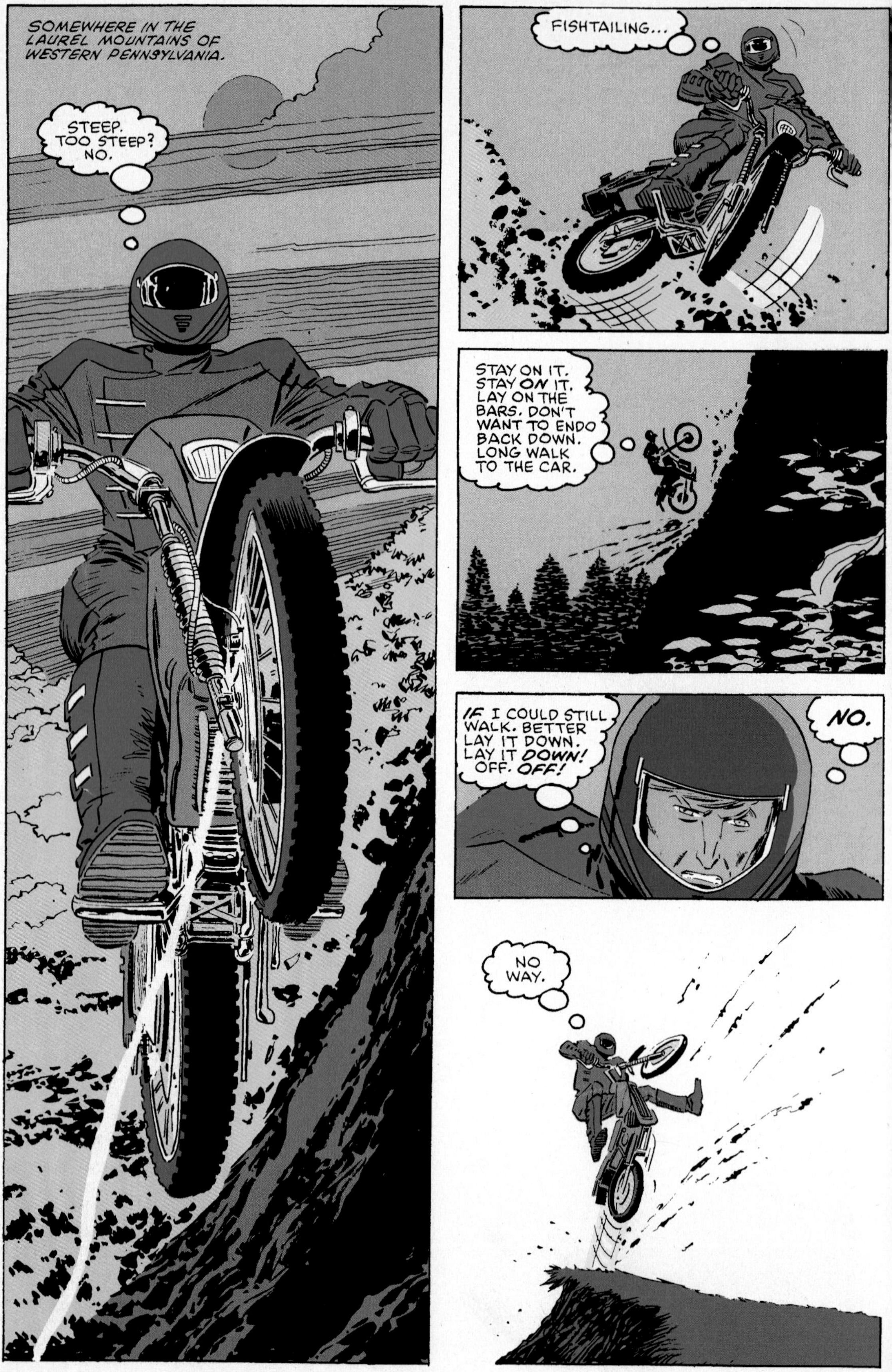
SOMEWHERE IN THE LAUREL MOUNTAINS OF WESTERN PENNSYLVANIA.
STEEP. TOO STEEP? NO.
FISHTAILING...
STAY ON IT. STAY ON IT. LAY ON THE BARS. DON'T WANT TO ENDO BACK DOWN. LONG WALK TO THE CAR.
IF I COULD STILL WALK. BETTER LAY IT DOWN. LAY IT DOWN! OFF. OFF!
NO.
NO WAY.

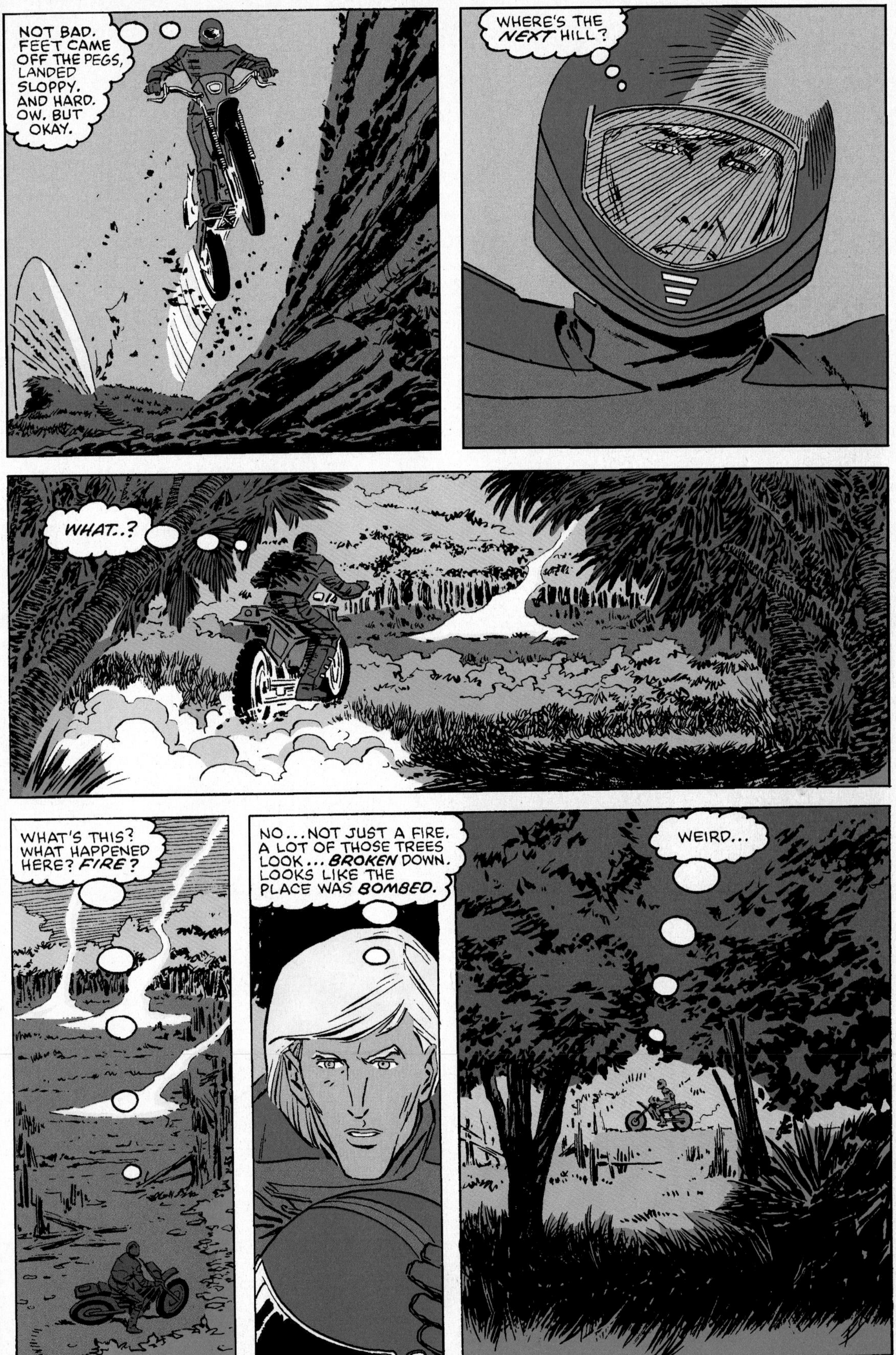
NOT BAD. FEET CAME OFF THE PEGS, LANDED SLOPPY. AND HARD. OW. BUT OKAY.
WHERE'S THE NEXT HILL?
WHAT..?
WHAT'S THIS? WHAT HAPPENED HERE? FIRE?
NO... NOT JUST A FIRE. A LOT OF THOSE TREES LOOK... BROKEN DOWN. LOOKS LIKE THE PLACE WAS BOMBED.
WEIRD...

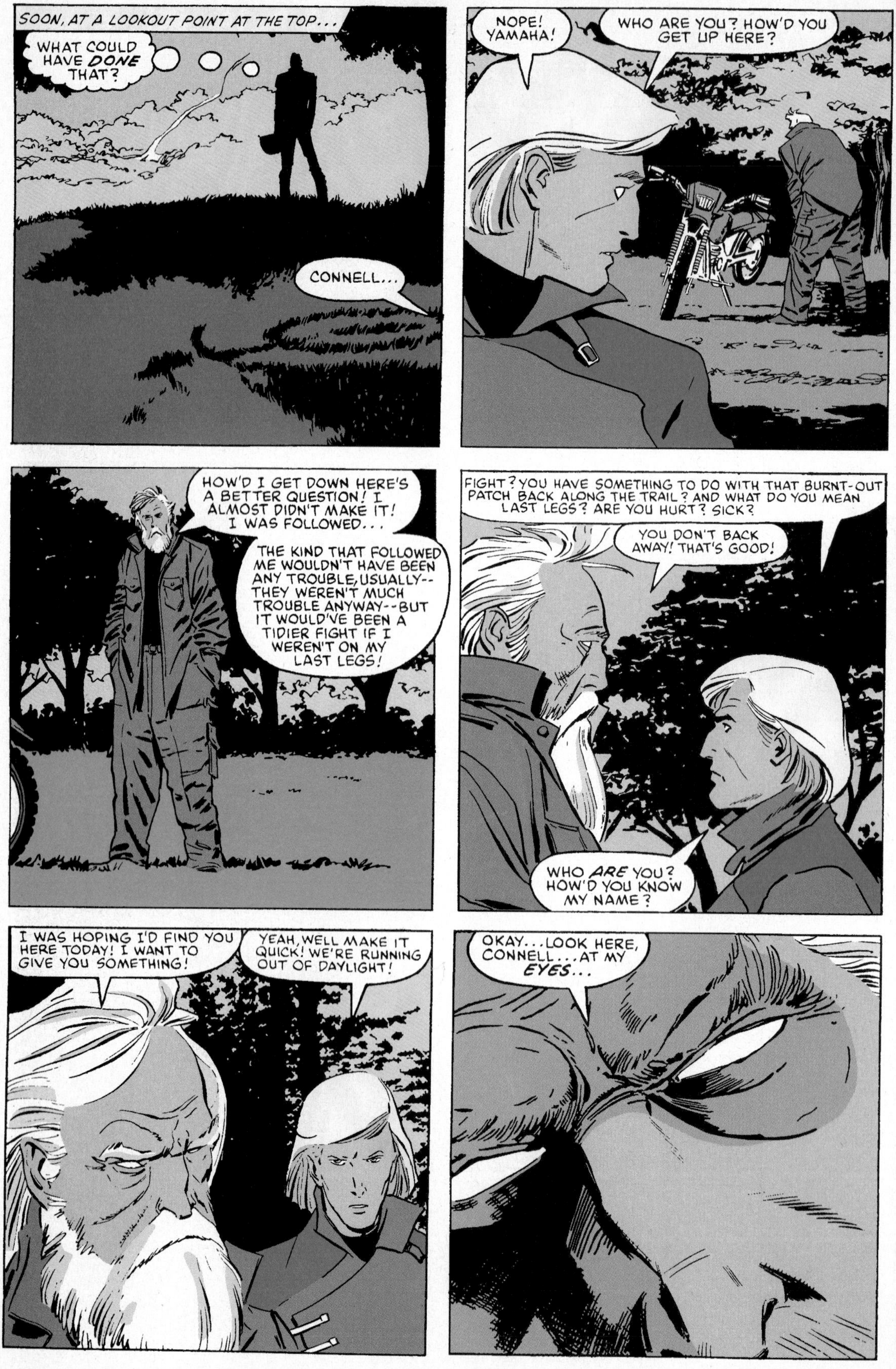
SOON, AT A LOOKOUT POINT AT THE TOP...
WHAT COULD HAVE DONE THAT?
CONNELL...
NOPE! YAMAHA!
WHO ARE YOU? HOW'D YOU GET UP HERE?
HOW'D I GET DOWN HERE'S A BETTER QUESTION! I ALMOST DIDN'T MAKE IT! I WAS FOLLOWED...
THE KIND THAT FOLLOWED ME WOULDN'T HAVE BEEN ANY TROUBLE, USUALLY-- THEY WEREN'T MUCH TROUBLE ANYWAY--BUT IT WOULD'VE BEEN A TIDIER FIGHT IF I WEREN'T ON MY LAST LEGS!
FIGHT? YOU HAVE SOMETHING TO DO WITH THAT BURNT-OUT PATCH BACK ALONG THE TRAIL? AND WHAT DO YOU MEAN LAST LEGS? ARE YOU HURT? SICK?
YOU DON'T BACK AWAY! THAT'S GOOD!
WHO ARE YOU? HOW'D YOU KNOW MY NAME?
I WAS HOPING I'D FIND YOU HERE TODAY! I WANT TO GIVE YOU SOMETHING!
YEAH, WELL MAKE IT QUICK! WE'RE RUNNING OUT OF DAYLIGHT!
OKAY... LOOK HERE, CONNELL... AT MY EYES...

HUH...

MORNING..? WHAT AM I DOING *HERE?*

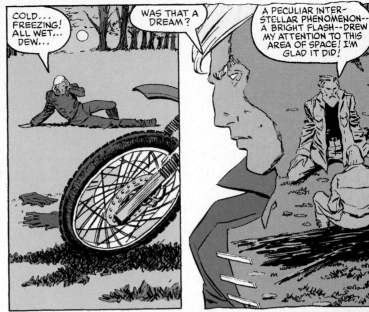

COLD... FREEZING! ALL WET... DEW...

WAS THAT A DREAM?

A PECULIAR INTER-STELLAR PHENOMENON-- A BRIGHT FLASH--DREW MY ATTENTION TO THIS AREA OF SPACE! I'M GLAD IT DID!

I'VE BEEN LOOKING FOR SOMEONE LIKE YOU FOR A LONG TIME! BEINGS LIKE YOU--AND ME--ARE A RARE BREED!

I SUPPOSE I DIDN'T PLAN THIS VERY WELL...YOU SEE, TIME IS RUNNING OUT FOR ME! I'M DYING! IF YOU WEREN'T AGREEABLE... WELL, I'M JUST GLAD YOU ARE!

THINK OF IT AS A TATTOO...

JUST PUT YOUR HAND ON IT! I'LL DO THE REST! DON'T WORRY, IF YOU DON'T WANT IT ON YOUR PALM YOU CAN *MOVE* IT LATER.

ON MY... *PALM--?*

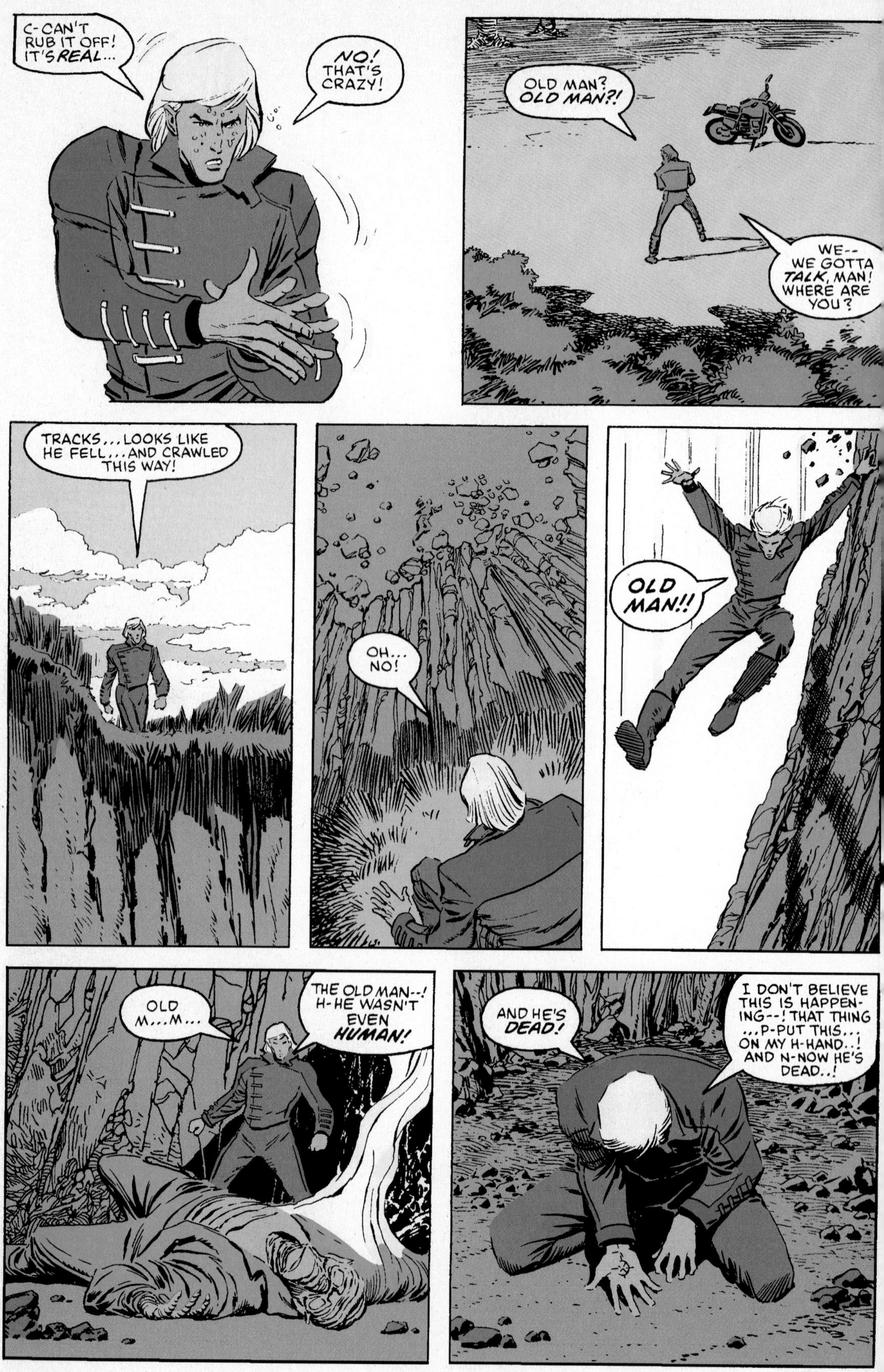
C-CAN'T RUB IT OFF! IT'S REAL...
NO! THAT'S CRAZY!
OLD MAN? OLD MAN?!
WE-- WE GOTTA TALK, MAN! WHERE ARE YOU?
TRACKS... LOOKS LIKE HE FELL... AND CRAWLED THIS WAY!
OH... NO!
OLD MAN!!
OLD M...M...
THE OLD MAN--! H-HE WASN'T EVEN HUMAN!
AND HE'S DEAD!
I DON'T BELIEVE THIS IS HAPPENING--! THAT THING ...P-PUT THIS... ON MY H-HAND..! AND N-NOW HE'S DEAD..!

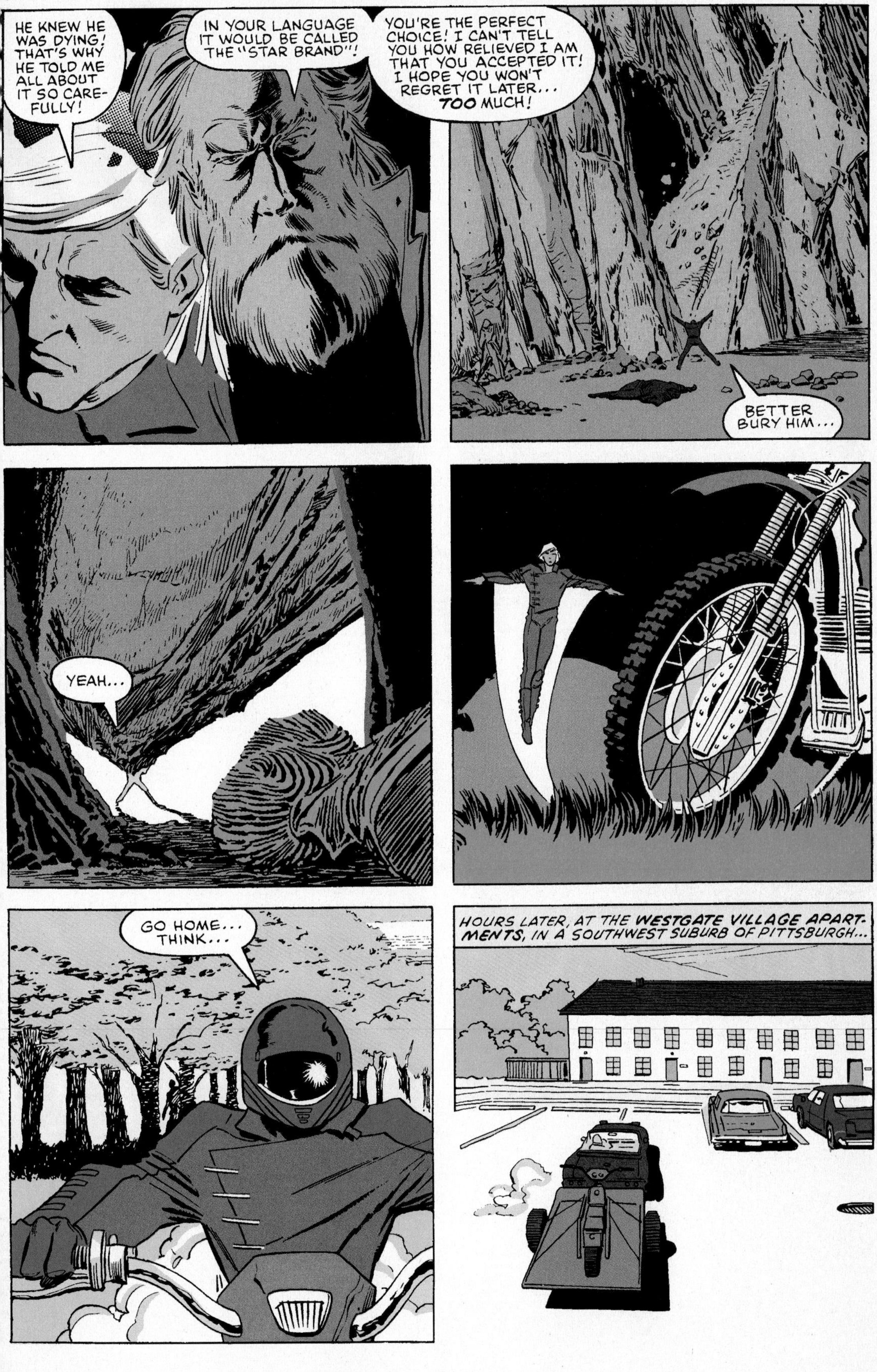
HE KNEW HE WAS DYING! THAT'S WHY HE TOLD ME ALL ABOUT IT SO CAREFULLY!
IN YOUR LANGUAGE IT WOULD BE CALLED THE "STAR BRAND"!
YOU'RE THE PERFECT CHOICE! I CAN'T TELL YOU HOW RELIEVED I AM THAT YOU ACCEPTED IT! I HOPE YOU WON'T REGRET IT LATER... TOO MUCH!
BETTER BURY HIM...
YEAH...
GO HOME... THINK...
HOURS LATER, AT THE WESTGATE VILLAGE APARTMENTS, IN A SOUTHWEST SUBURB OF PITTSBURGH...

WOW...

I CAN FEEL IT! IT'S ALWAYS WARMER THAN THE REST OF MY SKIN!

AND WHEN I THINK ABOUT IT-- CONCENTRATE, LIKE NOW--THE WARMTH SPREADS! IT SORT OF FLOWS... AND FILLS UP MY WHOLE BODY!

IT'S LIKE...IT *BECOMES* MY BODY-- AND THE REAL ME IS JUST...SMOKE...NOTHING...A TEMPLATE THAT TELLS MY ENERGY BODY WHAT SHAPE TO TAKE!

I DON'T LOOK ANY DIFFERENT... BUT THE FEELING IS INDESCRIBABLE...

...LIKE NOTHING CAN HURT ME!

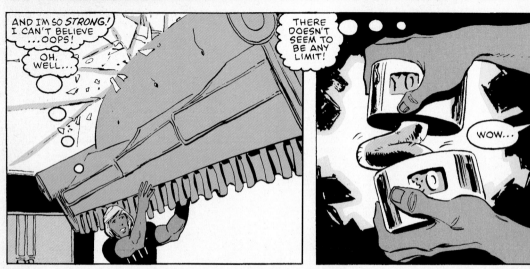

AND I'M SO *STRONG!* I CAN'T BELIEVE ...OOPS!

OH, WELL...

THERE DOESN'T SEEM TO BE ANY LIMIT!

WOW...

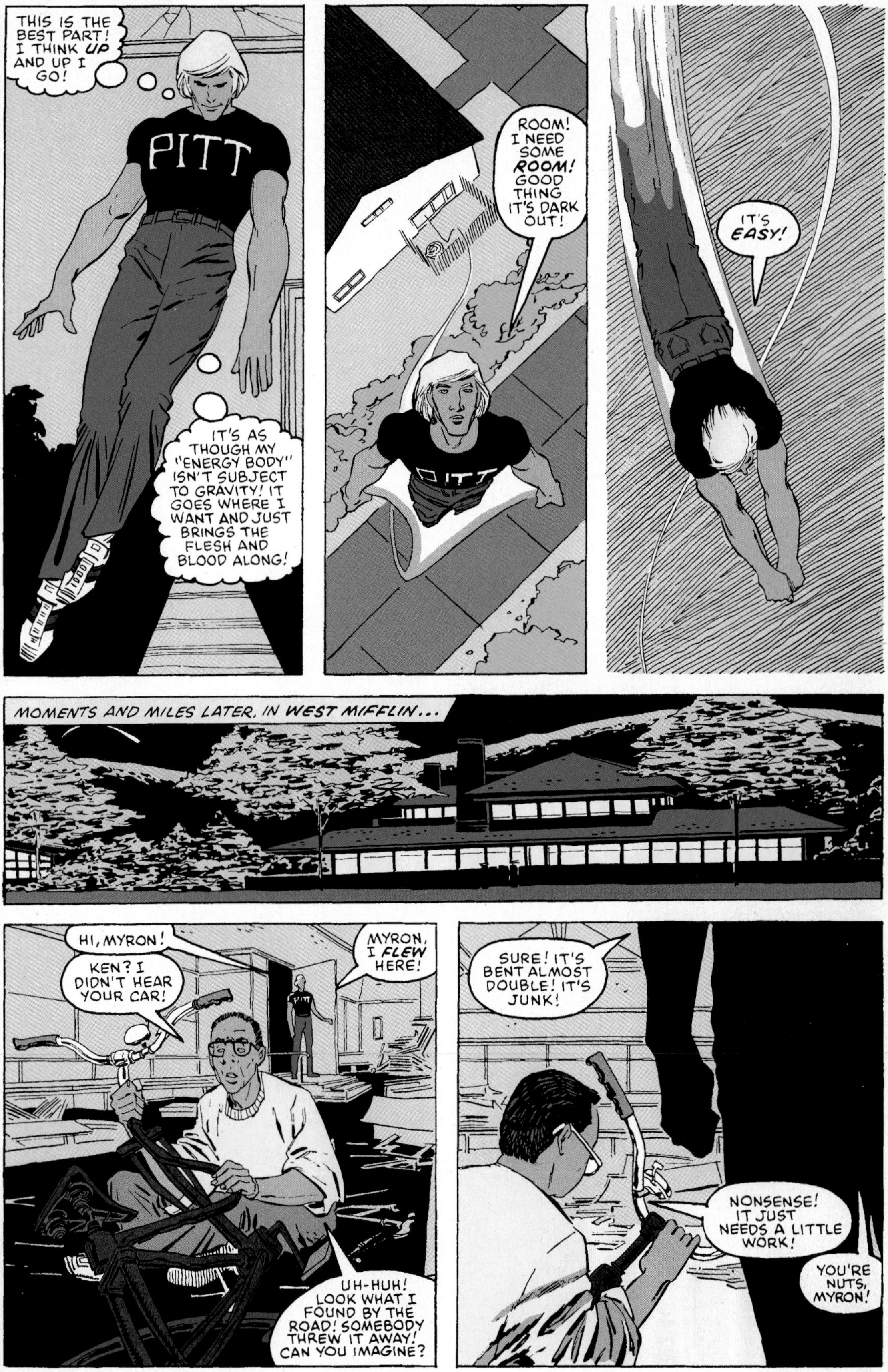
THIS IS THE BEST PART! I THINK UP AND UP I GO!
IT'S AS THOUGH MY "ENERGY BODY" ISN'T SUBJECT TO GRAVITY! IT GOES WHERE I WANT AND JUST BRINGS THE FLESH AND BLOOD ALONG!
ROOM! I NEED SOME ROOM! GOOD THING IT'S DARK OUT!
IT'S EASY!
MOMENTS AND MILES LATER, IN WEST MIFFLIN...
HI, MYRON!
KEN? I DIDN'T HEAR YOUR CAR!
MYRON, I FLEW HERE!
UH-HUH! LOOK WHAT I FOUND BY THE ROAD! SOMEBODY THREW IT AWAY! CAN YOU IMAGINE?
SURE! IT'S BENT ALMOST DOUBLE! IT'S JUNK!
NONSENSE! IT JUST NEEDS A LITTLE WORK!
YOU'RE NUTS, MYRON!

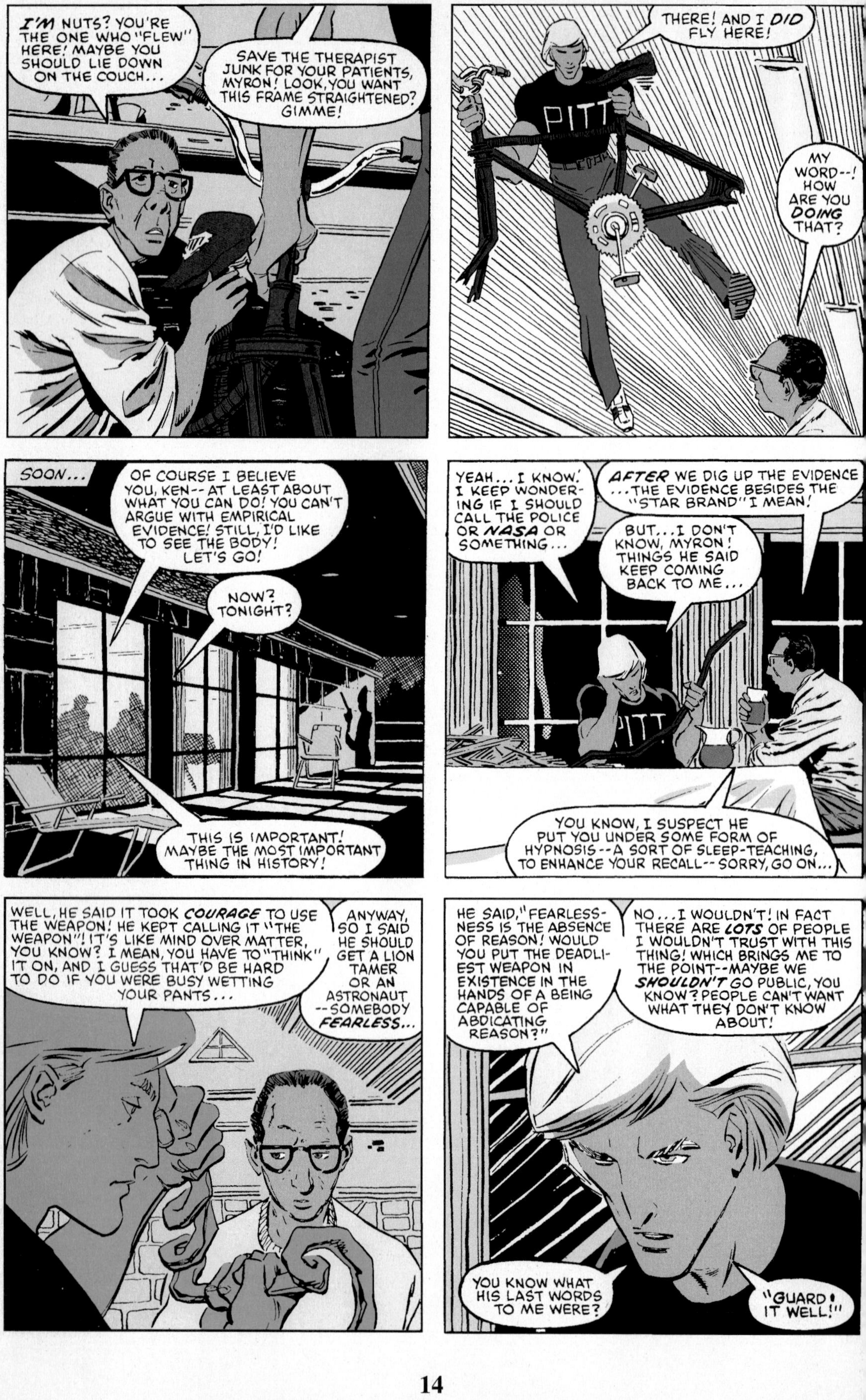
I'M NUTS? YOU'RE THE ONE WHO "FLEW" HERE! MAYBE YOU SHOULD LIE DOWN ON THE COUCH...
SAVE THE THERAPIST JUNK FOR YOUR PATIENTS, MYRON! LOOK, YOU WANT THIS FRAME STRAIGHTENED? GIMME!
THERE! AND I DID FLY HERE!
PITT
MY WORD--! HOW ARE YOU DOING THAT?
SOON...
OF COURSE I BELIEVE YOU, KEN-- AT LEAST ABOUT WHAT YOU CAN DO! YOU CAN'T ARGUE WITH EMPIRICAL EVIDENCE! STILL, I'D LIKE TO SEE THE BODY! LET'S GO!
NOW? TONIGHT?
THIS IS IMPORTANT! MAYBE THE MOST IMPORTANT THING IN HISTORY!
YEAH... I KNOW! I KEEP WONDERING IF I SHOULD CALL THE POLICE OR NASA OR SOMETHING...
AFTER WE DIG UP THE EVIDENCE ...THE EVIDENCE BESIDES THE "STAR BRAND" I MEAN!
BUT... I DON'T KNOW, MYRON! THINGS HE SAID KEEP COMING BACK TO ME...
PITT
YOU KNOW, I SUSPECT HE PUT YOU UNDER SOME FORM OF HYPNOSIS--A SORT OF SLEEP-TEACHING, TO ENHANCE YOUR RECALL--SORRY, GO ON...
WELL, HE SAID IT TOOK COURAGE TO USE THE WEAPON! HE KEPT CALLING IT "THE WEAPON"! IT'S LIKE MIND OVER MATTER, YOU KNOW? I MEAN, YOU HAVE TO "THINK" IT ON, AND I GUESS THAT'D BE HARD TO DO IF YOU WERE BUSY WETTING YOUR PANTS...
ANYWAY, SO I SAID HE SHOULD GET A LION TAMER OR AN ASTRONAUT --SOMEBODY FEARLESS...
HE SAID, "FEARLESSNESS IS THE ABSENCE OF REASON! WOULD YOU PUT THE DEADLIEST WEAPON IN EXISTENCE IN THE HANDS OF A BEING CAPABLE OF ABDICATING REASON?"
NO... I WOULDN'T! IN FACT THERE ARE LOTS OF PEOPLE I WOULDN'T TRUST WITH THIS THING! WHICH BRINGS ME TO THE POINT--MAYBE WE SHOULDN'T GO PUBLIC, YOU KNOW? PEOPLE CAN'T WANT WHAT THEY DON'T KNOW ABOUT!
YOU KNOW WHAT HIS LAST WORDS TO ME WERE?
"GUARD IT WELL!"

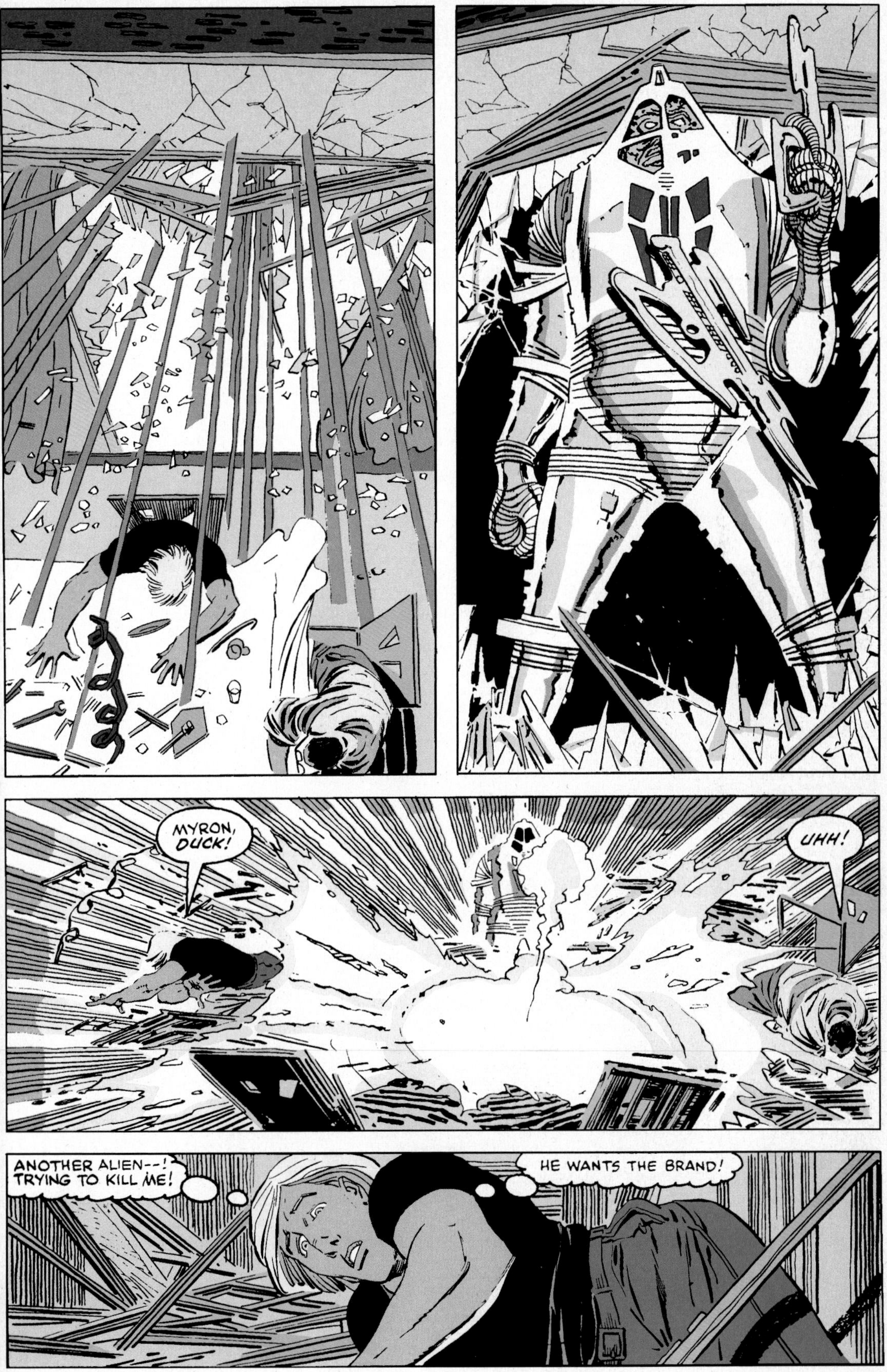

MYRON, DUCK!
UHH!
ANOTHER ALIEN--! TRYING TO KILL ME!
HE WANTS THE BRAND!

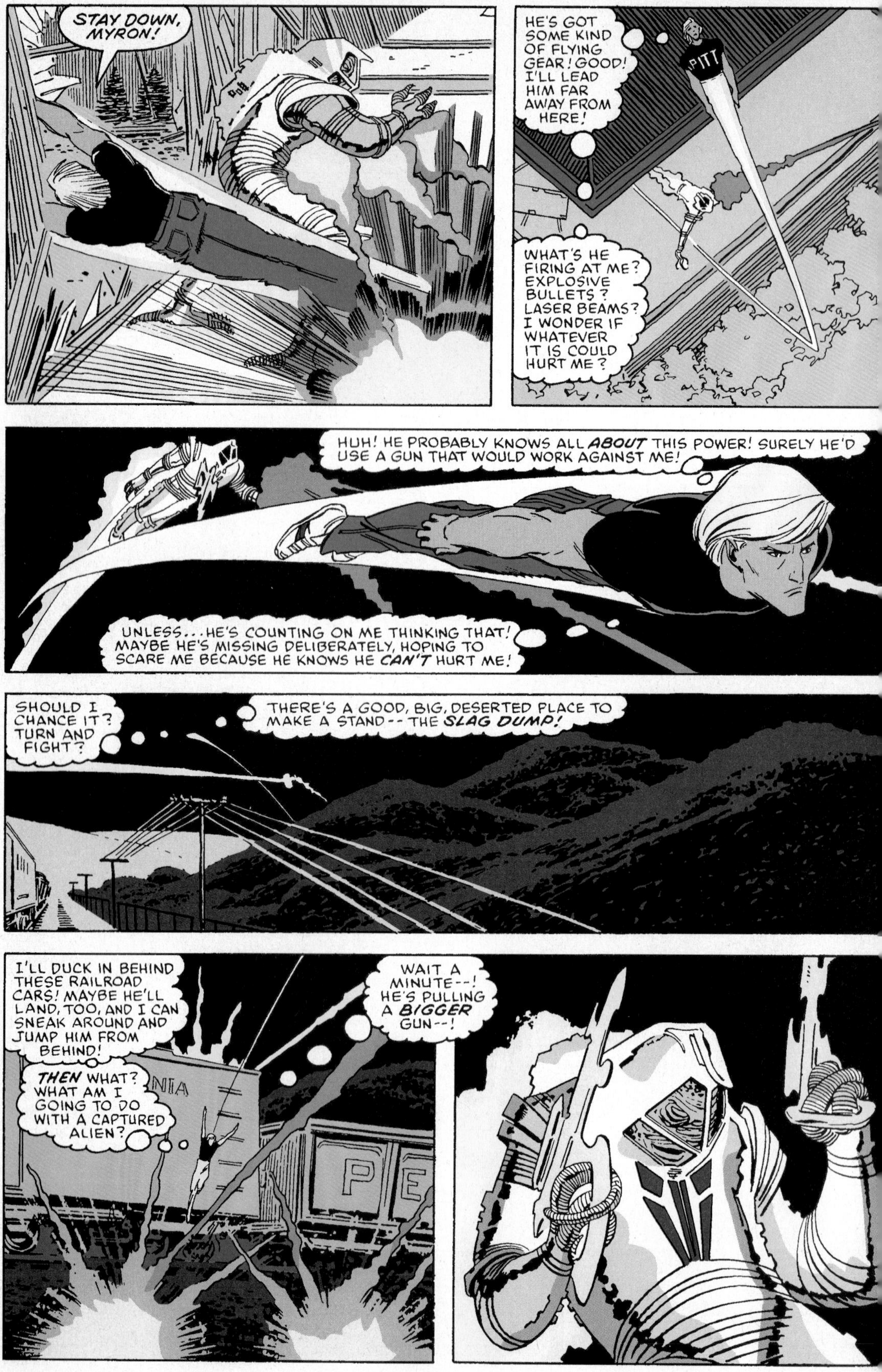
STAY DOWN, MYRON!
HE'S GOT SOME KIND OF FLYING GEAR! GOOD! I'LL LEAD HIM FAR AWAY FROM HERE!
PITT
WHAT'S HE FIRING AT ME? EXPLOSIVE BULLETS? LASER BEAMS? I WONDER IF WHATEVER IT IS COULD HURT ME?
HUH! HE PROBABLY KNOWS ALL ABOUT THIS POWER! SURELY HE'D USE A GUN THAT WOULD WORK AGAINST ME!
UNLESS...HE'S COUNTING ON ME THINKING THAT! MAYBE HE'S MISSING DELIBERATELY, HOPING TO SCARE ME BECAUSE HE KNOWS HE CAN'T HURT ME!
SHOULD I CHANCE IT? TURN AND FIGHT?
THERE'S A GOOD, BIG, DESERTED PLACE TO MAKE A STAND-- THE SLAG DUMP!
I'LL DUCK IN BEHIND THESE RAILROAD CARS! MAYBE HE'LL LAND, TOO, AND I CAN SNEAK AROUND AND JUMP HIM FROM BEHIND!
THEN WHAT? WHAT AM I GOING TO DO WITH A CAPTURED ALIEN?
WAIT A MINUTE--! HE'S PULLING A BIGGER GUN--!

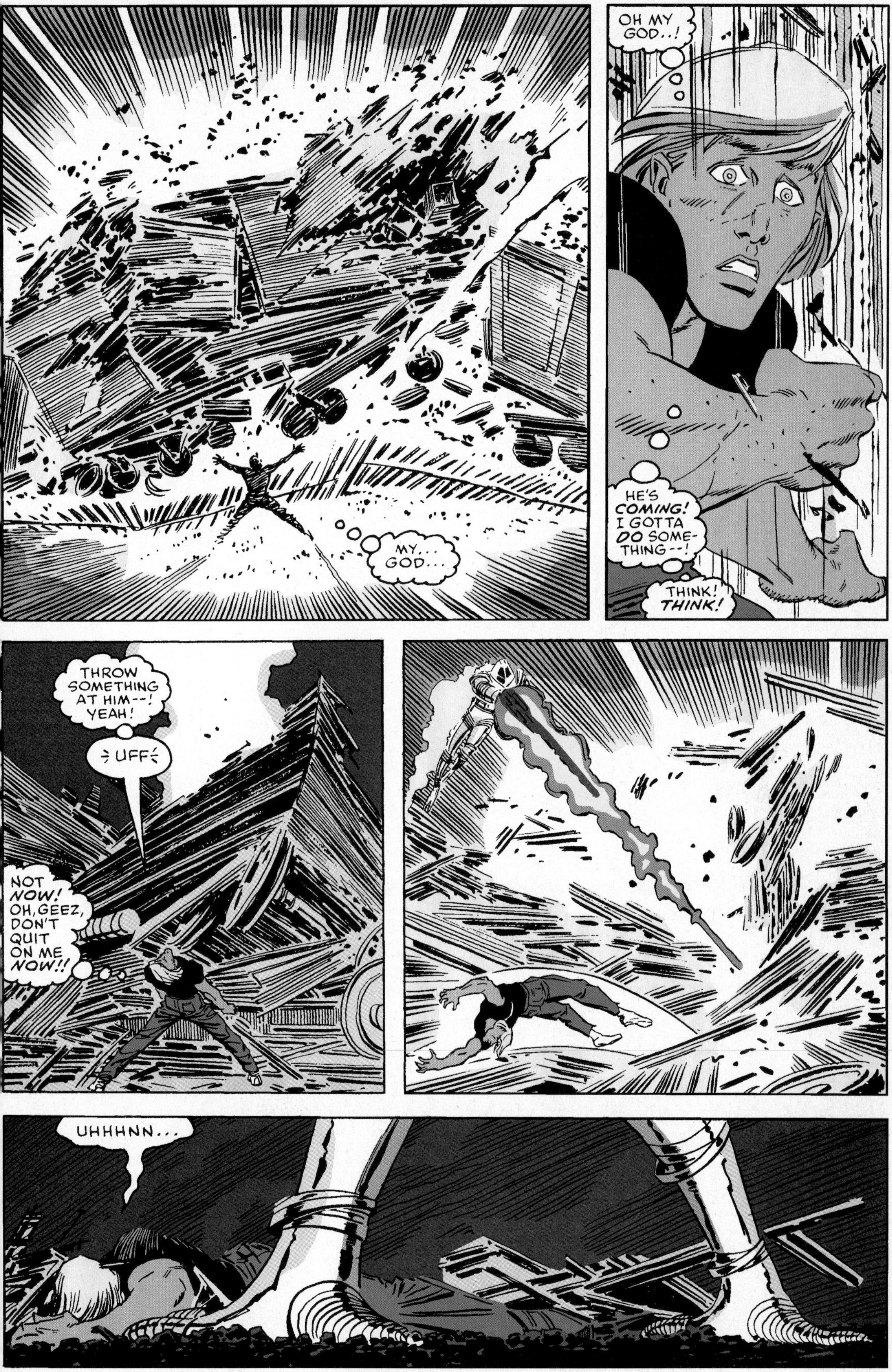
MY... GOD...
OH MY GOD..!
HE'S COMING! I GOTTA DO SOMETHING--!
THINK! THINK!
THROW SOMETHING AT HIM--! YEAH!
UFF
NOT NOW! OH, GEEZ, DON'T QUIT ON ME NOW!!
UHHHNN...

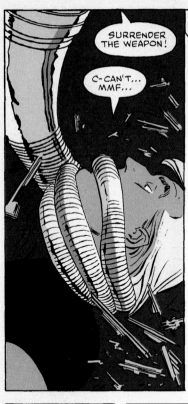

SURRENDER
THE WEAPON!

C-CAN'T...
MMF...

LISTEN TO ME!
LISTEN TO THE
TRUTH...

THE OLD MAN DECEIVED YOU.
HE WAS NOT DYING. HE IS
NOT DEAD!

YOU HAVE BEEN DUPED
INTO PLAYING A ROLE IN
AN INTRIGUE YOU CANNOT
BEGIN TO COMPREHEND--
A ROLE THAT WILL BRING
PAIN, SUFFERING, AND
DEATH TO YOU...

...AND UNIVERSAL
DOMINATION TO THE
OLD MAN AND HIS
ILK,

UNLESS...YOU
GIVE ME THE
WEAPON!

DO NOT
FORCE ME TO
TERMINATE
YOU!

GIVE IT TO ME! LET IT
GO! YOU ARE WEAK!
I AM STRONG! I SHALL
PROTECT IT! I SHALL
USE IT TO PROTECT
THE UNIVERSE! I AM
THE PERFECT ONE TO
POSSESS THE POWER
OF THE WEAPON!

BUT...
THE OLD
MAN SAID
I WAS...

SO
TIRED!
GIVE IT
UP?

NO! BUT...HE'S
PULLING IT
AWAY!

FIGHT BACK!
FIGHT BACK!
HOLD ON TO IT!
DON'T WANT TO
LOSE IT! LONG
WALK HOME...

WHAT AM I
THINKING--? HE'S
GOING TO KILL
ME! BETTER LET
IT GO! GIVE UP!
GIVE UP!

NO!

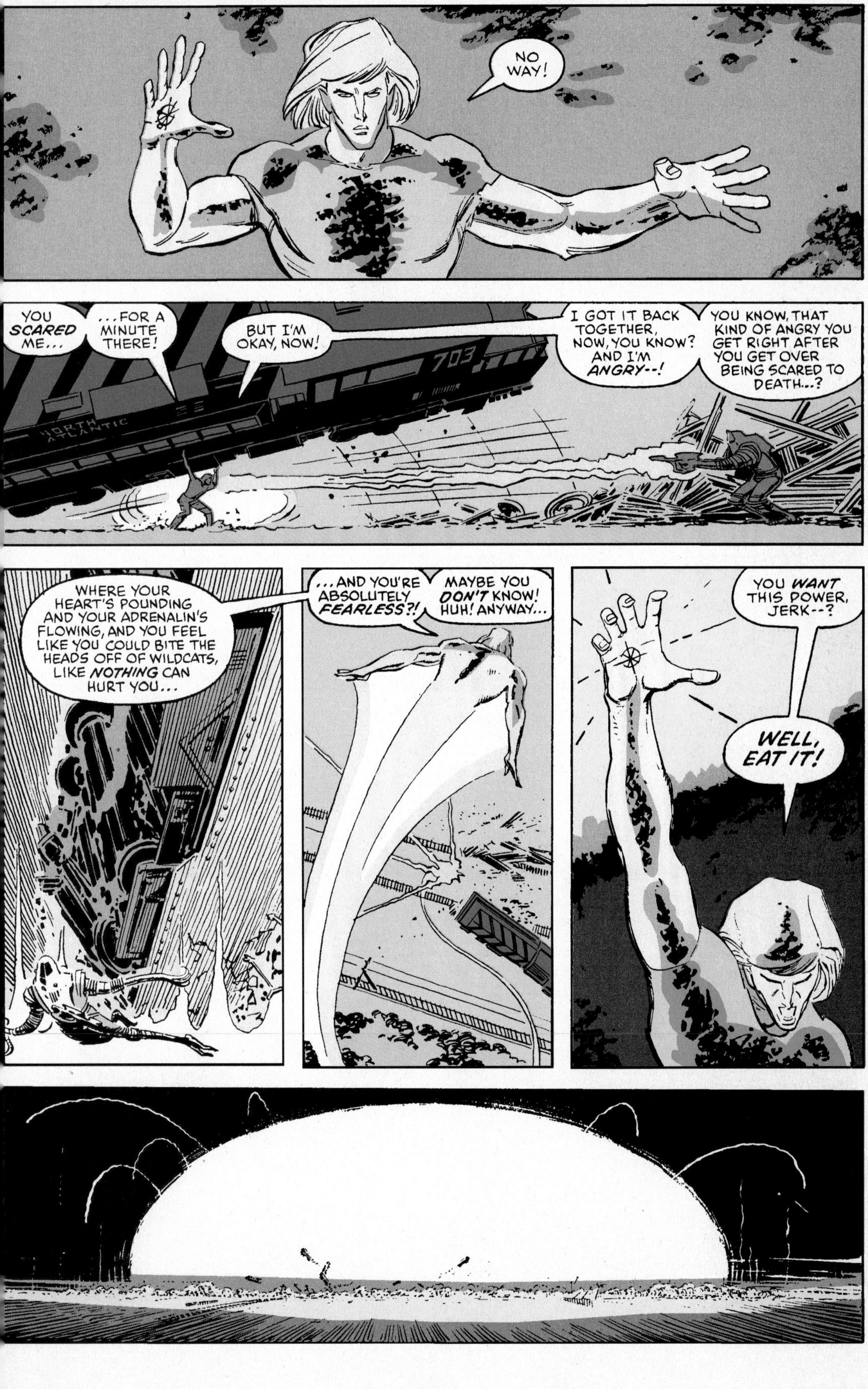
NO WAY!
YOU SCARED ME...
...FOR A MINUTE THERE!
BUT I'M OKAY, NOW!
I GOT IT BACK TOGETHER, NOW, YOU KNOW? AND I'M ANGRY--!
YOU KNOW, THAT KIND OF ANGRY YOU GET RIGHT AFTER YOU GET OVER BEING SCARED TO DEATH...?
703
NORTH ATLANTIC
WHERE YOUR HEART'S POUNDING AND YOUR ADRENALIN'S FLOWING, AND YOU FEEL LIKE YOU COULD BITE THE HEADS OFF OF WILDCATS, LIKE NOTHING CAN HURT YOU...
...AND YOU'RE ABSOLUTELY FEARLESS?!
MAYBE YOU DON'T KNOW! HUH! ANYWAY...
YOU WANT THIS POWER, JERK--?
WELL, EAT IT!

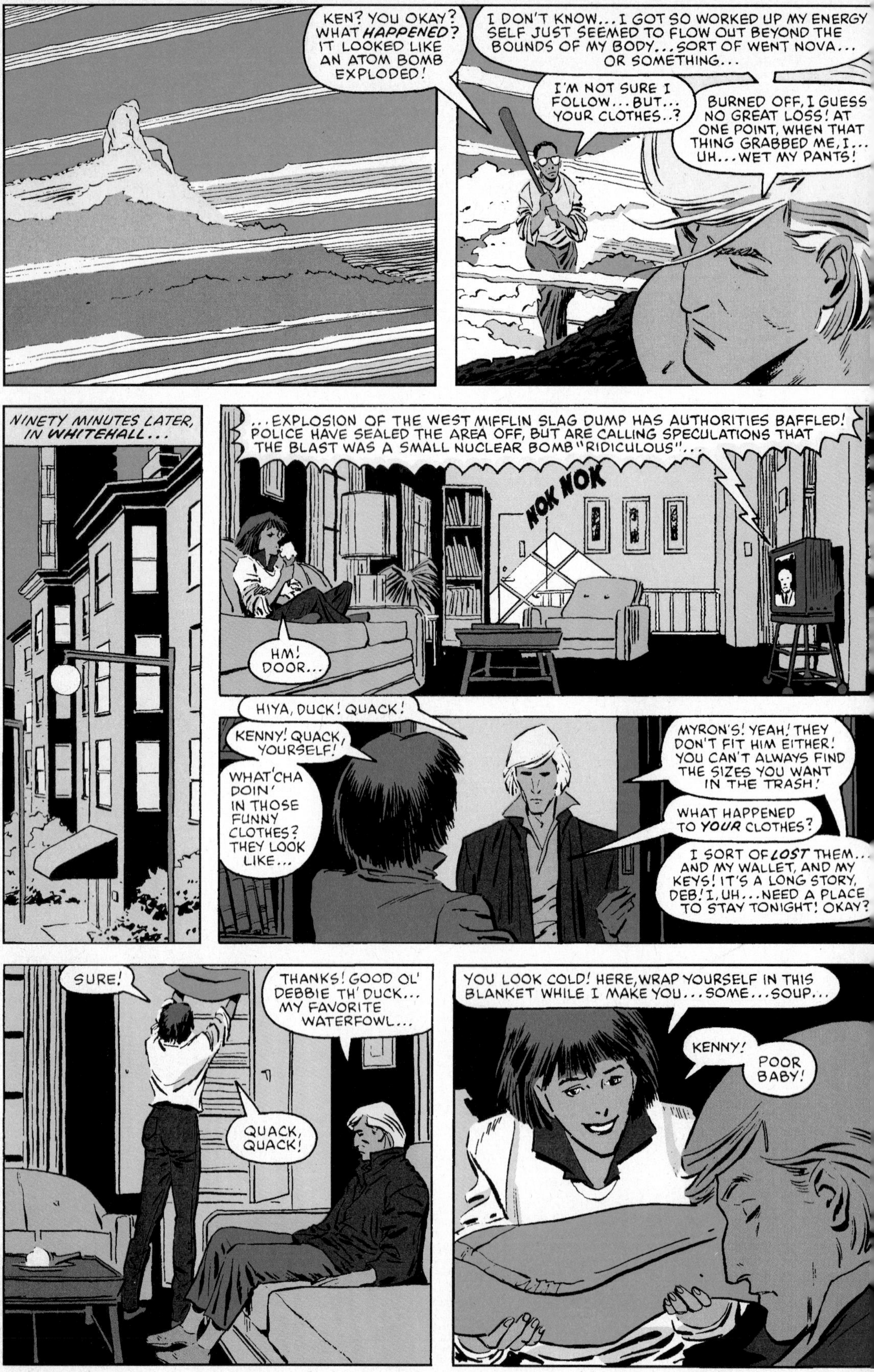

KEN? YOU OKAY? WHAT *HAPPENED*? IT LOOKED LIKE AN ATOM BOMB EXPLODED!
I DON'T KNOW... I GOT SO WORKED UP MY ENERGY SELF JUST SEEMED TO FLOW OUT BEYOND THE BOUNDS OF MY BODY... SORT OF WENT NOVA... OR SOMETHING...
I'M NOT SURE I FOLLOW... BUT... YOUR CLOTHES..?
BURNED OFF, I GUESS NO GREAT LOSS! AT ONE POINT, WHEN THAT THING GRABBED ME, I... UH... WET MY PANTS!
NINETY MINUTES LATER, IN *WHITEHALL*...
...EXPLOSION OF THE WEST MIFFLIN SLAG DUMP HAS AUTHORITIES BAFFLED! POLICE HAVE SEALED THE AREA OFF, BUT ARE CALLING SPECULATIONS THAT THE BLAST WAS A SMALL NUCLEAR BOMB "RIDICULOUS"...
NOK NOK
HM! DOOR...
HIYA, DUCK! QUACK!
KENNY! QUACK, YOURSELF!
WHAT'CHA DOIN' IN THOSE FUNNY CLOTHES? THEY LOOK LIKE...
MYRON'S! YEAH! THEY DON'T FIT HIM EITHER! YOU CAN'T ALWAYS FIND THE SIZES YOU WANT IN THE TRASH!
WHAT HAPPENED TO *YOUR* CLOTHES?
I SORT OF *LOST* THEM... AND MY WALLET, AND MY KEYS! IT'S A LONG STORY, DEB! I, UH... NEED A PLACE TO STAY TONIGHT! OKAY?
SURE!
THANKS! GOOD OL' DEBBIE TH' DUCK... MY FAVORITE WATERFOWL...
QUACK, QUACK!
YOU LOOK COLD! HERE, WRAP YOURSELF IN THIS BLANKET WHILE I MAKE YOU... SOME... SOUP...
KENNY!
POOR BABY!

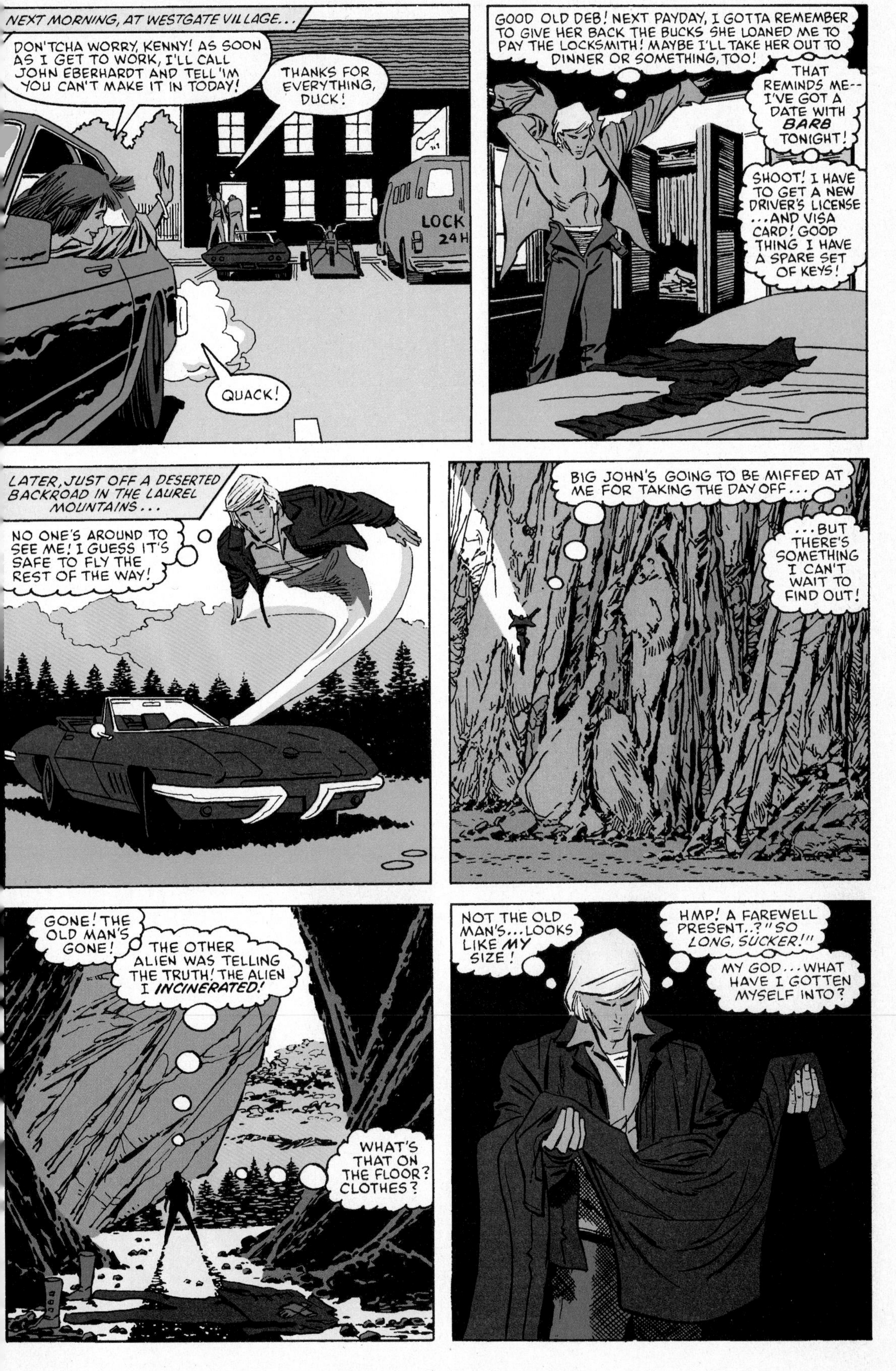
NEXT MORNING, AT WESTGATE VILLAGE...
DON'TCHA WORRY, KENNY! AS SOON AS I GET TO WORK, I'LL CALL JOHN EBERHARDT AND TELL 'IM YOU CAN'T MAKE IT IN TODAY!
THANKS FOR EVERYTHING, DUCK!
LOCK 24H
QUACK!
GOOD OLD DEB! NEXT PAYDAY, I GOTTA REMEMBER TO GIVE HER BACK THE BUCKS SHE LOANED ME TO PAY THE LOCKSMITH! MAYBE I'LL TAKE HER OUT TO DINNER OR SOMETHING, TOO!
THAT REMINDS ME-- I'VE GOT A DATE WITH BARB TONIGHT!
SHOOT! I HAVE TO GET A NEW DRIVER'S LICENSE ...AND VISA CARD! GOOD THING I HAVE A SPARE SET OF KEYS!
LATER, JUST OFF A DESERTED BACKROAD IN THE LAUREL MOUNTAINS...
NO ONE'S AROUND TO SEE ME! I GUESS IT'S SAFE TO FLY THE REST OF THE WAY!
BIG JOHN'S GOING TO BE MIFFED AT ME FOR TAKING THE DAY OFF...
...BUT THERE'S SOMETHING I CAN'T WAIT TO FIND OUT!
GONE! THE OLD MAN'S GONE!
THE OTHER ALIEN WAS TELLING THE TRUTH! THE ALIEN I INCINERATED!
WHAT'S THAT ON THE FLOOR? CLOTHES?
NOT THE OLD MAN'S...LOOKS LIKE MY SIZE!
HMP! A FAREWELL PRESENT..?" "SO LONG, SUCKER!"
MY GOD...WHAT HAVE I GOTTEN MYSELF INTO?

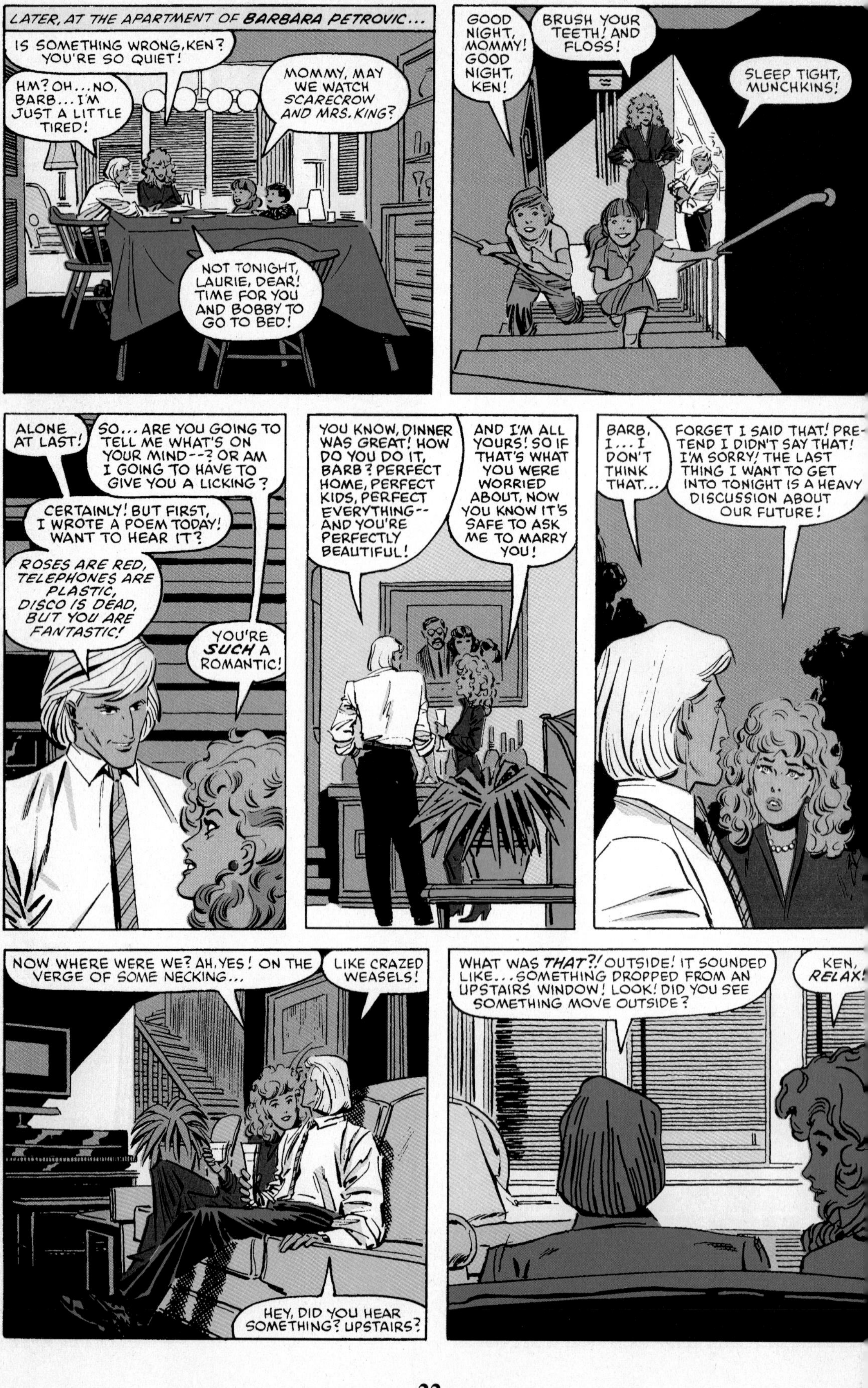
LATER, AT THE APARTMENT OF BARBARA PETROVIC...
IS SOMETHING WRONG, KEN? YOU'RE SO QUIET!
HM? OH...NO, BARB...I'M JUST A LITTLE TIRED!
MOMMY, MAY WE WATCH SCARECROW AND MRS. KING?
NOT TONIGHT, LAURIE, DEAR! TIME FOR YOU AND BOBBY TO GO TO BED!
GOOD NIGHT, MOMMY! GOOD NIGHT, KEN!
BRUSH YOUR TEETH! AND FLOSS!
SLEEP TIGHT, MUNCHKINS!
ALONE AT LAST!
SO... ARE YOU GOING TO TELL ME WHAT'S ON YOUR MIND--? OR AM I GOING TO HAVE TO GIVE YOU A LICKING?
CERTAINLY! BUT FIRST, I WROTE A POEM TODAY! WANT TO HEAR IT?
ROSES ARE RED, TELEPHONES ARE PLASTIC, DISCO IS DEAD, BUT YOU ARE FANTASTIC!
YOU'RE SUCH A ROMANTIC!
YOU KNOW, DINNER WAS GREAT! HOW DO YOU DO IT, BARB? PERFECT HOME, PERFECT KIDS, PERFECT EVERYTHING-- AND YOU'RE PERFECTLY BEAUTIFUL!
AND I'M ALL YOURS! SO IF THAT'S WHAT YOU WERE WORRIED ABOUT, NOW YOU KNOW IT'S SAFE TO ASK ME TO MARRY YOU!
BARB, I...I DON'T THINK THAT...
FORGET I SAID THAT! PRETEND I DIDN'T SAY THAT! I'M SORRY! THE LAST THING I WANT TO GET INTO TONIGHT IS A HEAVY DISCUSSION ABOUT OUR FUTURE!
NOW WHERE WERE WE? AH, YES! ON THE VERGE OF SOME NECKING...
LIKE CRAZED WEASELS!
HEY, DID YOU HEAR SOMETHING? UPSTAIRS?
WHAT WAS THAT?! OUTSIDE! IT SOUNDED LIKE...SOMETHING DROPPED FROM AN UPSTAIRS WINDOW! LOOK! DID YOU SEE SOMETHING MOVE OUTSIDE?
KEN, RELAX!

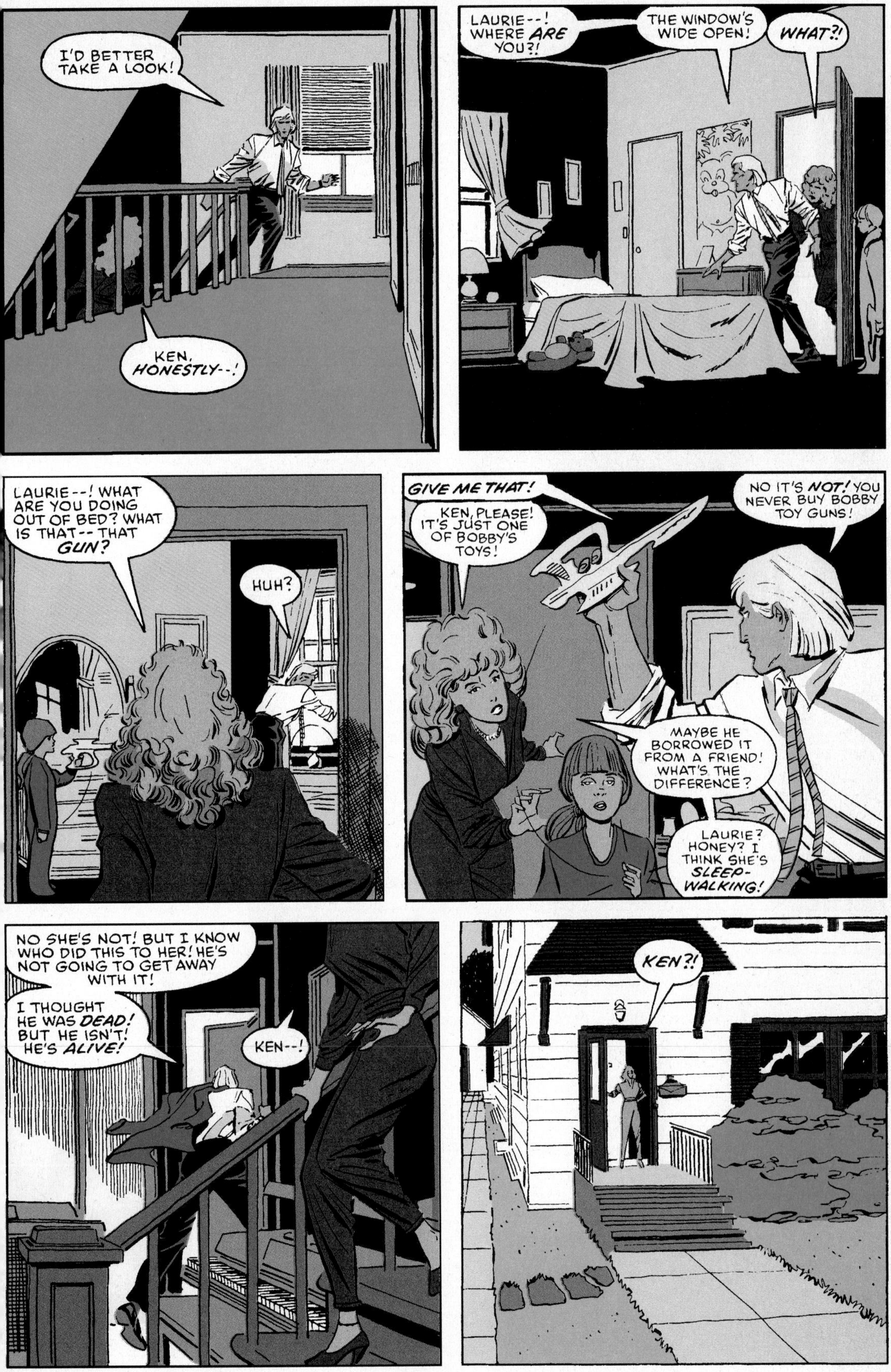
I'D BETTER TAKE A LOOK!
KEN, HONESTLY--!
LAURIE--! WHERE ARE YOU?!
THE WINDOW'S WIDE OPEN!
WHAT?!
LAURIE--! WHAT ARE YOU DOING OUT OF BED? WHAT IS THAT-- THAT GUN?
HUH?
GIVE ME THAT!
KEN, PLEASE! IT'S JUST ONE OF BOBBY'S TOYS!
NO IT'S NOT! YOU NEVER BUY BOBBY TOY GUNS!
MAYBE HE BORROWED IT FROM A FRIEND! WHAT'S THE DIFFERENCE?
LAURIE? HONEY? I THINK SHE'S SLEEP-WALKING!
NO SHE'S NOT! BUT I KNOW WHO DID THIS TO HER! HE'S NOT GOING TO GET AWAY WITH IT!
I THOUGHT HE WAS DEAD! BUT HE ISN'T! HE'S ALIVE!
KEN--!
KEN?!

WHERE IS HE? WHERE *IS* HE?!

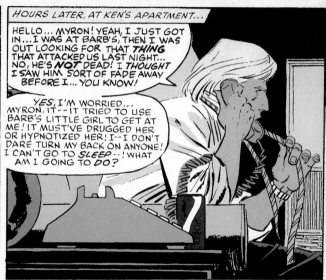

HOURS LATER, AT KEN'S APARTMENT...

HELLO... MYRON! YEAH, I JUST GOT IN...I WAS AT BARB'S, THEN I WAS OUT LOOKING FOR THAT *THING* THAT ATTACKED US LAST NIGHT... NO, HE'S *NOT* DEAD! I *THOUGHT* I SAW HIM SORT OF FADE AWAY BEFORE I... YOU KNOW!

YES, I'M WORRIED... MYRON, IT--IT TRIED TO USE BARB'S LITTLE GIRL TO GET AT ME! IT MUST'VE DRUGGED HER OR HYPNOTIZED HER! I--I DON'T DARE TURN MY BACK ON ANYONE! I CAN'T GO TO *SLEEP*--! WHAT AM I GOING TO *DO*?

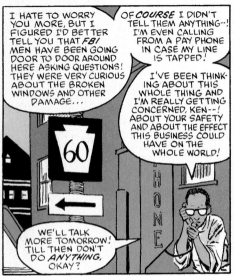

I HATE TO WORRY YOU MORE, BUT I FIGURED I'D BETTER TELL YOU THAT *FBI* MEN HAVE BEEN GOING DOOR TO DOOR AROUND HERE ASKING QUESTIONS! THEY WERE VERY CURIOUS ABOUT THE BROKEN WINDOWS AND OTHER DAMAGE...

OF *COURSE* I DIDN'T TELL THEM ANYTHING--! I'M EVEN CALLING FROM A PAY PHONE IN CASE MY LINE IS TAPPED!

I'VE BEEN THINK-ING ABOUT THIS WHOLE THING AND I'M REALLY GETTING CONCERNED, KEN--! ABOUT YOUR SAFETY AND ABOUT THE EFFECT THIS BUSINESS COULD HAVE ON THE WHOLE WORLD!

WE'LL TALK MORE TOMORROW! TILL THEN DON'T DO *ANYTHING*, OKAY?

60

KENNY? YOU ALONE?

TAP TAP

YEAH...

I'VE BEEN TRYIN' TO CALL YOU ALL DAY! I JUST CAME TO LEAVE A NOTE ON YOUR DOOR!

WHEN I CALLED JOHN EBERHARDT THIS MORNING, HE SAID IF YOU DINT COME TO WORK TOMORROW YOU SHOONT COME IN EVER AGAIN!

GREAT...

WHAT'S WRONG, KENNY? IS IT... SOMETHING WITH... BARB?

NO...BUT I PROBABLY SCREWED THAT UP, TOO!

I WISH I COULD MAKE WHATEVER IT IS ALL BETTER! HEY, YOU'LL ALWAYS HAVE ME, Y'KNOW!

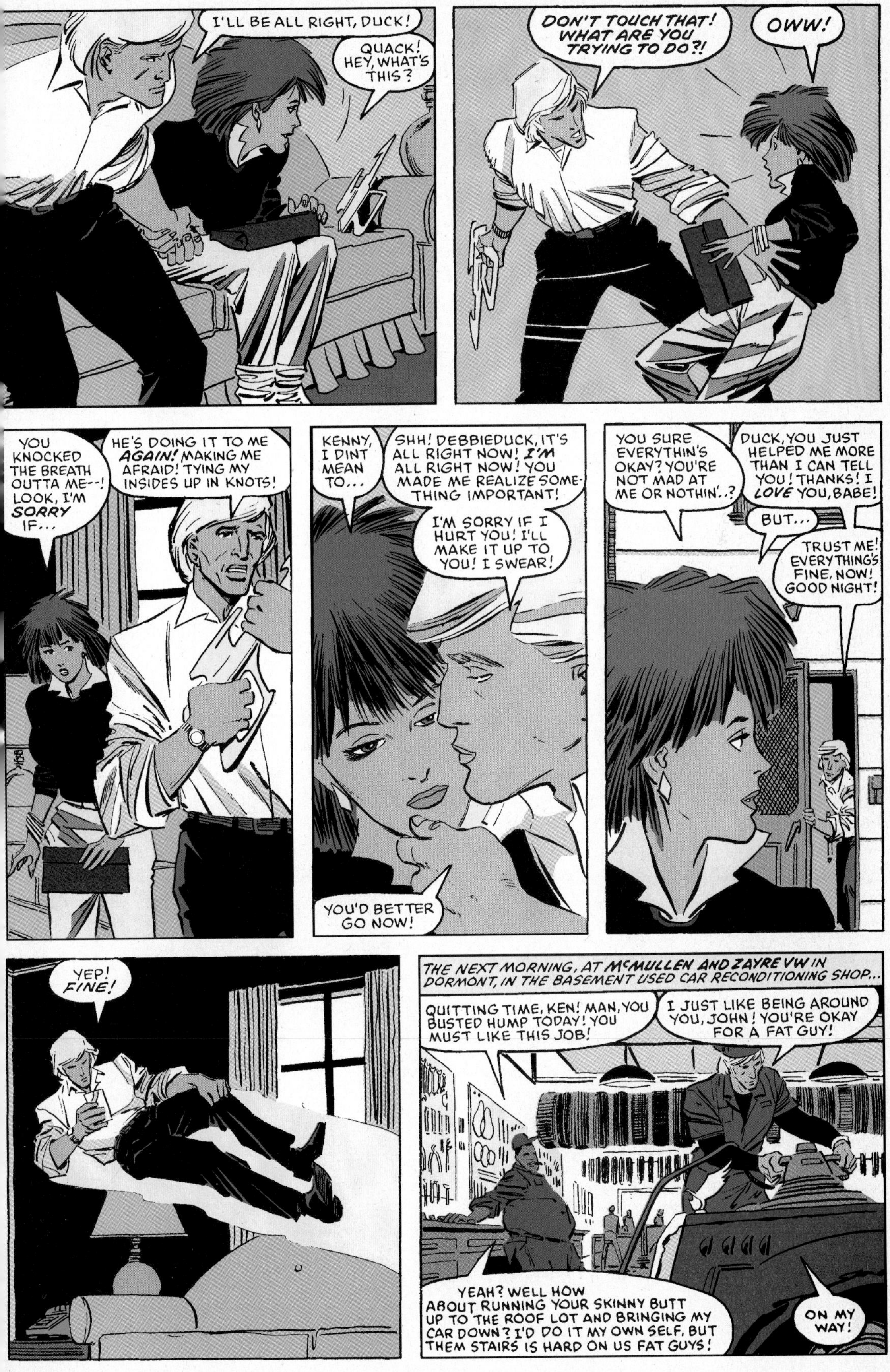
I'LL BE ALL RIGHT, DUCK!
QUACK! HEY, WHAT'S THIS?
DON'T TOUCH THAT! WHAT ARE YOU TRYING TO DO?!
OWW!
YOU KNOCKED THE BREATH OUTTA ME--! LOOK, I'M SORRY IF...
HE'S DOING IT TO ME AGAIN! MAKING ME AFRAID! TYING MY INSIDES UP IN KNOTS!
KENNY, I DINT MEAN TO...
SHH! DEBBIEDUCK, IT'S ALL RIGHT NOW! I'M ALL RIGHT NOW! YOU MADE ME REALIZE SOMETHING IMPORTANT!
I'M SORRY IF I HURT YOU! I'LL MAKE IT UP TO YOU! I SWEAR!
YOU'D BETTER GO NOW!
YOU SURE EVERYTHIN'S OKAY? YOU'RE NOT MAD AT ME OR NOTHIN'..?
DUCK, YOU JUST HELPED ME MORE THAN I CAN TELL YOU! THANKS! I LOVE YOU, BABE!
BUT...
TRUST ME! EVERYTHING'S FINE, NOW! GOOD NIGHT!
YEP! FINE!
THE NEXT MORNING, AT McMULLEN AND ZAYRE VW IN DORMONT, IN THE BASEMENT USED CAR RECONDITIONING SHOP...
QUITTING TIME, KEN! MAN, YOU BUSTED HUMP TODAY! YOU MUST LIKE THIS JOB!
I JUST LIKE BEING AROUND YOU, JOHN! YOU'RE OKAY FOR A FAT GUY!
YEAH? WELL HOW ABOUT RUNNING YOUR SKINNY BUTT UP TO THE ROOF LOT AND BRINGING MY CAR DOWN? I'D DO IT MY OWN SELF, BUT THEM STAIRS IS HARD ON US FAT GUYS!
ON MY WAY!

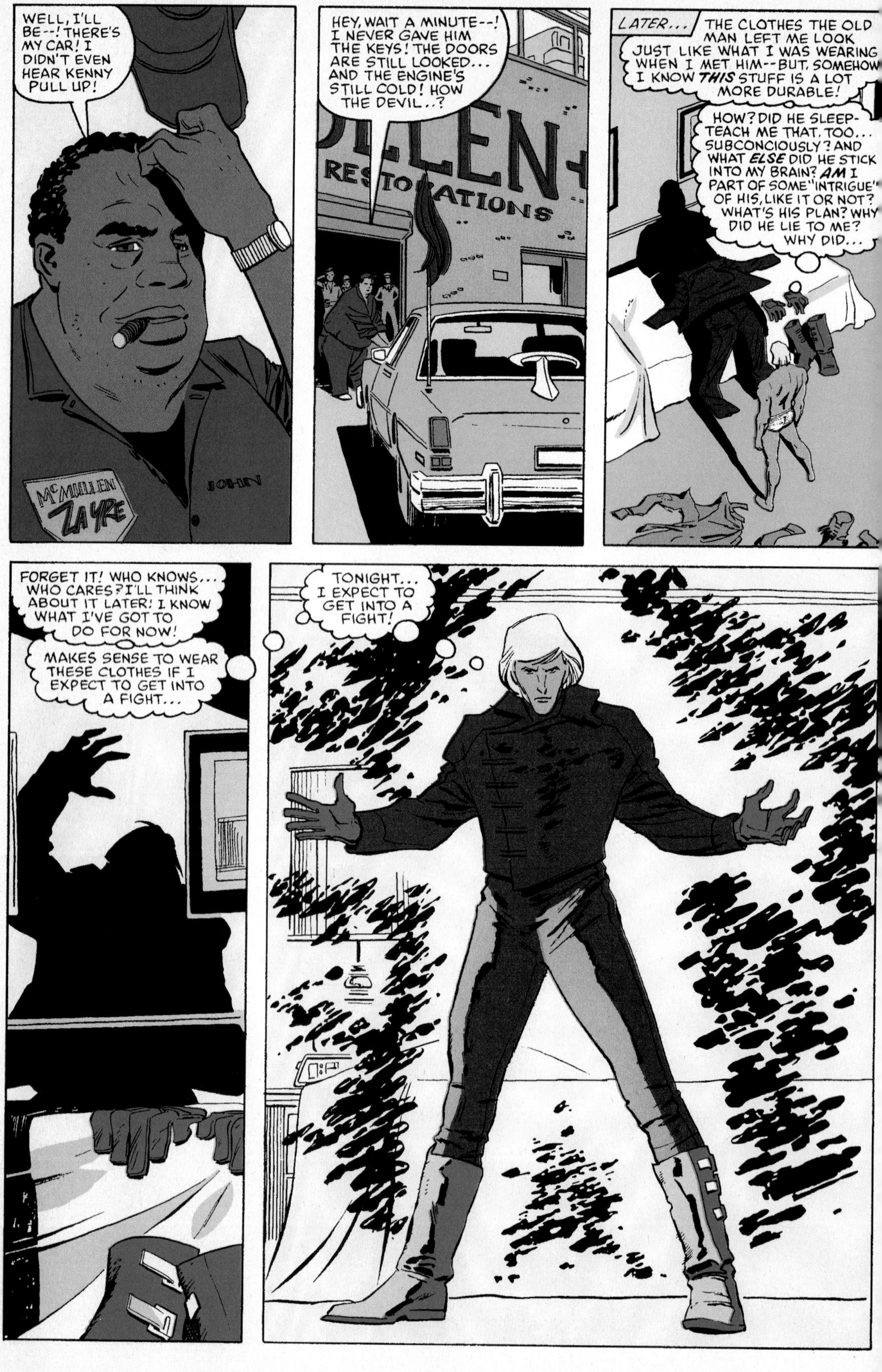
WELL, I'LL BE--! THERE'S MY CAR! I DIDN'T EVEN HEAR KENNY PULL UP!
McMILLEN ZAYRE
JOHN
HEY, WAIT A MINUTE--! I NEVER GAVE HIM THE KEYS! THE DOORS ARE STILL LOOKED... AND THE ENGINE'S STILL COLD! HOW THE DEVIL..?
RESTORATIONS
LATER...
THE CLOTHES THE OLD MAN LEFT ME LOOK JUST LIKE WHAT I WAS WEARING WHEN I MET HIM--BUT, SOMEHOW I KNOW THIS STUFF IS A LOT MORE DURABLE!
HOW? DID HE SLEEP-TEACH ME THAT, TOO... SUBCONCIOUSLY? AND WHAT ELSE DID HE STICK INTO MY BRAIN? AM I PART OF SOME "INTRIGUE" OF HIS, LIKE IT OR NOT? WHAT'S HIS PLAN? WHY DID HE LIE TO ME? WHY DID...
FORGET IT! WHO KNOWS... WHO CARES? I'LL THINK ABOUT IT LATER! I KNOW WHAT I'VE GOT TO DO FOR NOW!
MAKES SENSE TO WEAR THESE CLOTHES IF I EXPECT TO GET INTO A FIGHT...
TONIGHT... I EXPECT TO GET INTO A FIGHT!

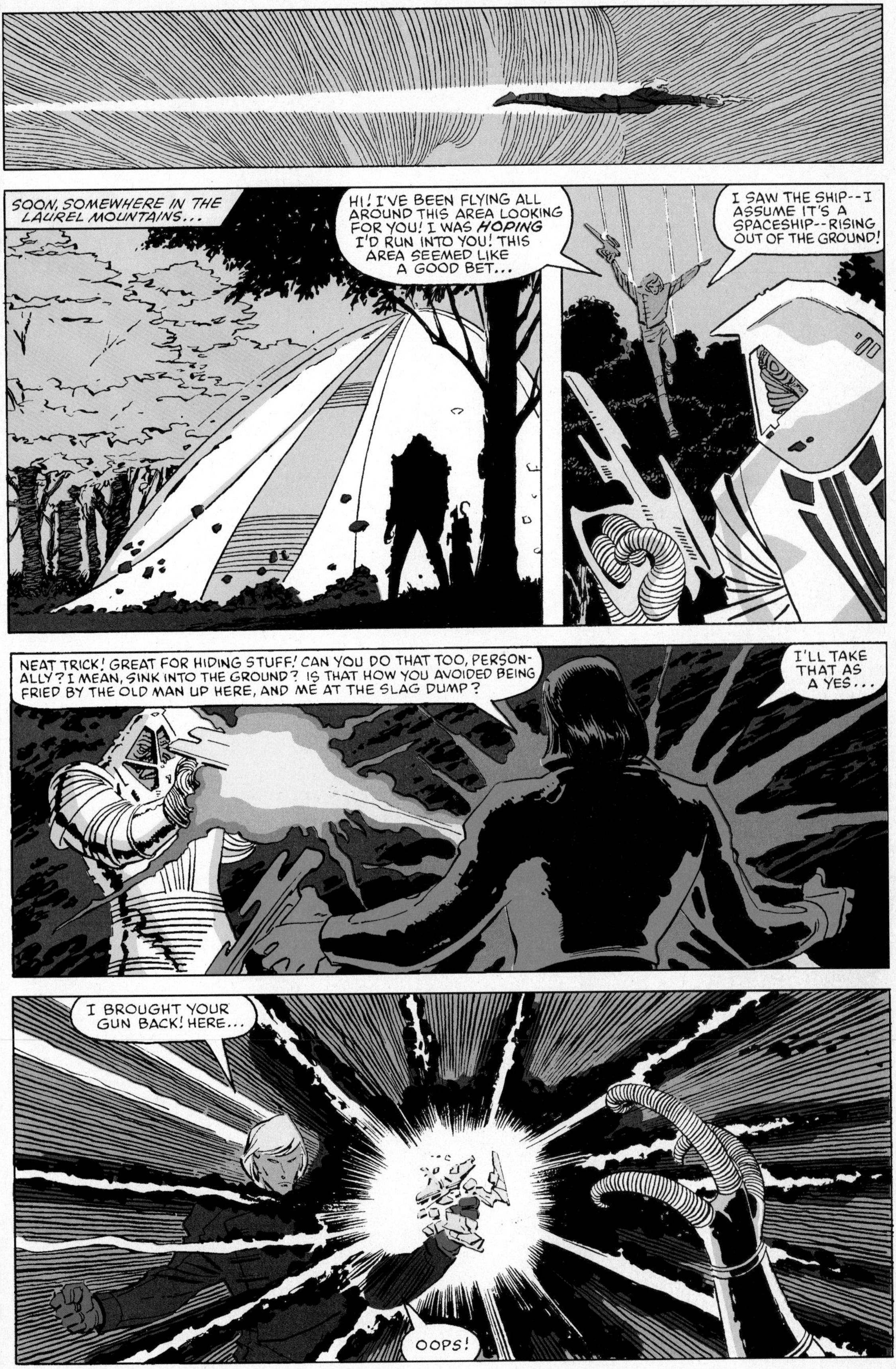
SOON, SOMEWHERE IN THE LAUREL MOUNTAINS...
HI! I'VE BEEN FLYING ALL AROUND THIS AREA LOOKING FOR YOU! I WAS HOPING I'D RUN INTO YOU! THIS AREA SEEMED LIKE A GOOD BET...
I SAW THE SHIP--I ASSUME IT'S A SPACESHIP--RISING OUT OF THE GROUND!
NEAT TRICK! GREAT FOR HIDING STUFF! CAN YOU DO THAT TOO, PERSON-ALLY? I MEAN, SINK INTO THE GROUND? IS THAT HOW YOU AVOIDED BEING FRIED BY THE OLD MAN UP HERE, AND ME AT THE SLAG DUMP?
I'LL TAKE THAT AS A YES...
I BROUGHT YOUR GUN BACK! HERE...
OOPS!

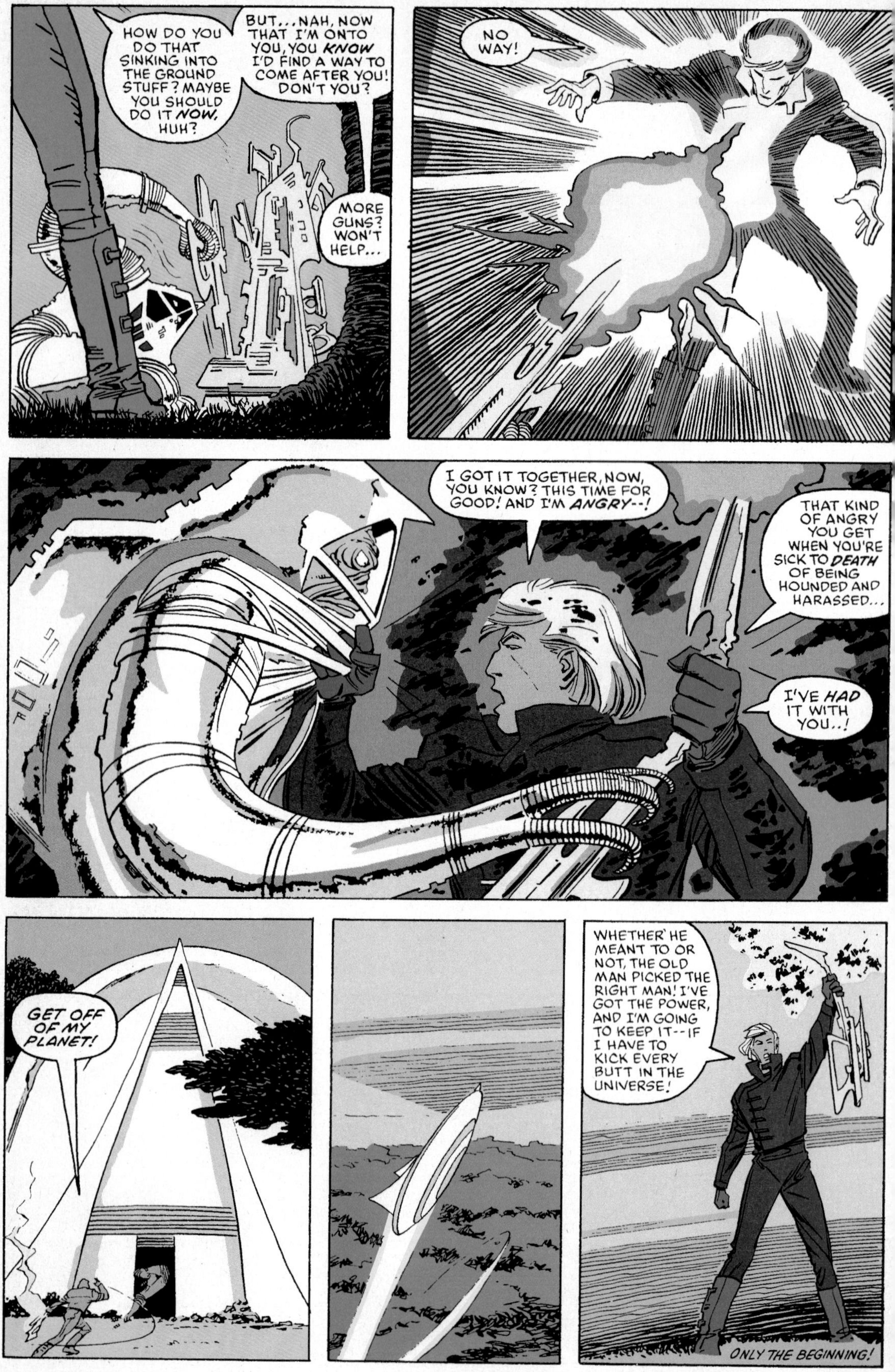
HOW DO YOU DO THAT SINKING INTO THE GROUND STUFF? MAYBE YOU SHOULD DO IT NOW, HUH?
BUT...NAH, NOW THAT I'M ONTO YOU, YOU KNOW I'D FIND A WAY TO COME AFTER YOU! DON'T YOU?
MORE GUNS? WON'T HELP...
NO WAY!
I GOT IT TOGETHER, NOW, YOU KNOW? THIS TIME FOR GOOD! AND I'M ANGRY--!
THAT KIND OF ANGRY YOU GET WHEN YOU'RE SICK TO DEATH OF BEING HOUNDED AND HARASSED...
I'VE HAD IT WITH YOU..!
GET OFF OF MY PLANET!
WHETHER HE MEANT TO OR NOT, THE OLD MAN PICKED THE RIGHT MAN! I'VE GOT THE POWER, AND I'M GOING TO KEEP IT--IF I HAVE TO KICK EVERY BUTT IN THE UNIVERSE!
ONLY THE BEGINNING!

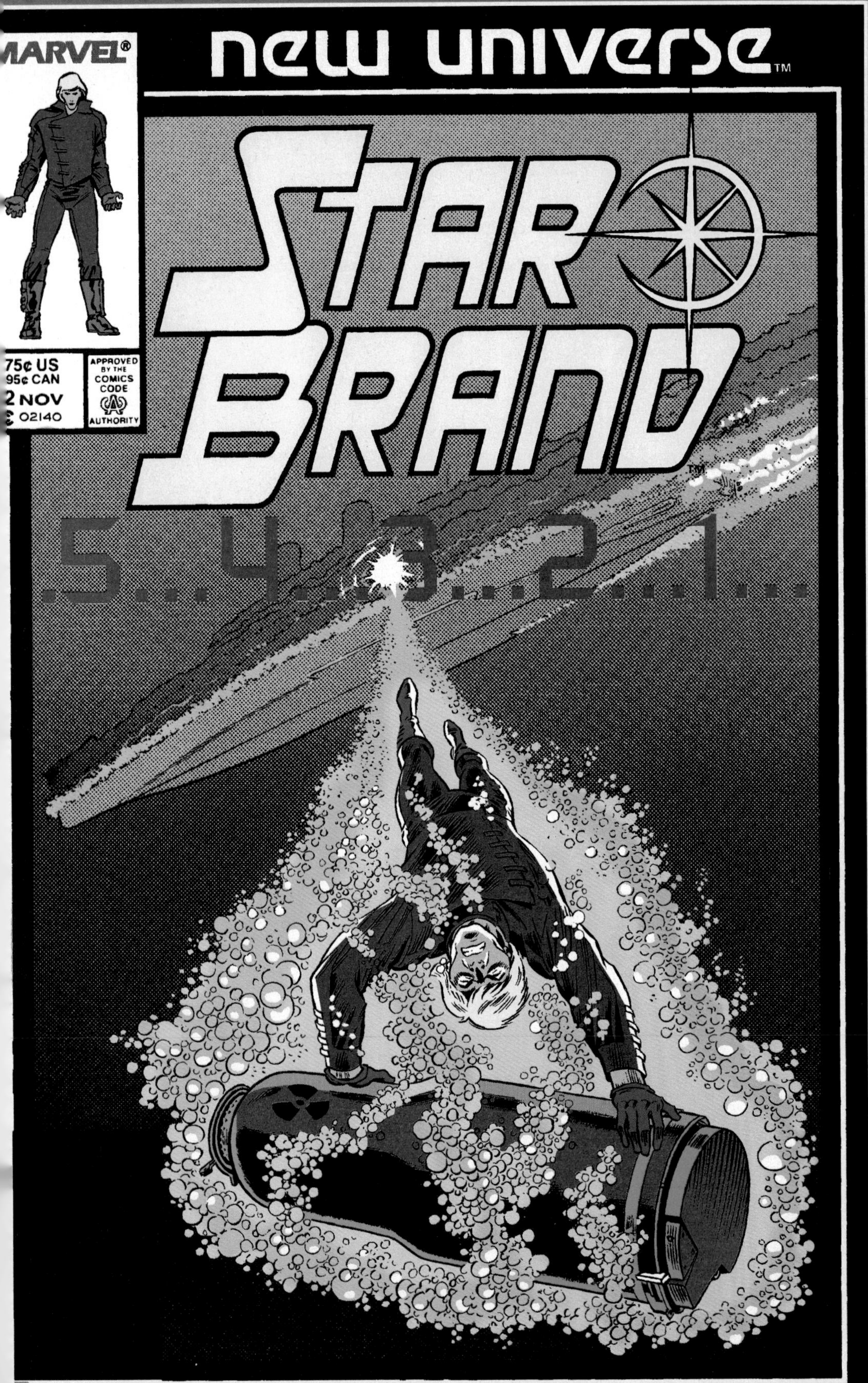

MARVEL
new universe
STAR BRAND
75¢ US
95¢ CAN
2 NOV
02140
APPROVED BY THE COMICS CODE AUTHORITY
5...4...3...2...1...

TAKING CHARGE!

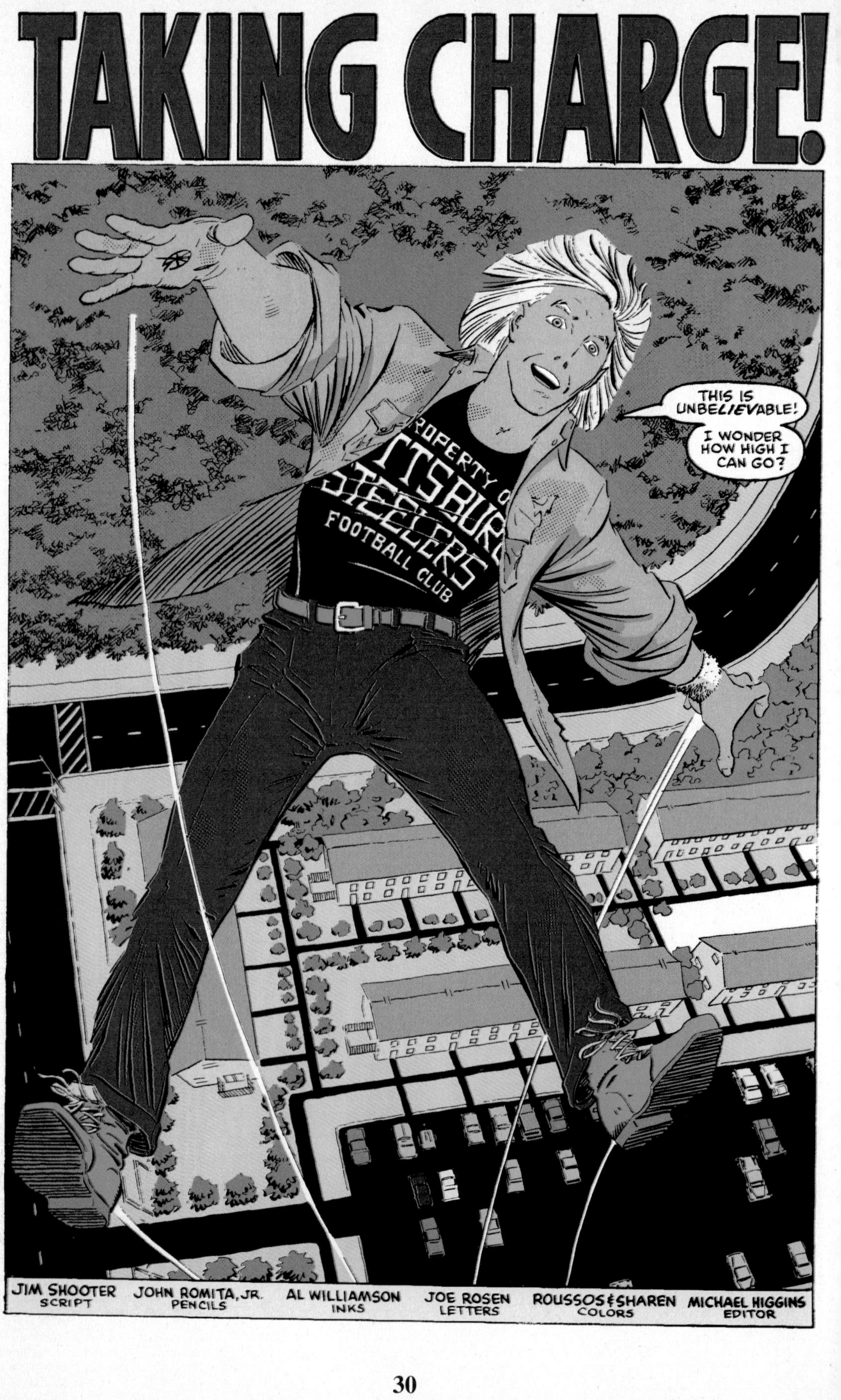
THIS IS UNBELIEVABLE!
I WONDER HOW HIGH I CAN GO?
FOOTBALL CLUB
JIM SHOOTER SCRIPT
JOHN ROMITA, JR. PENCILS
AL WILLIAMSON INKS
JOE ROSEN LETTERS
ROUSSOS & SHAREN COLORS
MICHAEL HIGGINS EDITOR

LET'S SEE...

AMAZING...

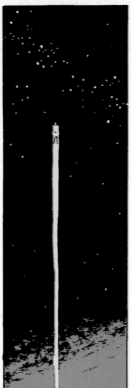

IT'S COLD! I KNOW IT'S COLD. I CAN *FEEL* IT... BUT IT DOESN'T BOTHER ME.

HEY--! NO *AIR* UP HERE! BETTER GET *DOWN! FAST!*

WAIT A MINUTE. DON'T *PANIC.* WHEN I PANIC, I LOSE CONTROL OF THE POWER! AND IF IT FADED OUT ON ME *NOW,* LACK OF AIR WOULD BE THE LEAST OF MY PROBLEMS. THINK. IT ISN'T REALLY *BOTHERING* ME. LIKE THE COLD. DON'T PANIC.

HEAD HOME... BUT CALMLY.

HMM... WHERE *IS* HOME? I GUESS I'M STILL OVER WESTERN PENNSYLVANIA. HARD TO TELL FROM UP HERE...

SOON... WHERE *AM* I?

MAYBE IF I FOLLOW THIS STREAM I'LL WIND UP SOMEPLACE I RECOGNIZE.

TWENTY MINUTES OF RIVER-FOLLOWING LATER...

PITTSBURGH! ALL *RIGHT...*

31

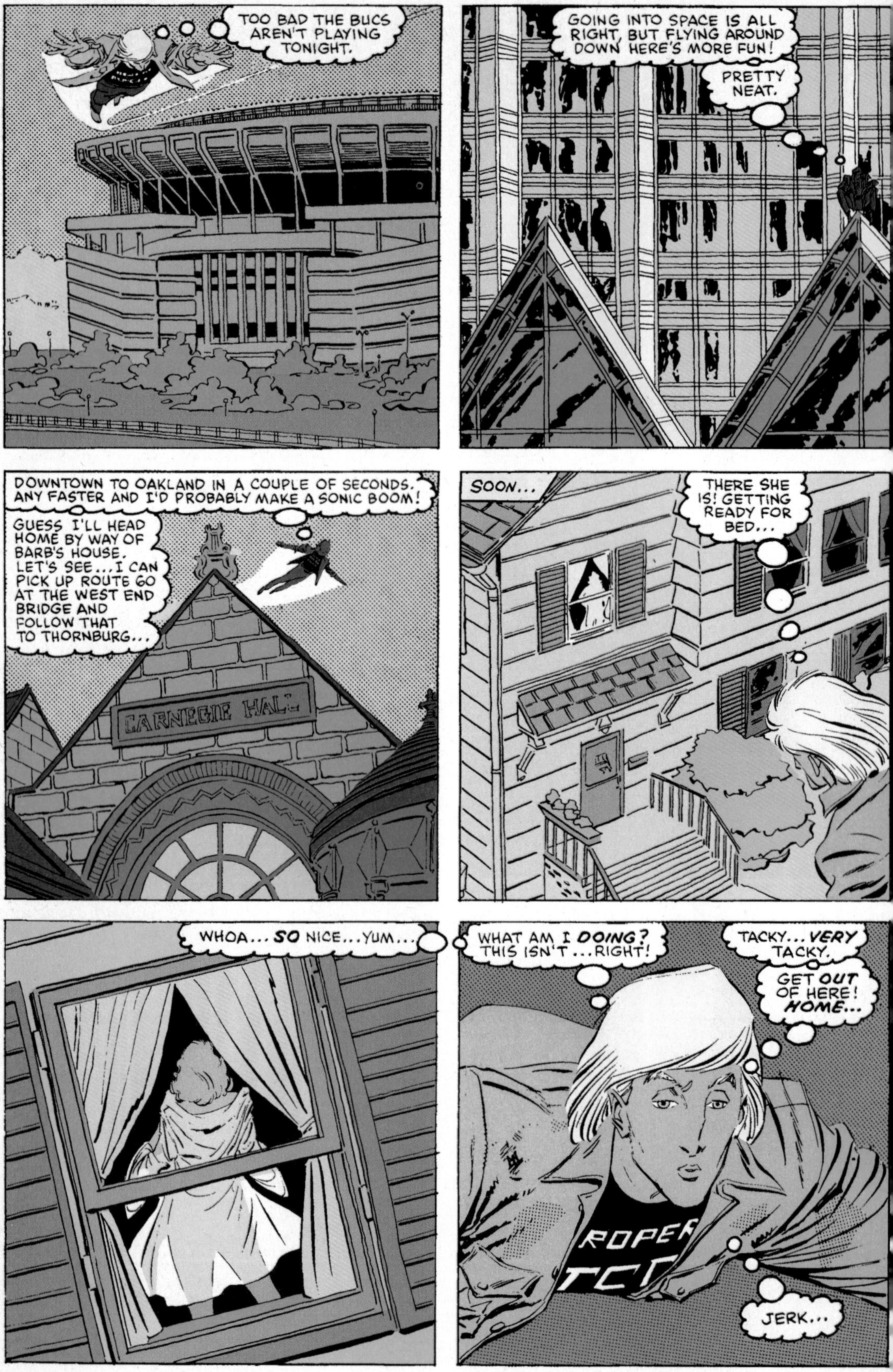
TOO BAD THE BUCS AREN'T PLAYING TONIGHT.
GOING INTO SPACE IS ALL RIGHT, BUT FLYING AROUND DOWN HERE'S MORE FUN!
PRETTY NEAT.
DOWNTOWN TO OAKLAND IN A COUPLE OF SECONDS. ANY FASTER AND I'D PROBABLY MAKE A SONIC BOOM!
GUESS I'LL HEAD HOME BY WAY OF BARB'S HOUSE. LET'S SEE... I CAN PICK UP ROUTE 60 AT THE WEST END BRIDGE AND FOLLOW THAT TO THORNBURG...
CARNEGIE HALL
SOON...
THERE SHE IS! GETTING READY FOR BED...
WHOA... SO NICE... YUM...
WHAT AM I DOING? THIS ISN'T... RIGHT!
TACKY... VERY TACKY.
GET OUT OF HERE! HOME...
JERK...

SOON, AT NEARBY WESTGATE VILLAGE...

IT'D BE SO EASY TO BECOME A TOTAL SLIMEBALL WITH THIS POWER.

SO WHAT *SHOULD* I BECOME?

...COMING UP AT ELEVEN, THE LATEST ON THE TERRORIST HIJACKING OF THE CRUISE SHIP AJAX.

SHOULD I BEAT UP TERRORISTS?

NOK! NOK!

DOOR...

KENNY! YOU'RE HOME!

HI, DUCK! QUACK.

MYRON'S BEEN TRYING TO CALL YOU! HE WANTS YOU TO COME OVER AT SIX TOMORROW. HE SAID IT'S IMPORTANT. HE ASKED ME TO LEAVE A NOTE ON YOUR DOOR...

SO MYRON'S GOT THE DEBBIE THE DUCK MESSENGER SERVICE DOING HIS ERRANDS NOW, HUH?

S'OKAY, I LIVE CLOSER. QUACK.

UM...SINCE I'M HERE ANYWAY, KENNY... CAN I STAY?

DO DUCKS LIKE WATER?

I *HATE* WATER. I'M A DESERT DUCK. QUACK.

YEAH? WELL, YOU CAN STAY ANYWAY.

NEXT AFTERNOON...

YOU NEED GAS, KENNY?

YEAH. HAVE TO MAKE A PHONE CALL, TOO.

BARB? HI! I WANTED TO CALL YOU BEFORE, BUT...I, UH, CAN'T MAKE IT TONIGHT. SOMETHING'S COME UP. IT'S MYRON...HE LEFT AN URGENT MESSAGE. NO, I DON'T KNOW WHAT IT'S ABOUT YET.

GETTY

PHONE

FOREIGN DOMESTIC REPAIR

WHY DIDN'T YOU CALL ME LAST NIGHT?

I KNOW I SAID I WOULD, BUT...I- I'M SORRY. MY LIFE'S BEEN A LITTLE STRANGE LATELY.

NO, NOTHING MAJOR'S WRONG. REALLY, BARB. SURE, I--I FEEL THAT WAY ABOUT YOU, TOO. NO, I'M NOT AFRAID TO SAY IT. I LOVE YOU. THERE, OKAY?

I'LL TALK TO YOU LATER, OKAY? BYE.

KENNY...IF YOU WANTED TO CALL BARB LAST NIGHT I COULD'A LEFT. I HOPE I DINT ROON EVERYTHING.

IT'S ALL RIGHT. NOT YOUR FAULT.

I JUST WANT YOU TO BE HAPPY. I WISH...I WISH I COULD...

COOL IT, DEB, HUH?

WHATEVER MYRON WANTS HAD BETTER BE IMPORTANT.

SOON...

HIYA, MYRON. WHAT'S THAT? MORE JUNK?

IT JUST MAY BE THE FUTURE, KEN! ELECTRIC CARS WILL MAKE A COMEBACK WHEN THE NEXT OIL CRISIS COMES. I SAW THIS OLD BEAUTY SITTING IN A FARMER'S FIELD. HE GAVE IT TO ME FOR NOTHING! I JUST HAD TO HAUL IT AWAY.

I HOPE YOU DIDN'T CALL ME HERE TO HELP YOU FIX THIS "OLD BEAUTY"...

OH, NO! THAT'S LATER. LET'S GO INSIDE. EVERYONE'S PROBABLY HERE BY NOW.

EVERYONE WHO?

I WANTED YOU TO SIT IN WITH THE GROUP TONIGHT, KEN!

YOUR THERAPY GROUP? YOU'VE GOT TO BE KIDDING! YOU ASKED ME HERE TO PLAY ENCOUNTER GAMES WITH YOUR PATIENTS?!

NOT ALL PATIENTS. SOME ARE JUST FRIENDS, LIKE YOU. YOU KNOW MOST OF THEM. COME ON, IT'LL BE FUN!

HELLO, EVERYBODY! THIS IS KEN CONNELL AND DEBBIE.

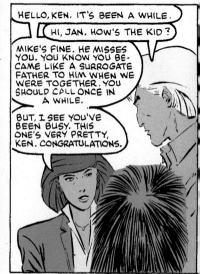

HELLO, KEN. IT'S BEEN A WHILE.

HI, JAN, HOW'S THE KID?

MIKE'S FINE. HE MISSES YOU. YOU KNOW YOU BECAME LIKE A SURROGATE FATHER TO HIM WHEN WE WERE TOGETHER. YOU SHOULD CALL ONCE IN A WHILE.

BUT, I SEE YOU'VE BEEN BUSY. THIS ONE'S VERY PRETTY, KEN. CONGRATULATIONS.

KEN! WHERE ARE YOU GOING? WE'RE ABOUT TO START.

MYRON, THIS IS TOO WEIRD, TOO SIXTIES, AND I DON'T *NEED* THERAPY.

OF COURSE YOU DON'T NEED THE GROUP, BUT YOU'RE SO BRIGHT AND PERCEPTIVE--! YOU'RE GOOD FOR *THEM!*

COME *ON!*

AND...

LET'S PLAY THAT FALLING-BACKWARD-OFF-THE-CHAIR THING. YOU KNOW-- THE *TRUST* GAME.

IN A WHILE, SHEILA. FOR NOW, I WANT EACH OF YOU TO THINK ABOUT IT, AND THEN TELL THE GROUP WHAT YOU WOULD DO...

...IF YOU SUDDENLY ACQUIRED THE POWER TO CONTROL OR EVEN DESTROY THE WORLD!

JANET?

HMM...BOY, FIRST, I'D BE TEMPTED TO HAVE ALL THE PARKING METERS ON WASHINGTON ROAD REMOVED...

GOOD GRIEF! I-- I CAN'T BELIEVE MYRON'S *DOING* THIS TO ME!

KEN, WAIT! WHERE ARE YOU *GOING?* I THOUGHT THIS MIGHT *HELP* YOU...YOU KNOW, FIGURE THINGS OUT.

GET YOUR MANIPULATIVE BUTT OFF MY CASE, MYRON! I'LL FIGURE THINGS OUT MYSELF. I'M SORRY I CONFIDED IN YOU!

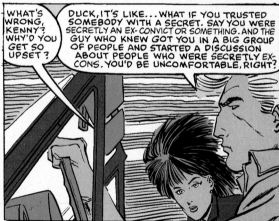

WHAT'S WRONG, KENNY? WHY'D YOU GET SO UPSET?

DUCK, IT'S LIKE...WHAT IF YOU TRUSTED SOMEBODY WITH A SECRET. SAY YOU WERE SECRETLY AN EX-CONVICT OR SOMETHING. AND THE GUY WHO KNEW GOT YOU IN A BIG GROUP OF PEOPLE AND STARTED A DISCUSSION ABOUT PEOPLE WHO WERE SECRETLY EX-CONS. YOU'D BE UNCOMFORTABLE, RIGHT?

YOU MEAN... YOU'RE AN EX-CON?

NO...GEEZ, DUCK, YOU'RE SO DUMB.

I KNOW I CAN TRUST YOU, THOUGH. GET OUT. I'LL *SHOW* YOU WHAT I'M TALKING ABOUT.

SPEED LIMIT 45

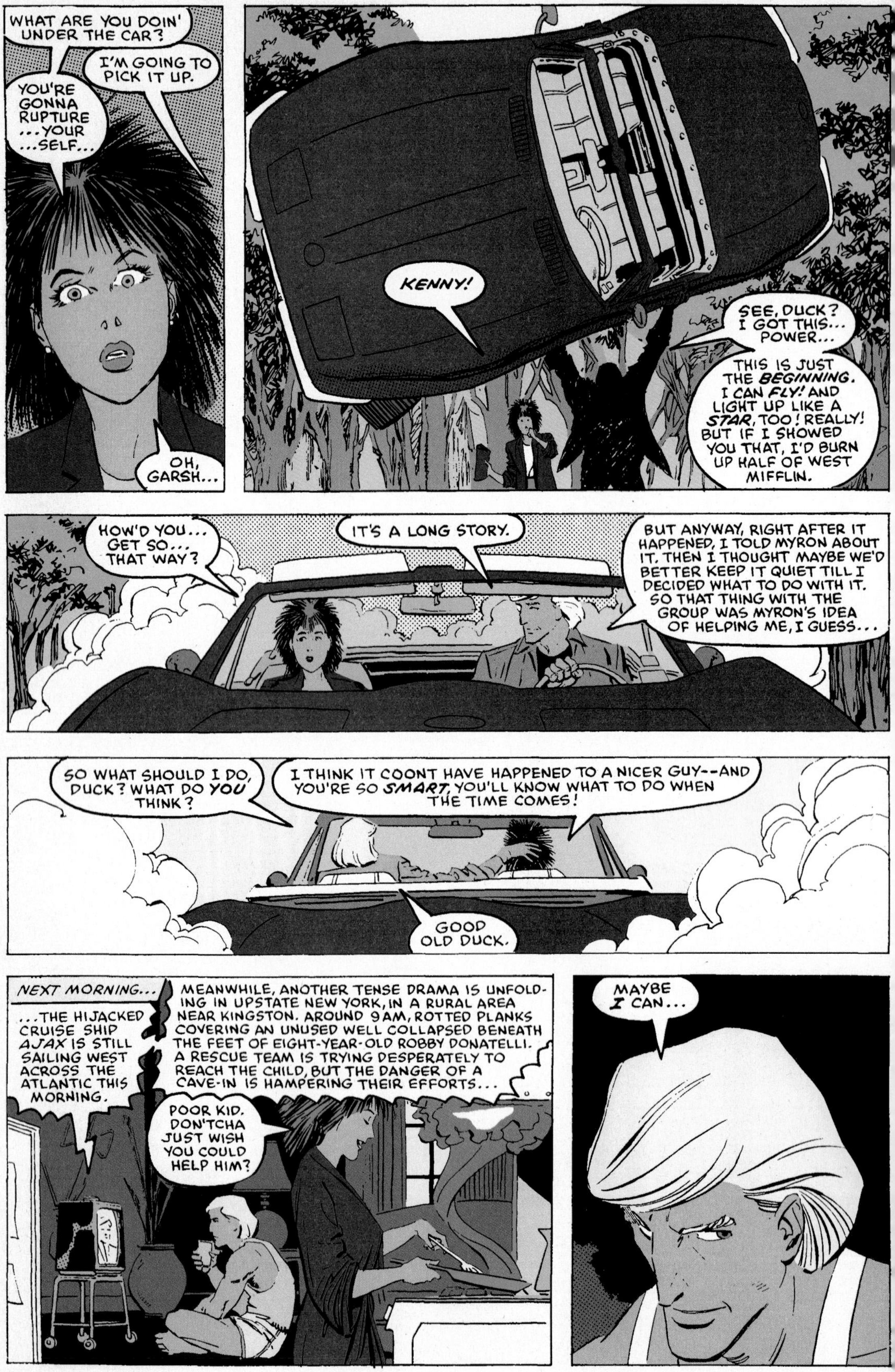
WHAT ARE YOU DOIN' UNDER THE CAR?
I'M GOING TO PICK IT UP.
YOU'RE GONNA RUPTURE ...YOUR ...SELF...
OH, GARSH...
KENNY!
SEE, DUCK? I GOT THIS... POWER...
THIS IS JUST THE BEGINNING. I CAN FLY! AND LIGHT UP LIKE A STAR, TOO! REALLY! BUT IF I SHOWED YOU THAT, I'D BURN UP HALF OF WEST MIFFLIN.
HOW'D YOU... GET SO... THAT WAY?
IT'S A LONG STORY.
BUT ANYWAY, RIGHT AFTER IT HAPPENED, I TOLD MYRON ABOUT IT. THEN I THOUGHT MAYBE WE'D BETTER KEEP IT QUIET TILL I DECIDED WHAT TO DO WITH IT. SO THAT THING WITH THE GROUP WAS MYRON'S IDEA OF HELPING ME, I GUESS...
SO WHAT SHOULD I DO, DUCK? WHAT DO YOU THINK?
I THINK IT COONT HAVE HAPPENED TO A NICER GUY--AND YOU'RE SO SMART, YOU'LL KNOW WHAT TO DO WHEN THE TIME COMES!
GOOD OLD DUCK.
NEXT MORNING...
...THE HIJACKED CRUISE SHIP AJAX IS STILL SAILING WEST ACROSS THE ATLANTIC THIS MORNING.
MEANWHILE, ANOTHER TENSE DRAMA IS UNFOLDING IN UPSTATE NEW YORK, IN A RURAL AREA NEAR KINGSTON. AROUND 9AM, ROTTED PLANKS COVERING AN UNUSED WELL COLLAPSED BENEATH THE FEET OF EIGHT-YEAR-OLD ROBBY DONATELLI. A RESCUE TEAM IS TRYING DESPERATELY TO REACH THE CHILD, BUT THE DANGER OF A CAVE-IN IS HAMPERING THEIR EFFORTS...
POOR KID. DON'TCHA JUST WISH YOU COULD HELP HIM?
MAYBE I CAN...

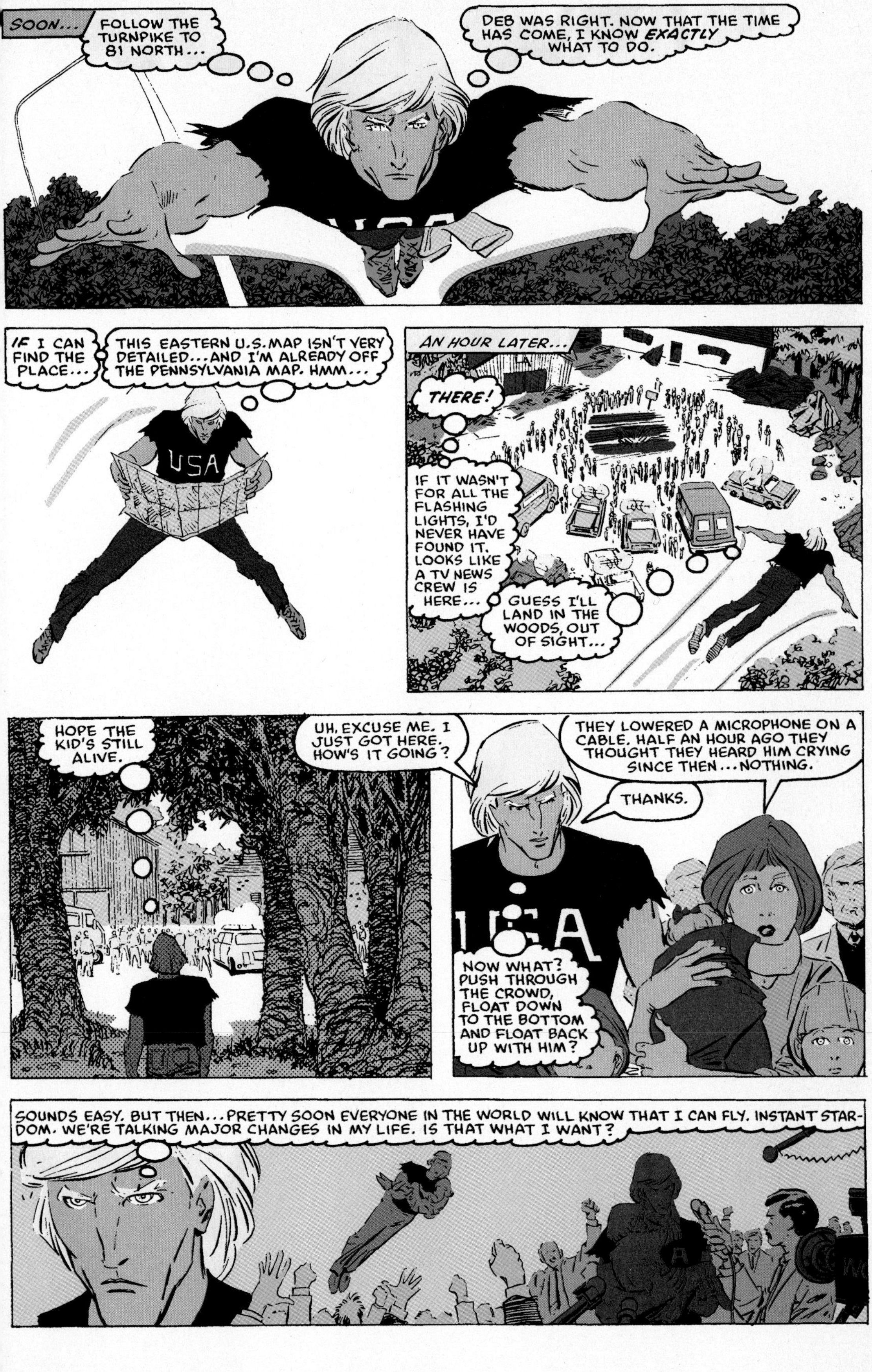
SOON...
FOLLOW THE TURNPIKE TO 81 NORTH...
DEB WAS RIGHT. NOW THAT THE TIME HAS COME, I KNOW EXACTLY WHAT TO DO.
USA
IF I CAN FIND THE PLACE...
THIS EASTERN U.S. MAP ISN'T VERY DETAILED...AND I'M ALREADY OFF THE PENNSYLVANIA MAP. HMM...
USA
AN HOUR LATER...
THERE!
IF IT WASN'T FOR ALL THE FLASHING LIGHTS, I'D NEVER HAVE FOUND IT. LOOKS LIKE A TV NEWS CREW IS HERE...
GUESS I'LL LAND IN THE WOODS, OUT OF SIGHT...
HOPE THE KID'S STILL ALIVE.
UH, EXCUSE ME. I JUST GOT HERE. HOW'S IT GOING?
THEY LOWERED A MICROPHONE ON A CABLE. HALF AN HOUR AGO THEY THOUGHT THEY HEARD HIM CRYING SINCE THEN...NOTHING.
THANKS.
USA
NOW WHAT? PUSH THROUGH THE CROWD, FLOAT DOWN TO THE BOTTOM AND FLOAT BACK UP WITH HIM?
SOUNDS EASY. BUT THEN...PRETTY SOON EVERYONE IN THE WORLD WILL KNOW THAT I CAN FLY. INSTANT STARDOM. WE'RE TALKING MAJOR CHANGES IN MY LIFE. IS THAT WHAT I WANT?

IT MIGHT BE WORTH IT IF I SAVED HIS LIFE. BUT WHAT IF HE'S ALREADY *DEAD*? OR WHAT IF HE'S BADLY HURT AND BY MOVING HIM I CRIPPLE HIM PERMANENTLY...OR *KILL* HIM?

THIS IS MORE COMPLICATED THAN I THOUGHT...

WAIT! I HAVE AN IDEA!

I'LL JUST ZIP BACK INTO THE WOODS WHILE NOBODY'S LOOKING...

MAYBE I CAN *TUNNEL* DOWN TO THE KID... SEE IF HE'S ALIVE, WITHOUT ANYBODY SEEING *ME*. IF HE IS, I'LL BRING HIM UP. IF NOT, I'LL LEAVE THE WAY I CAME, NO ONE THE WISER.

HEY, IT *WORKS*! I'M SO STRONG I CAN SORT OF *SWIM* THROUGH SOLID EARTH.

CAN'T SEE WHERE I'M GOING, THOUGH. *BLUHH! PHFF! YUCHH!*

STUPID. STUPID. STUPID.

I'LL HAVE TO GO DOWN THE WELL. MAYBE I CAN FIND A BAG TO PUT OVER MY HEAD.

HMP, WHY BOTHER? I'M SO COVERED WITH MUD EVEN MUM AND DAD WOULDN'T RECOGNIZE ME.

OKAY, SO THE WORLD WILL KNOW *SOMEONE* CAN FLY...

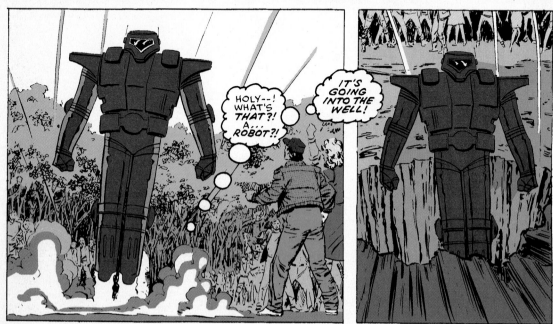

HOLY--! WHAT'S *THAT*?! A...ROBOT?!

IT'S GOING INTO THE WELL!

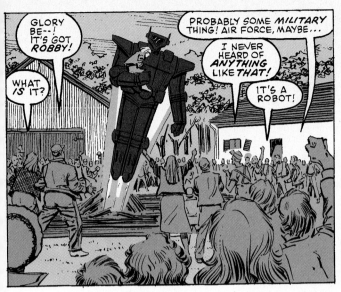

GLORY BE---! IT'S GOT *ROBBY!*

WHAT *IS* IT?

PROBABLY SOME *MILITARY* THING! AIR FORCE, MAYBE...

I NEVER HEARD OF *ANYTHING* LIKE *THAT!*

IT'S A ROBOT!

ROBBY! ROBBY!

MAMA...

YA-A YY!

I WISH I'D DONE THAT!

I *HAVE* TO FOLLOW THAT THING AND SEE WHAT IT IS!

IF I STAY LOW, THE TREES WILL SCREEN ME TILL I'M OUT OF EYEBALL RANGE OF THAT CROWD.

TWENTY MINUTES LATER...

THOSE TRUCKS MUST HAVE SOMETHING TO DO WITH IT.

NO SENSE TIPPING *MY* HAND...YET.

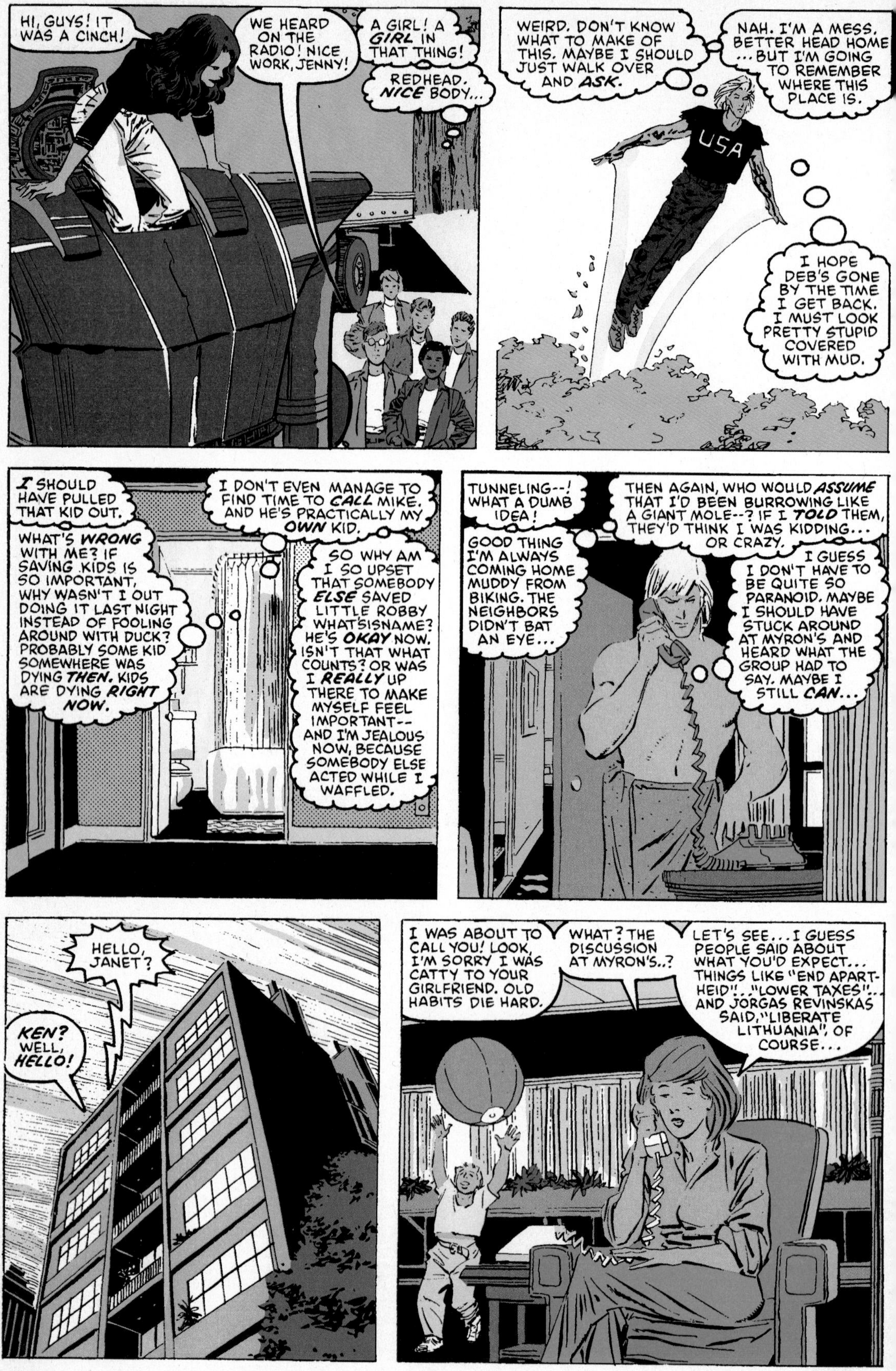

HI, GUYS! IT WAS A CINCH!
WE HEARD ON THE RADIO! NICE WORK, JENNY!
A GIRL! A GIRL IN THAT THING!
REDHEAD. NICE BODY...
WEIRD. DON'T KNOW WHAT TO MAKE OF THIS. MAYBE I SHOULD JUST WALK OVER AND ASK.
NAH. I'M A MESS. BETTER HEAD HOME ...BUT I'M GOING TO REMEMBER WHERE THIS PLACE IS.
USA
I HOPE DEB'S GONE BY THE TIME I GET BACK. I MUST LOOK PRETTY STUPID COVERED WITH MUD.
I SHOULD HAVE PULLED THAT KID OUT.
I DON'T EVEN MANAGE TO FIND TIME TO CALL MIKE. AND HE'S PRACTICALLY MY OWN KID.
WHAT'S WRONG WITH ME? IF SAVING KIDS IS SO IMPORTANT, WHY WASN'T I OUT DOING IT LAST NIGHT INSTEAD OF FOOLING AROUND WITH DUCK? PROBABLY SOME KID SOMEWHERE WAS DYING THEN. KIDS ARE DYING RIGHT NOW.
SO WHY AM I SO UPSET THAT SOMEBODY ELSE SAVED LITTLE ROBBY WHAT'SISNAME? HE'S OKAY NOW. ISN'T THAT WHAT COUNTS? OR WAS I REALLY UP THERE TO MAKE MYSELF FEEL IMPORTANT-- AND I'M JEALOUS NOW, BECAUSE SOMEBODY ELSE ACTED WHILE I WAFFLED.
TUNNELING--! WHAT A DUMB IDEA!
THEN AGAIN, WHO WOULD ASSUME THAT I'D BEEN BURROWING LIKE A GIANT MOLE--? IF I TOLD THEM, THEY'D THINK I WAS KIDDING... OR CRAZY.
GOOD THING I'M ALWAYS COMING HOME MUDDY FROM BIKING. THE NEIGHBORS DIDN'T BAT AN EYE...
I GUESS I DON'T HAVE TO BE QUITE SO PARANOID. MAYBE I SHOULD HAVE STUCK AROUND AT MYRON'S AND HEARD WHAT THE GROUP HAD TO SAY. MAYBE I STILL CAN...
...HELLO, JANET?
KEN? WELL, HELLO!
I WAS ABOUT TO CALL YOU! LOOK, I'M SORRY I WAS CATTY TO YOUR GIRLFRIEND. OLD HABITS DIE HARD.
WHAT? THE DISCUSSION AT MYRON'S..?
LET'S SEE... I GUESS PEOPLE SAID ABOUT WHAT YOU'D EXPECT... THINGS LIKE "END APARTHEID"..."LOWER TAXES"... AND JORGAS REVINSKAS SAID, "LIBERATE LITHUANIA", OF COURSE...

SHEILA LEONETTI SAID SHE'D SIMPLY *ENLIGHTEN* EVERYONE IN THE WORLD SO WE'D ALL BE LIKE HER. WHEN SHE SAID *THAT,* ROB LEONETTI LOOKED LIKE HE'D SWALLOWED A LIVE RAT.

AND YOU?

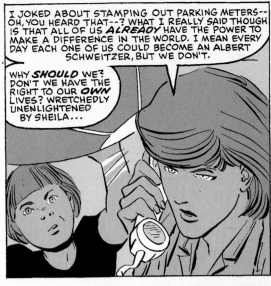

I JOKED ABOUT STAMPING OUT PARKING METERS-- OH, YOU HEARD THAT--? WHAT I REALLY SAID THOUGH IS THAT ALL OF US *ALREADY* HAVE THE POWER TO MAKE A DIFFERENCE IN THE WORLD. I MEAN EVERY DAY EACH ONE OF US COULD BECOME AN ALBERT SCHWEITZER, BUT WE DON'T.

WHY *SHOULD* WE? DON'T WE HAVE THE RIGHT TO OUR *OWN* LIVES? WRETCHEDLY UNENLIGHTENED BY SHEILA...

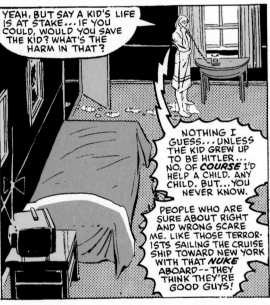

YEAH, BUT SAY A KID'S LIFE IS AT STAKE...IF YOU COULD, WOULD YOU SAVE THE KID? WHAT'S THE HARM IN THAT?

NOTHING I GUESS...UNLESS THE KID GREW UP TO BE HITLER... NO, OF *COURSE* I'D HELP A CHILD. ANY CHILD, BUT...YOU NEVER KNOW.

PEOPLE WHO ARE SURE ABOUT RIGHT AND WRONG SCARE ME. LIKE THOSE TERROR- ISTS SAILING THE CRUISE SHIP TOWARD NEW YORK WITH THAT *NUKE* ABOARD--THEY THINK THEY'RE GOOD GUYS!

YES, A NUKE... THEY *THINK.* IT'S ON THE NEWS!

OH, OKAY, KEN, I'LL TALK TO YOU LATER. NO, I DON'T MIND. THANKS FOR CALLING.

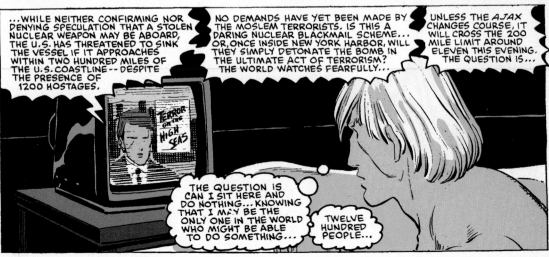

...WHILE NEITHER CONFIRMING NOR DENYING SPECULATION THAT A STOLEN NUCLEAR WEAPON MAY BE ABOARD, THE U.S. HAS THREATENED TO SINK THE VESSEL IF IT APPROACHES WITHIN TWO HUNDRED MILES OF THE U.S. COASTLINE--DESPITE THE PRESENCE OF 1200 HOSTAGES.

NO DEMANDS HAVE YET BEEN MADE BY THE MOSLEM TERRORISTS. IS THIS A DARING NUCLEAR BLACKMAIL SCHEME... OR, ONCE INSIDE NEW YORK HARBOR, WILL THEY SIMPLY DETONATE THE BOMB IN THE ULTIMATE ACT OF TERRORISM? THE WORLD WATCHES FEARFULLY...

UNLESS THE *AJAX* CHANGES COURSE, IT WILL CROSS THE 200 MILE LIMIT AROUND ELEVEN THIS EVENING. THE QUESTION IS...

TERROR ON THE HIGH SEAS

THE QUESTION IS CAN I SIT HERE AND DO NOTHING...KNOWING THAT I MAY BE THE ONLY ONE IN THE WORLD WHO MIGHT BE ABLE TO DO SOMETHING...

TWELVE HUNDRED PEOPLE...

41

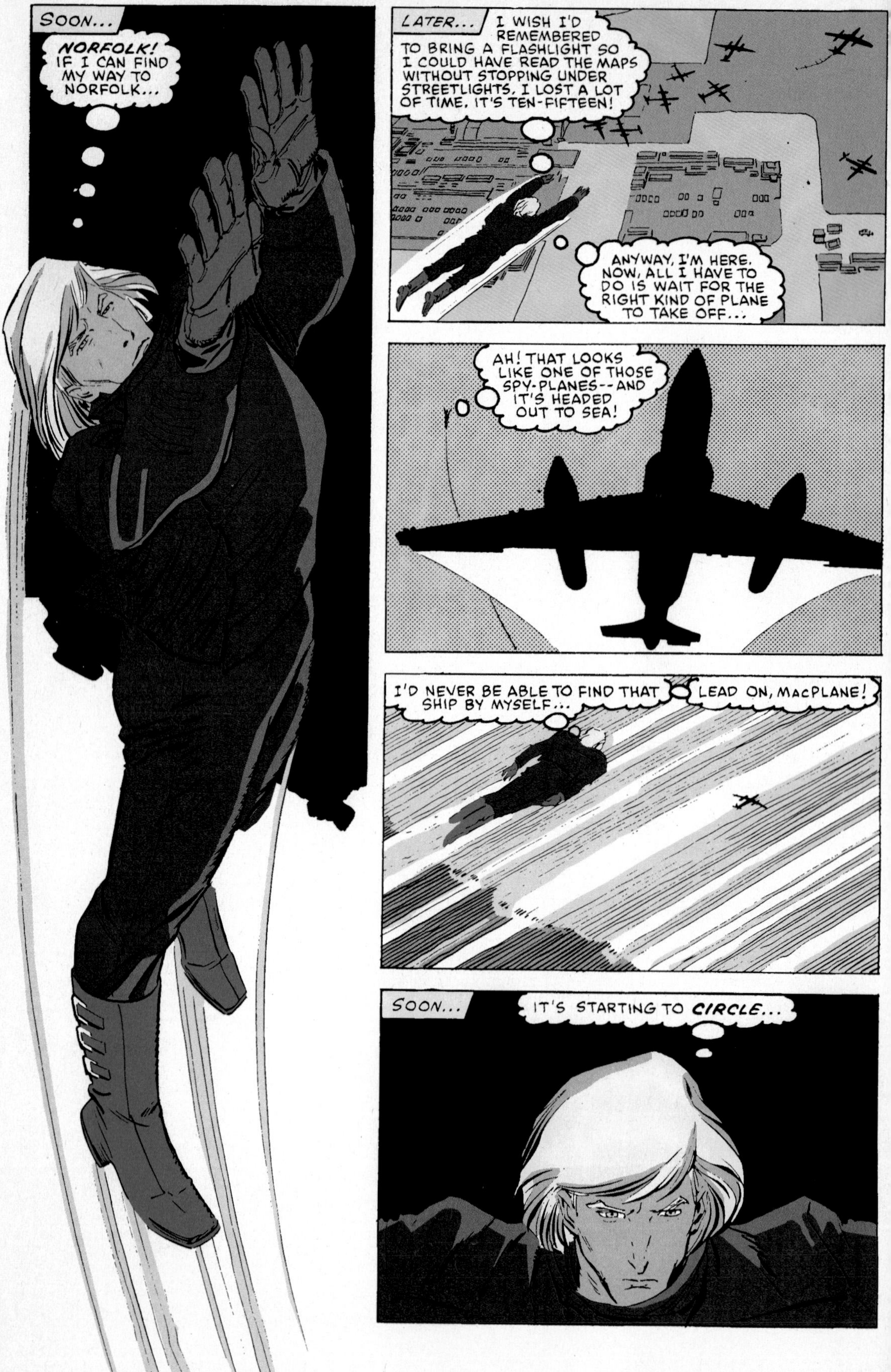
SOON...
NORFOLK! IF I CAN FIND MY WAY TO NORFOLK...
LATER...
I WISH I'D REMEMBERED TO BRING A FLASHLIGHT SO I COULD HAVE READ THE MAPS WITHOUT STOPPING UNDER STREETLIGHTS. I LOST A LOT OF TIME. IT'S TEN-FIFTEEN!
ANYWAY, I'M HERE. NOW, ALL I HAVE TO DO IS WAIT FOR THE RIGHT KIND OF PLANE TO TAKE OFF...
AH! THAT LOOKS LIKE ONE OF THOSE SPY-PLANES--AND IT'S HEADED OUT TO SEA!
I'D NEVER BE ABLE TO FIND THAT SHIP BY MYSELF...
LEAD ON, MACPLANE!
SOON...
IT'S STARTING TO CIRCLE...

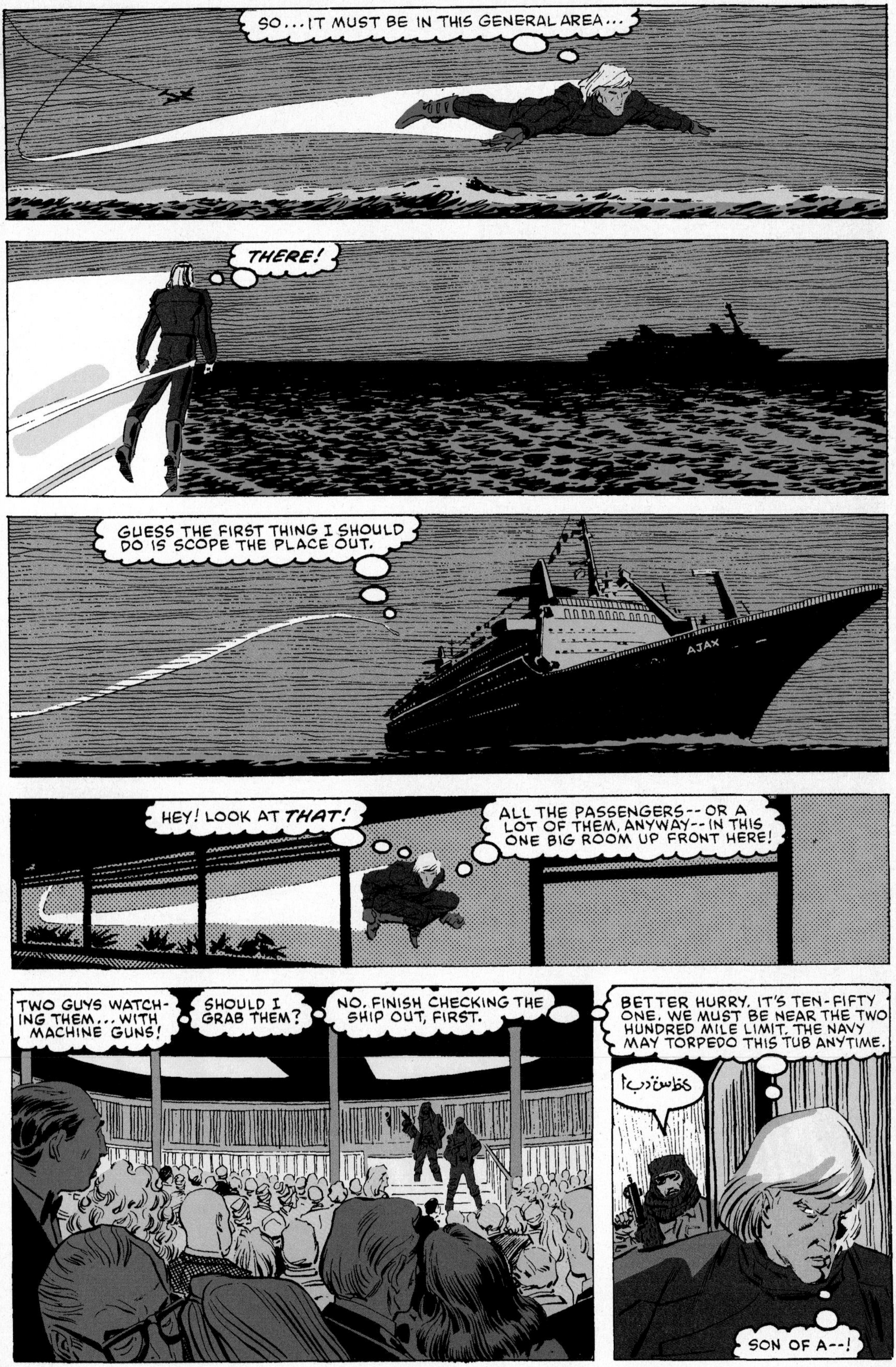
SO... IT MUST BE IN THIS GENERAL AREA...
THERE!
GUESS THE FIRST THING I SHOULD DO IS SCOPE THE PLACE OUT.
AJAX
HEY! LOOK AT *THAT!*
ALL THE PASSENGERS-- OR A LOT OF THEM, ANYWAY-- IN THIS ONE BIG ROOM UP FRONT HERE!
TWO GUYS WATCHING THEM... WITH MACHINE GUNS!
SHOULD I GRAB THEM?
NO. FINISH CHECKING THE SHIP OUT, FIRST.
BETTER HURRY. IT'S TEN-FIFTY ONE. WE MUST BE NEAR THE TWO HUNDRED MILE LIMIT. THE NAVY MAY TORPEDO THIS TUB ANYTIME.
SON OF A--!

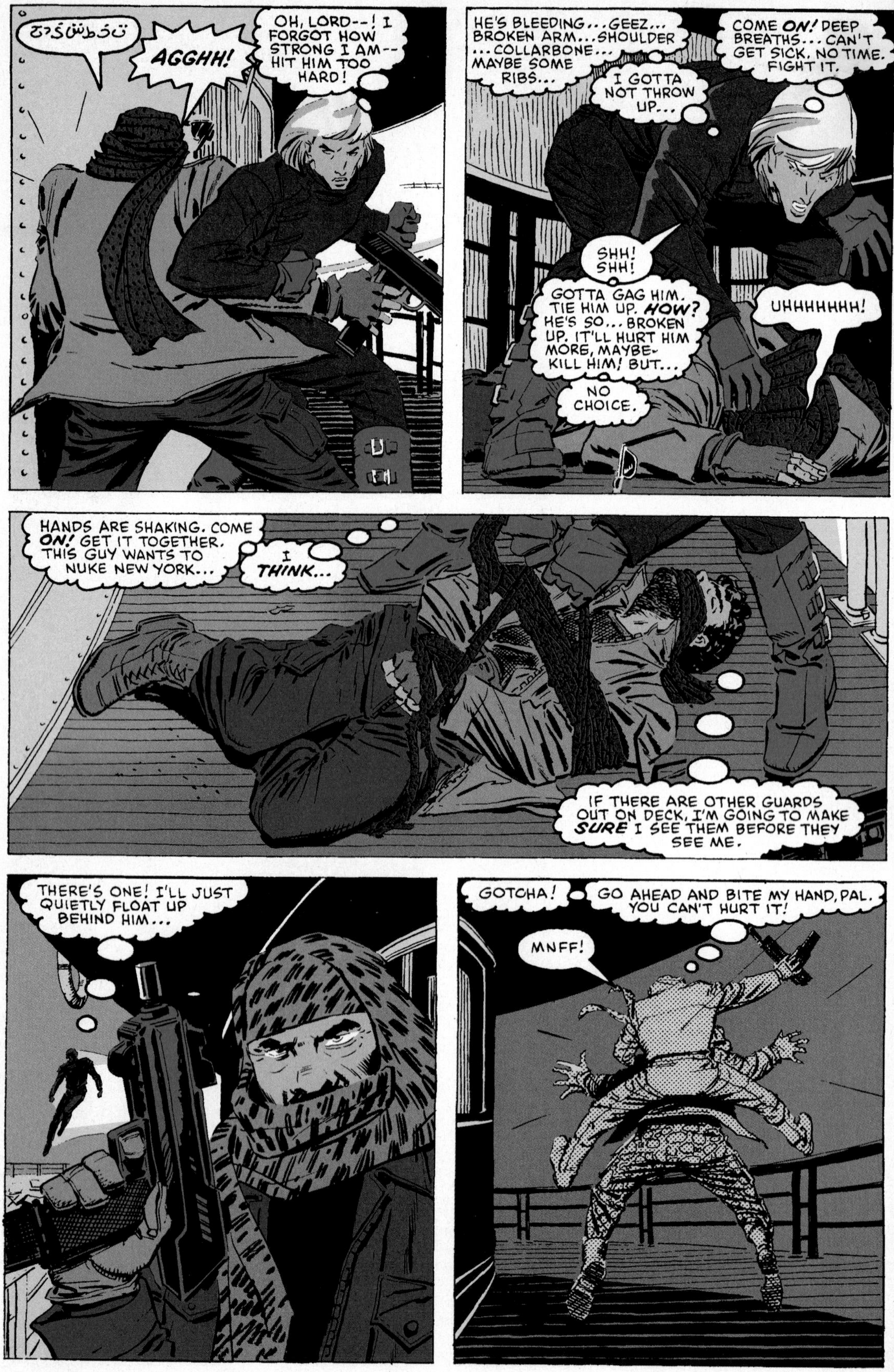

AGGHH!
OH, LORD--! I FORGOT HOW STRONG I AM-- HIT HIM TOO HARD!
HE'S BLEEDING...GEEZ... BROKEN ARM...SHOULDER ...COLLARBONE... MAYBE SOME RIBS...
COME ON! DEEP BREATHS... CAN'T GET SICK. NO TIME. FIGHT IT.
I GOTTA NOT THROW UP...
SHH! SHH!
GOTTA GAG HIM. TIE HIM UP. HOW? HE'S SO... BROKEN UP. IT'LL HURT HIM MORE, MAYBE KILL HIM! BUT...
UHHHHHHH!
NO CHOICE.
HANDS ARE SHAKING. COME ON! GET IT TOGETHER. THIS GUY WANTS TO NUKE NEW YORK...
I THINK...
IF THERE ARE OTHER GUARDS OUT ON DECK, I'M GOING TO MAKE SURE I SEE THEM BEFORE THEY SEE ME.
THERE'S ONE! I'LL JUST QUIETLY FLOAT UP BEHIND HIM...
GOTCHA!
GO AHEAD AND BITE MY HAND, PAL. YOU CAN'T HURT IT!
MNFF!

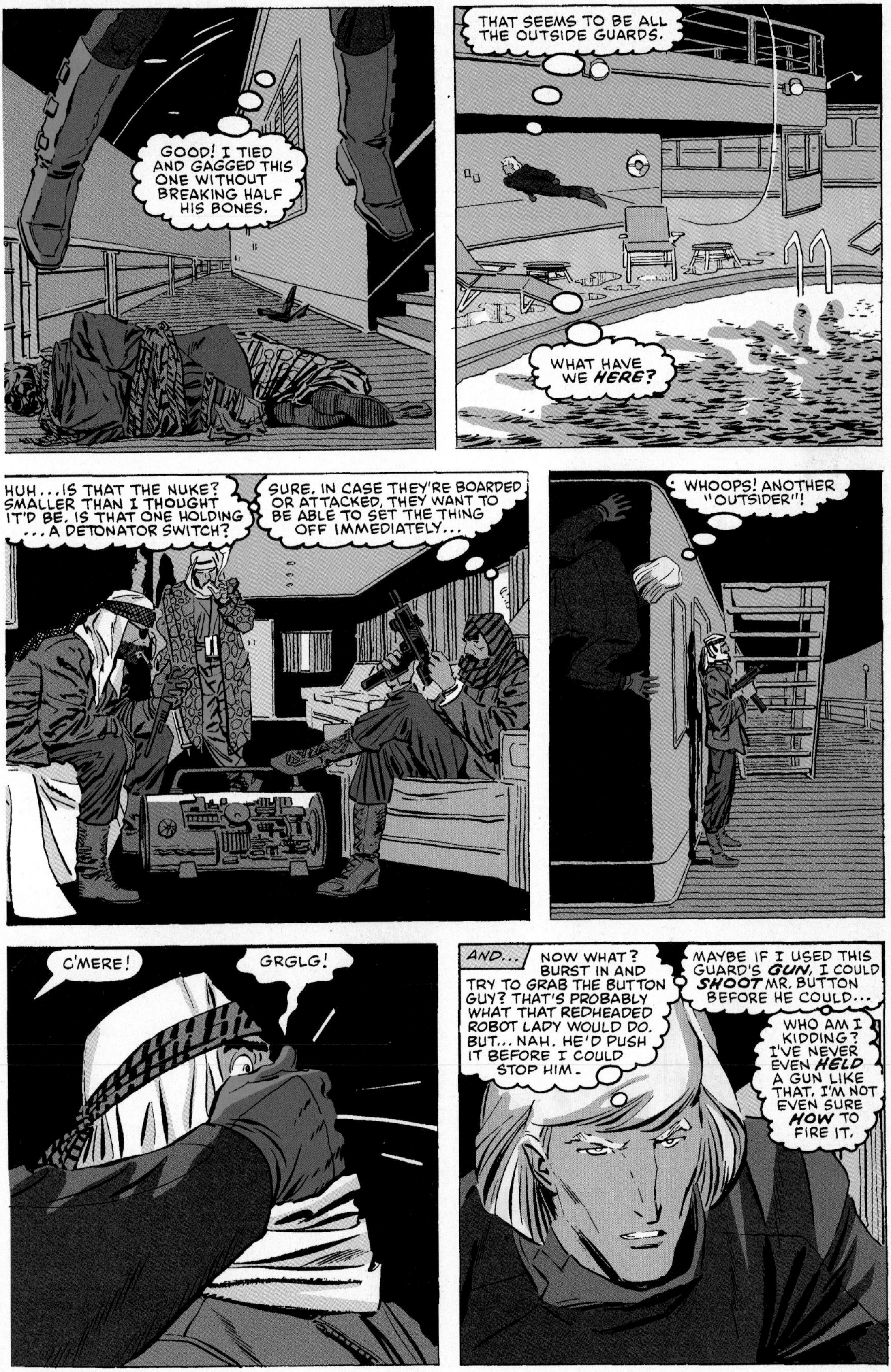
GOOD! I TIED AND GAGGED THIS ONE WITHOUT BREAKING HALF HIS BONES.
THAT SEEMS TO BE ALL THE OUTSIDE GUARDS.
WHAT HAVE WE HERE?
HUH...IS THAT THE NUKE? SMALLER THAN I THOUGHT IT'D BE. IS THAT ONE HOLDING ...A DETONATOR SWITCH?
SURE. IN CASE THEY'RE BOARDED OR ATTACKED, THEY WANT TO BE ABLE TO SET THE THING OFF IMMEDIATELY...
WHOOPS! ANOTHER "OUTSIDER"!
C'MERE!
GRGLG!
AND...
NOW WHAT? BURST IN AND TRY TO GRAB THE BUTTON GUY? THAT'S PROBABLY WHAT THAT REDHEADED ROBOT LADY WOULD DO. BUT... NAH. HE'D PUSH IT BEFORE I COULD STOP HIM.
MAYBE IF I USED THIS GUARD'S GUN, I COULD SHOOT MR. BUTTON BEFORE HE COULD...
WHO AM I KIDDING? I'VE NEVER EVEN HELD A GUN LIKE THAT. I'M NOT EVEN SURE HOW TO FIRE IT.

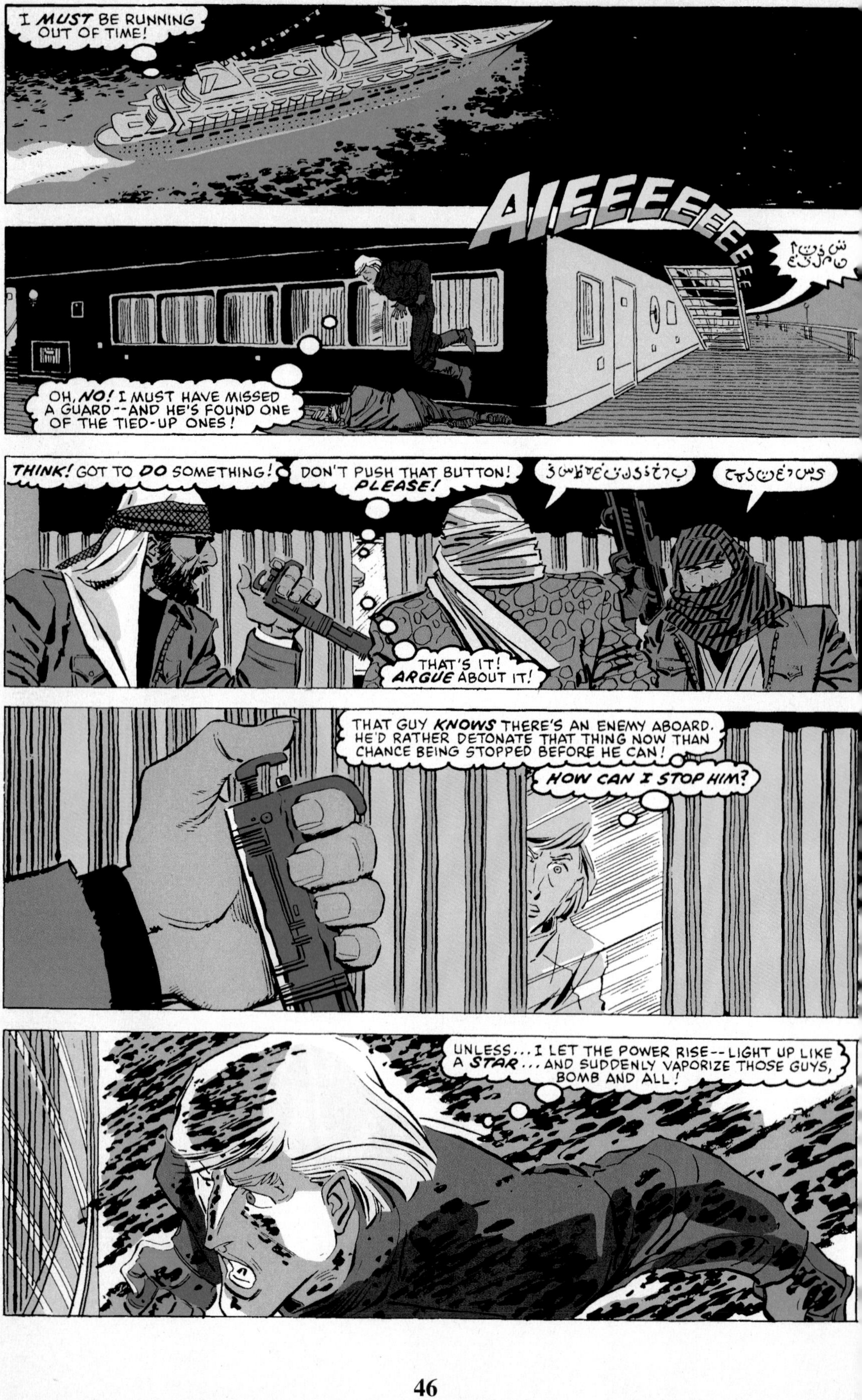
I MUST BE RUNNING OUT OF TIME!
AIEEEEEEEEEE
OH, NO! I MUST HAVE MISSED A GUARD--AND HE'S FOUND ONE OF THE TIED-UP ONES!
THINK! GOT TO DO SOMETHING!
DON'T PUSH THAT BUTTON! PLEASE!
THAT'S IT! ARGUE ABOUT IT!
THAT GUY KNOWS THERE'S AN ENEMY ABOARD. HE'D RATHER DETONATE THAT THING NOW THAN CHANCE BEING STOPPED BEFORE HE CAN!
HOW CAN I STOP HIM?
UNLESS... I LET THE POWER RISE--LIGHT UP LIKE A STAR... AND SUDDENLY VAPORIZE THOSE GUYS, BOMB AND ALL!

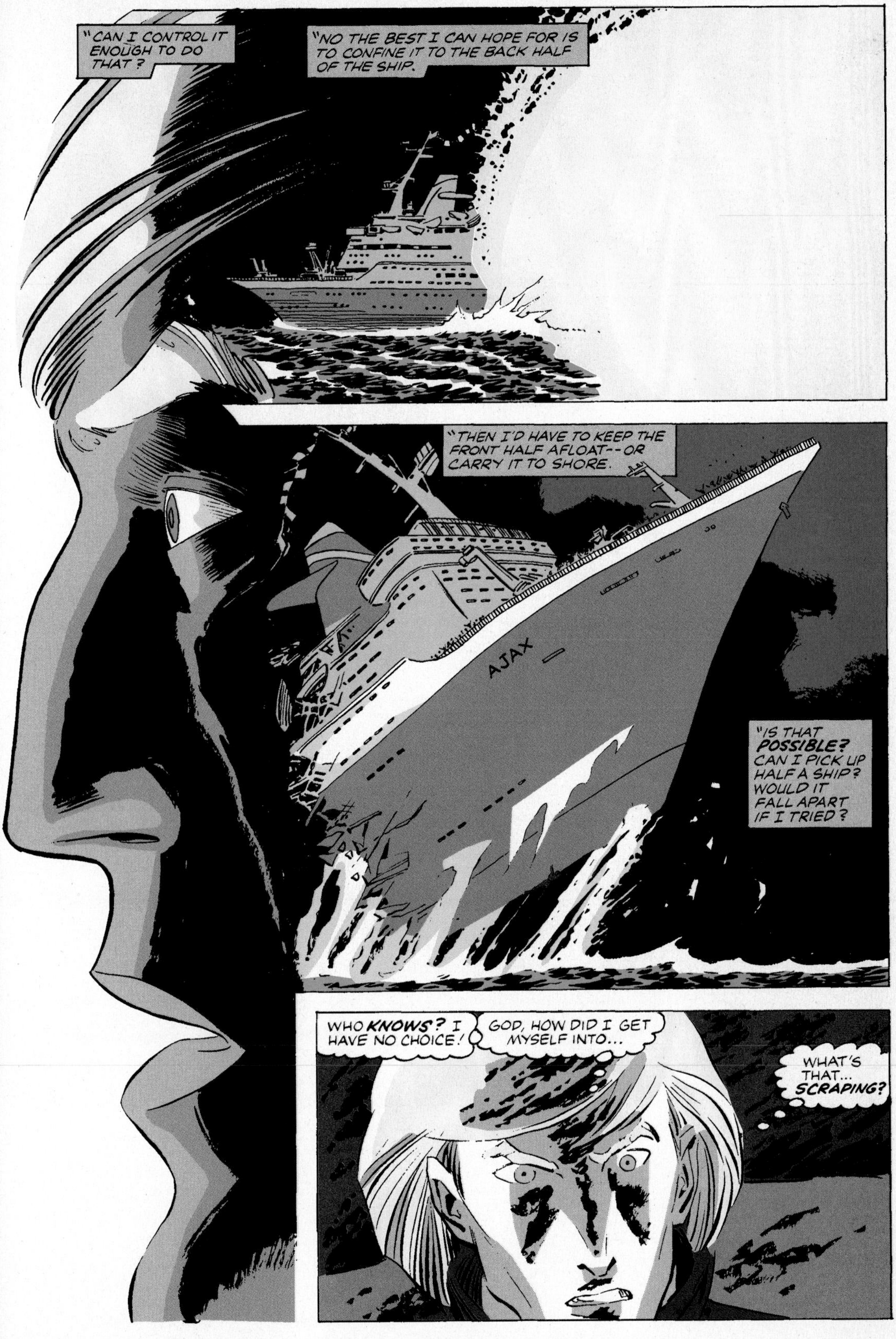
"CAN I CONTROL IT ENOUGH TO DO THAT?
"NO THE BEST I CAN HOPE FOR IS TO CONFINE IT TO THE BACK HALF OF THE SHIP.
"THEN I'D HAVE TO KEEP THE FRONT HALF AFLOAT--OR CARRY IT TO SHORE.
AJAX
"IS THAT POSSIBLE? CAN I PICK UP HALF A SHIP? WOULD IT FALL APART IF I TRIED?
WHO KNOWS? I HAVE NO CHOICE!
GOD, HOW DID I GET MYSELF INTO...
WHAT'S THAT... SCRAPING?

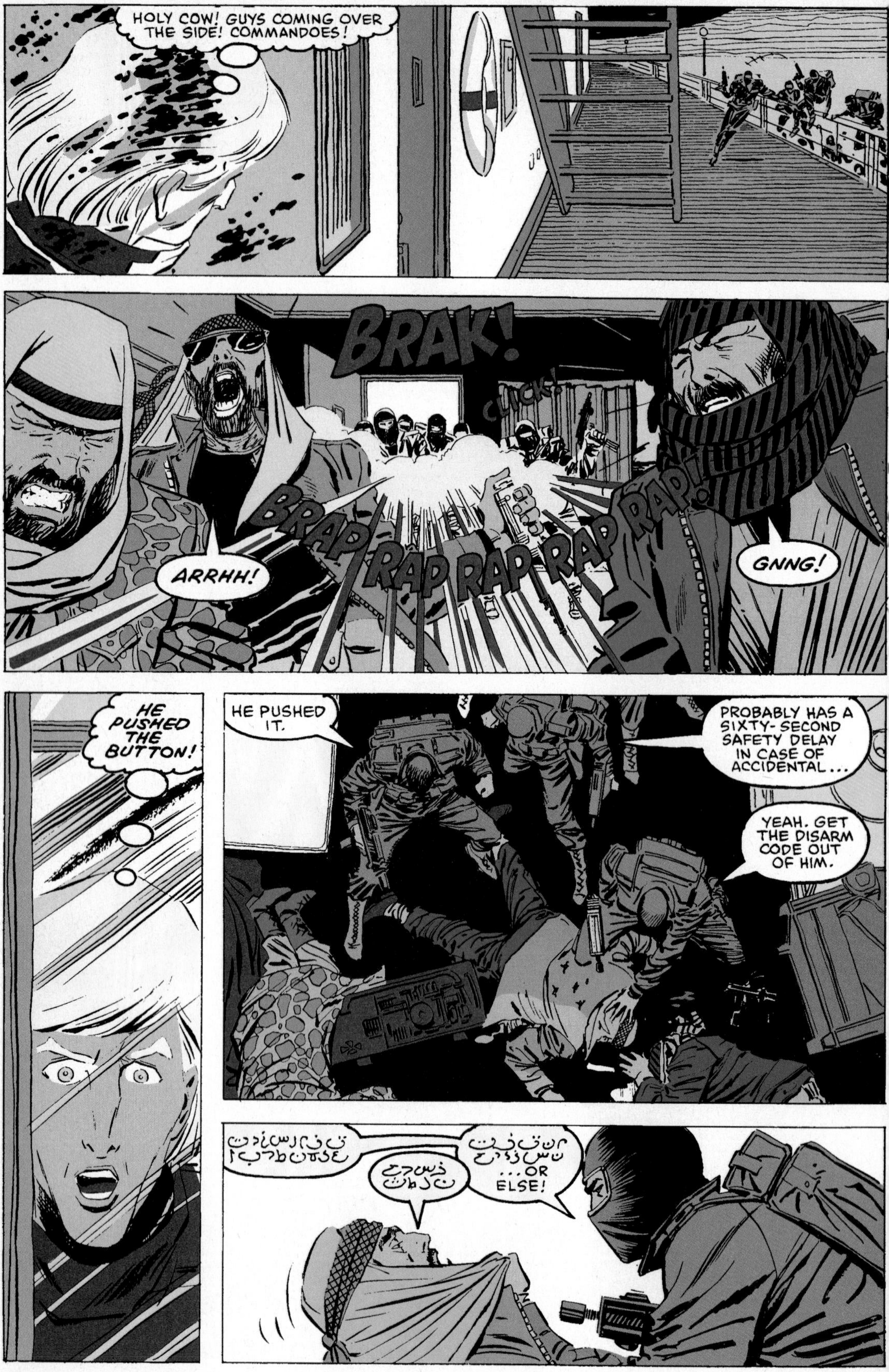
HOLY COW! GUYS COMING OVER THE SIDE! COMMANDOES!
BRAK!
CLICK!
ARRHH!
BRAP RAP RAP RAP RAP RAP!
GNNG!
HE PUSHED THE BUTTON!
HE PUSHED IT.
PROBABLY HAS A SIXTY-SECOND SAFETY DELAY IN CASE OF ACCIDENTAL...
YEAH. GET THE DISARM CODE OUT OF HIM.
...OR ELSE!

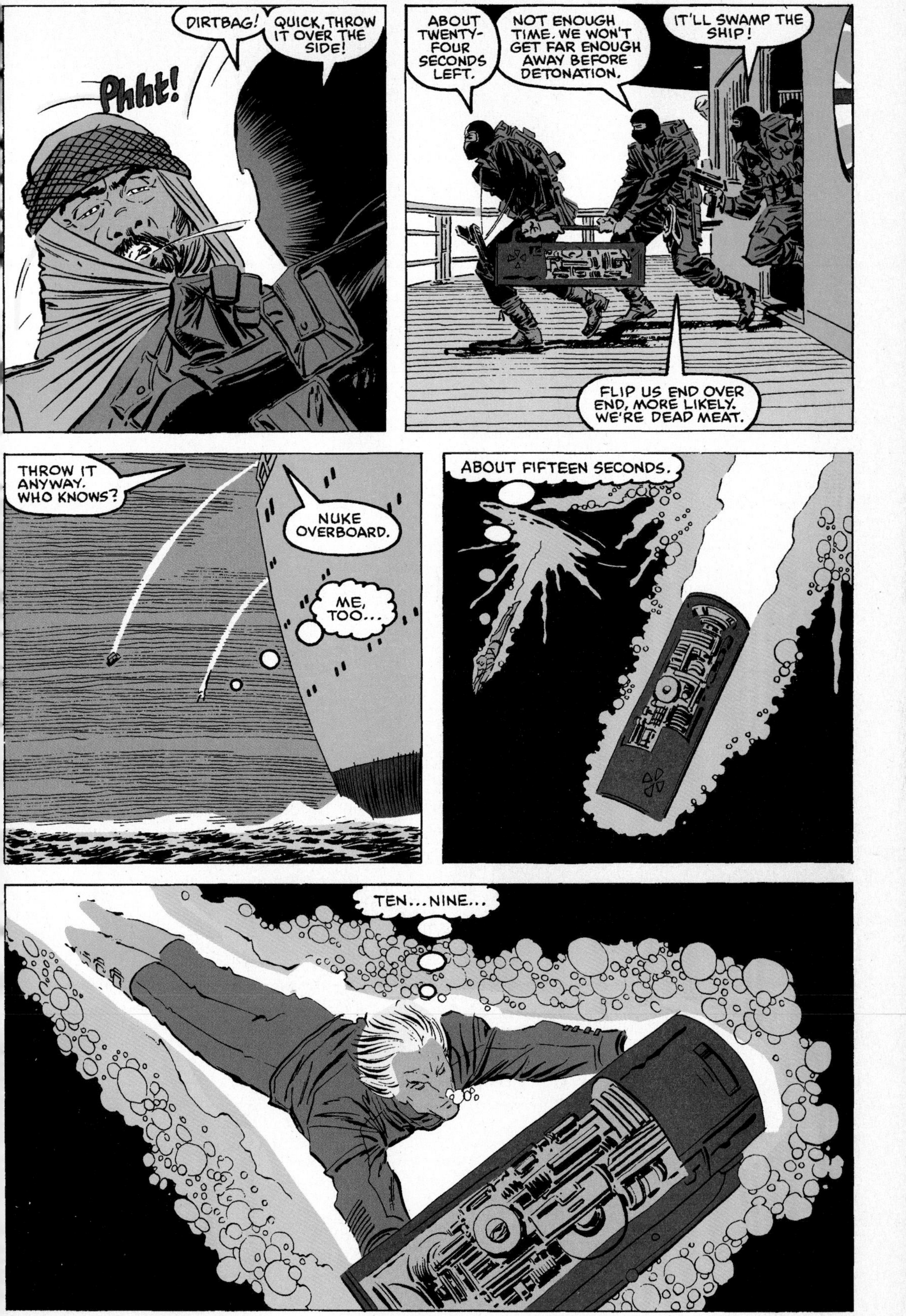
DIRTBAG!
QUICK, THROW IT OVER THE SIDE!
Phht!
ABOUT TWENTY-FOUR SECONDS LEFT.
NOT ENOUGH TIME. WE WON'T GET FAR ENOUGH AWAY BEFORE DETONATION.
IT'LL SWAMP THE SHIP!
FLIP US END OVER END, MORE LIKELY. WE'RE DEAD MEAT.
THROW IT ANYWAY. WHO KNOWS?
NUKE OVERBOARD.
ME, TOO...
ABOUT FIFTEEN SECONDS.
TEN...NINE...

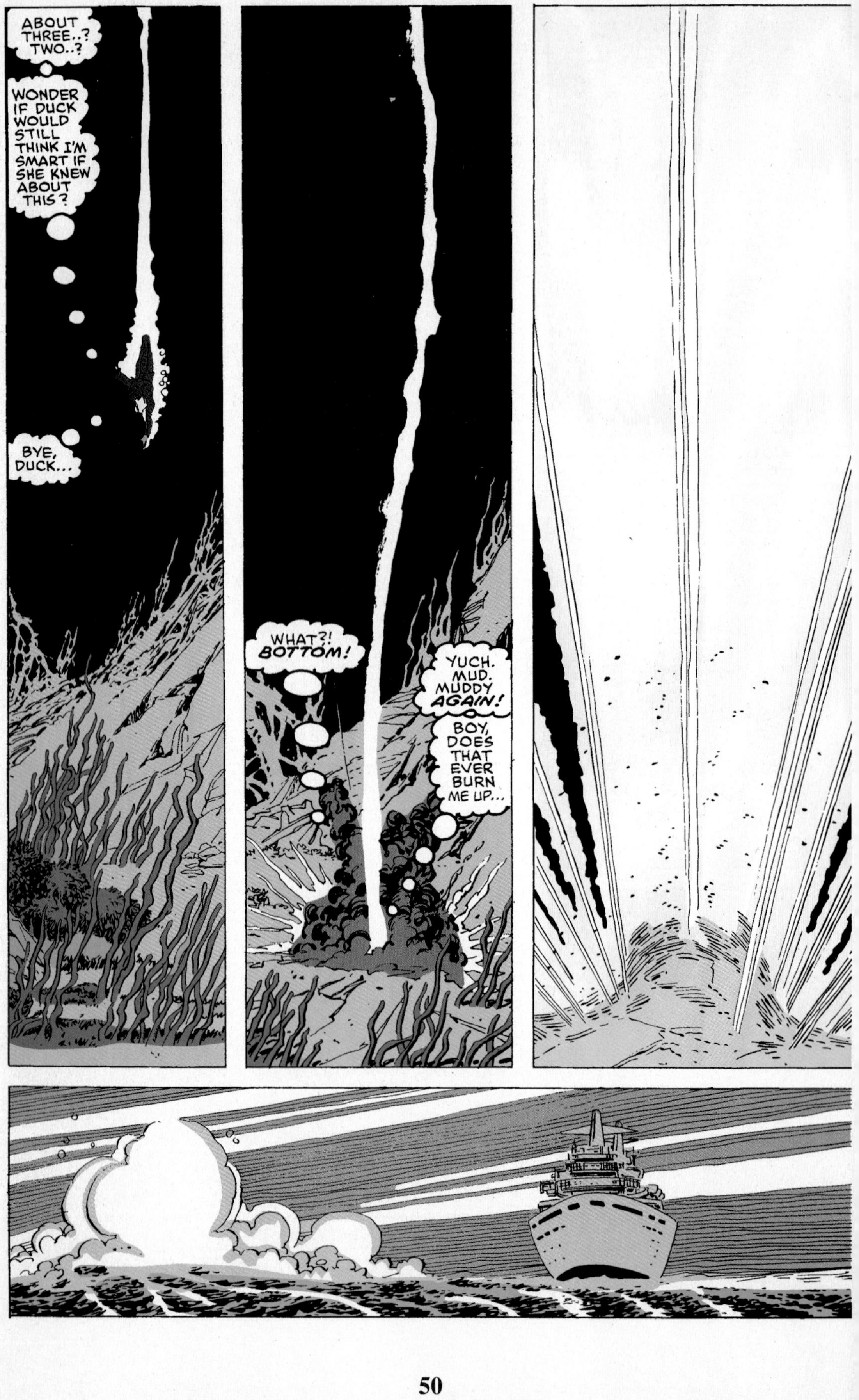
ABOUT THREE..? TWO..?
WONDER IF DUCK WOULD STILL THINK I'M SMART IF SHE KNEW ABOUT THIS?
BYE, DUCK...
WHAT?! BOTTOM!
YUCH. MUD. MUDDY AGAIN!
BOY, DOES THAT EVER BURN ME UP...

OWW...

I HOPE ALL THE MUD AND WATER MUTED THE BLAST ENOUGH SO THE SHIP SURVIVED. GUESS I'LL SOON FIND OUT.

I CAN'T BELIEVE *I* SURVIVED-- SURVIVED A *NUKE*, POINT BLANK!

THE *MUD* DID IT--MADE ME TOO *MAD* TO DIE!

AT LEAST THE BLAST CLEANED ME OFF...

GO HOME NOW. HMM. MAYBE I'LL MAKE A STOP ALONG THE WAY.

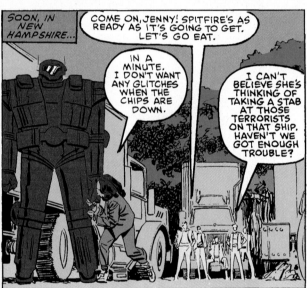

SOON, IN NEW HAMPSHIRE...

COME ON, JENNY! SPITFIRE'S AS READY AS IT'S GOING TO GET. LET'S GO EAT.

IN A MINUTE. I DON'T WANT ANY GLITCHES WHEN THE CHIPS ARE DOWN.

I CAN'T BELIEVE SHE'S THINKING OF TAKING A STAB AT THOSE TERRORISTS ON THAT SHIP. HAVEN'T WE GOT ENOUGH TROUBLE?

NO NEED TO WORRY ABOUT THE SHIP. IT WAS RESCUED. SOME COMMANDO GROUP.

YEAH? PROBABLY *DELTA FORCE*. BUT WHO ARE YOU, PAL?

SOMEONE WHO KNOWS A LOT ABOUT YOU AND THAT ...ROBOT SUIT, SO NO GAMES, HUH? LET'S TALK.

MOMENTS LATER, IN-SIDE ONE OF THE TRAILERS...

FIRST... UH, WITH ALL THIS EQUIPMENT COULD YOU TELL IF THERE'S, UH... ANY UNUSUAL RADIOACTIVITY AROUND?

YES. AND NO, THERE ISN'T. WHY?

WHAT IS THAT... ROBOT?

I SUPPOSE IT CAN'T HURT TO TELL YOU THIS MUCH-- THAT "ROBOT" IS THE *MAN-AMPLIFIED CONSTRUCTION SUIT*--A SOPHISTI-CATED MOBILE ARMORED EXO-SKELETON USEFUL FOR...LOTS OF STUFF.

LIKE SAVING KIDS FROM WELLS. I SAW IT. WHY ARE YOU HIDING OUT HERE IN THE MOUNTAINS?

LET'S JUST SAY WE HAVE A *MISUNDER-STANDING* WITH THE LAW. NOTHING THAT CONCERNS YOU.

RIGHT. WHAT DOES CONCERN ME, THOUGH, IS THE DAMAGE YOU MIGHT CAUSE WITH WELL-INTENTIONED INTERFERING. I JUST HAD A HARD LESSON ON THAT SCORE. A CLOSE CALL.

IF YOU'RE GOING TO TAKE CHARGE OF SOME SITUATION --JUST BE AWARE OF ALL THAT CAN GO WRONG...ALL THE POTENTIAL CONSEQUENCES AND WHO'S GOING TO BEAR THEM.

THINK ABOUT IT.

WHERE DO YOU THINK YOU'RE GOING?

HOME.

NOT YET, MISTER. IT'S OUR TURN FOR QUESTIONS. YOU'RE GOING NOWHERE UNTIL WE GET SOME ANSWERS!

USE THIS WRENCH MUCH?

NO...

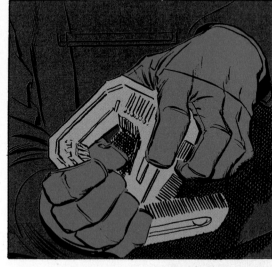

IT'S SCULPTURE NOW.

SEE YOU AROUND.

OY.

LATER...

...DARING RESCUE OF THE CRUISE SHIP *AJAX* BY A DELTA FORCE ANTI-TERRORIST SQUADRON. A PENTAGON SPOKESMAN SAID NO NUCLEAR DEVICE WAS FOUND ON BOARD. PASSENGERS REPORTED HEARING A SMALL MUFFLED EXPLOSION, POSSIBLY A *GRENADE* THROWN OVERBOARD DURING THE SCUFFLE.

NEXT: *CLOSE ENCOUNTER*

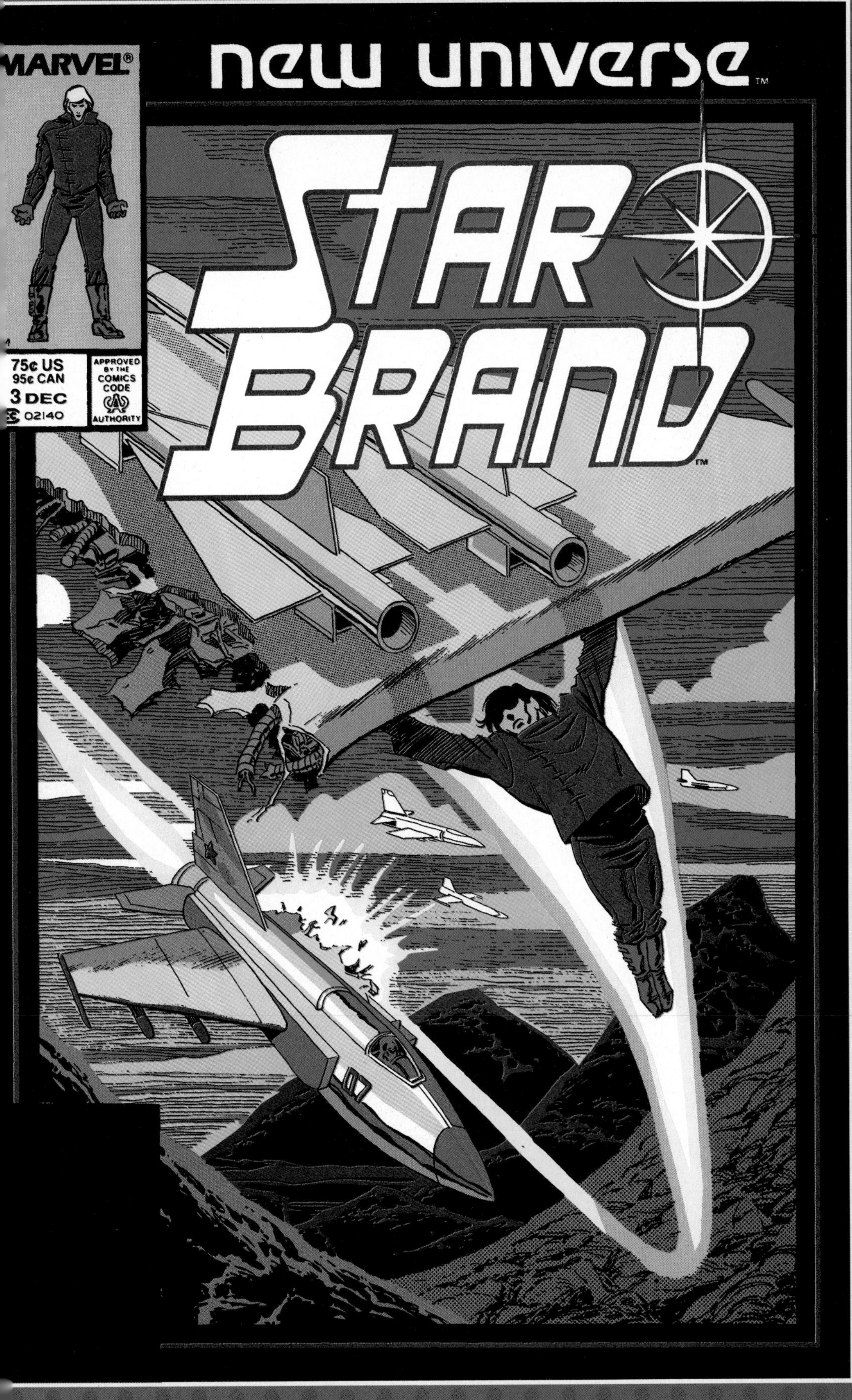
MARVEL®
NEW UNIVERSE™
STAR BRAND™
75¢ US
95¢ CAN
3 DEC
02140
APPROVED BY THE COMICS CODE AUTHORITY

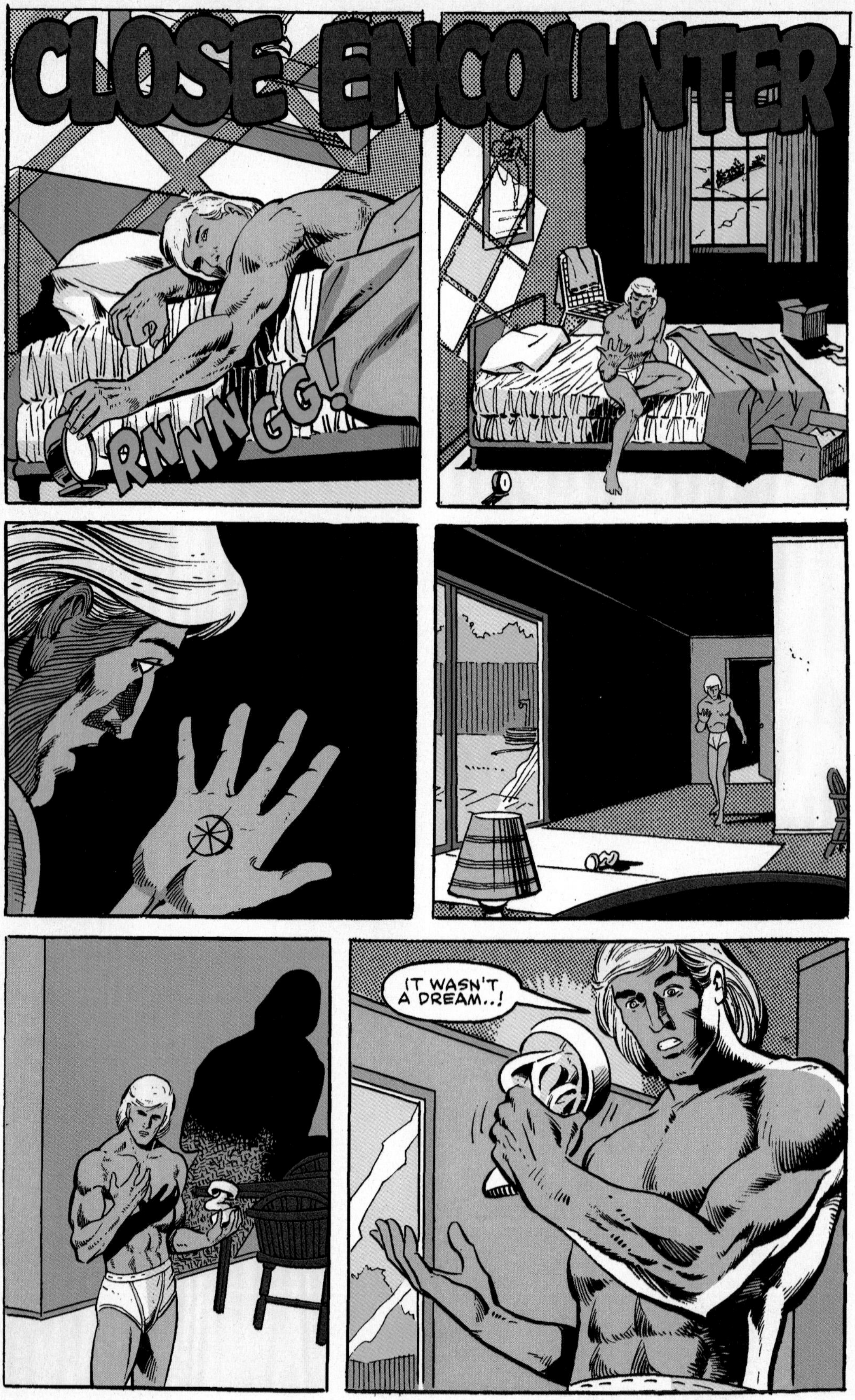
CLOSE ENCOUNTER
RNNNGG!
IT WASN'T A DREAM..!

JIM SHOOTER WRITER | ALEX SAVIUK PENCILER | VINCE COLLETTA INKER | JOE ROSEN LETTERER | BOB SHAREN COLORIST | MICHAEL HIGGINS EDITOR

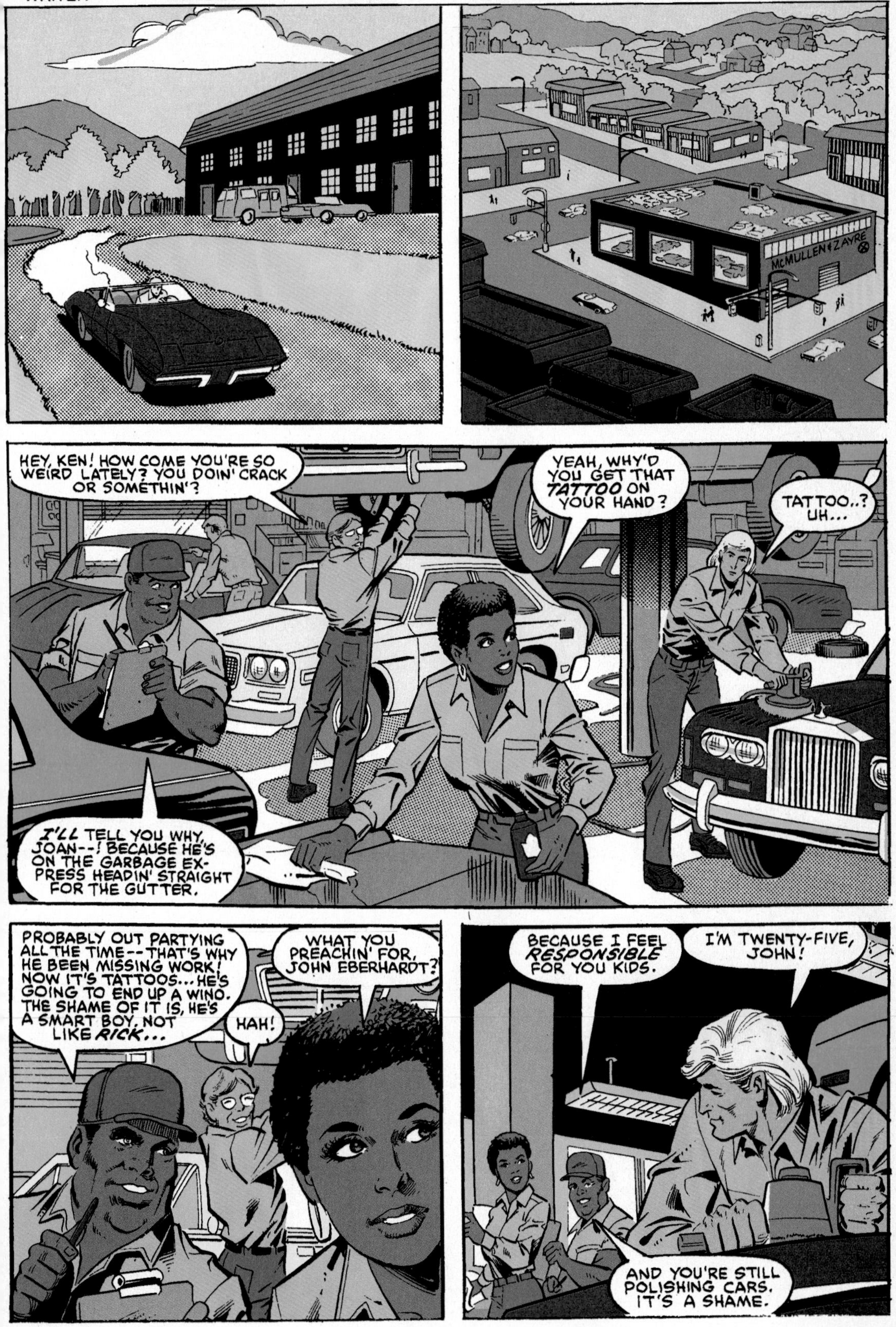

McMULLEN & ZAYRE
HEY, KEN! HOW COME YOU'RE SO WEIRD LATELY? YOU DOIN' CRACK OR SOMETHIN'?
YEAH, WHY'D YOU GET THAT *TATTOO* ON YOUR HAND?
TATTOO..? UH...
I'LL TELL YOU WHY, JOAN--! BECAUSE HE'S ON THE GARBAGE EXPRESS HEADIN' STRAIGHT FOR THE GUTTER.
PROBABLY OUT PARTYING ALL THE TIME--THAT'S WHY HE BEEN MISSING WORK! NOW IT'S TATTOOS... HE'S GOING TO END UP A WINO. THE SHAME OF IT IS, HE'S A SMART BOY, NOT LIKE *RICK*...
HAH!
WHAT YOU PREACHIN' FOR, JOHN EBERHARDT?
BECAUSE I FEEL *RESPONSIBLE* FOR YOU KIDS.
I'M TWENTY-FIVE, JOHN!
AND YOU'RE STILL POLISHING CARS. IT'S A SHAME.

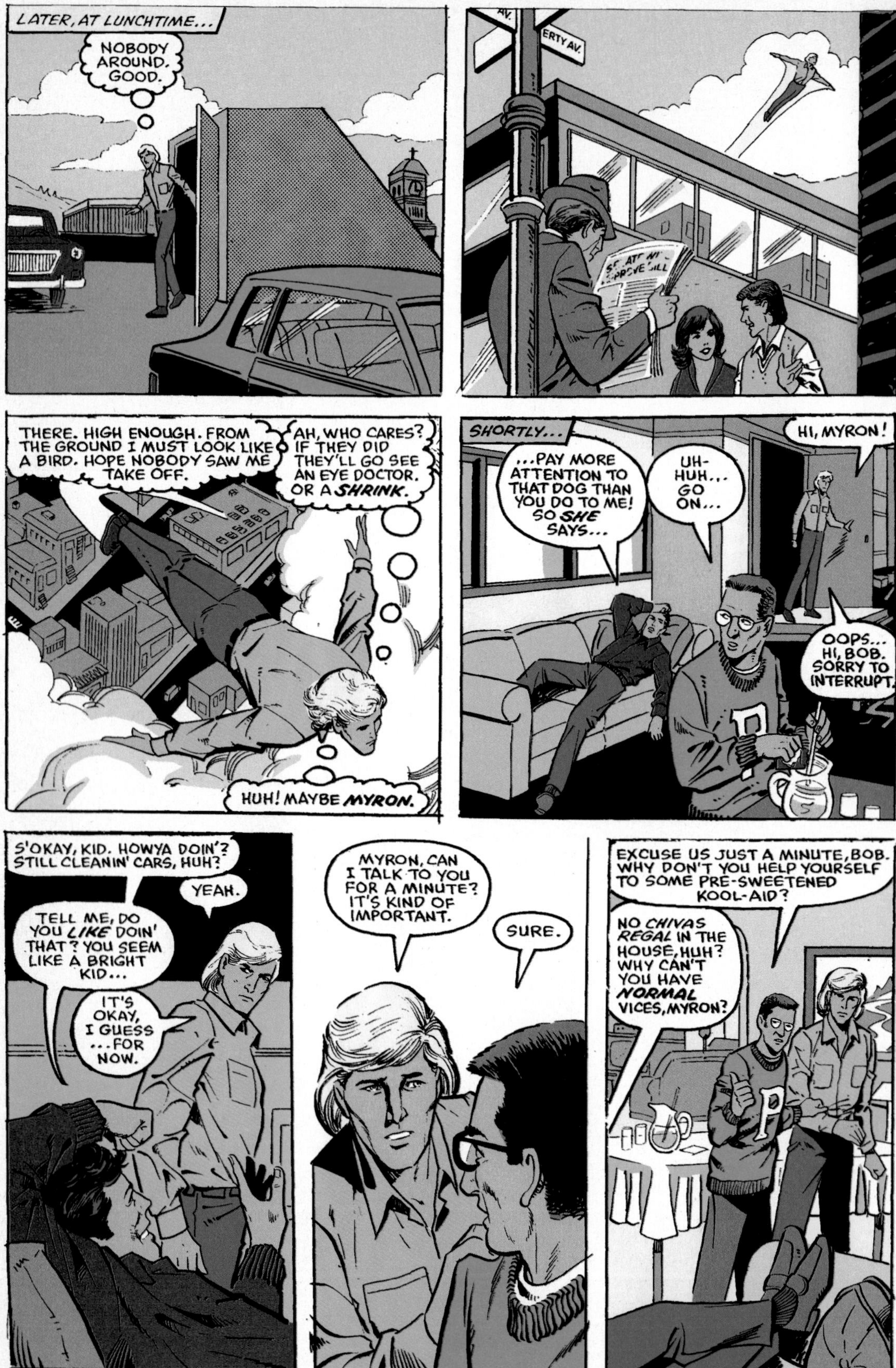
LATER, AT LUNCHTIME...
NOBODY AROUND. GOOD.
THERE. HIGH ENOUGH. FROM THE GROUND I MUST LOOK LIKE A BIRD. HOPE NOBODY SAW ME TAKE OFF.
AH, WHO CARES? IF THEY DID THEY'LL GO SEE AN EYE DOCTOR. OR A SHRINK.
HUH! MAYBE MYRON.
SHORTLY...
...PAY MORE ATTENTION TO THAT DOG THAN YOU DO TO ME! SO SHE SAYS...
UH-HUH... GO ON...
HI, MYRON!
OOPS... HI, BOB. SORRY TO INTERRUPT.
S'OKAY, KID. HOWYA DOIN'? STILL CLEANIN' CARS, HUH?
YEAH.
TELL ME, DO YOU LIKE DOIN' THAT? YOU SEEM LIKE A BRIGHT KID...
IT'S OKAY, I GUESS ...FOR NOW.
MYRON, CAN I TALK TO YOU FOR A MINUTE? IT'S KIND OF IMPORTANT.
SURE.
EXCUSE US JUST A MINUTE, BOB. WHY DON'T YOU HELP YOURSELF TO SOME PRE-SWEETENED KOOL-AID?
NO CHIVAS REGAL IN THE HOUSE, HUH? WHY CAN'T YOU HAVE NORMAL VICES, MYRON?

WHAT'S SO URGENT? IS IT ABOUT THE STAR BRAND?

YES, I GUESS. I DON'T KNOW. I JUST NEED SOMEBODY TO *TALK* TO.

HMPH! LAST WEEK YOU TOLD ME TO GET MY "MANIPULATIVE BUTT" OFF YOUR CASE.

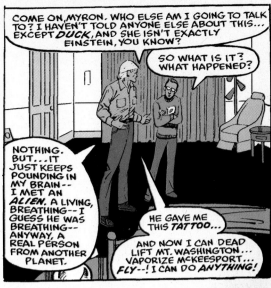

COME ON, MYRON. WHO ELSE AM I GOING TO TALK TO? I HAVEN'T TOLD ANYONE ELSE ABOUT THIS... EXCEPT *DUCK*, AND SHE ISN'T EXACTLY EINSTEIN, YOU KNOW?

SO WHAT IS IT? WHAT HAPPENED?

NOTHING. BUT... IT JUST KEEPS POUNDING IN MY BRAIN-- I MET AN *ALIEN.* A LIVING, BREATHING-- I GUESS HE WAS BREATHING-- ANYWAY, A REAL PERSON FROM ANOTHER PLANET.

HE GAVE ME THIS *TATTOO*...

AND NOW I CAN DEAD LIFT MT. WASHINGTON... VAPORIZE McKEESPORT... *FLY*--! I CAN DO *ANYTHING!*

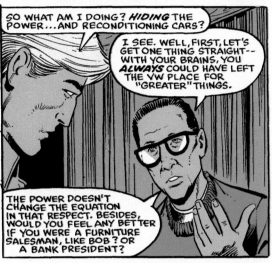

SO WHAT AM I DOING? *HIDING* THE POWER... AND RECONDITIONING CARS?

I SEE. WELL, FIRST, LET'S GET ONE THING STRAIGHT-- WITH YOUR BRAINS, YOU *ALWAYS* COULD HAVE LEFT THE VW PLACE FOR "GREATER" THINGS.

THE POWER DOESN'T CHANGE THE EQUATION IN THAT RESPECT. BESIDES, WOULD YOU FEEL ANY BETTER IF YOU WERE A FURNITURE SALESMAN, LIKE BOB? OR A BANK PRESIDENT?

SECOND-- WHAT DO YOU *WANT* TO DO? WHAT DO YOU THINK YOU *SHOULD* DO?

I DON'T KNOW. SOMETHING IMPORTANT.

THEN FIGURE OUT WHAT IT IS AND DO IT. BUT REMEMBER, ONCE YOU LET IT OUT THAT YOU *HAVE* THIS POWER--OR EVEN THAT SUCH POWER EXISTS--THERE'S NO TURNING BACK.

UH-HUH. I'D BETTER GO. LUNCHTIME'S OVER IN FIVE MINUTES.

YOU'LL NEVER MAKE IT... OR ...DID YOU..?

YEAH, I FLEW HERE. IT'S OKAY.

THANKS, MYRON.

BOB--!

OH--! I, UH... WAS JUST ON MY WAY TO THE BATHROOM!

RIGHT. CARRYING YOUR DRINK.

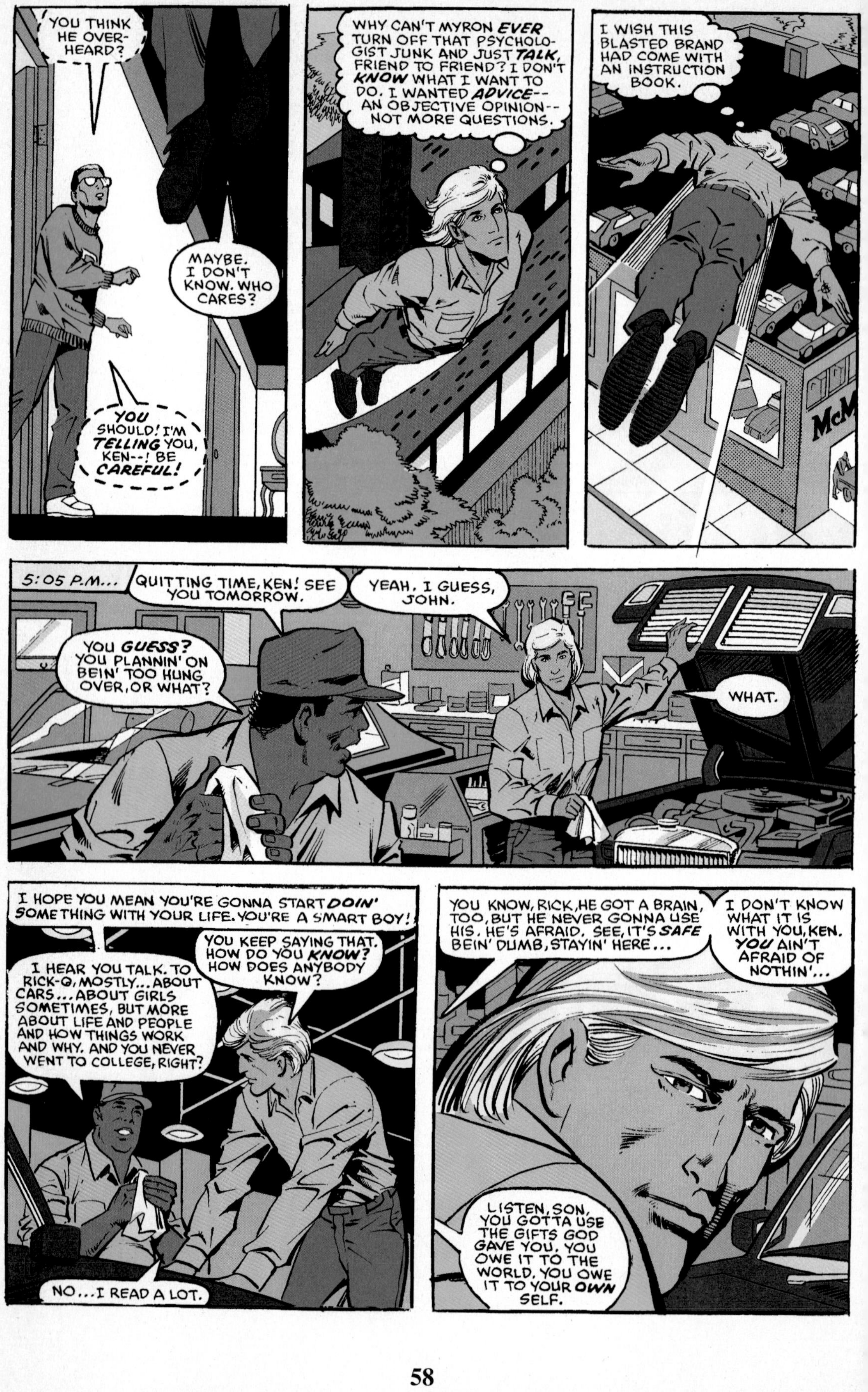
YOU THINK HE OVER-HEARD?
MAYBE. I DON'T KNOW. WHO CARES?
YOU SHOULD! I'M TELLING YOU, KEN--! BE CAREFUL!
WHY CAN'T MYRON EVER TURN OFF THAT PSYCHOLOGIST JUNK AND JUST TALK, FRIEND TO FRIEND? I DON'T KNOW WHAT I WANT TO DO. I WANTED ADVICE-- AN OBJECTIVE OPINION-- NOT MORE QUESTIONS.
I WISH THIS BLASTED BRAND HAD COME WITH AN INSTRUCTION BOOK.
McM
5:05 P.M...
QUITTING TIME, KEN! SEE YOU TOMORROW.
YEAH. I GUESS, JOHN.
YOU GUESS? YOU PLANNIN' ON BEIN' TOO HUNG OVER, OR WHAT?
WHAT.
I HOPE YOU MEAN YOU'RE GONNA START DOIN' SOMETHING WITH YOUR LIFE. YOU'RE A SMART BOY!
I HEAR YOU TALK. TO RICK-O, MOSTLY... ABOUT CARS... ABOUT GIRLS SOMETIMES, BUT MORE ABOUT LIFE AND PEOPLE AND HOW THINGS WORK AND WHY. AND YOU NEVER WENT TO COLLEGE, RIGHT?
YOU KEEP SAYING THAT. HOW DO YOU KNOW? HOW DOES ANYBODY KNOW?
NO... I READ A LOT.
YOU KNOW, RICK, HE GOT A BRAIN, TOO, BUT HE NEVER GONNA USE HIS. HE'S AFRAID, SEE, IT'S SAFE BEIN' DUMB, STAYIN' HERE...
I DON'T KNOW WHAT IT IS WITH YOU, KEN. YOU AIN'T AFRAID OF NOTHIN'...
LISTEN, SON, YOU GOTTA USE THE GIFTS GOD GAVE YOU. YOU OWE IT TO THE WORLD. YOU OWE IT TO YOUR OWN SELF.

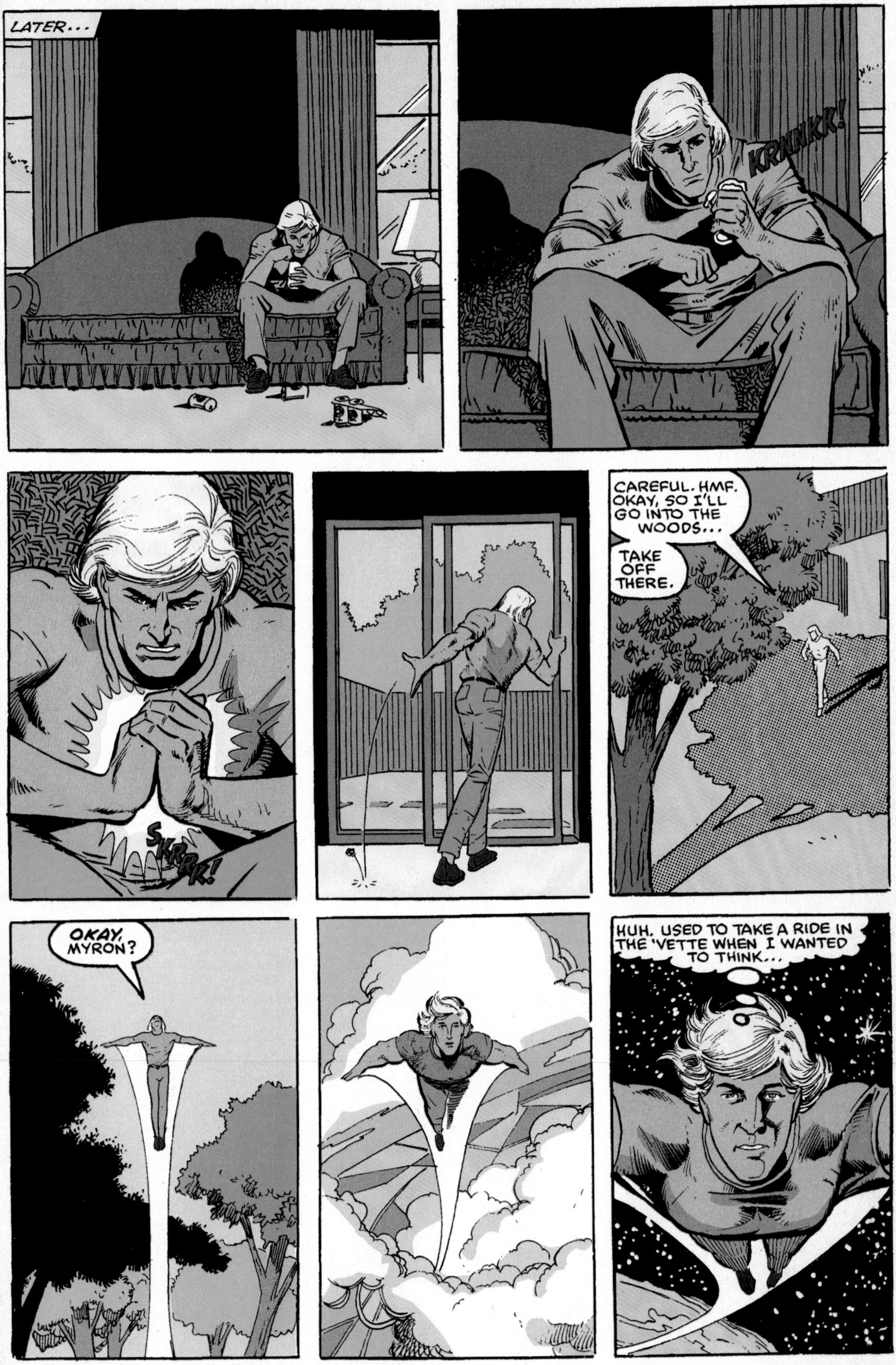
LATER...
KRNNKK!
SKRRK!
CAREFUL. HMF. OKAY, SO I'LL GO INTO THE WOODS...
TAKE OFF THERE.
OKAY, MYRON?
HUH. USED TO TAKE A RIDE IN THE 'VETTE WHEN I WANTED TO THINK...

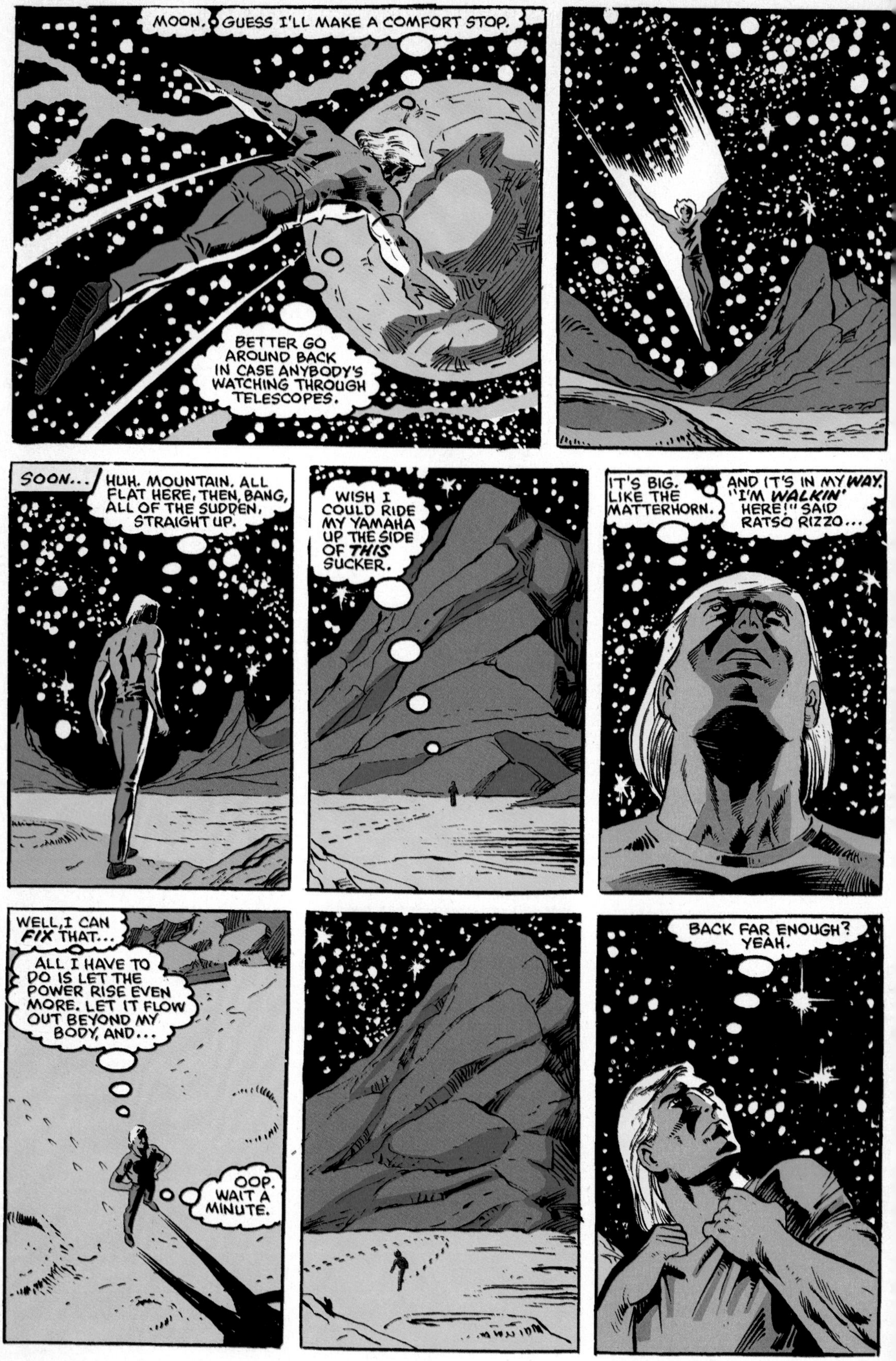
MOON. GUESS I'LL MAKE A COMFORT STOP.
BETTER GO AROUND BACK IN CASE ANYBODY'S WATCHING THROUGH TELESCOPES.
SOON...
HUH. MOUNTAIN. ALL FLAT HERE, THEN, BANG, ALL OF THE SUDDEN, STRAIGHT UP.
WISH I COULD RIDE MY YAMAHA UP THE SIDE OF THIS SUCKER.
IT'S BIG. LIKE THE MATTERHORN.
AND IT'S IN MY WAY. "I'M WALKIN' HERE!" SAID RATSO RIZZO...
WELL, I CAN FIX THAT...
ALL I HAVE TO DO IS LET THE POWER RISE EVEN MORE. LET IT FLOW OUT BEYOND MY BODY, AND...
OOP. WAIT A MINUTE.
BACK FAR ENOUGH? YEAH.

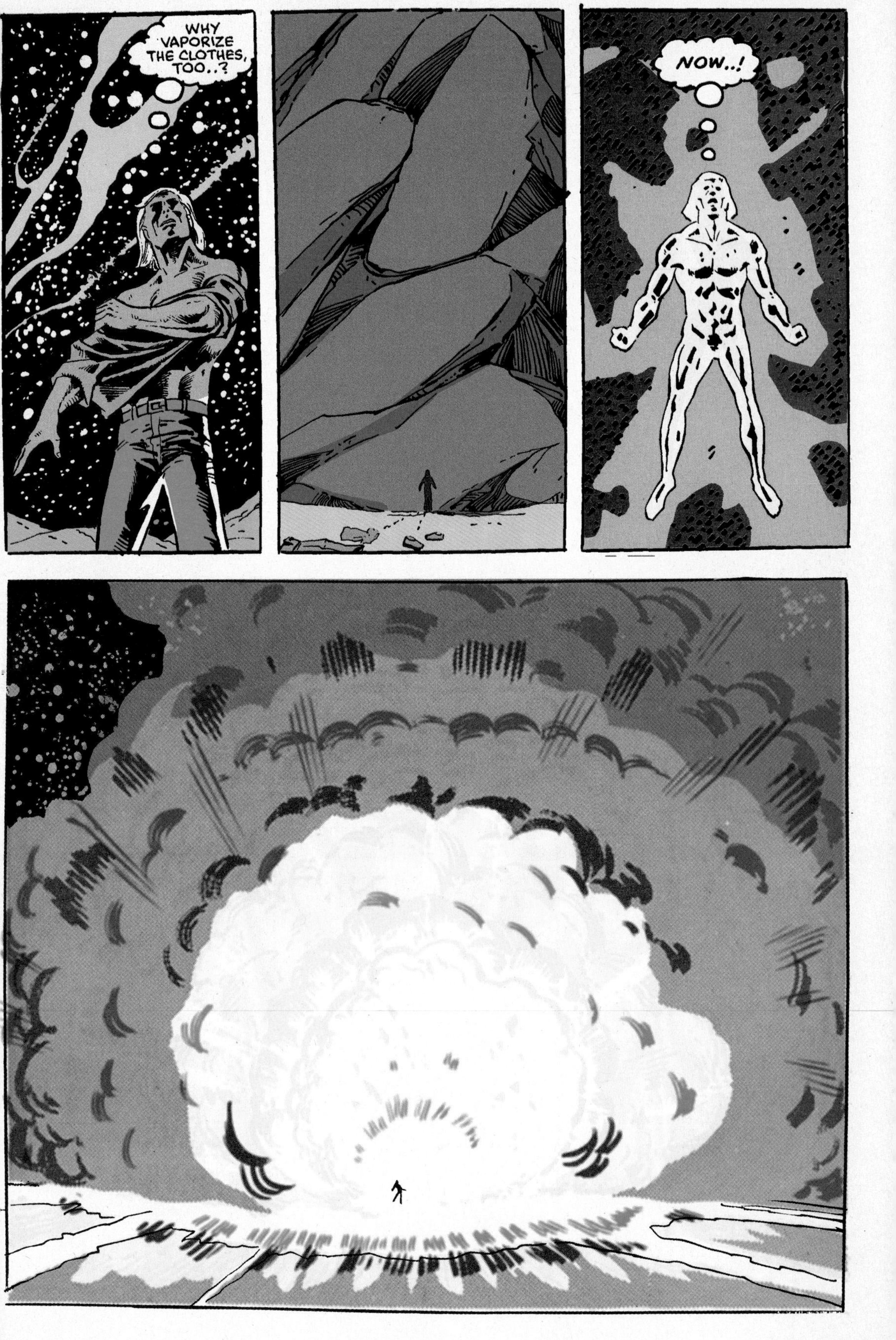
WHY VAPORIZE THE CLOTHES, TOO..?
NOW..!

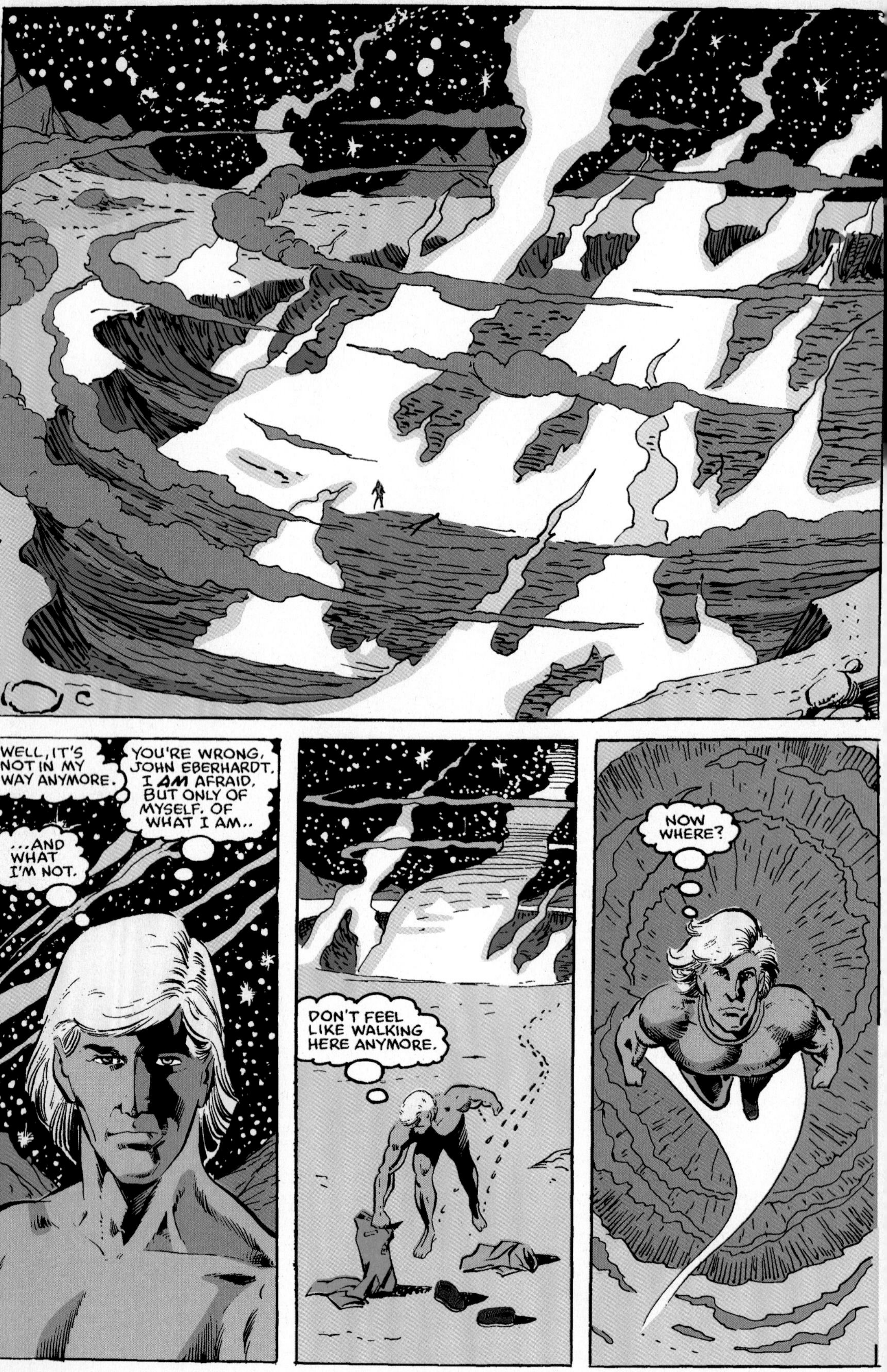
WELL, IT'S NOT IN MY WAY ANYMORE.
YOU'RE WRONG, JOHN EBERHARDT. I AM AFRAID, BUT ONLY OF MYSELF. OF WHAT I AM..
...AND WHAT I'M NOT.
DON'T FEEL LIKE WALKING HERE ANYMORE.
NOW WHERE?

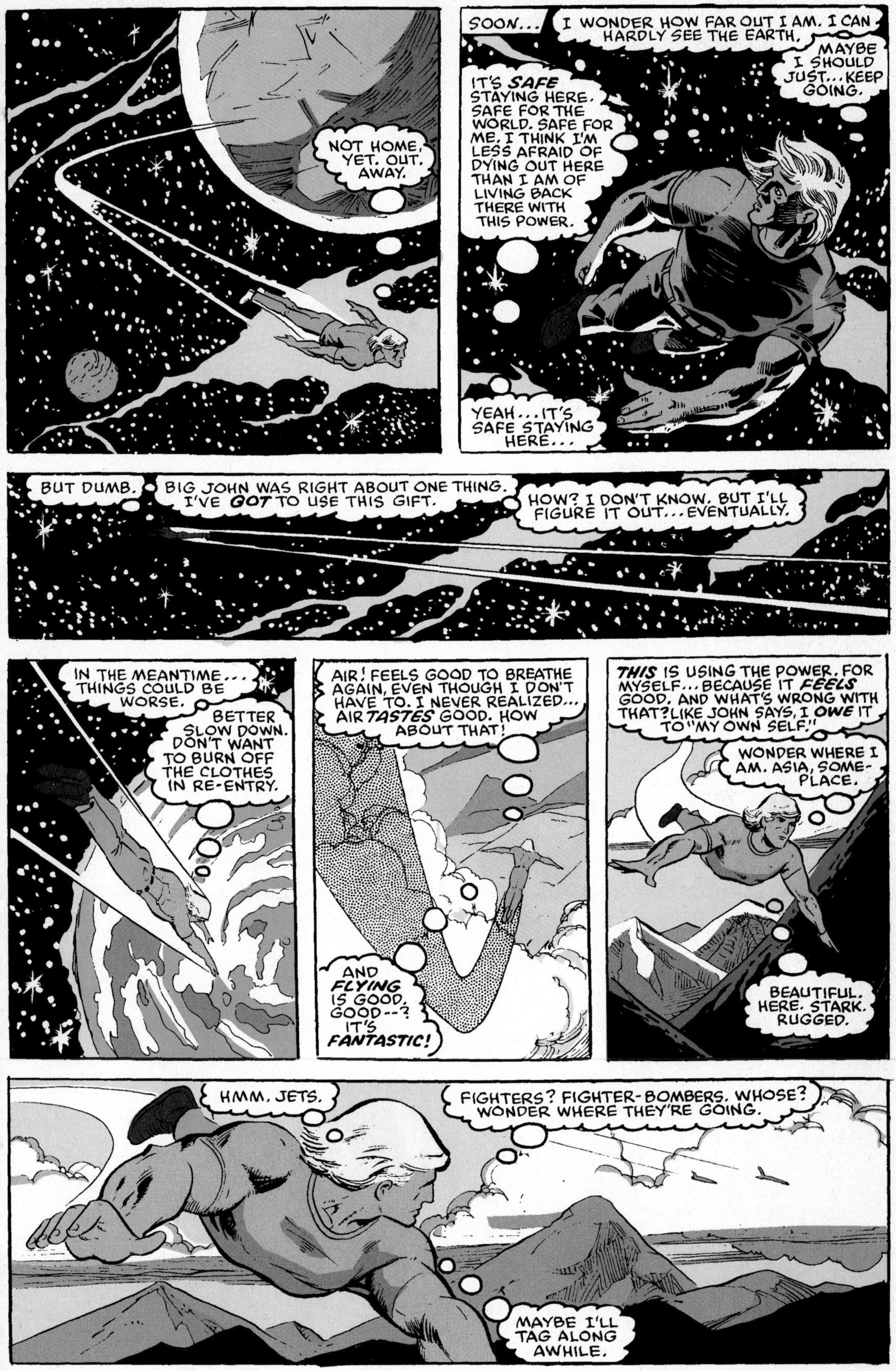
NOT HOME. YET. OUT. AWAY.
SOON...
I WONDER HOW FAR OUT I AM. I CAN HARDLY SEE THE EARTH.
MAYBE I SHOULD JUST...KEEP GOING.
IT'S SAFE STAYING HERE. SAFE FOR THE WORLD. SAFE FOR ME. I THINK I'M LESS AFRAID OF DYING OUT HERE THAN I AM OF LIVING BACK THERE WITH THIS POWER.
YEAH...IT'S SAFE STAYING HERE...
BUT DUMB.
BIG JOHN WAS RIGHT ABOUT ONE THING. I'VE GOT TO USE THIS GIFT.
HOW? I DON'T KNOW. BUT I'LL FIGURE IT OUT...EVENTUALLY.
IN THE MEANTIME... THINGS COULD BE WORSE.
BETTER SLOW DOWN. DON'T WANT TO BURN OFF THE CLOTHES IN RE-ENTRY.
AIR! FEELS GOOD TO BREATHE AGAIN, EVEN THOUGH I DON'T HAVE TO. I NEVER REALIZED... AIR TASTES GOOD. HOW ABOUT THAT!
AND FLYING IS GOOD. GOOD--? IT'S FANTASTIC!
THIS IS USING THE POWER. FOR MYSELF... BECAUSE IT FEELS GOOD. AND WHAT'S WRONG WITH THAT? LIKE JOHN SAYS, I OWE IT TO "MY OWN SELF."
WONDER WHERE I AM. ASIA, SOME-PLACE.
BEAUTIFUL. HERE. STARK. RUGGED.
HMM. JETS.
FIGHTERS? FIGHTER-BOMBERS. WHOSE? WONDER WHERE THEY'RE GOING.
MAYBE I'LL TAG ALONG AWHILE.

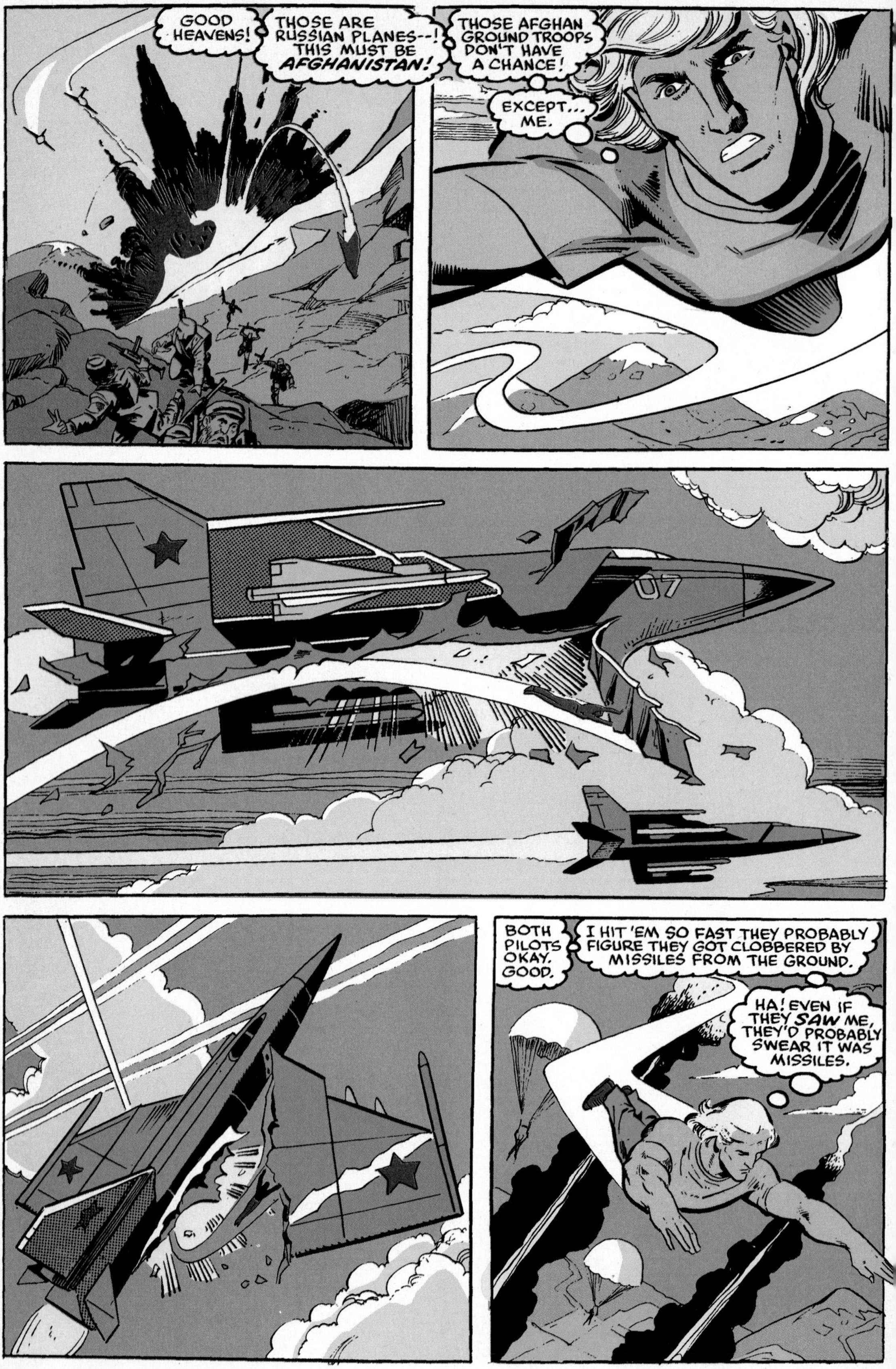
GOOD HEAVENS!
THOSE ARE RUSSIAN PLANES--! THIS MUST BE AFGHANISTAN!
THOSE AFGHAN GROUND TROOPS DON'T HAVE A CHANCE!
EXCEPT... ME.
BOTH PILOTS OKAY. GOOD.
I HIT 'EM SO FAST THEY PROBABLY FIGURE THEY GOT CLOBBERED BY MISSILES FROM THE GROUND.
HA! EVEN IF THEY SAW ME, THEY'D PROBABLY SWEAR IT WAS MISSILES.

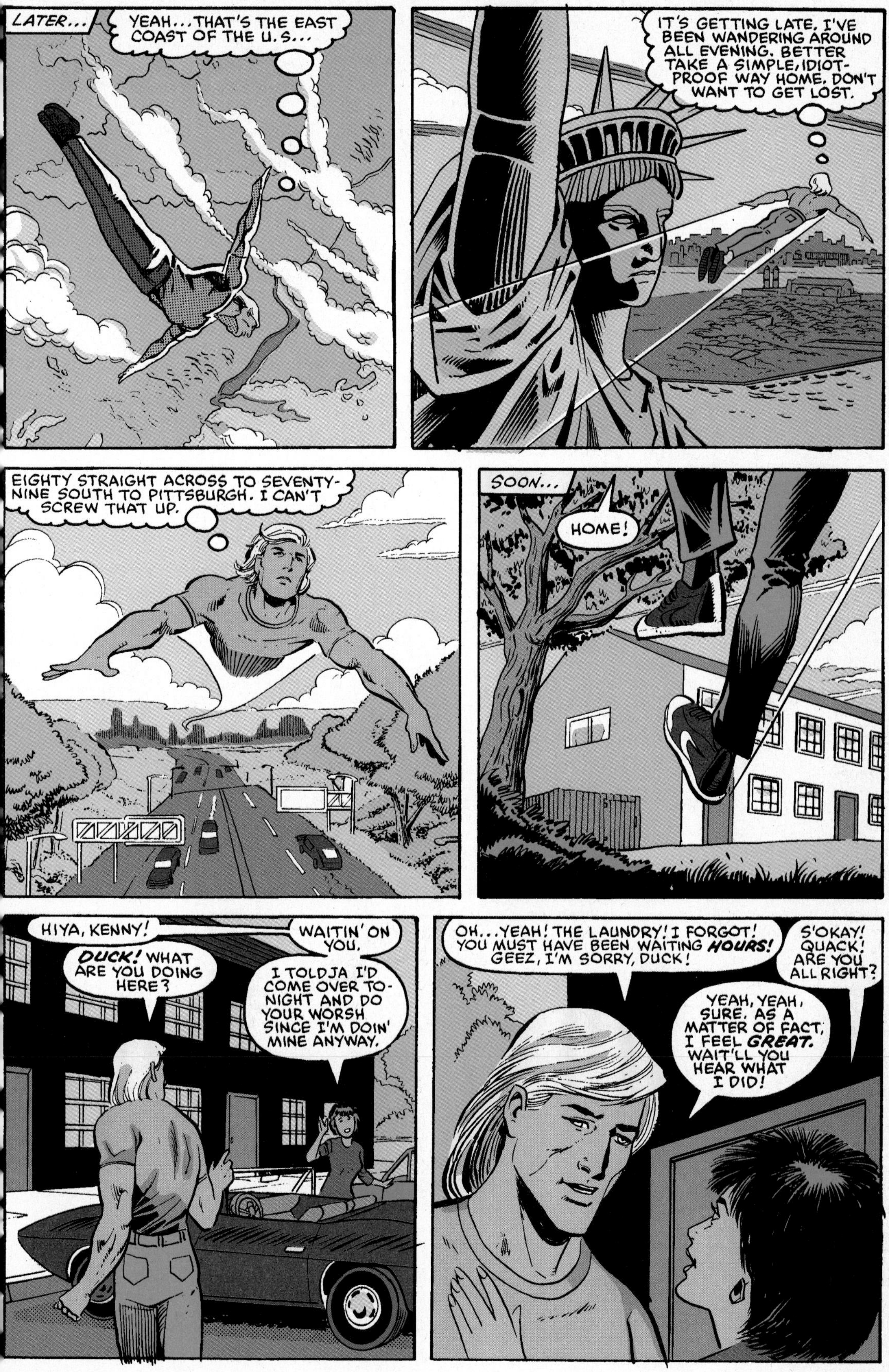
LATER...
YEAH...THAT'S THE EAST COAST OF THE U. S...
IT'S GETTING LATE. I'VE BEEN WANDERING AROUND ALL EVENING. BETTER TAKE A SIMPLE, IDIOT-PROOF WAY HOME. DON'T WANT TO GET LOST.
EIGHTY STRAIGHT ACROSS TO SEVENTY-NINE SOUTH TO PITTSBURGH. I CAN'T SCREW THAT UP.
SOON...
HOME!
HIYA, KENNY!
DUCK! WHAT ARE YOU DOING HERE?
WAITIN' ON YOU.
I TOLDJA I'D COME OVER TO-NIGHT AND DO YOUR WORSH SINCE I'M DOIN' MINE ANYWAY.
OH...YEAH! THE LAUNDRY! I FORGOT! YOU MUST HAVE BEEN WAITING HOURS! GEEZ, I'M SORRY, DUCK!
S'OKAY! QUACK! ARE YOU ALL RIGHT?
YEAH, YEAH, SURE. AS A MATTER OF FACT, I FEEL GREAT. WAIT'LL YOU HEAR WHAT I DID!

MAN, IT WAS AWESOME, DUCK! *TWO* FIGHTER-BOMBERS--! AND RIP, WHAM, THANK YOU, MA'AM, THEY WERE *SCRAP!*

WOW! I WISH I COULD'A SEEN YA! AND, I WISH I COULD'A SEEN WHERE YOU THREW YOUR OTHER BROWN SOCK! QUACK!

TRY UNDER THE TABLE.

PITTSBURGH PRESS
SENATE REFORM BILL PASSES

DOES THIS NEED TO BE WORSHED? OR DO YOU DRY CLEAN IT?

THE OUTFIT THE ALIEN GAVE ME-- I DON'T EVEN KNOW WHAT IT'S MADE OF. HMM. COULD HAVE USED IT ON THE MOON...

THERE'S NO FABRIC CARE LABEL INSIDE. I BETTER NOT WORSH IT. IT MIGHT SHRINK.

EEYAHH!

KENNY!

WHAT *HAPPENED?*

MMH! PAPER CUT...

YOU?

YEAH. THE POWER ONLY PROTECTS ME WHEN IT'S *ON.* I HAVE TO "THINK" IT ON. I JUST RELAXED A LITTLE THERE...

UH-HUH. SPEAKING OF RELAXING...IT'S KINDA LATE TO DO THE WORSH TONIGHT. I'LL DO IT TOMORROW, OKAY? SO HOW'S ABOUT IF I TAKE YA OUT AND TREAT'CHA TO A KLONDIKE?

I'LL THROW IN A BACK RUB...OR A FRONT RUB...? OKAY?

SURE, DUCK, BUT *I'LL* BUY THE ICE CREAM

HEY, WAIT A MINUTE! LOOK AT THIS BIG CLASSIFIED--! "FLYING MAN! I WAIT FOR YOU EVERY EVENING AT THE PLACE WHERE YOU BURNED LIKE THE SUN. DESPERATELY NEED YOU. HELP ME, PLEASE," SIGNED "DAMSEL IN DISTRESS."

THEY MEAN *ME.* "...BURNED LIKE THE SUN." THEY'RE TALKING ABOUT THE FIRST TIME I LET THE POWER FLARE UP.

SPORTS EXTRA
STEELERS WIN!

SOMEBODY MUST HAVE *SEEN* THAT.

UNLESS YOU *TOLD* SOMEBODY.

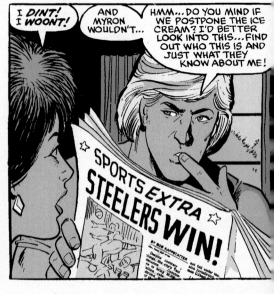

I *DINT!* I *WOONT!*

AND MYRON WOULDN'T...

HMM...DO YOU MIND IF WE POSTPONE THE ICE CREAM? I'D BETTER LOOK INTO THIS...FIND OUT WHO THIS IS AND JUST WHAT THEY KNOW ABOUT ME!

SPORTS EXTRA
STEELERS WIN!

BY BOB KAMPSTATTER

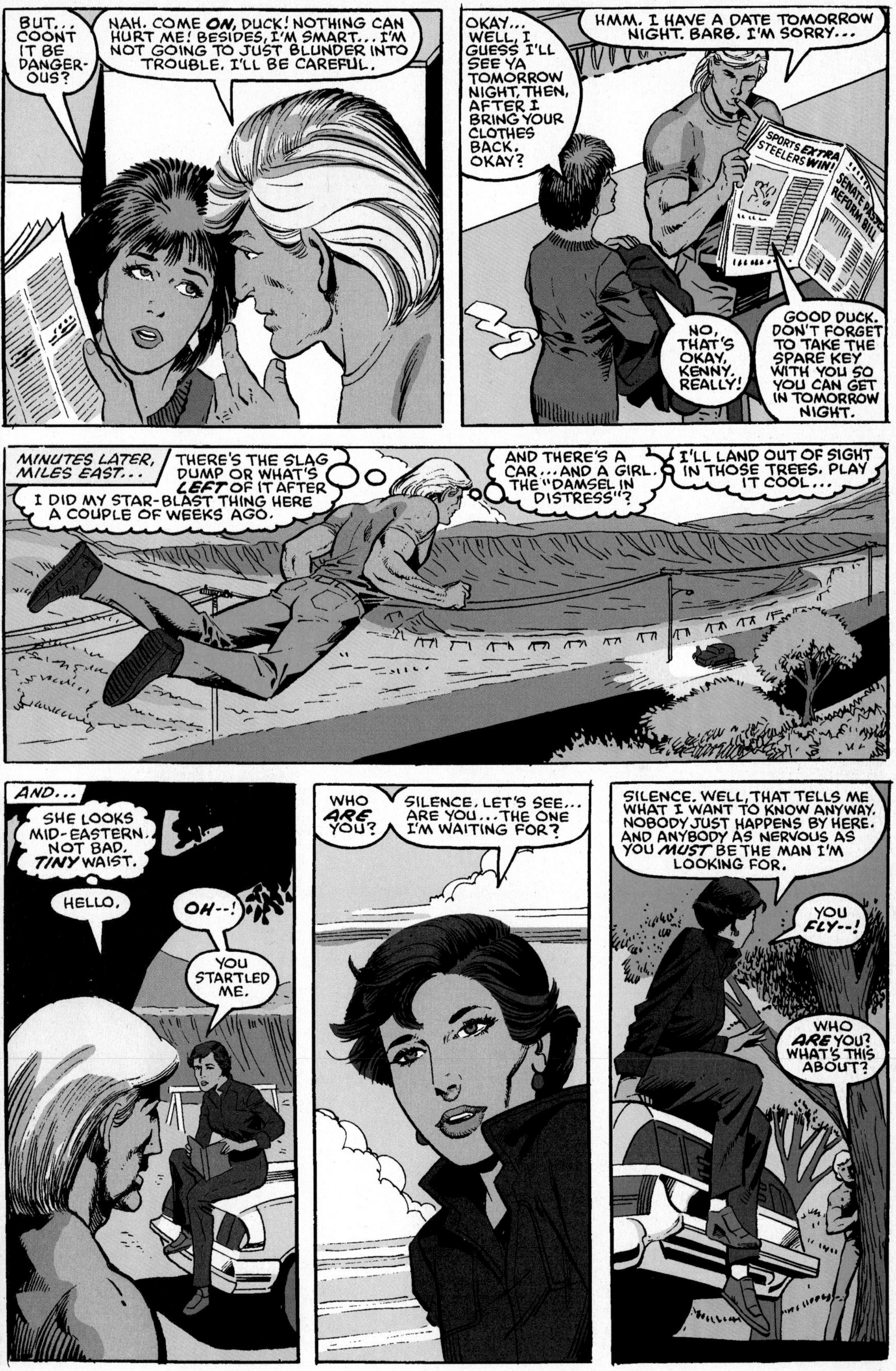

BUT... COONT IT BE DANGER-OUS?
NAH. COME ON, DUCK! NOTHING CAN HURT ME! BESIDES, I'M SMART... I'M NOT GOING TO JUST BLUNDER INTO TROUBLE. I'LL BE CAREFUL.
OKAY... WELL, I GUESS I'LL SEE YA TOMORROW NIGHT, THEN, AFTER I BRING YOUR CLOTHES BACK. OKAY?
HMM. I HAVE A DATE TOMORROW NIGHT, BARB. I'M SORRY...
SPORTS EXTRA
STEELERS WIN!
REFORM BILL
NO, THAT'S OKAY, KENNY, REALLY!
GOOD DUCK. DON'T FORGET TO TAKE THE SPARE KEY WITH YOU SO YOU CAN GET IN TOMORROW NIGHT.
MINUTES LATER, MILES EAST...
THERE'S THE SLAG DUMP OR WHAT'S LEFT OF IT AFTER I DID MY STAR-BLAST THING HERE A COUPLE OF WEEKS AGO.
AND THERE'S A CAR... AND A GIRL. THE "DAMSEL IN DISTRESS"?
I'LL LAND OUT OF SIGHT IN THOSE TREES. PLAY IT COOL...
AND...
SHE LOOKS MID-EASTERN. NOT BAD. TINY WAIST.
HELLO.
OH--!
YOU STARTLED ME.
WHO ARE YOU?
SILENCE. LET'S SEE... ARE YOU... THE ONE I'M WAITING FOR?
SILENCE. WELL, THAT TELLS ME WHAT I WANT TO KNOW ANYWAY. NOBODY JUST HAPPENS BY HERE. AND ANYBODY AS NERVOUS AS YOU MUST BE THE MAN I'M LOOKING FOR.
YOU FLY--!
WHO ARE YOU? WHAT'S THIS ABOUT?

ME? I'M A STUDENT, AT PITT. I'M JUST, UM... INTERESTED IN FLYING, YOU KNOW? I'M WRITING A THESIS...?

ALL RIGHT, THE TRUTH. MY BOYFRIEND PUT ME UP TO THIS.

YOU SEE, THE C.I.A. INVESTIGATED THE SLAG DUMP BLAST. THEY TURNED UP NOTHING MUCH-- EXCEPT ONE LESS-THAN-RELIABLE WITNESS WHO CLAIMED THAT A FLYING MAN BLEW UP THE DUMP.

A TRAITOR IN THE C.I.A. *SOLD* THAT REPORT TO, UH... AN ENEMY GOVERNMENT, HEADED BY SOMEONE CRAZY ENOUGH TO *BELIEVE* ... IN *YOU!*

SINCE THEN, *HIS* "AGENTS"-- MOSTLY STUDENTS LIKE MY BOY-FRIEND--HAVE BEEN STAKED OUT AROUND HERE WATCHING. SURE ENOUGH, SEVERAL TIMES THEY CAUGHT A GLIMPSE OF OF A FLYING MAN.

WHOOPS! NO MORE FLYING TO MYRON'S.

SO, THEY HATCHED THIS BIG PLAN TO MAKE CONTACT. I'VE BEEN SIT-TING OUT HERE FOR A *WEEK*, TRYING TO READ, GETTING EYE-STRAIN. AM I GLAD YOU SHOWED UP!

WHAT DO YOU WANT?

WELL... WHATEVER IT *IS*. HOW DO YOU *DO* WHAT YOU DO?

SILENCE, AGAIN, OF COURSE. I MAKE A LOUSY SPY. WHY ON EARTH WOULD YOU TELL ME ANYTHING FOR NOTHING?

I'M SORRY I'M SO BAD AT THIS, I *DO* HAVE SOMETHING TO OFFER YOU IN RETURN.

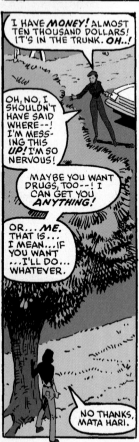

I HAVE *MONEY!* ALMOST TEN THOUSAND DOLLARS! IT'S IN THE TRUNK. *OH...!*

OH, NO, I SHOULDN'T HAVE SAID WHERE--! I'M MESS-ING THIS *UP!* I'M SO NERVOUS!

MAYBE YOU WANT DRUGS, TOO--! I CAN GET YOU *ANYTHING!*

OR... *ME.* THAT IS... I MEAN... IF YOU WANT ...I'LL DO... WHATEVER.

NO THANKS, MATA HARI.

LOOK, THIS ISN'T WHAT YOU THINK. IT'S NOTHING. JUST A TRICK. A GIMMICK. *FORGET* IT.

IF IT'S NOTHING, THEN *TELL* ME! *SHOW* ME!

YOU DON'T UNDER-STAND. MY BOY-FRIEND AND THE OTHERS ARE WATCHING FROM A DISTANCE. THEY KNOW I'VE BEEN TALKING TO YOU. IF I DON'T GET WHAT THEY WANT FROM YOU THEY'LL BE *ANGRY!* THEY'LL *HURT* ME-- OR WORSE! *PLEASE!*

SORRY!

I'LL TELL THEM YOU SAID YOU'LL COME BACK TO-MORROW NIGHT! ALL RIGHT? PLEASE COME BACK! TO-MORROW NIGHT, OKAY? IF YOU DON'T THEY'LL *KILL* ME!

IF ONLY YOU HADN'T COME AT *ALL--!*

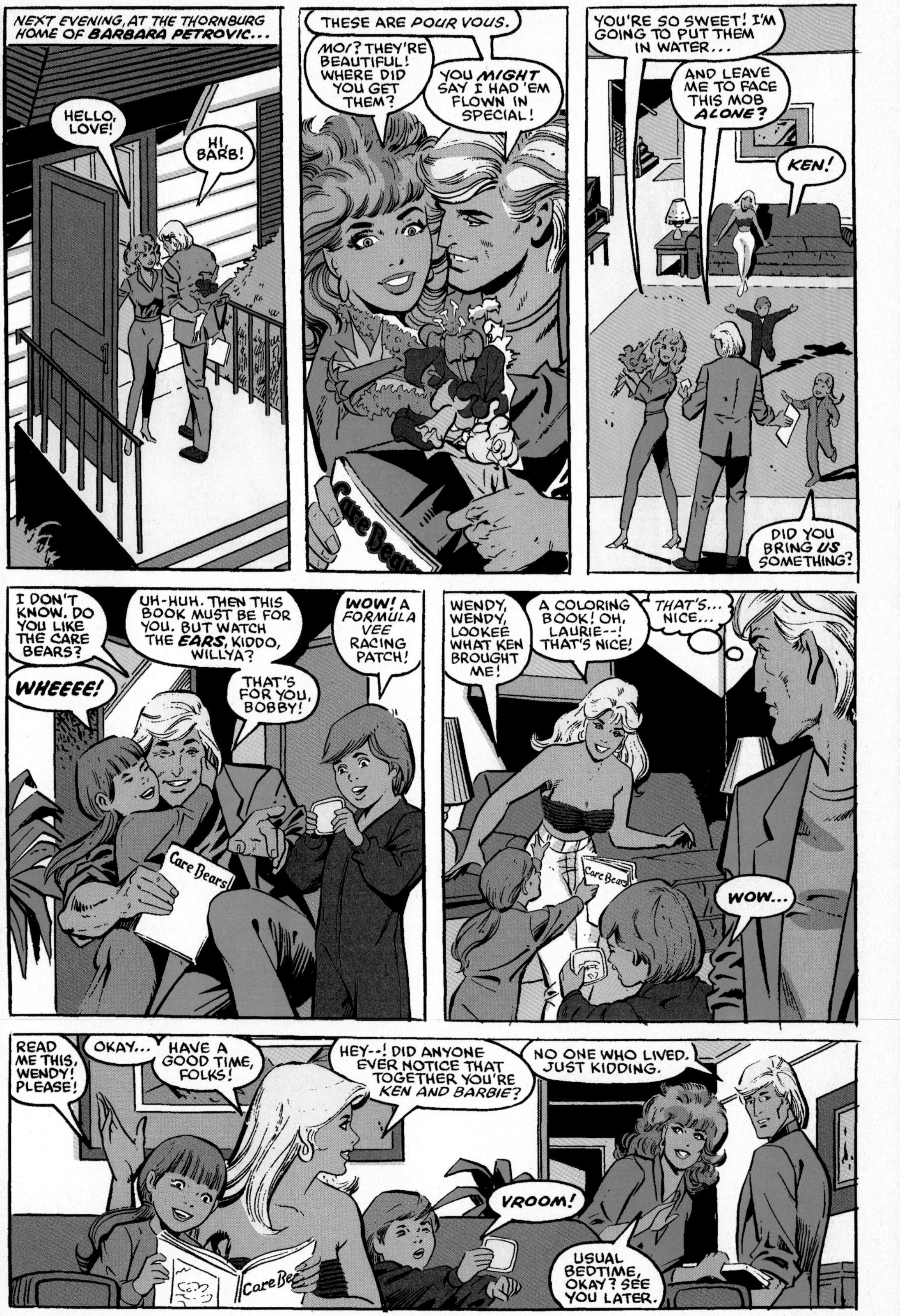

NEXT EVENING, AT THE THORNBURG HOME OF BARBARA PETROVIC...
HELLO, LOVE!
HI, BARB!
THESE ARE POUR VOUS.
MOI? THEY'RE BEAUTIFUL! WHERE DID YOU GET THEM?
YOU MIGHT SAY I HAD 'EM FLOWN IN SPECIAL!
Care Bears
YOU'RE SO SWEET! I'M GOING TO PUT THEM IN WATER...
AND LEAVE ME TO FACE THIS MOB ALONE?
KEN!
DID YOU BRING US SOMETHING?
I DON'T KNOW. DO YOU LIKE THE CARE BEARS?
WHEEEE!
UH-HUH. THEN THIS BOOK MUST BE FOR YOU. BUT WATCH THE EARS, KIDDO, WILLYA?
WOW! A FORMULA VEE RACING PATCH!
THAT'S FOR YOU, BOBBY!
Care Bears
WENDY, WENDY, LOOKEE WHAT KEN BROUGHT ME!
A COLORING BOOK! OH, LAURIE--! THAT'S NICE!
THAT'S... NICE...
Care Bears
WOW...
READ ME THIS, WENDY! PLEASE!
OKAY...
HAVE A GOOD TIME, FOLKS!
HEY--! DID ANYONE EVER NOTICE THAT TOGETHER YOU'RE KEN AND BARBIE?
NO ONE WHO LIVED. JUST KIDDING.
VROOM!
USUAL BEDTIME, OKAY? SEE YOU LATER.

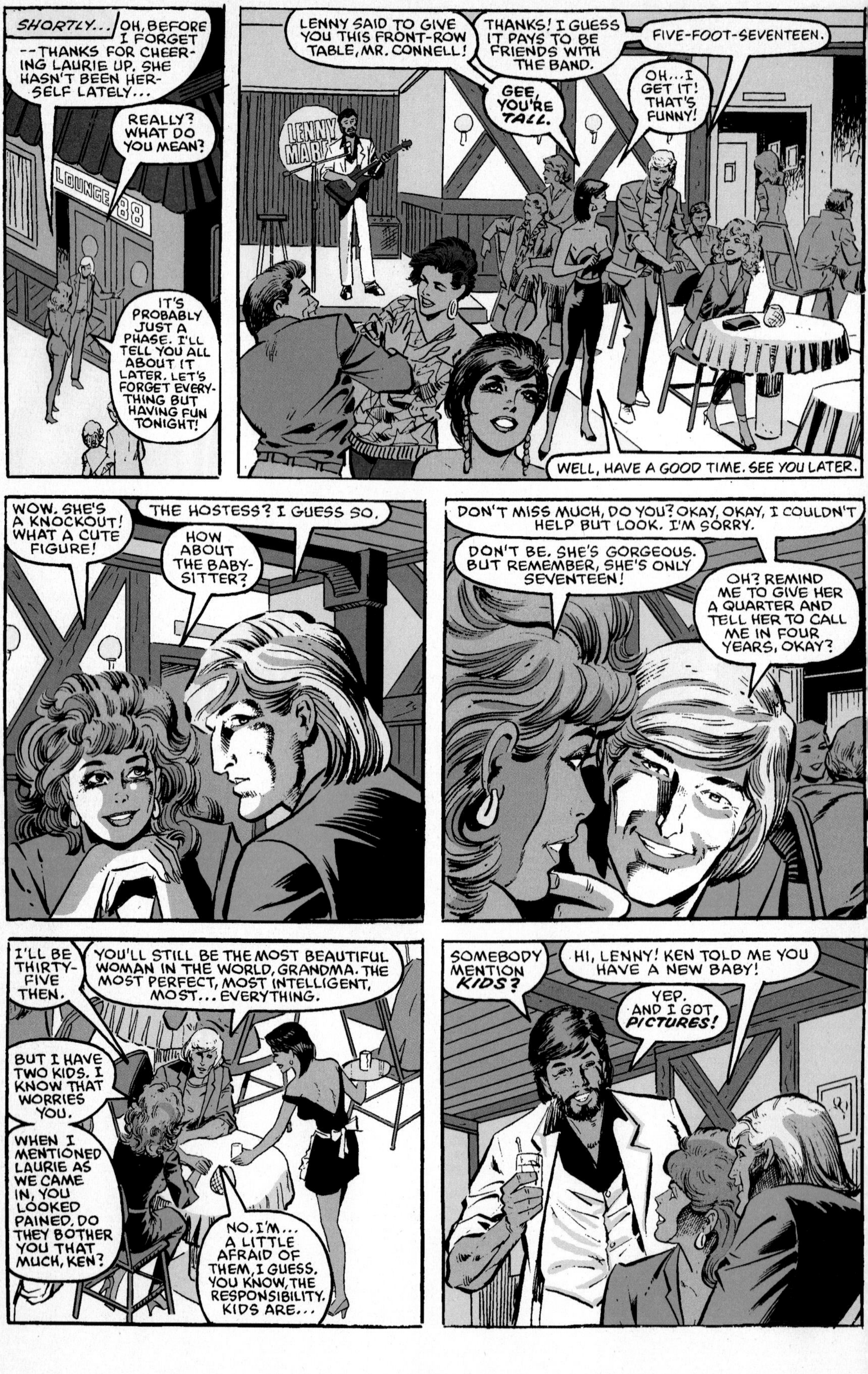
SHORTLY...
OH, BEFORE I FORGET --THANKS FOR CHEERING LAURIE UP. SHE HASN'T BEEN HERSELF LATELY...
REALLY? WHAT DO YOU MEAN?
LOUNGE 88
IT'S PROBABLY JUST A PHASE. I'LL TELL YOU ALL ABOUT IT LATER. LET'S FORGET EVERYTHING BUT HAVING FUN TONIGHT!
LENNY SAID TO GIVE YOU THIS FRONT-ROW TABLE, MR. CONNELL!
THANKS! I GUESS IT PAYS TO BE FRIENDS WITH THE BAND.
GEE, YOU'RE TALL.
FIVE-FOOT-SEVENTEEN.
OH...I GET IT! THAT'S FUNNY!
WELL, HAVE A GOOD TIME. SEE YOU LATER.
WOW. SHE'S A KNOCKOUT! WHAT A CUTE FIGURE!
THE HOSTESS? I GUESS SO.
HOW ABOUT THE BABY-SITTER?
DON'T MISS MUCH, DO YOU? OKAY, OKAY, I COULDN'T HELP BUT LOOK. I'M SORRY.
DON'T BE. SHE'S GORGEOUS. BUT REMEMBER, SHE'S ONLY SEVENTEEN!
OH? REMIND ME TO GIVE HER A QUARTER AND TELL HER TO CALL ME IN FOUR YEARS, OKAY?
I'LL BE THIRTY-FIVE THEN.
YOU'LL STILL BE THE MOST BEAUTIFUL WOMAN IN THE WORLD, GRANDMA. THE MOST PERFECT, MOST INTELLIGENT, MOST... EVERYTHING.
BUT I HAVE TWO KIDS. I KNOW THAT WORRIES YOU.
WHEN I MENTIONED LAURIE AS WE CAME IN, YOU LOOKED PAINED. DO THEY BOTHER YOU THAT MUCH, KEN?
NO. I'M... A LITTLE AFRAID OF THEM, I GUESS. YOU KNOW, THE RESPONSIBILITY. KIDS ARE...
SOMEBODY MENTION KIDS?
HI, LENNY! KEN TOLD ME YOU HAVE A NEW BABY!
YEP. AND I GOT PICTURES!

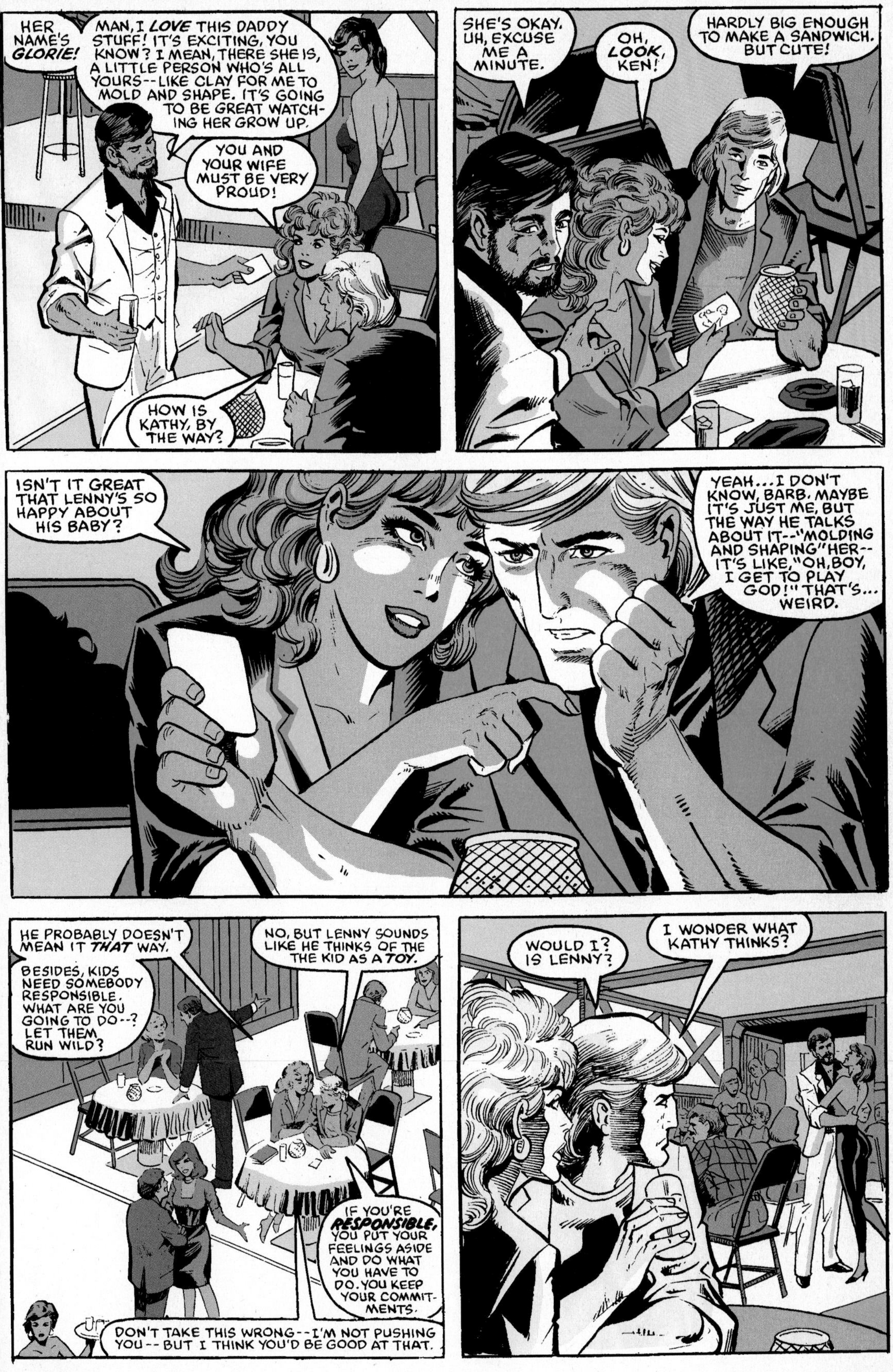
HER NAME'S GLORIE!
MAN, I LOVE THIS DADDY STUFF! IT'S EXCITING, YOU KNOW? I MEAN, THERE SHE IS, A LITTLE PERSON WHO'S ALL YOURS--LIKE CLAY FOR ME TO MOLD AND SHAPE. IT'S GOING TO BE GREAT WATCHING HER GROW UP.
YOU AND YOUR WIFE MUST BE VERY PROUD!
HOW IS KATHY, BY THE WAY?
SHE'S OKAY. UH, EXCUSE ME A MINUTE.
OH, LOOK, KEN!
HARDLY BIG ENOUGH TO MAKE A SANDWICH. BUT CUTE!
ISN'T IT GREAT THAT LENNY'S SO HAPPY ABOUT HIS BABY?
YEAH...I DON'T KNOW, BARB. MAYBE IT'S JUST ME, BUT THE WAY HE TALKS ABOUT IT--"MOLDING AND SHAPING" HER--IT'S LIKE, "OH, BOY, I GET TO PLAY GOD!" THAT'S... WEIRD.
HE PROBABLY DOESN'T MEAN IT THAT WAY.
BESIDES, KIDS NEED SOMEBODY RESPONSIBLE. WHAT ARE YOU GOING TO DO--? LET THEM RUN WILD?
NO, BUT LENNY SOUNDS LIKE HE THINKS OF THE THE KID AS A TOY.
IF YOU'RE RESPONSIBLE, YOU PUT YOUR FEELINGS ASIDE AND DO WHAT YOU HAVE TO DO. YOU KEEP YOUR COMMITMENTS.
DON'T TAKE THIS WRONG--I'M NOT PUSHING YOU--BUT I THINK YOU'D BE GOOD AT THAT.
WOULD I? IS LENNY?
I WONDER WHAT KATHY THINKS?

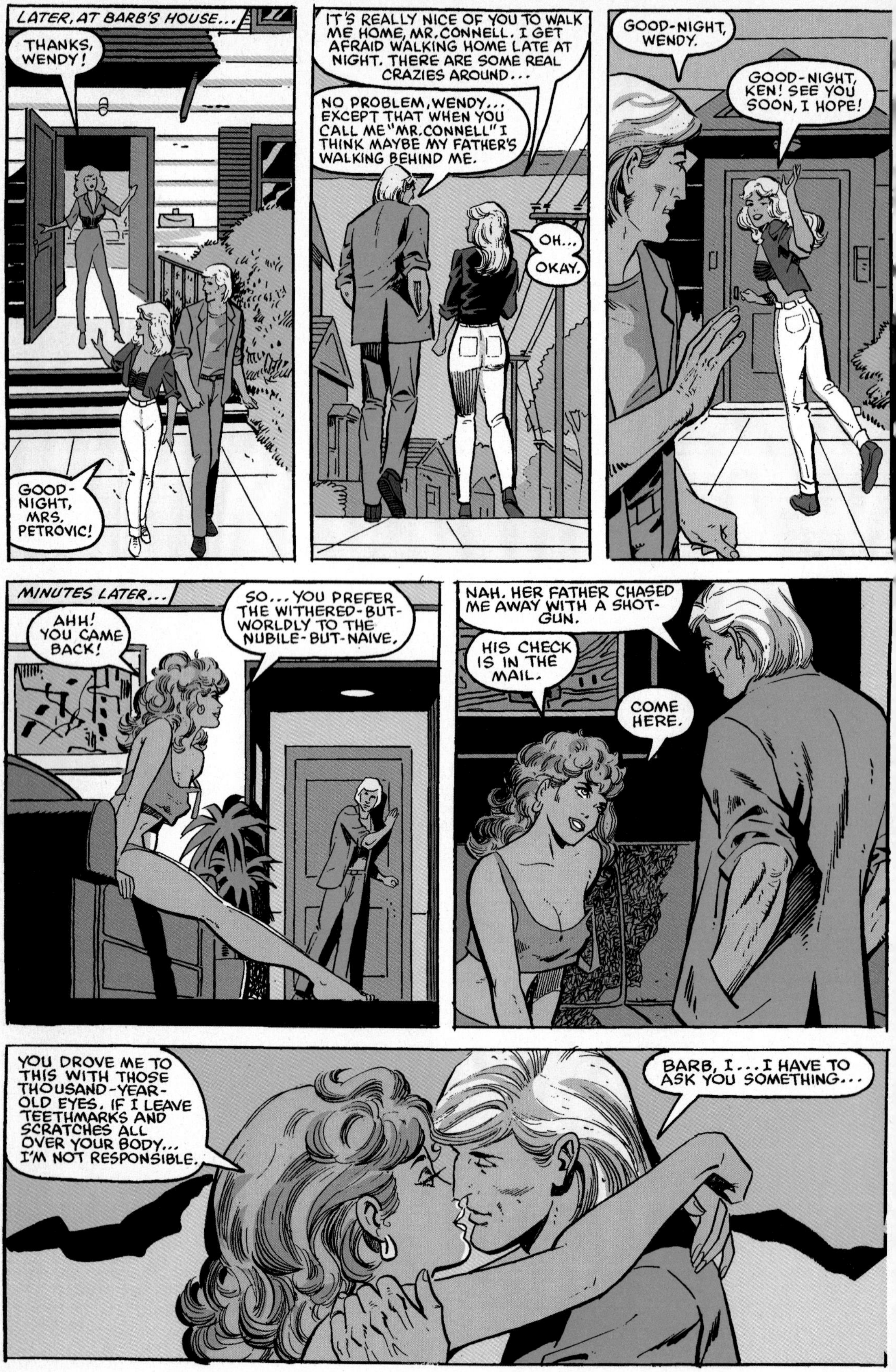

LATER, AT BARB'S HOUSE...
THANKS, WENDY!
GOOD-NIGHT, MRS. PETROVIC!
IT'S REALLY NICE OF YOU TO WALK ME HOME, MR. CONNELL. I GET AFRAID WALKING HOME LATE AT NIGHT. THERE ARE SOME REAL CRAZIES AROUND...
NO PROBLEM, WENDY... EXCEPT THAT WHEN YOU CALL ME "MR. CONNELL" I THINK MAYBE MY FATHER'S WALKING BEHIND ME.
OH... OKAY.
GOOD-NIGHT, WENDY.
GOOD-NIGHT, KEN! SEE YOU SOON, I HOPE!
MINUTES LATER...
AHH! YOU CAME BACK!
SO... YOU PREFER THE WITHERED-BUT-WORLDLY TO THE NUBILE-BUT-NAIVE.
NAH. HER FATHER CHASED ME AWAY WITH A SHOT-GUN.
HIS CHECK IS IN THE MAIL.
COME HERE.
YOU DROVE ME TO THIS WITH THOSE THOUSAND-YEAR-OLD EYES. IF I LEAVE TEETHMARKS AND SCRATCHES ALL OVER YOUR BODY... I'M NOT RESPONSIBLE.
BARB, I... I HAVE TO ASK YOU SOMETHING...

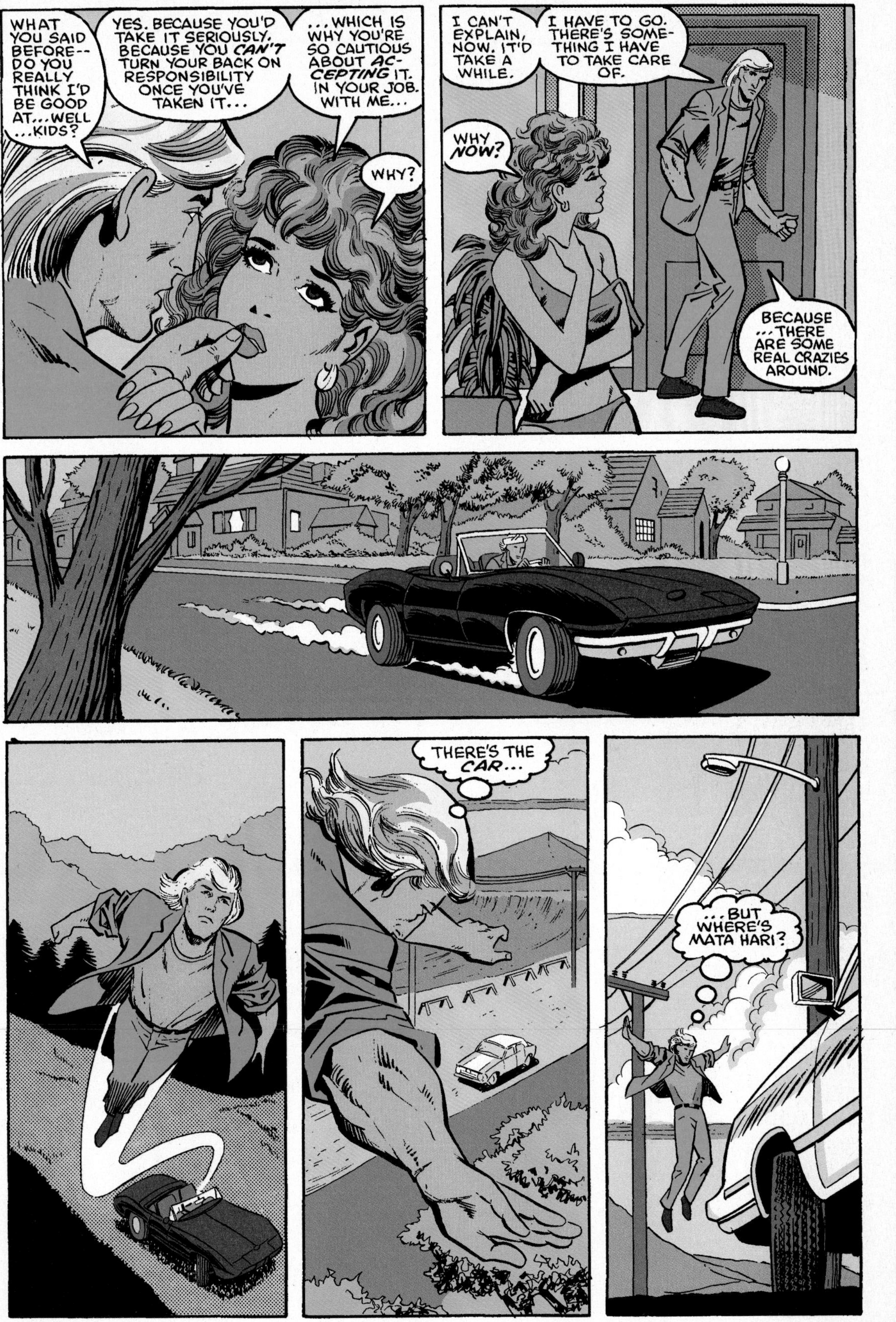
WHAT YOU SAID BEFORE--DO YOU REALLY THINK I'D BE GOOD AT...WELL ...KIDS?
YES. BECAUSE YOU'D TAKE IT SERIOUSLY. BECAUSE YOU CAN'T TURN YOUR BACK ON RESPONSIBILITY ONCE YOU'VE TAKEN IT...
...WHICH IS WHY YOU'RE SO CAUTIOUS ABOUT ACCEPTING IT. IN YOUR JOB. WITH ME...
WHY?
I CAN'T EXPLAIN, NOW. IT'D TAKE A WHILE.
I HAVE TO GO. THERE'S SOMETHING I HAVE TO TAKE CARE OF.
WHY NOW?
BECAUSE ...THERE ARE SOME REAL CRAZIES AROUND.
THERE'S THE CAR...
...BUT WHERE'S MATA HARI?

IT'S LATE. MAYBE SHE FELL ASLEEP IN THE CAR.

WON'T HURT TO LOOK, I SUPPOSE.

NOBODY COULD HAVE SEEN ME LAND. TOO DARK.

HOLY--!

SHE LOOKS... HURT!

LOCKED--!

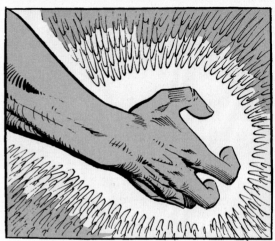

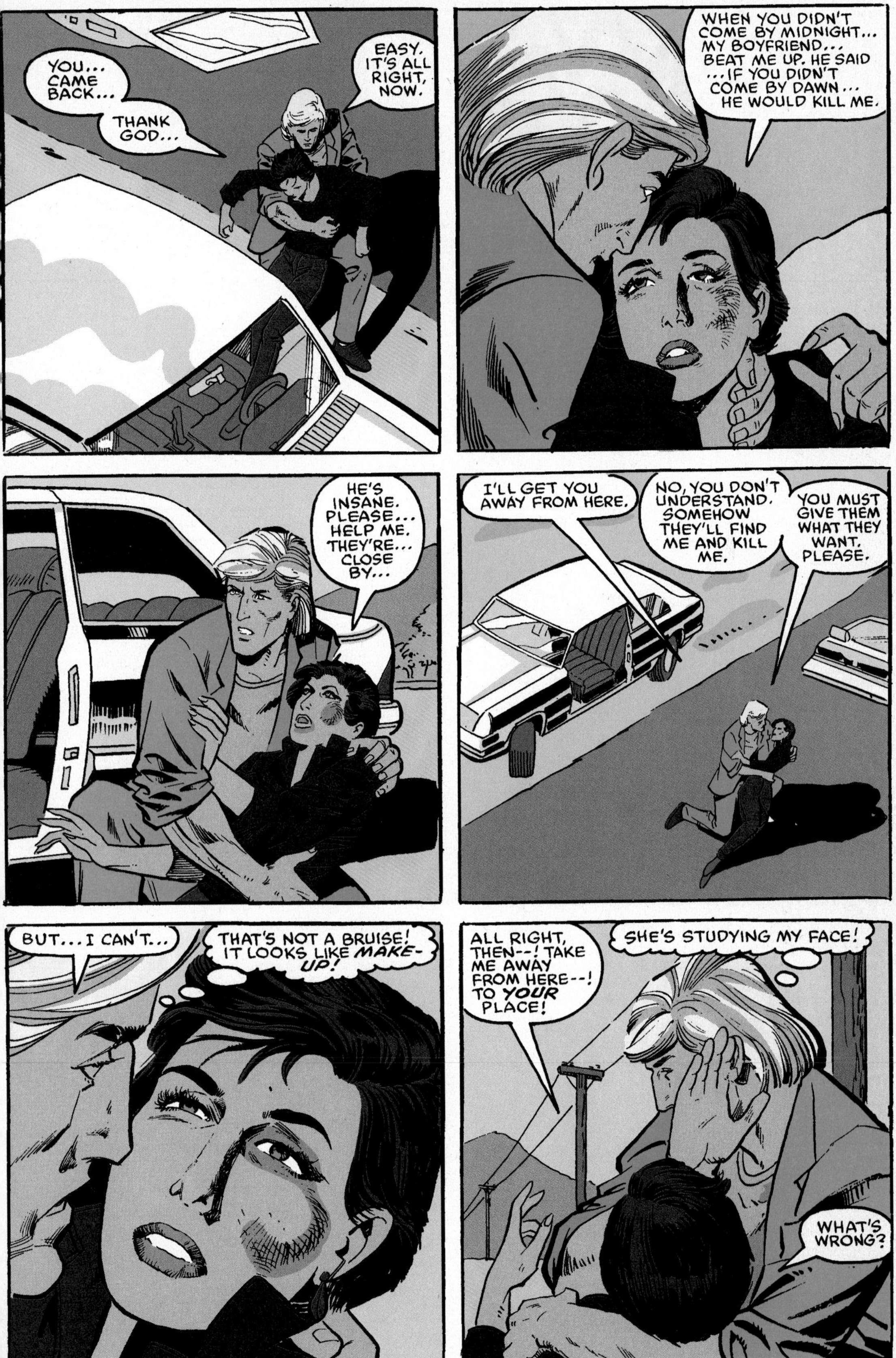
YOU... CAME BACK...
THANK GOD...
EASY. IT'S ALL RIGHT, NOW.
WHEN YOU DIDN'T COME BY MIDNIGHT... MY BOYFRIEND... BEAT ME UP. HE SAID ...IF YOU DIDN'T COME BY DAWN... HE WOULD KILL ME.
HE'S INSANE. PLEASE... HELP ME. THEY'RE... CLOSE BY...
I'LL GET YOU AWAY FROM HERE.
NO, YOU DON'T UNDERSTAND. SOMEHOW THEY'LL FIND ME AND KILL ME.
YOU MUST GIVE THEM WHAT THEY WANT. PLEASE.
BUT... I CAN'T...
THAT'S NOT A BRUISE! IT LOOKS LIKE *MAKE-UP!*
ALL RIGHT, THEN--! TAKE ME AWAY FROM HERE--! TO *YOUR* PLACE!
SHE'S STUDYING MY FACE!
WHAT'S WRONG?

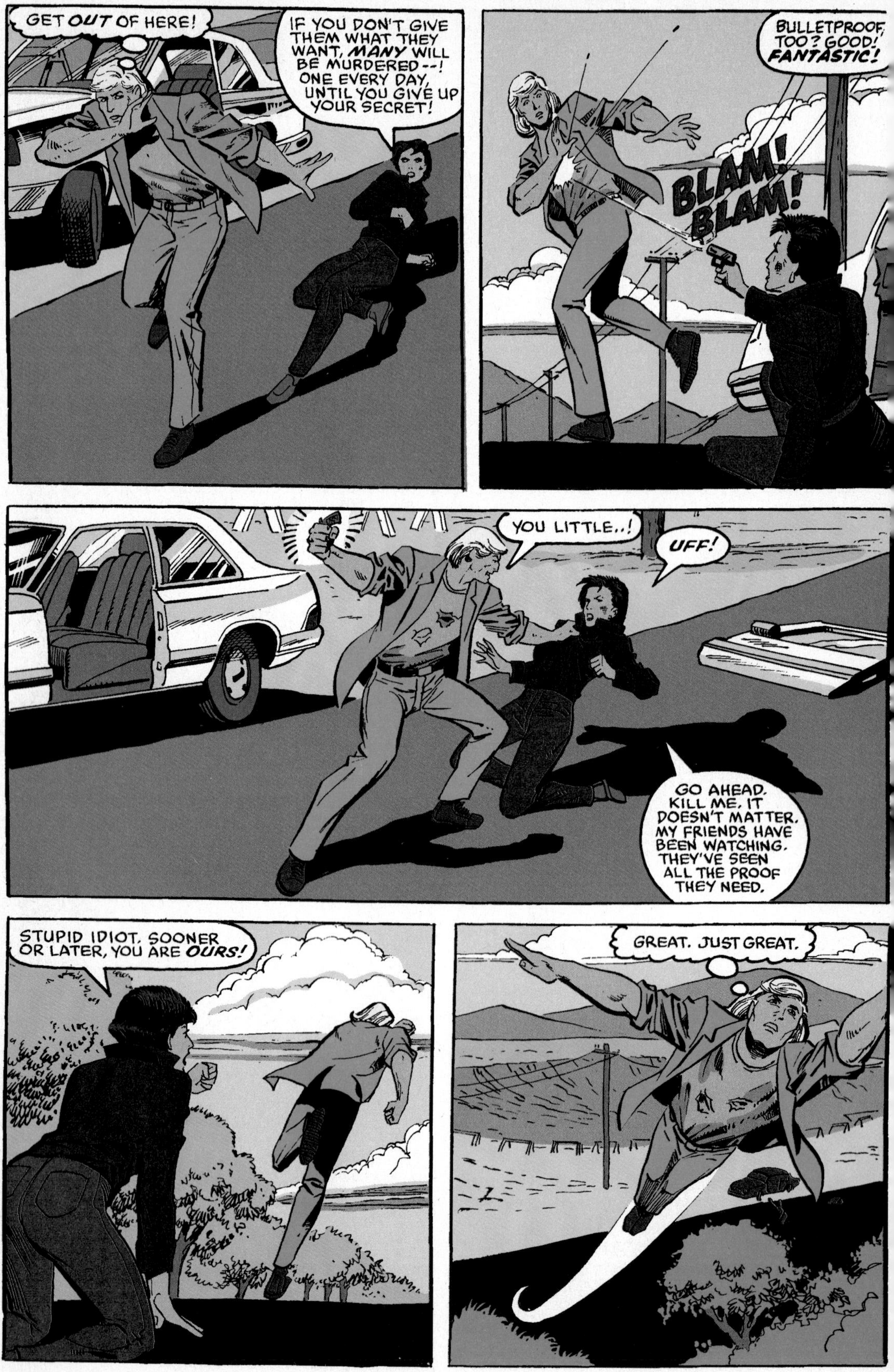
GET OUT OF HERE!
IF YOU DON'T GIVE THEM WHAT THEY WANT, MANY WILL BE MURDERED--! ONE EVERY DAY, UNTIL YOU GIVE UP YOUR SECRET!
BULLETPROOF, TOO? GOOD! FANTASTIC!
BLAM! BLAM!
YOU LITTLE..!
UFF!
GO AHEAD. KILL ME. IT DOESN'T MATTER. MY FRIENDS HAVE BEEN WATCHING. THEY'VE SEEN ALL THE PROOF THEY NEED.
STUPID IDIOT. SOONER OR LATER, YOU ARE OURS!
GREAT. JUST GREAT.

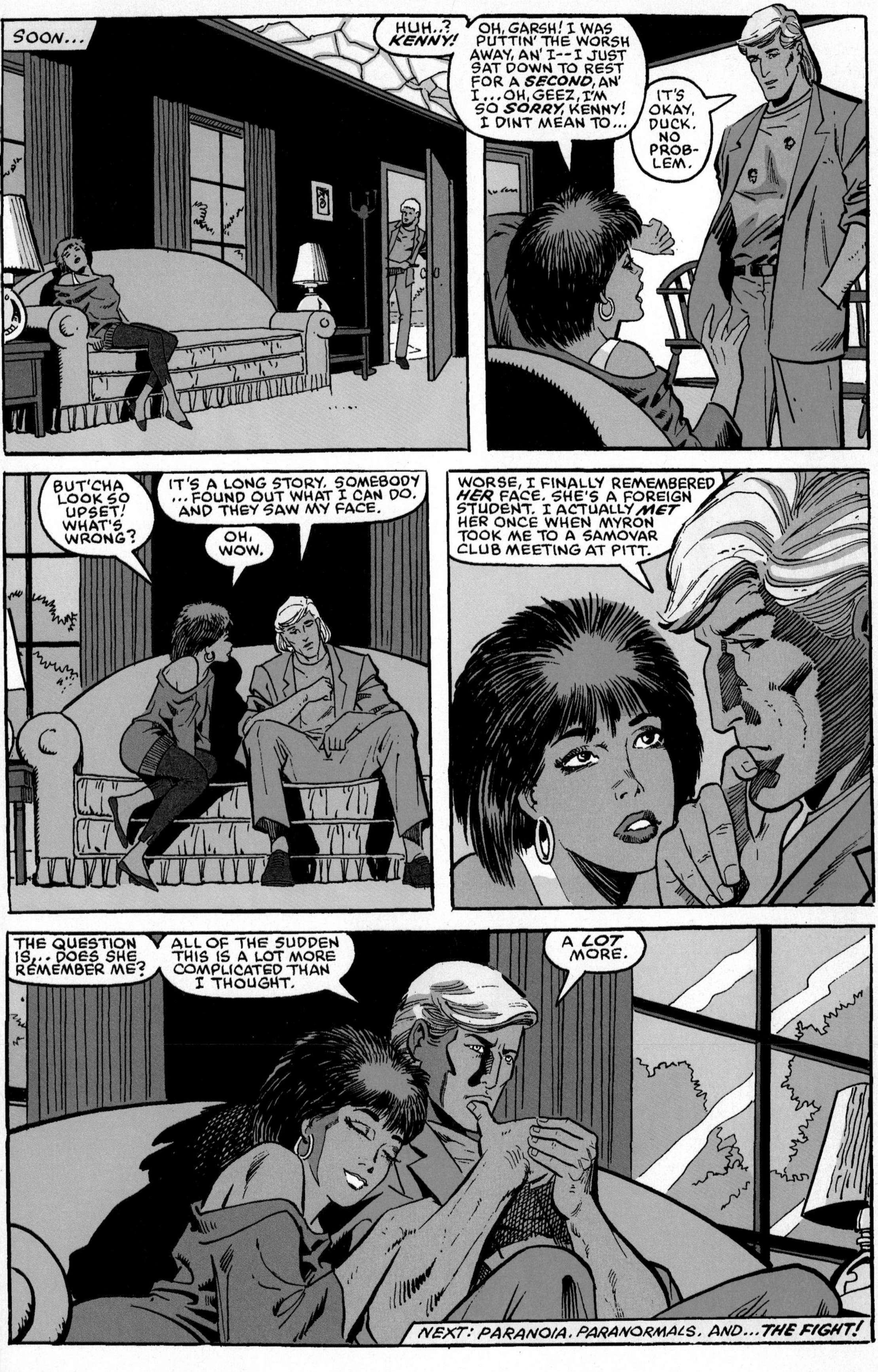
SOON...
HUH..? KENNY!
OH, GARSH! I WAS PUTTIN' THE WORSH AWAY, AN' I--I JUST SAT DOWN TO REST FOR A SECOND, AN' I...OH, GEEZ, I'M SO SORRY, KENNY! I DINT MEAN TO...
IT'S OKAY, DUCK. NO PROB-LEM.
BUT'CHA LOOK SO UPSET! WHAT'S WRONG?
IT'S A LONG STORY. SOMEBODY ...FOUND OUT WHAT I CAN DO. AND THEY SAW MY FACE.
OH, WOW.
WORSE, I FINALLY REMEMBERED HER FACE. SHE'S A FOREIGN STUDENT. I ACTUALLY MET HER ONCE WHEN MYRON TOOK ME TO A SAMOVAR CLUB MEETING AT PITT.
THE QUESTION IS... DOES SHE REMEMBER ME?
ALL OF THE SUDDEN THIS IS A LOT MORE COMPLICATED THAN I THOUGHT.
A LOT MORE.
NEXT: PARANOIA, PARANORMALS, AND... THE FIGHT!

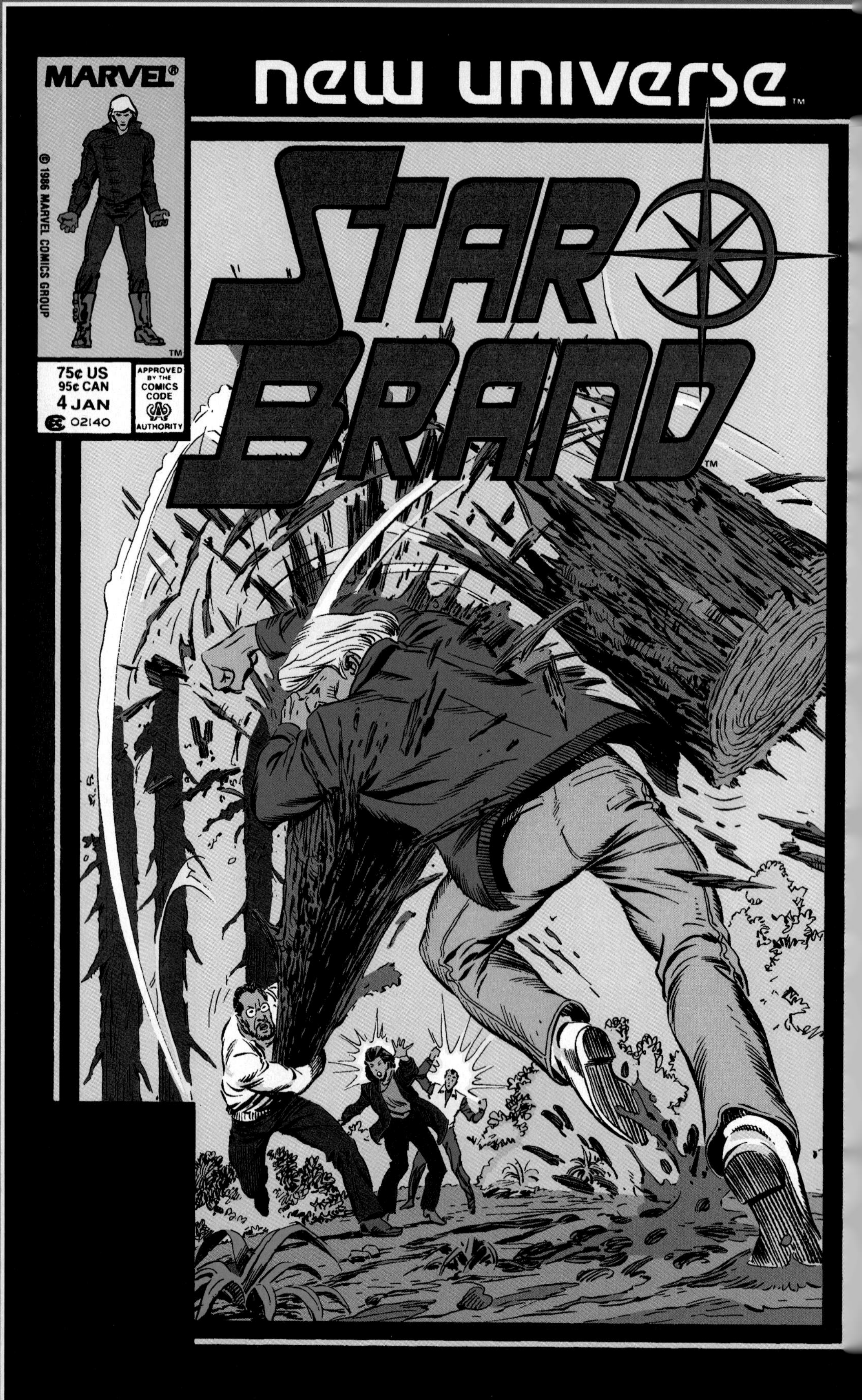
MARVEL®
NEW UNIVERSE™
STAR BRAND™
© 1986 MARVEL COMICS GROUP
75¢ US
95¢ CAN
4 JAN
02140
APPROVED BY THE COMICS CODE AUTHORITY

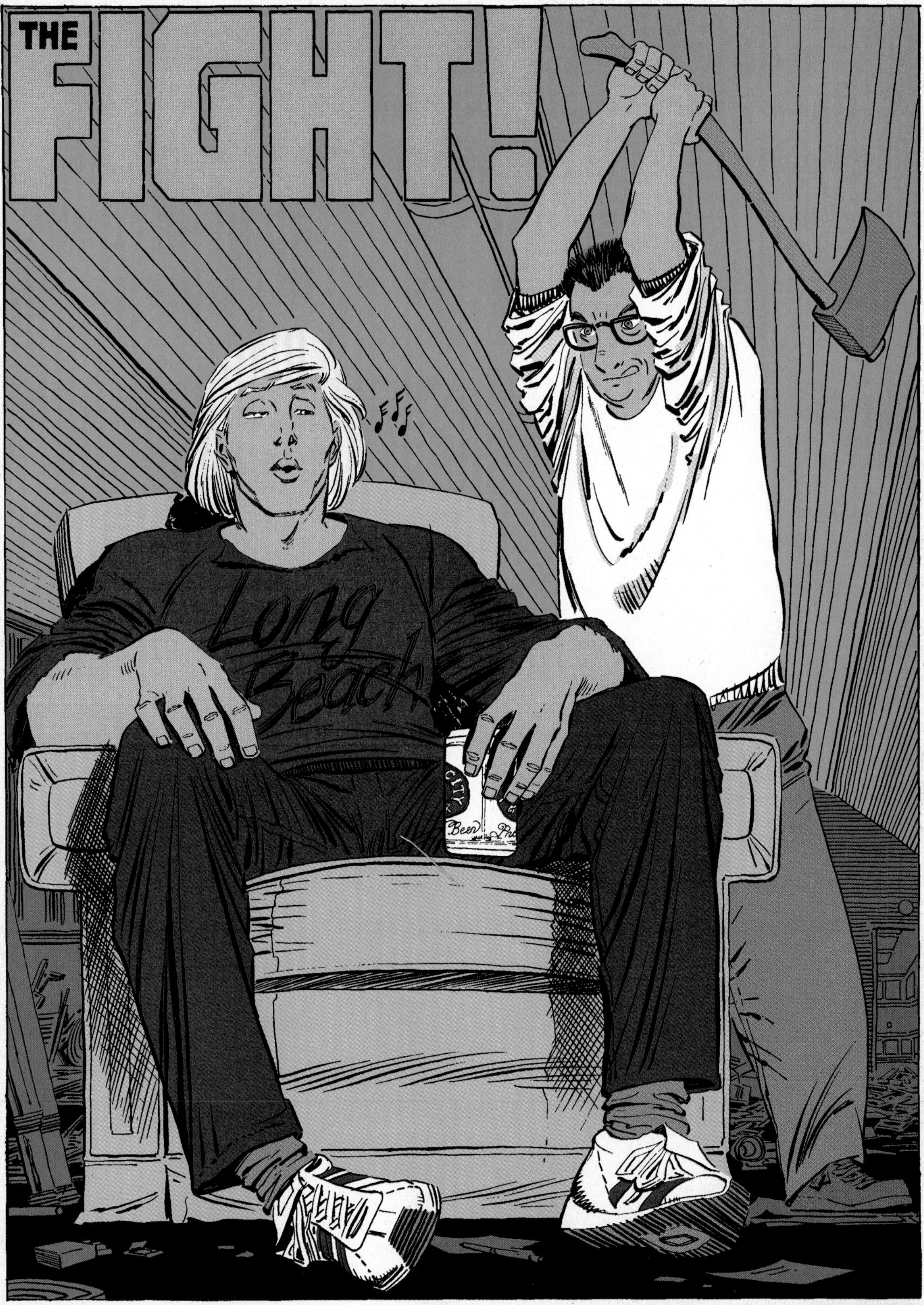
THE FIGHT!
Long Beach
City
Beer

JIM SHOOTER SCRIPT · JOHN ROMITA, JR. PENCILS · AL WILLIAMSON INKS · JOE ROSEN LETTERS · CHRISTIE SCHEELE COLORS · MICHAEL HIGGINS EDITING

UNNNN!

A DOLLAR FIFTY AT THE FLEA MARKET, AND LOOK AT IT NOW! RUINED!

YOU OWE ME AN AXE, KEN!

MYRON, I *TOLD* YOU --A WHILE BACK, A *NUKE* WENT OFF IN MY HANDS AND DIDN'T HURT ME. DON'T YOU BELIEVE ME?

THIS WHOLE THING IS *SO* IMPOSSIBLE THAT EVEN *SEEING* ISN'T BELIEVING.

HM. THANKS FOR REMINDING ME THAT I NEED A HAIRCUT.

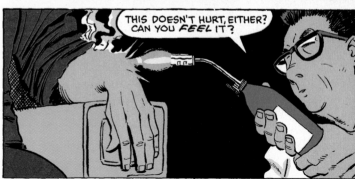

THIS DOESN'T HURT, EITHER? CAN YOU *FEEL* IT?

I CAN FEEL THAT IT'S HOT... BUT IT DOESN'T HURT. *NOTHING* CAN HURT ME--

--UNLESS I LOSE MY CONCENTRATION...

OH, *MY GOD*--!

HUH? KATHY--!

OH--!

RELAX, KATH. NO BIG DEAL. MYRON AND I WERE, UH... JUST TRYING TO GET THE TORCH TO WORK RIGHT.

GRAB THAT THING AND CLOSE THE VALVE, WILLYA, MYRON?

VALVE. RIGHT.

BUT YOU'RE ON *FIRE!*

IT'S OKAY. IT'S OUT. HERE, LET ME HELP YOU.

AREN'T YOU BURNED?

NAH. I SMOTHERED IT TOO FAST.

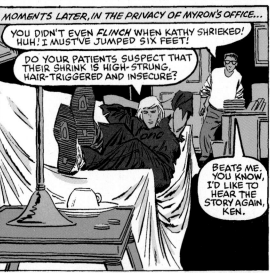

MOMENTS LATER, IN THE PRIVACY OF MYRON'S OFFICE...

YOU DIDN'T EVEN *FLINCH* WHEN KATHY SHRIEKED! HUH! I MUST'VE JUMPED SIX FEET!

DO YOUR PATIENTS SUSPECT THAT THEIR SHRINK IS HIGH-STRUNG, HAIR-TRIGGERED AND INSECURE?

BEATS ME. YOU KNOW, I'D LIKE TO HEAR THE STORY AGAIN, KEN.

OKAY...

I WAS RIDING MY BIKE UP IN THE LAUREL MOUNTAINS ...IT WAS SATURDAY, AUGUST SECOND...

I SAW THIS BURNED OUT AREA. IT LOOKED LIKE A *BATTLEFIELD.* I DIDN'T KNOW WHAT TO MAKE OF IT.

"THEN THIS *OLD MAN* WALKED UP TO ME. BIG GUY. MAYBE A FOOT TALLER THAN *I* AM!

"I GATHERED FROM WHAT HE SAID THAT THERE *HAD* BEEN A FIGHT THERE, HIM AGAINST SOME ENEMIES WHO'D BEEN FOLLOWING HIM. SURE, I THOUGHT-- WITH A FLAME THROWER AND GRENADES?

"ANYWAY, HE SAID HE WAS *DYING.* HE SAID THAT HE'D BEEN LOOKING FOR ME FOR A LONG TIME. THAT I WAS LIKE HIM -- AND WE WERE A 'RARE BREED.'

"HE TOLD ME HE WANTED TO GIVE ME SOMETHING. ASKED ME TO LOOK AT HIS EYES. HIS EYES WERE *WEIRD*...

81

"THERE WAS THIS *MARK* ON HIS ARM...HE SAID IT GAVE ITS BEARER *POWER*. HE TOLD ME IT WAS LIKE A TATTOO, BUT MOVEABLE. HE CALLED IT THE *STAR BRAND*...AND HE *GAVE* IT TO ME.

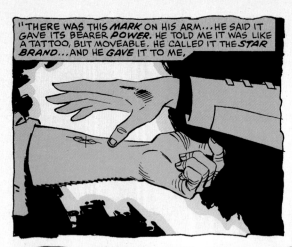

"NEXT, I REMEMBER WAKING UP. THE OLD MAN WAS GONE...

"...BUT I FOLLOWED HIS TRAIL THROUGH THE DEW-SOAKED GRASS AND BRUSH. IT LOOKED LIKE HE'D *STAGGERED* AWAY...

"...AND STUMBLED OFF A CLIFF.

"I WENT DOWN THAT CLIFF WITH-OUT A SECOND THOUGHT. I GUESS, SOMEHOW, I *KNEW* I COULD FLY.

"THE BODY WAS HIS, BUT...IT WASN'T *HUMAN*, REALLY, MYRON. IT WAS THIS GRAYISH-GREEN...

"I--I FELT...NUMB..."

I BURIED THE BODY...RIPPED A HUGE BLOCK OF SHALE OUT OF THE HILLSIDE--MADE A LITTLE CAVE, SORT OF--SEALED HIM IN. I DON'T KNOW HOW I KNEW I COULD DO *THAT*, EITHER.

AND NOW I WONDER *WHY* I DID IT. WHY *BURY* HIM? WHY NOT BRING THE BODY TO THE POLICE OR SOME-BODY?

I TRY TO REMEMBER WHAT I WAS *THINKING*, THEN... BUT IT'S JUST A BLANK. I WAS ON AUTOPILOT.

OR POST-HYPNOTIC *SUGGESTION*, MORE LIKELY. IT SOUNDS AS THOUGH THE "OLD MAN" PUT YOU UNDER SOME FORM OF HYPNOSIS.

ANYWAY, ONCE I STARTED THINKING STRAIGHT, I KNEW I NEEDED SOMEBODY TO *TALK* TO, A FRIEND I COULD *TRUST*. SO, I CAME HERE.

I HAD TO *PROVE* TO YOU WHAT I COULD DO. BEEN PROVING IT TO YOU, AND TO *MYSELF*, EVER SINCE. LIKE TONIGHT.

82

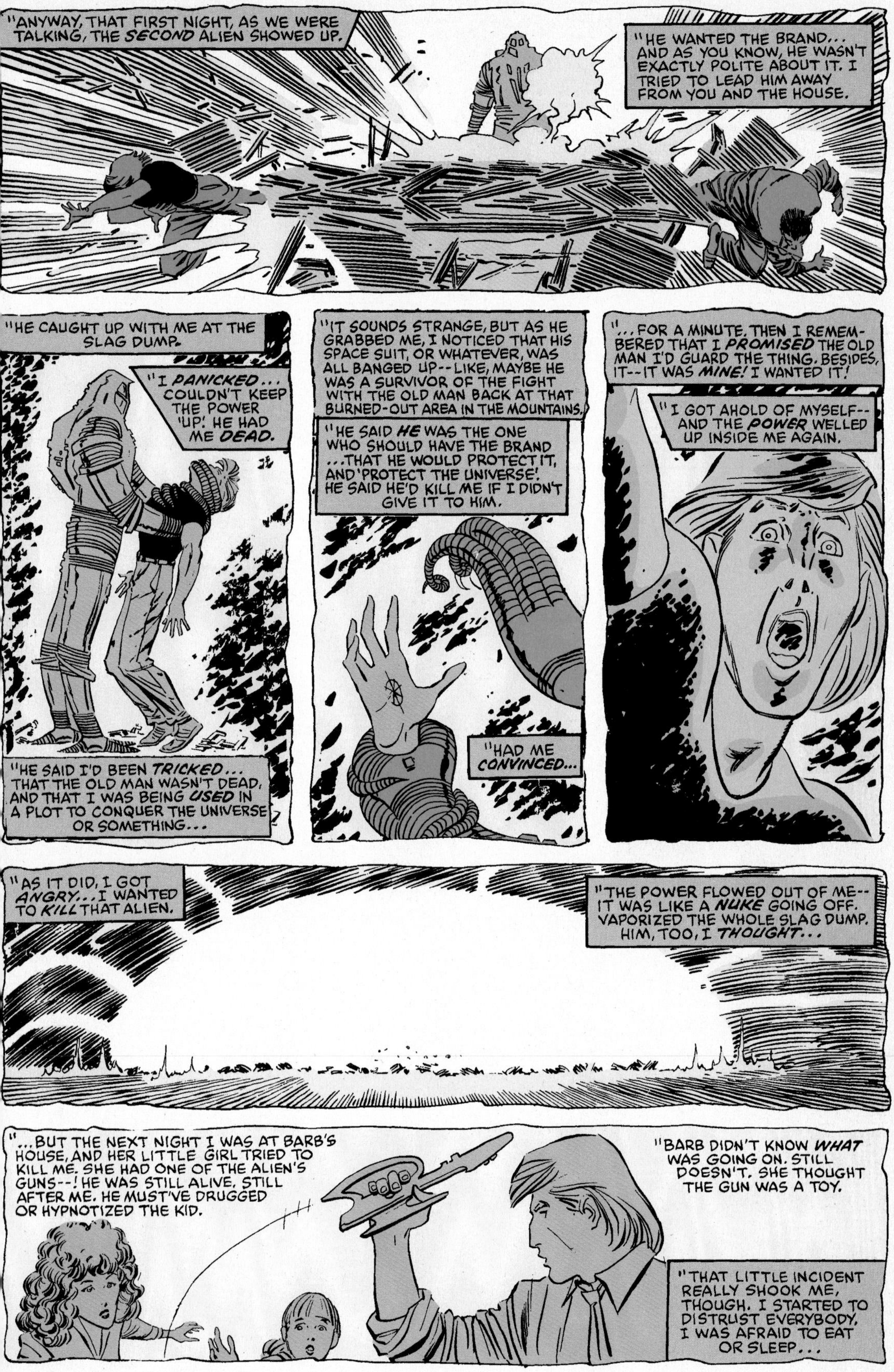
"ANYWAY, THAT FIRST NIGHT, AS WE WERE TALKING, THE *SECOND* ALIEN SHOWED UP.
"HE WANTED THE BRAND... AND AS YOU KNOW, HE WASN'T EXACTLY POLITE ABOUT IT. I TRIED TO LEAD HIM AWAY FROM YOU AND THE HOUSE.
"HE CAUGHT UP WITH ME AT THE SLAG DUMP.
"I *PANICKED*... COULDN'T KEEP THE POWER 'UP.' HE HAD ME *DEAD*.
"HE SAID I'D BEEN *TRICKED*... THAT THE OLD MAN WASN'T DEAD, AND THAT I WAS BEING *USED* IN A PLOT TO CONQUER THE UNIVERSE OR SOMETHING...
"IT SOUNDS STRANGE, BUT AS HE GRABBED ME, I NOTICED THAT HIS SPACE SUIT, OR WHATEVER, WAS ALL BANGED UP--LIKE, MAYBE HE WAS A SURVIVOR OF THE FIGHT WITH THE OLD MAN BACK AT THAT BURNED-OUT AREA IN THE MOUNTAINS.
"HE SAID *HE* WAS THE ONE WHO SHOULD HAVE THE BRAND ...THAT HE WOULD PROTECT IT, AND 'PROTECT THE UNIVERSE!' HE SAID HE'D KILL ME IF I DIDN'T GIVE IT TO HIM.
"HAD ME *CONVINCED*...
"...FOR A MINUTE. THEN I REMEMBERED THAT I *PROMISED* THE OLD MAN I'D GUARD THE THING. BESIDES, IT--IT WAS *MINE!* I WANTED IT!
"I GOT AHOLD OF MYSELF-- AND THE *POWER* WELLED UP INSIDE ME AGAIN.
"AS IT DID, I GOT *ANGRY*... I WANTED TO *KILL* THAT ALIEN.
"THE POWER FLOWED OUT OF ME-- IT WAS LIKE A *NUKE* GOING OFF. VAPORIZED THE WHOLE SLAG DUMP. HIM, TOO, I *THOUGHT*...
"...BUT THE NEXT NIGHT I WAS AT BARB'S HOUSE, AND HER LITTLE GIRL TRIED TO KILL ME. SHE HAD ONE OF THE ALIEN'S GUNS--! HE WAS STILL ALIVE. STILL AFTER ME. HE MUST'VE DRUGGED OR HYPNOTIZED THE KID.
"BARB DIDN'T KNOW *WHAT* WAS GOING ON. STILL DOESN'T. SHE THOUGHT THE GUN WAS A TOY.
"THAT LITTLE INCIDENT REALLY SHOOK ME, THOUGH. I STARTED TO DISTRUST EVERYBODY. I WAS AFRAID TO EAT OR SLEEP...

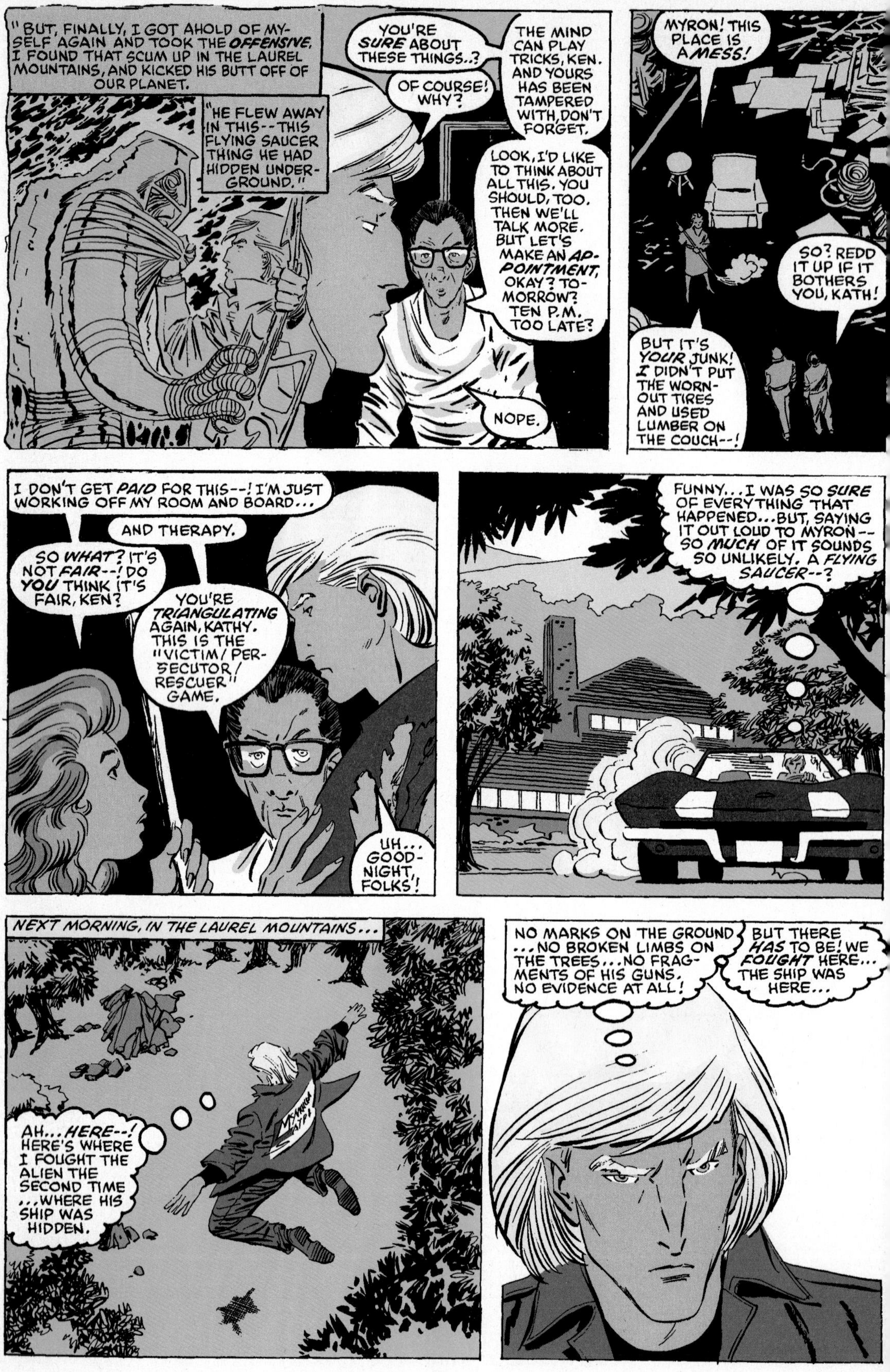
"BUT, FINALLY, I GOT AHOLD OF MYSELF AGAIN AND TOOK THE OFFENSIVE. I FOUND THAT SCUM UP IN THE LAUREL MOUNTAINS, AND KICKED HIS BUTT OFF OF OUR PLANET.
"HE FLEW AWAY IN THIS--THIS FLYING SAUCER THING HE HAD HIDDEN UNDERGROUND."
YOU'RE SURE ABOUT THESE THINGS..?
OF COURSE! WHY?
THE MIND CAN PLAY TRICKS, KEN. AND YOURS HAS BEEN TAMPERED WITH, DON'T FORGET.
LOOK, I'D LIKE TO THINK ABOUT ALL THIS. YOU SHOULD, TOO. THEN WE'LL TALK MORE. BUT LET'S MAKE AN APPOINTMENT, OKAY? TOMORROW? TEN P.M. TOO LATE?
NOPE.
MYRON! THIS PLACE IS A MESS!
SO? REDD IT UP IF IT BOTHERS YOU, KATH!
BUT IT'S YOUR JUNK! I DIDN'T PUT THE WORN-OUT TIRES AND USED LUMBER ON THE COUCH--!
I DON'T GET PAID FOR THIS--! I'M JUST WORKING OFF MY ROOM AND BOARD...
AND THERAPY.
SO WHAT? IT'S NOT FAIR--! DO YOU THINK IT'S FAIR, KEN?
YOU'RE TRIANGULATING AGAIN, KATHY. THIS IS THE "VICTIM/PERSECUTOR/RESCUER" GAME.
UH... GOOD-NIGHT, FOLKS!
FUNNY...I WAS SO SURE OF EVERYTHING THAT HAPPENED...BUT, SAYING IT OUT LOUD TO MYRON--SO MUCH OF IT SOUNDS SO UNLIKELY. A FLYING SAUCER--?
NEXT MORNING, IN THE LAUREL MOUNTAINS...
AH...HERE--! HERE'S WHERE I FOUGHT THE ALIEN THE SECOND TIME...WHERE HIS SHIP WAS HIDDEN.
NO MARKS ON THE GROUND...NO BROKEN LIMBS ON THE TREES...NO FRAGMENTS OF HIS GUNS. NO EVIDENCE AT ALL!
BUT THERE HAS TO BE! WE FOUGHT HERE... THE SHIP WAS HERE...

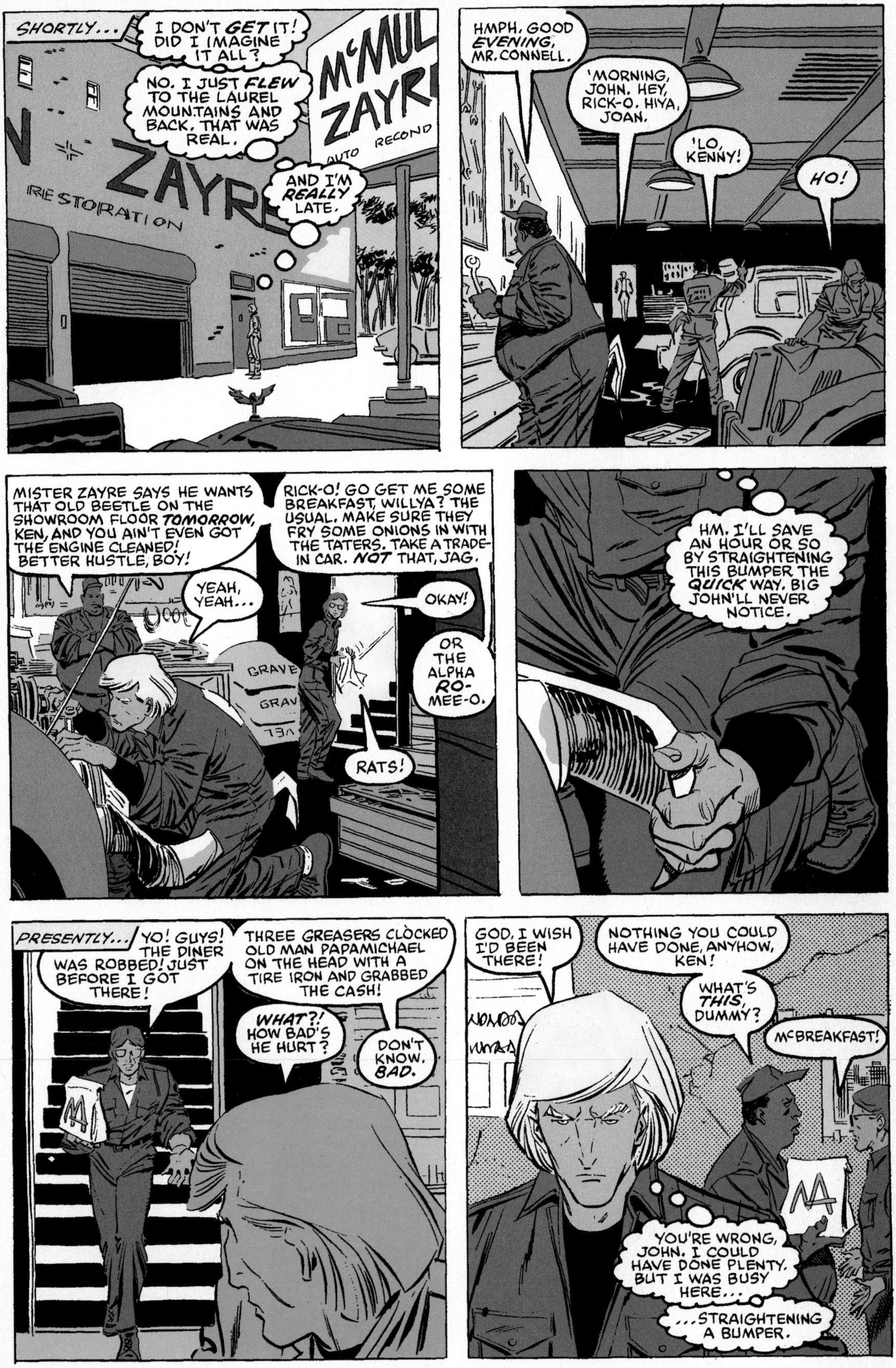

SHORTLY...
I DON'T GET IT! DID I IMAGINE IT ALL?
NO. I JUST FLEW TO THE LAUREL MOUNTAINS AND BACK. THAT WAS REAL.
AND I'M REALLY LATE.
McMUL ZAYR
AUTO RECOND
ZAYRE
RESTORATION
HMPH. GOOD EVENING, MR. CONNELL.
'MORNING, JOHN. HEY, RICK-O. HIYA, JOAN.
'LO, KENNY!
HO!
MISTER ZAYRE SAYS HE WANTS THAT OLD BEETLE ON THE SHOWROOM FLOOR TOMORROW, KEN, AND YOU AIN'T EVEN GOT THE ENGINE CLEANED! BETTER HUSTLE, BOY!
YEAH, YEAH...
RICK-O! GO GET ME SOME BREAKFAST, WILLYA? THE USUAL. MAKE SURE THEY FRY SOME ONIONS IN WITH THE TATERS. TAKE A TRADE-IN CAR. NOT THAT, JAG.
OKAY!
OR THE ALPHA RO-MEE-O.
RATS!
HM. I'LL SAVE AN HOUR OR SO BY STRAIGHTENING THIS BUMPER THE QUICK WAY. BIG JOHN'LL NEVER NOTICE.
PRESENTLY...
YO! GUYS! THE DINER WAS ROBBED! JUST BEFORE I GOT THERE!
THREE GREASERS CLOCKED OLD MAN PAPAMICHAEL ON THE HEAD WITH A TIRE IRON AND GRABBED THE CASH!
WHAT?! HOW BAD'S HE HURT?
DON'T KNOW. BAD.
GOD, I WISH I'D BEEN THERE!
NOTHING YOU COULD HAVE DONE, ANYHOW, KEN!
WHAT'S THIS, DUMMY?
McBREAKFAST!
YOU'RE WRONG, JOHN. I COULD HAVE DONE PLENTY. BUT I WAS BUSY HERE...
...STRAIGHTENING A BUMPER.

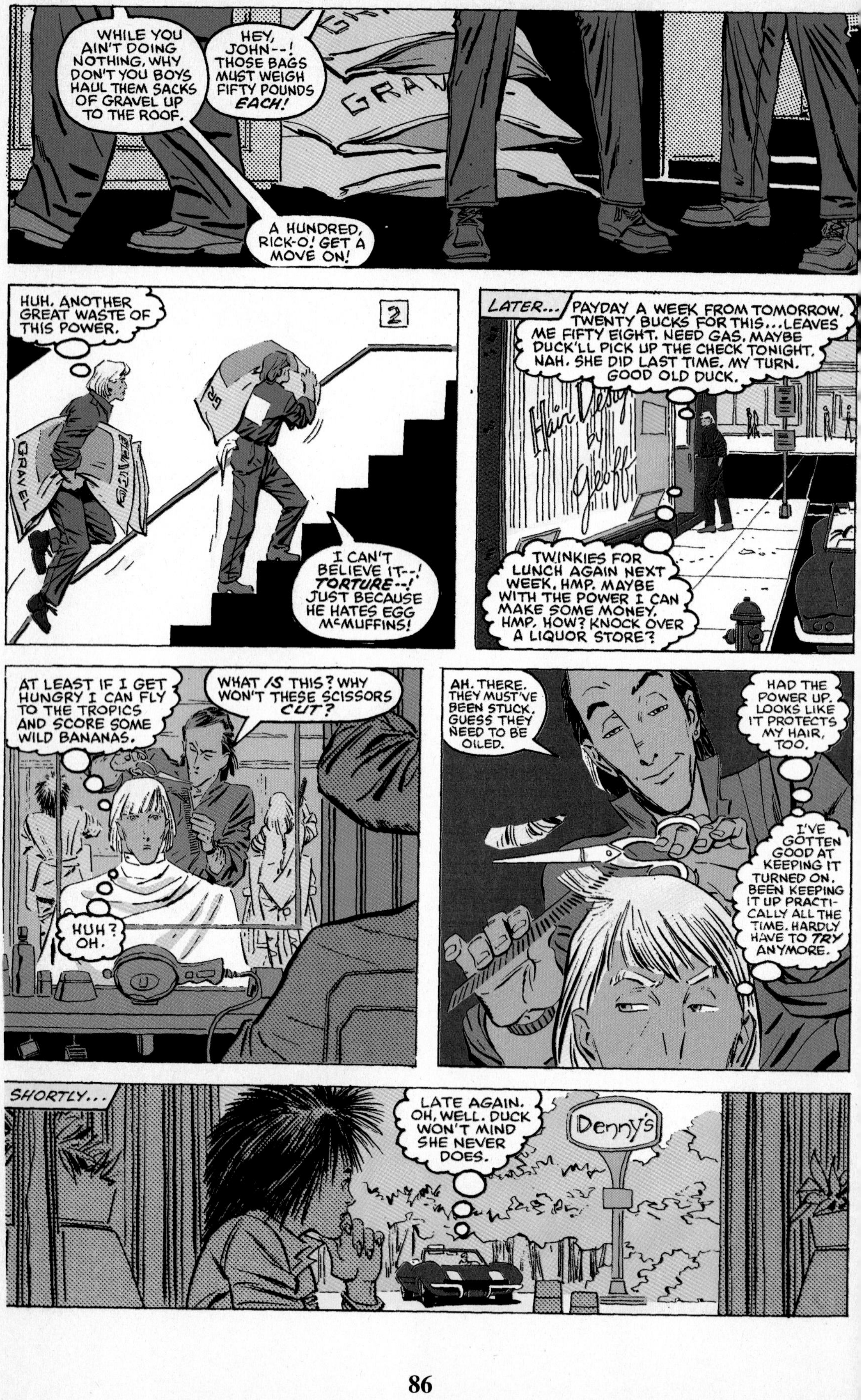
WHILE YOU AIN'T DOING NOTHING, WHY DON'T YOU BOYS HAUL THEM SACKS OF GRAVEL UP TO THE ROOF.
HEY, JOHN--! THOSE BAGS MUST WEIGH FIFTY POUNDS EACH!
A HUNDRED, RICK-O! GET A MOVE ON!
HUH. ANOTHER GREAT WASTE OF THIS POWER.
2
GRAVEL
I CAN'T BELIEVE IT--! TORTURE--! JUST BECAUSE HE HATES EGG McMUFFINS!
LATER...
PAYDAY A WEEK FROM TOMORROW. TWENTY BUCKS FOR THIS...LEAVES ME FIFTY EIGHT. NEED GAS. MAYBE DUCK'LL PICK UP THE CHECK TONIGHT. NAH. SHE DID LAST TIME. MY TURN. GOOD OLD DUCK.
Hair Design by Geoff
TWINKIES FOR LUNCH AGAIN NEXT WEEK. HMP. MAYBE WITH THE POWER I CAN MAKE SOME MONEY. HMP. HOW? KNOCK OVER A LIQUOR STORE?
AT LEAST IF I GET HUNGRY I CAN FLY TO THE TROPICS AND SCORE SOME WILD BANANAS.
WHAT IS THIS? WHY WON'T THESE SCISSORS CUT?
HUH? OH.
AH. THERE. THEY MUST'VE BEEN STUCK. GUESS THEY NEED TO BE OILED.
HAD THE POWER UP. LOOKS LIKE IT PROTECTS MY HAIR, TOO.
I'VE GOTTEN GOOD AT KEEPING IT TURNED ON. BEEN KEEPING IT UP PRACTICALLY ALL THE TIME. HARDLY HAVE TO TRY ANYMORE.
SHORTLY...
LATE AGAIN. OH, WELL. DUCK WON'T MIND. SHE NEVER DOES.
Denny's

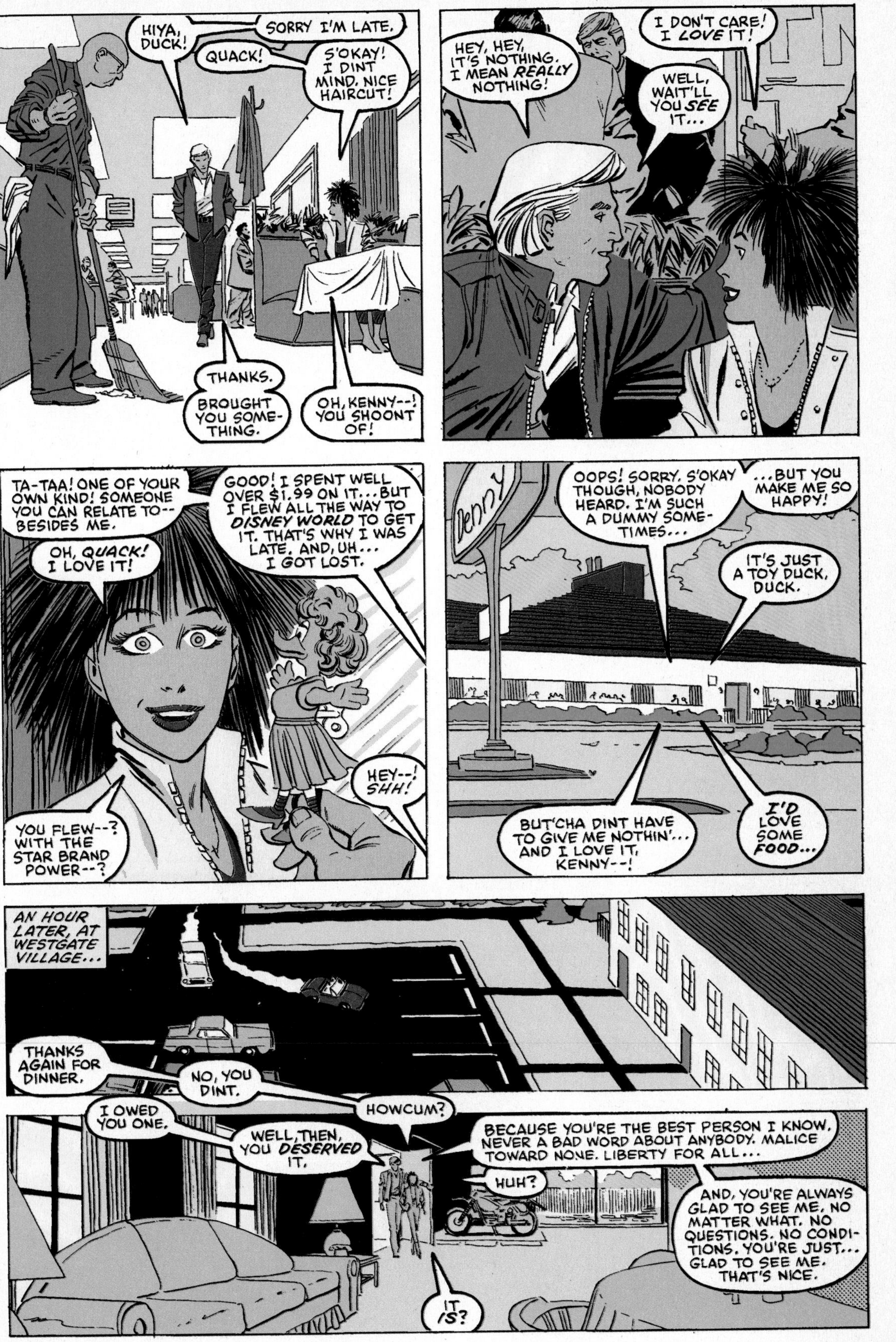
HIYA, DUCK!
SORRY I'M LATE.
QUACK!
S'OKAY! I DINT MIND. NICE HAIRCUT!
THANKS.
BROUGHT YOU SOME-THING.
OH, KENNY--! YOU SHOONT OF!
HEY, HEY, IT'S NOTHING. I MEAN REALLY NOTHING!
I DON'T CARE! I LOVE IT!
WELL, WAIT'LL YOU SEE IT...
TA-TAA! ONE OF YOUR OWN KIND! SOMEONE YOU CAN RELATE TO-- BESIDES ME.
OH, QUACK! I LOVE IT!
GOOD! I SPENT WELL OVER $1.99 ON IT... BUT I FLEW ALL THE WAY TO DISNEY WORLD TO GET IT. THAT'S WHY I WAS LATE. AND, UH... I GOT LOST.
HEY--! SHH!
YOU FLEW--? WITH THE STAR BRAND POWER--?
OOPS! SORRY. S'OKAY THOUGH, NOBODY HEARD. I'M SUCH A DUMMY SOME-TIMES...
...BUT YOU MAKE ME SO HAPPY!
IT'S JUST A TOY DUCK, DUCK.
BUT'CHA DINT HAVE TO GIVE ME NOTHIN'... AND I LOVE IT, KENNY--!
I'D LOVE SOME FOOD...
AN HOUR LATER, AT WESTGATE VILLAGE...
THANKS AGAIN FOR DINNER.
NO, YOU DINT.
I OWED YOU ONE.
HOWCUM?
WELL, THEN, YOU DESERVED IT.
BECAUSE YOU'RE THE BEST PERSON I KNOW. NEVER A BAD WORD ABOUT ANYBODY. MALICE TOWARD NONE. LIBERTY FOR ALL...
HUH?
AND, YOU'RE ALWAYS GLAD TO SEE ME. NO MATTER WHAT. NO QUESTIONS. NO CONDI-TIONS. YOU'RE JUST... GLAD TO SEE ME. THAT'S NICE.
IT IS?

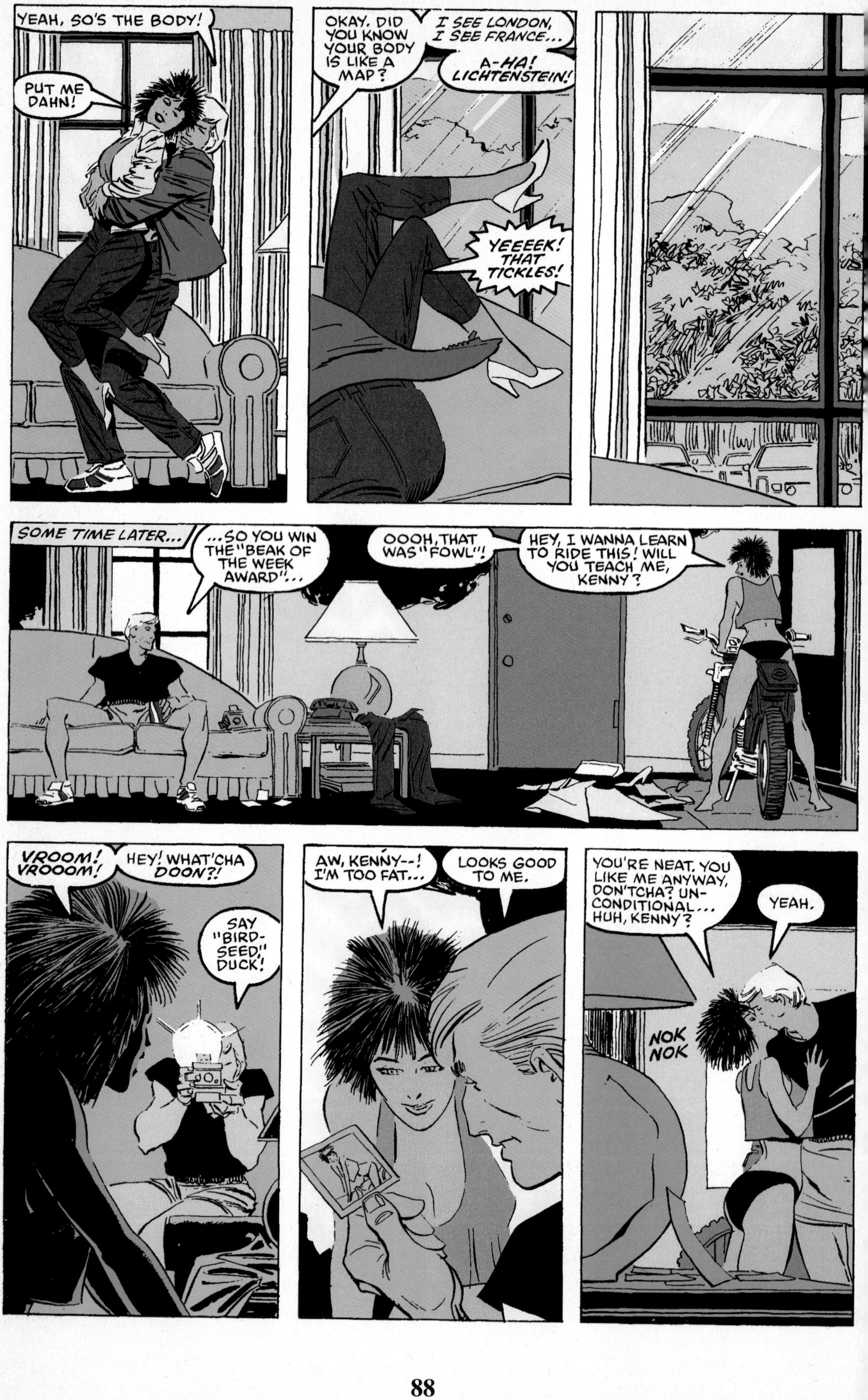
YEAH, SO'S THE BODY!
PUT ME DAHN!
OKAY, DID YOU KNOW YOUR BODY IS LIKE A MAP?
I SEE LONDON, I SEE FRANCE...
A-HA! LICHTENSTEIN!
YEEEEK! THAT TICKLES!
SOME TIME LATER...
...SO YOU WIN THE "BEAK OF THE WEEK AWARD"...
OOOH, THAT WAS "FOWL"!
HEY, I WANNA LEARN TO RIDE THIS! WILL YOU TEACH ME, KENNY?
VROOM! VROOOM!
HEY! WHAT'CHA DOON?!
SAY "BIRD-SEED," DUCK!
AW, KENNY--! I'M TOO FAT...
LOOKS GOOD TO ME.
YOU'RE NEAT. YOU LIKE ME ANYWAY, DON'TCHA? UN-CONDITIONAL... HUH, KENNY?
YEAH.
NOK NOK

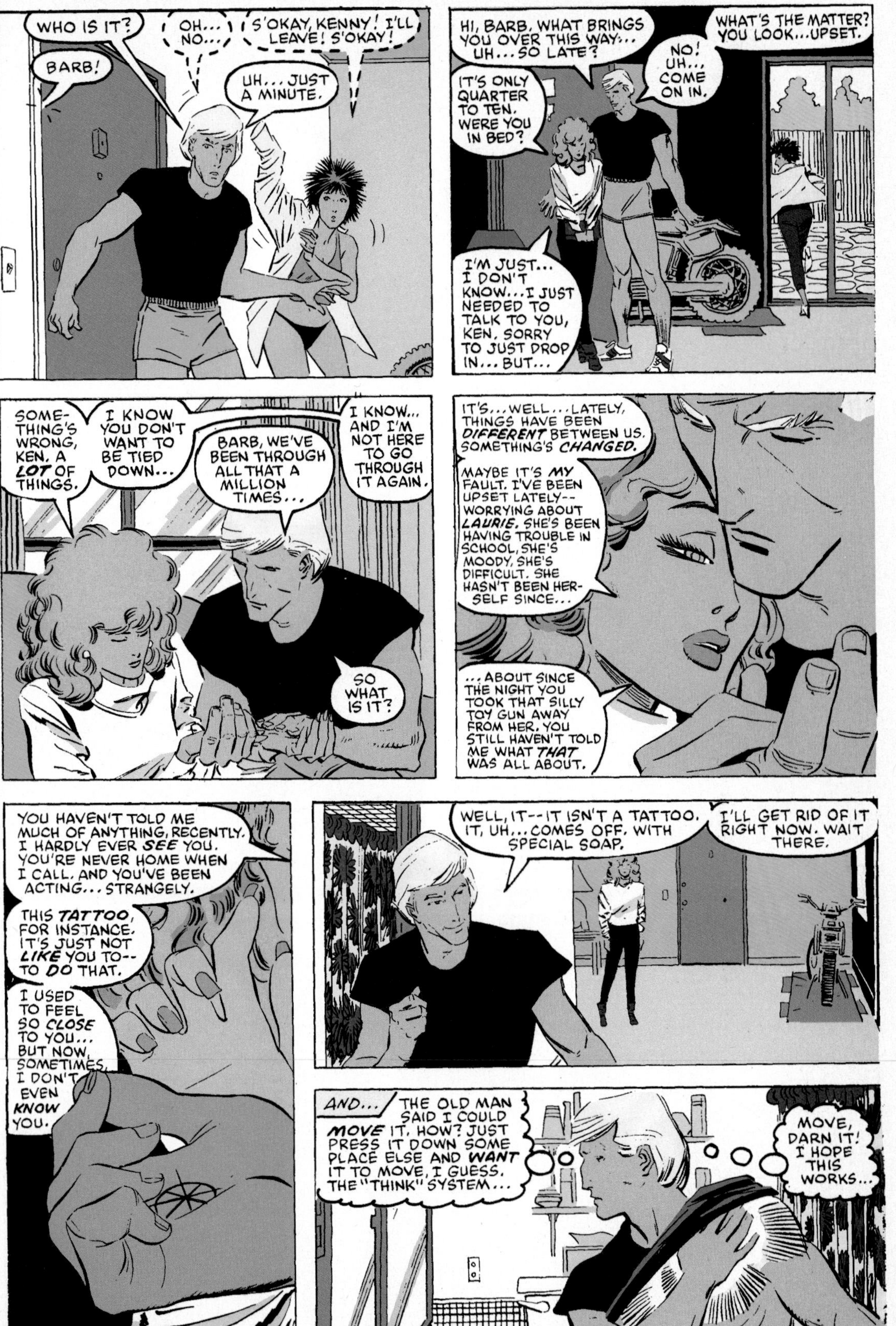
WHO IS IT?
OH... NO...
S'OKAY, KENNY! I'LL LEAVE! S'OKAY!
BARB!
UH... JUST A MINUTE.
HI, BARB. WHAT BRINGS YOU OVER THIS WAY... UH... SO LATE?
WHAT'S THE MATTER? YOU LOOK... UPSET.
IT'S ONLY QUARTER TO TEN. WERE YOU IN BED?
NO! UH... COME ON IN.
I'M JUST... I DON'T KNOW... I JUST NEEDED TO TALK TO YOU, KEN. SORRY TO JUST DROP IN... BUT...
SOMETHING'S WRONG, KEN. A LOT OF THINGS.
I KNOW YOU DON'T WANT TO BE TIED DOWN...
BARB, WE'VE BEEN THROUGH ALL THAT A MILLION TIMES...
I KNOW... AND I'M NOT HERE TO GO THROUGH IT AGAIN.
SO WHAT IS IT?
IT'S... WELL... LATELY, THINGS HAVE BEEN DIFFERENT BETWEEN US. SOMETHING'S CHANGED.
MAYBE IT'S MY FAULT. I'VE BEEN UPSET LATELY-- WORRYING ABOUT LAURIE. SHE'S BEEN HAVING TROUBLE IN SCHOOL, SHE'S MOODY, SHE'S DIFFICULT. SHE HASN'T BEEN HER-SELF SINCE...
...ABOUT SINCE THE NIGHT YOU TOOK THAT SILLY TOY GUN AWAY FROM HER. YOU STILL HAVEN'T TOLD ME WHAT THAT WAS ALL ABOUT.
YOU HAVEN'T TOLD ME MUCH OF ANYTHING, RECENTLY. I HARDLY EVER SEE YOU. YOU'RE NEVER HOME WHEN I CALL, AND YOU'VE BEEN ACTING... STRANGELY.
THIS TATTOO, FOR INSTANCE. IT'S JUST NOT LIKE YOU TO-- TO DO THAT.
I USED TO FEEL SO CLOSE TO YOU... BUT NOW, SOMETIMES, I DON'T EVEN KNOW YOU.
WELL, IT--IT ISN'T A TATTOO. IT, UH... COMES OFF. WITH SPECIAL SOAP.
I'LL GET RID OF IT RIGHT NOW. WAIT THERE.
AND...
THE OLD MAN SAID I COULD MOVE IT. HOW? JUST PRESS IT DOWN SOME PLACE ELSE AND WANT IT TO MOVE, I GUESS. THE "THINK" SYSTEM...
MOVE, DARN IT! I HOPE THIS WORKS...

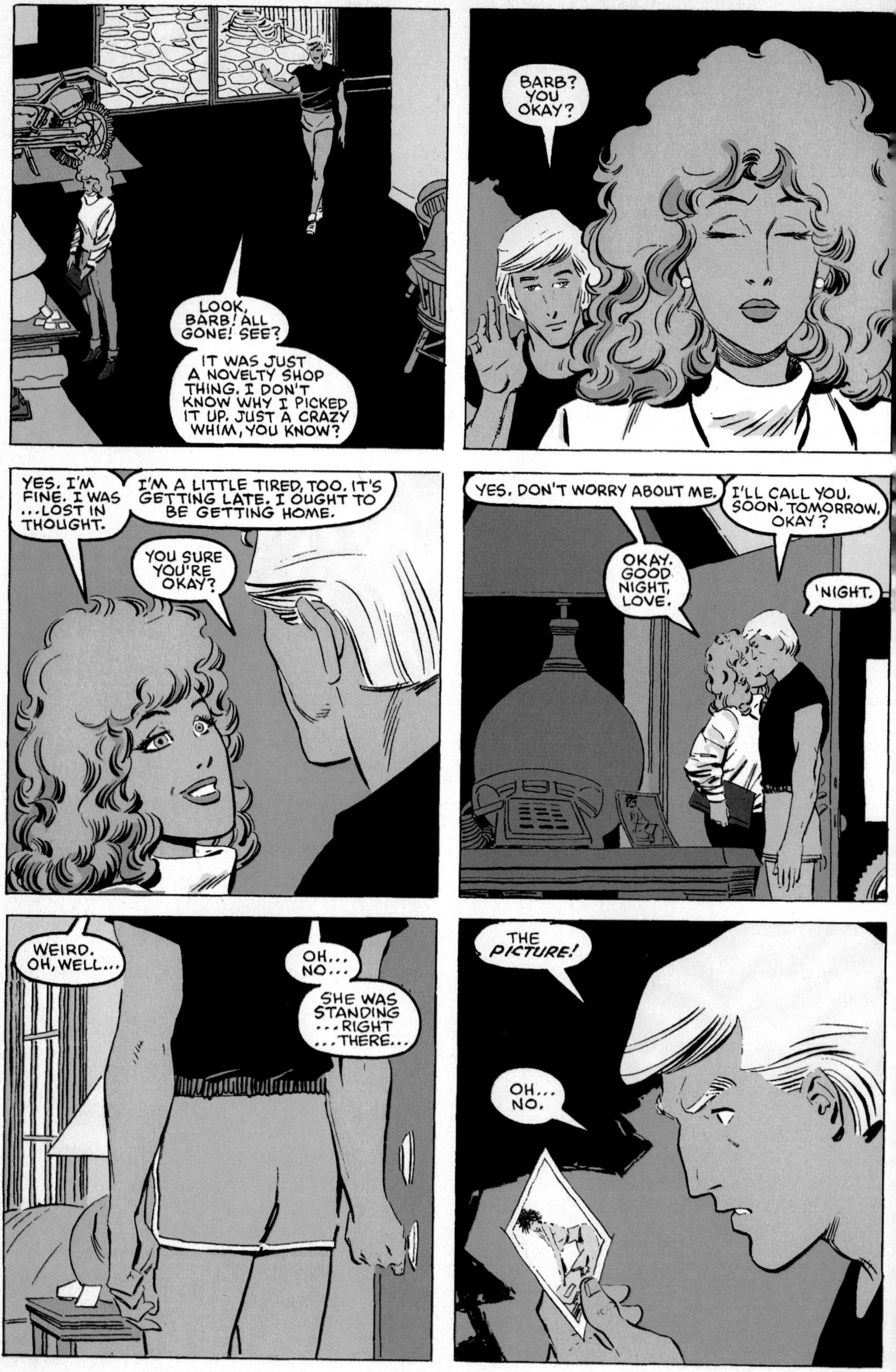
LOOK, BARB! ALL GONE! SEE?
IT WAS JUST A NOVELTY SHOP THING. I DON'T KNOW WHY I PICKED IT UP. JUST A CRAZY WHIM, YOU KNOW?
BARB? YOU OKAY?
YES. I'M FINE. I WAS ...LOST IN THOUGHT.
I'M A LITTLE TIRED, TOO. IT'S GETTING LATE. I OUGHT TO BE GETTING HOME.
YOU SURE YOU'RE OKAY?
YES. DON'T WORRY ABOUT ME.
I'LL CALL YOU. SOON. TOMORROW, OKAY?
OKAY. GOOD NIGHT, LOVE.
'NIGHT.
WEIRD. OH, WELL...
OH... NO...
SHE WAS STANDING ...RIGHT ...THERE...
THE *PICTURE!*
OH... NO.

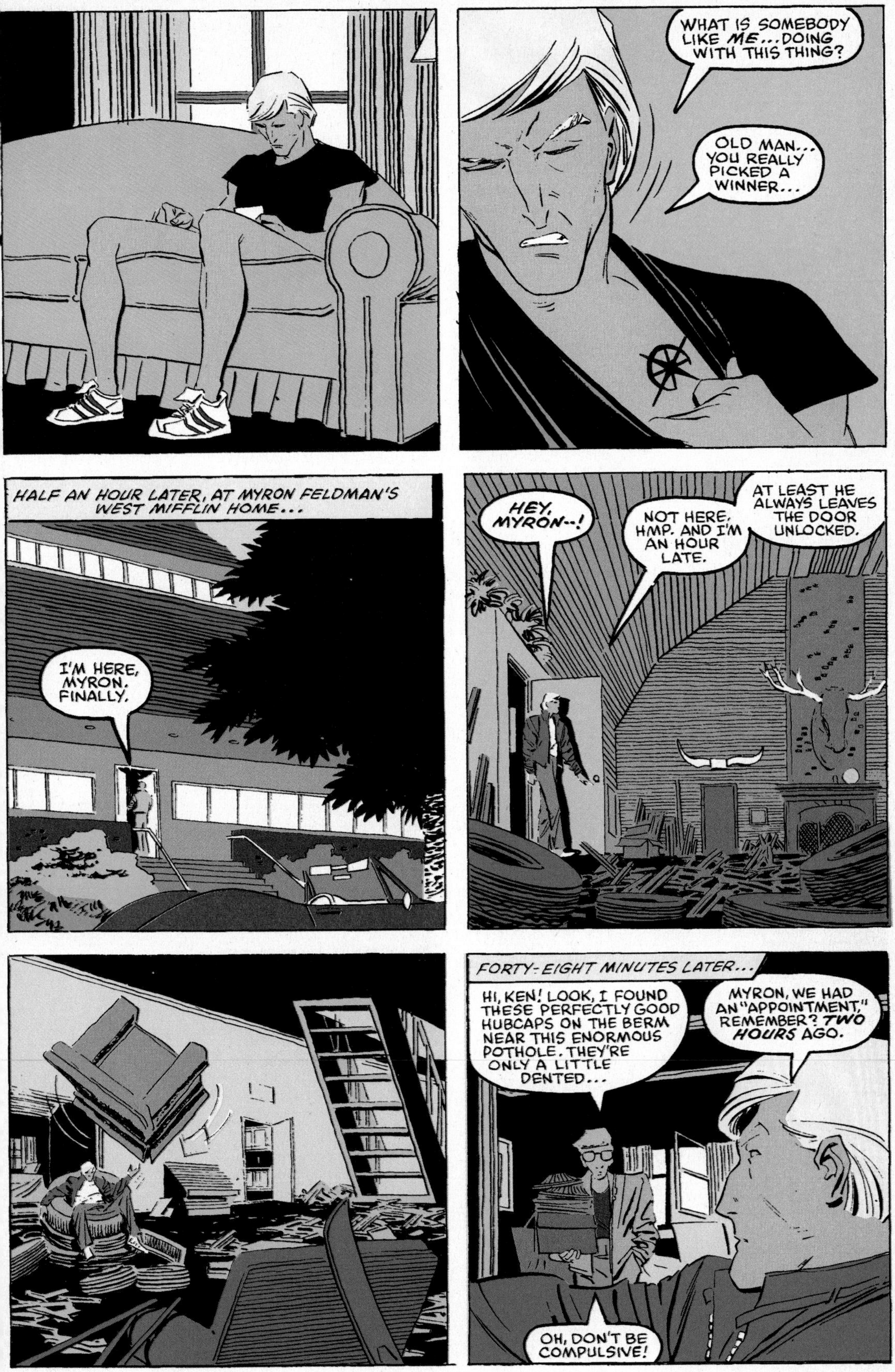
WHAT IS SOMEBODY LIKE ME...DOING WITH THIS THING?
OLD MAN... YOU REALLY PICKED A WINNER...
HALF AN HOUR LATER, AT MYRON FELDMAN'S WEST MIFFLIN HOME...
I'M HERE, MYRON. FINALLY.
HEY, MYRON--!
NOT HERE. HMP. AND I'M AN HOUR LATE.
AT LEAST HE ALWAYS LEAVES THE DOOR UNLOCKED.
FORTY-EIGHT MINUTES LATER...
HI, KEN! LOOK, I FOUND THESE PERFECTLY GOOD HUBCAPS ON THE BERM NEAR THIS ENORMOUS POTHOLE. THEY'RE ONLY A LITTLE DENTED...
MYRON, WE HAD AN "APPOINTMENT," REMEMBER? TWO HOURS AGO.
OH, DON'T BE COMPULSIVE!

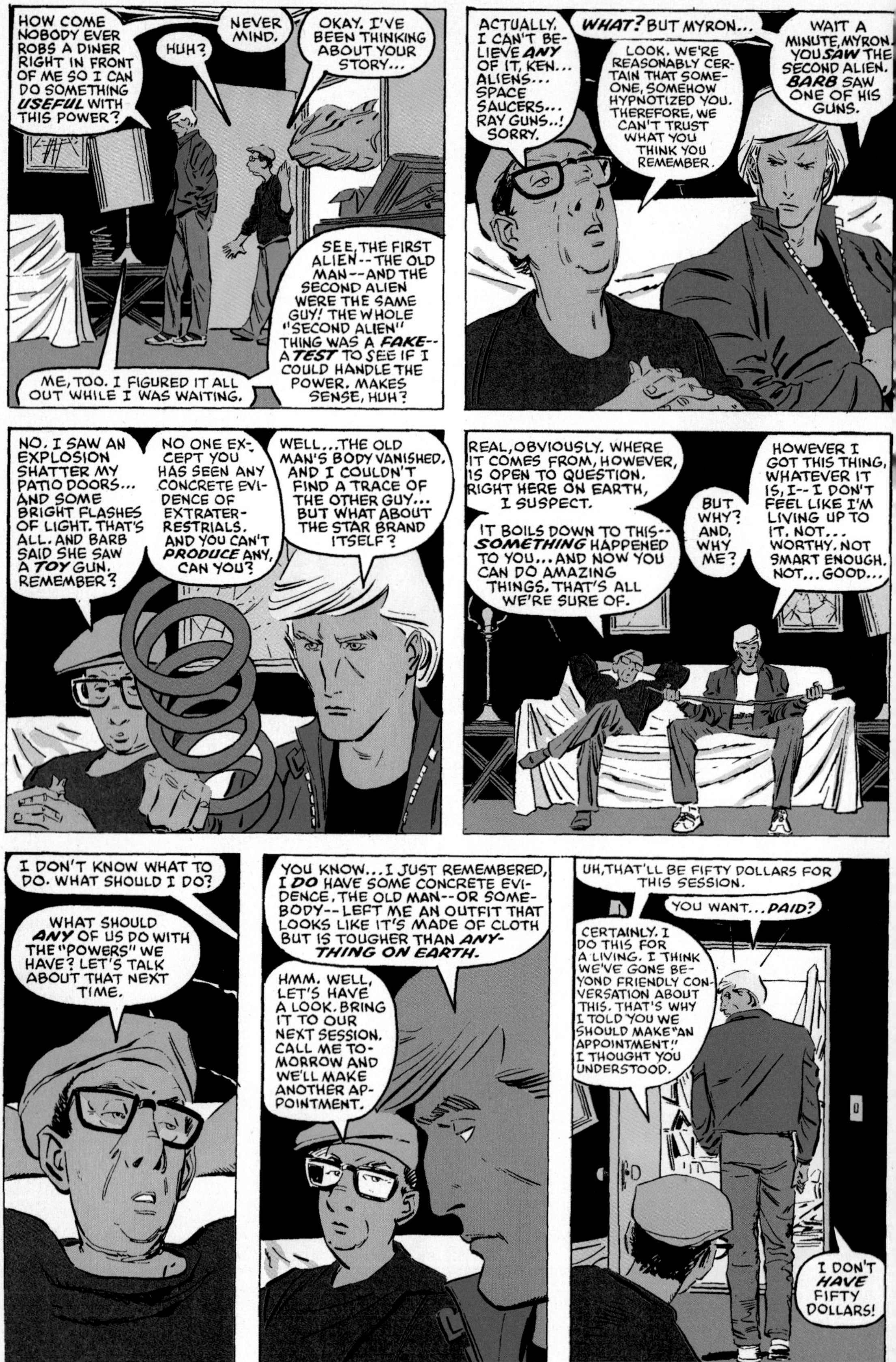
HOW COME NOBODY EVER ROBS A DINER RIGHT IN FRONT OF ME SO I CAN DO SOMETHING USEFUL WITH THIS POWER?
HUH?
NEVER MIND.
OKAY. I'VE BEEN THINKING ABOUT YOUR STORY...
SEE, THE FIRST ALIEN--THE OLD MAN--AND THE SECOND ALIEN WERE THE SAME GUY! THE WHOLE "SECOND ALIEN" THING WAS A FAKE--A TEST TO SEE IF I COULD HANDLE THE POWER. MAKES SENSE, HUH?
ME, TOO. I FIGURED IT ALL OUT WHILE I WAS WAITING.
ACTUALLY, I CAN'T BELIEVE ANY OF IT, KEN... ALIENS... SPACE SAUCERS... RAY GUNS..! SORRY.
WHAT? BUT MYRON...
LOOK. WE'RE REASONABLY CERTAIN THAT SOMEONE, SOMEHOW HYPNOTIZED YOU. THEREFORE, WE CAN'T TRUST WHAT YOU THINK YOU REMEMBER.
WAIT A MINUTE, MYRON. YOU SAW THE SECOND ALIEN. BARB SAW ONE OF HIS GUNS.
NO. I SAW AN EXPLOSION SHATTER MY PATIO DOORS... AND SOME BRIGHT FLASHES OF LIGHT. THAT'S ALL. AND BARB SAID SHE SAW A TOY GUN. REMEMBER?
NO ONE EXCEPT YOU HAS SEEN ANY CONCRETE EVIDENCE OF EXTRATERRESTRIALS. AND YOU CAN'T PRODUCE ANY, CAN YOU?
WELL...THE OLD MAN'S BODY VANISHED, AND I COULDN'T FIND A TRACE OF THE OTHER GUY... BUT WHAT ABOUT THE STAR BRAND ITSELF?
REAL, OBVIOUSLY. WHERE IT COMES FROM, HOWEVER, IS OPEN TO QUESTION. RIGHT HERE ON EARTH, I SUSPECT.
IT BOILS DOWN TO THIS--SOMETHING HAPPENED TO YOU...AND NOW YOU CAN DO AMAZING THINGS. THAT'S ALL WE'RE SURE OF.
BUT WHY? AND, WHY ME?
HOWEVER I GOT THIS THING, WHATEVER IT IS, I--I DON'T FEEL LIKE I'M LIVING UP TO IT. NOT... WORTHY. NOT SMART ENOUGH. NOT...GOOD...
I DON'T KNOW WHAT TO DO. WHAT SHOULD I DO?
WHAT SHOULD ANY OF US DO WITH THE "POWERS" WE HAVE? LET'S TALK ABOUT THAT NEXT TIME.
YOU KNOW...I JUST REMEMBERED, I DO HAVE SOME CONCRETE EVIDENCE. THE OLD MAN--OR SOMEBODY--LEFT ME AN OUTFIT THAT LOOKS LIKE IT'S MADE OF CLOTH BUT IS TOUGHER THAN ANYTHING ON EARTH.
HMM. WELL, LET'S HAVE A LOOK. BRING IT TO OUR NEXT SESSION. CALL ME TOMORROW AND WE'LL MAKE ANOTHER APPOINTMENT.
UH, THAT'LL BE FIFTY DOLLARS FOR THIS SESSION.
YOU WANT...PAID?
CERTAINLY. I DO THIS FOR A LIVING. I THINK WE'VE GONE BEYOND FRIENDLY CONVERSATION ABOUT THIS. THAT'S WHY I TOLD YOU WE SHOULD MAKE "AN APPOINTMENT." I THOUGHT YOU UNDERSTOOD.
I DON'T HAVE FIFTY DOLLARS!

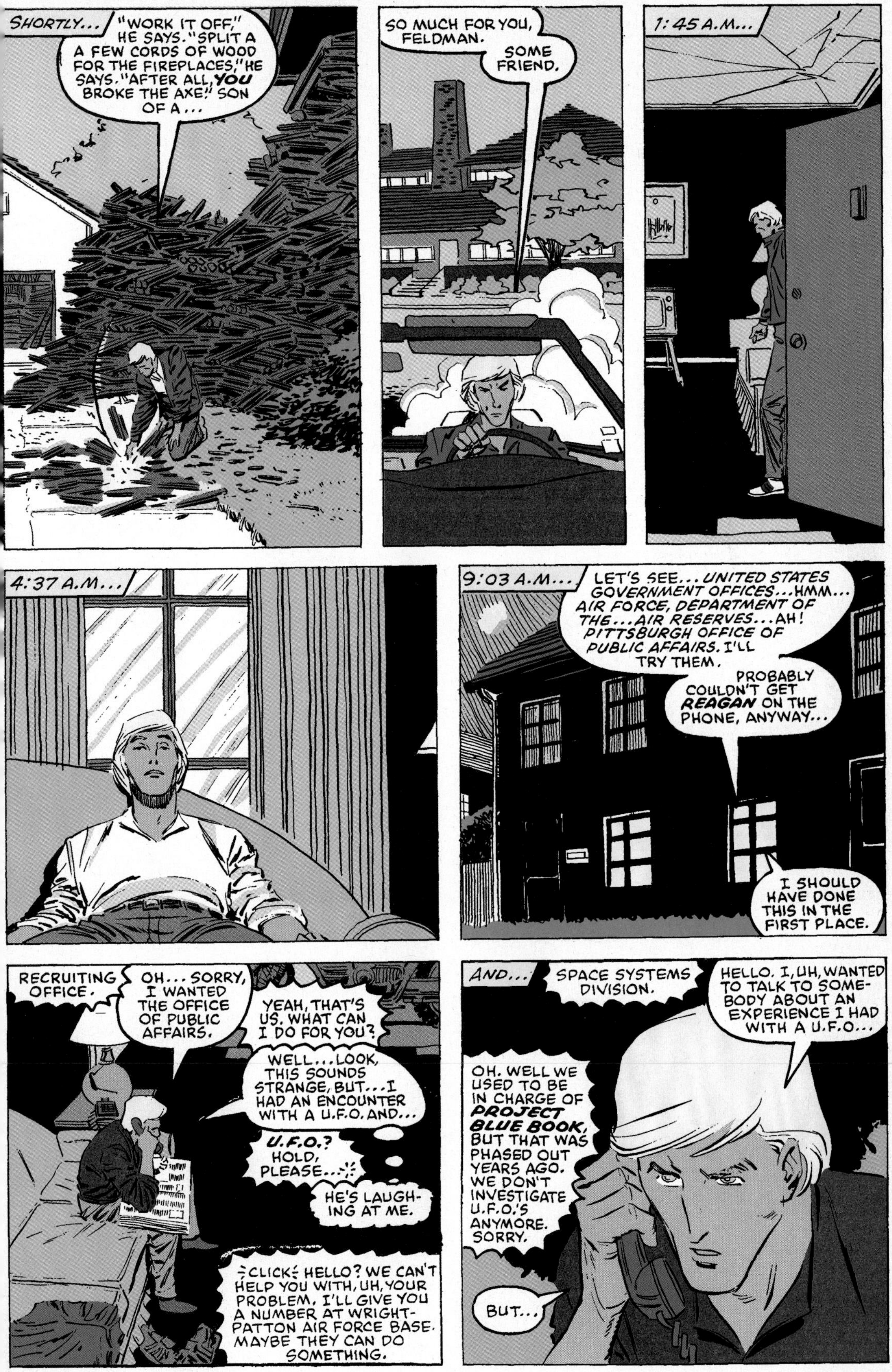

SHORTLY...
"WORK IT OFF," HE SAYS. "SPLIT A A FEW CORDS OF WOOD FOR THE FIREPLACES," HE SAYS. "AFTER ALL, YOU BROKE THE AXE!" SON OF A...
SO MUCH FOR YOU, FELDMAN.
SOME FRIEND.
1:45 A.M...
4:37 A.M...
9:03 A.M...
LET'S SEE... UNITED STATES GOVERNMENT OFFICES... HMM... AIR FORCE, DEPARTMENT OF THE... AIR RESERVES... AH! PITTSBURGH OFFICE OF PUBLIC AFFAIRS. I'LL TRY THEM.
PROBABLY COULDN'T GET REAGAN ON THE PHONE, ANYWAY...
I SHOULD HAVE DONE THIS IN THE FIRST PLACE.
RECRUITING OFFICE.
OH... SORRY, I WANTED THE OFFICE OF PUBLIC AFFAIRS.
YEAH, THAT'S US. WHAT CAN I DO FOR YOU?
WELL... LOOK, THIS SOUNDS STRANGE, BUT... I HAD AN ENCOUNTER WITH A U.F.O. AND...
U.F.O.? HOLD, PLEASE...
HE'S LAUGHING AT ME.
CLICK HELLO? WE CAN'T HELP YOU WITH, UH, YOUR PROBLEM. I'LL GIVE YOU A NUMBER AT WRIGHT-PATTON AIR FORCE BASE. MAYBE THEY CAN DO SOMETHING.
AND...
SPACE SYSTEMS DIVISION.
HELLO. I, UH, WANTED TO TALK TO SOMEBODY ABOUT AN EXPERIENCE I HAD WITH A U.F.O...
OH. WELL WE USED TO BE IN CHARGE OF PROJECT BLUE BOOK, BUT THAT WAS PHASED OUT YEARS AGO. WE DON'T INVESTIGATE U.F.O.'S ANYMORE. SORRY.
BUT...

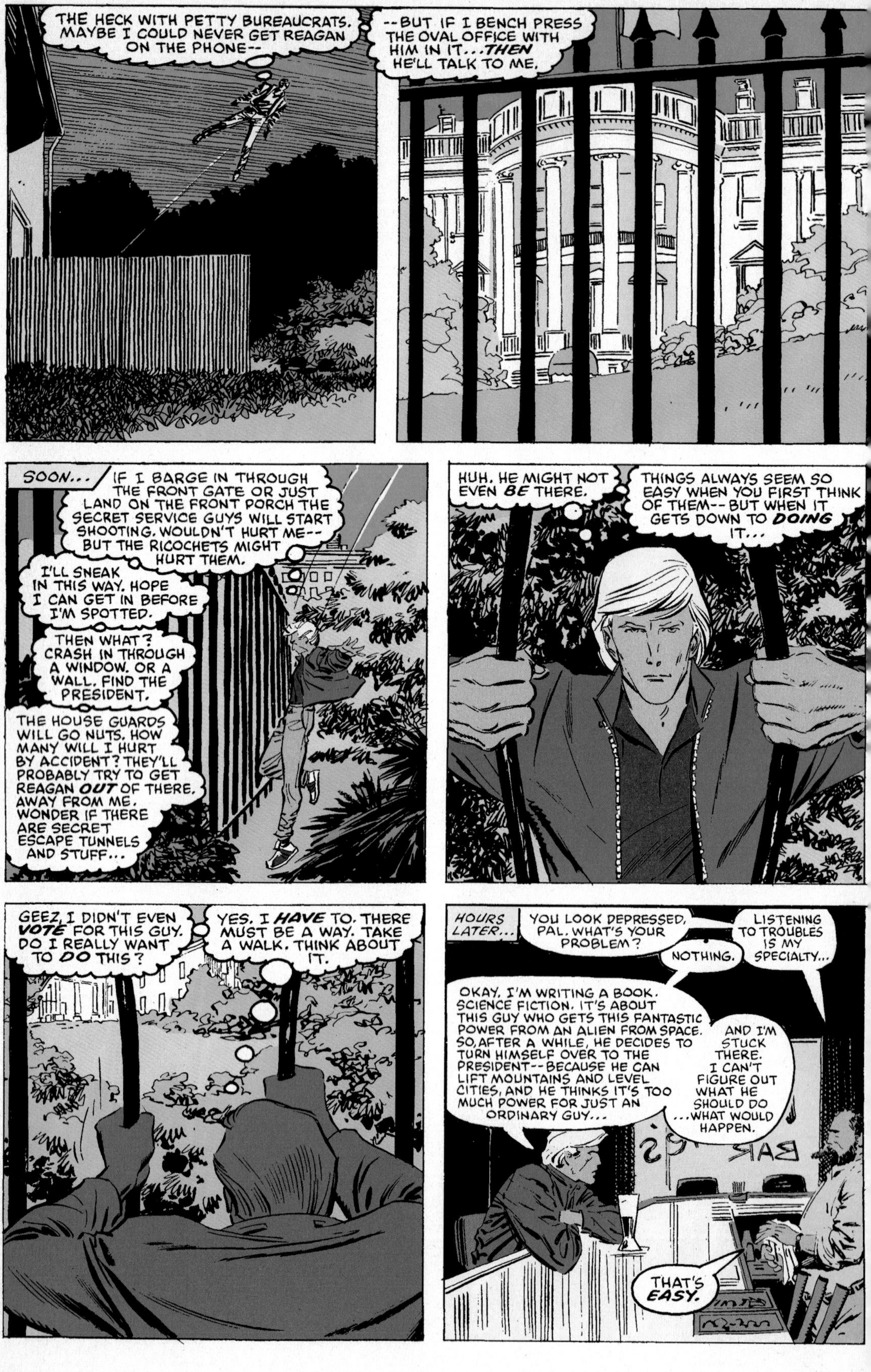
THE HECK WITH PETTY BUREAUCRATS. MAYBE I COULD NEVER GET REAGAN ON THE PHONE--
--BUT IF I BENCH PRESS THE OVAL OFFICE WITH HIM IN IT... THEN HE'LL TALK TO ME.
SOON...
IF I BARGE IN THROUGH THE FRONT GATE OR JUST LAND ON THE FRONT PORCH THE SECRET SERVICE GUYS WILL START SHOOTING. WOULDN'T HURT ME-- BUT THE RICOCHETS MIGHT HURT THEM.
I'LL SNEAK IN THIS WAY. HOPE I CAN GET IN BEFORE I'M SPOTTED.
THEN WHAT? CRASH IN THROUGH A WINDOW. OR A WALL. FIND THE PRESIDENT.
THE HOUSE GUARDS WILL GO NUTS. HOW MANY WILL I HURT BY ACCIDENT? THEY'LL PROBABLY TRY TO GET REAGAN OUT OF THERE. AWAY FROM ME. WONDER IF THERE ARE SECRET ESCAPE TUNNELS AND STUFF...
HUH. HE MIGHT NOT EVEN BE THERE.
THINGS ALWAYS SEEM SO EASY WHEN YOU FIRST THINK OF THEM-- BUT WHEN IT GETS DOWN TO DOING IT...
GEEZ, I DIDN'T EVEN VOTE FOR THIS GUY. DO I REALLY WANT TO DO THIS?
YES. I HAVE TO. THERE MUST BE A WAY. TAKE A WALK. THINK ABOUT IT.
HOURS LATER...
YOU LOOK DEPRESSED, PAL. WHAT'S YOUR PROBLEM?
LISTENING TO TROUBLES IS MY SPECIALTY...
NOTHING.
OKAY. I'M WRITING A BOOK. SCIENCE FICTION. IT'S ABOUT THIS GUY WHO GETS THIS FANTASTIC POWER FROM AN ALIEN FROM SPACE. SO, AFTER A WHILE, HE DECIDES TO TURN HIMSELF OVER TO THE PRESIDENT--BECAUSE HE CAN LIFT MOUNTAINS AND LEVEL CITIES, AND HE THINKS IT'S TOO MUCH POWER FOR JUST AN ORDINARY GUY...
AND I'M STUCK THERE. I CAN'T FIGURE OUT WHAT HE SHOULD DO ...WHAT WOULD HAPPEN.
THAT'S EASY.

AT FIRST, THEY'D PANIC. THEN, IF HE SEEMED PEACEFUL, THEY'D GET *REAL* FRIENDLY-- AND TALK HIM INTO BEING TESTED AT SOME SECRET LAB. THEY WOULDN'T BELIEVE HE WAS FOR REAL--HE'D HAVE TO PROVE IT WASN'T A TRICK OR A GIMMICK AGAIN AND AGAIN. AND, FINALLY, WHEN THEY WERE CONVINCED HE WAS AS POWERFUL AS YOU SAID--

--THEY'D KILL HIM IN HIS SLEEP.

WHAT?! WHY?

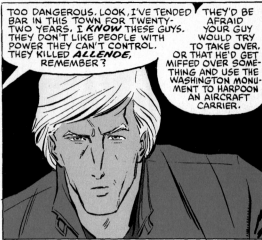

TOO DANGEROUS. LOOK, I'VE TENDED BAR IN THIS TOWN FOR TWENTY-TWO YEARS. I *KNOW* THESE GUYS. THEY DON'T LIKE PEOPLE WITH POWER THEY CAN'T CONTROL. THEY KILLED *ALLENDE,* REMEMBER?

THEY'D BE AFRAID YOUR GUY WOULD TRY TO TAKE OVER. OR THAT HE'D GET MIFFED OVER SOMETHING AND USE THE WASHINGTON MONUMENT TO HARPOON AN AIRCRAFT CARRIER.

LATER...

WISH THERE WAS SOMEBODY I COULD TALK TO. CAN'T *AFFORD* MYRON, WHO NEEDS THAT GREEDY JERK, ANYWAY?

DUCK? SHE *IS* THE ONLY OTHER PERSON I TOLD ABOUT THE POWER.

NAH. SHE WOULDN'T BE ANY HELP. NOT THE BRIGHTEST WOMAN IN THE WORLD.

MAYBE I'LL STOP AND SEE *BARB.* YEAH, SHE'S SMART. I SHOULD HAVE CONFIDED IN HER FROM THE START.

SOON...

HI, WENDY. BARB'S OUT, HUH?

HI, MISTER CONNELL-- I MEAN *KEN!*

MRS. PETROVIC WENT TO THE HOCKEY GAME WITH ONE OF HER GIRLFRIENDS.

I ALREADY PUT THE KIDS TO BED. WANT TO, UM...COME IN AND WATCH TEEVEE WITH ME?

WHOA! WHAT'S *THIS?!*

UH...THANKS, BUT I'D BETTER NOT. MAYBE, UH... SOME *OTHER* TIME, OKAY?

PROMISE? *GREAT!* SEEYA!

WHY DID I *SAY* THAT?

SHE'S *SEVENTEEN.* THE *BABYSITTER,* FOR PETE'S SAKE--! BOY, IF BARB WAS UPSET OVER DEBBIE THE DUCK..! WOW...

BUT THAT *BODY--*! WHEW...

MAYBE I'LL HANG AROUND... WAIT FOR BARB. I REALLY NEED TO TALK TO HER...

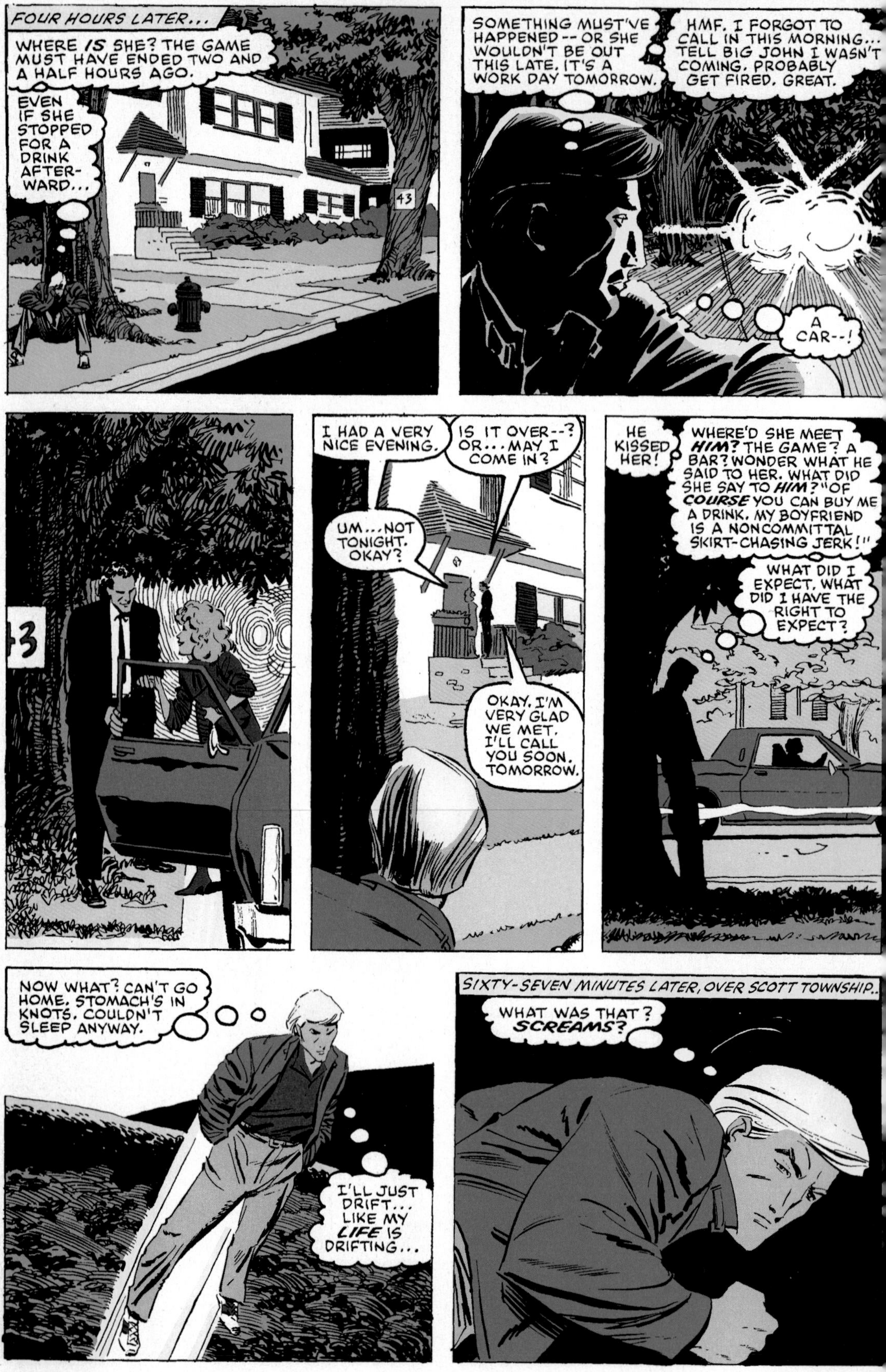
FOUR HOURS LATER...
WHERE IS SHE? THE GAME MUST HAVE ENDED TWO AND A HALF HOURS AGO.
EVEN IF SHE STOPPED FOR A DRINK AFTER-WARD...
43
SOMETHING MUST'VE HAPPENED -- OR SHE WOULDN'T BE OUT THIS LATE. IT'S A WORK DAY TOMORROW.
HMF. I FORGOT TO CALL IN THIS MORNING... TELL BIG JOHN I WASN'T COMING. PROBABLY GET FIRED. GREAT.
A CAR--!
43
I HAD A VERY NICE EVENING.
IS IT OVER--? OR... MAY I COME IN?
UM... NOT TONIGHT. OKAY?
OKAY. I'M VERY GLAD WE MET. I'LL CALL YOU SOON. TOMORROW.
HE KISSED HER!
WHERE'D SHE MEET HIM? THE GAME? A BAR? WONDER WHAT HE SAID TO HER. WHAT DID SHE SAY TO HIM? "OF COURSE YOU CAN BUY ME A DRINK. MY BOYFRIEND IS A NONCOMMITTAL SKIRT-CHASING JERK!"
WHAT DID I EXPECT. WHAT DID I HAVE THE RIGHT TO EXPECT?
NOW WHAT? CAN'T GO HOME. STOMACH'S IN KNOTS. COULDN'T SLEEP ANYWAY.
I'LL JUST DRIFT... LIKE MY LIFE IS DRIFTING...
SIXTY-SEVEN MINUTES LATER, OVER SCOTT TOWNSHIP...
WHAT WAS THAT? SCREAMS?

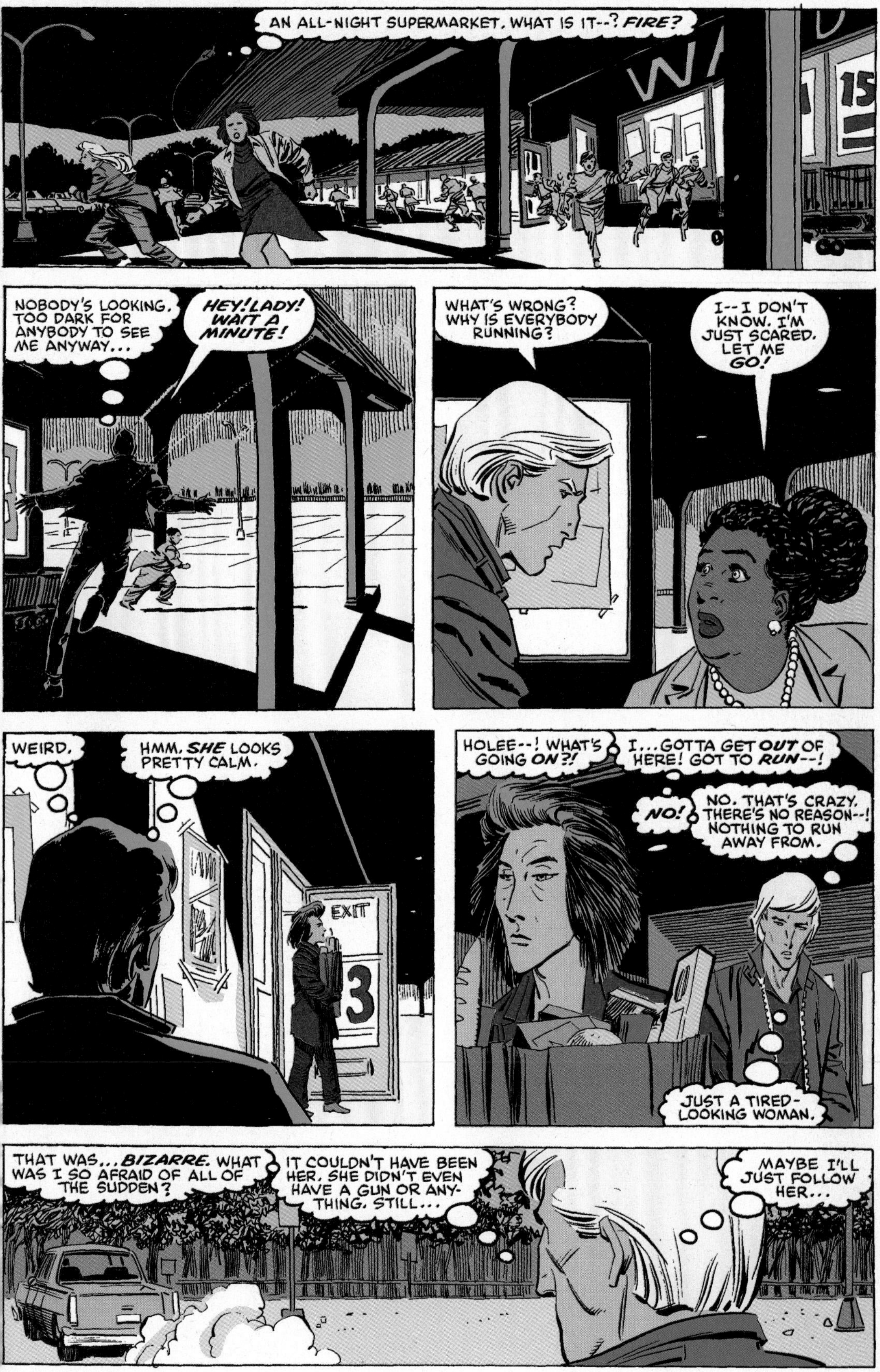
AN ALL-NIGHT SUPERMARKET. WHAT IS IT--? *FIRE?*
NOBODY'S LOOKING. TOO DARK FOR ANYBODY TO SEE ME ANYWAY...
HEY! LADY! WAIT A MINUTE!
WHAT'S WRONG? WHY IS EVERYBODY RUNNING?
I-- I DON'T KNOW. I'M JUST SCARED. LET ME *GO!*
WEIRD.
HMM. *SHE* LOOKS PRETTY CALM.
EXIT
HOLEE--! WHAT'S GOING *ON?!*
I...GOTTA GET *OUT* OF HERE! GOT TO *RUN*--!
NO!
NO. THAT'S CRAZY. THERE'S NO REASON--! NOTHING TO RUN AWAY FROM.
JUST A TIRED-LOOKING WOMAN.
THAT WAS... *BIZARRE.* WHAT WAS I SO AFRAID OF ALL OF THE SUDDEN?
IT COULDN'T HAVE BEEN HER. SHE DIDN'T EVEN HAVE A GUN OR ANY-THING. STILL...
MAYBE I'LL JUST FOLLOW HER...

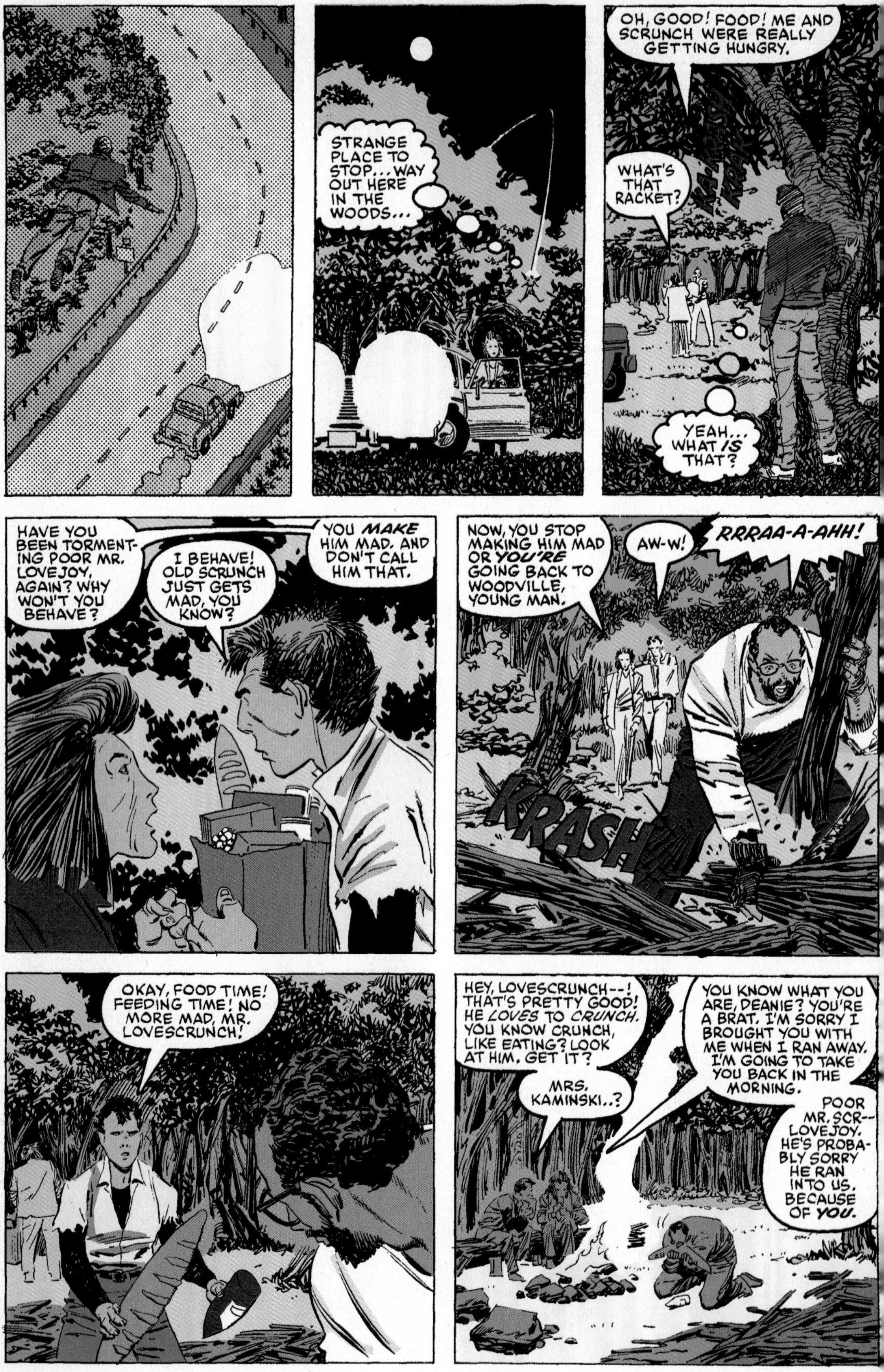
STRANGE PLACE TO STOP... WAY OUT HERE IN THE WOODS...
OH, GOOD! FOOD! ME AND SCRUNCH WERE REALLY GETTING HUNGRY.
WHAT'S THAT RACKET?
YEAH... WHAT IS THAT?
HAVE YOU BEEN TORMENTING POOR MR. LOVEJOY, AGAIN? WHY WON'T YOU BEHAVE?
I BEHAVE! OLD SCRUNCH JUST GETS MAD, YOU KNOW?
YOU MAKE HIM MAD. AND DON'T CALL HIM THAT.
NOW, YOU STOP MAKING HIM MAD OR YOU'RE GOING BACK TO WOODVILLE, YOUNG MAN.
AW-W!
RRRAA-A-AHH!
KRASH
OKAY, FOOD TIME! FEEDING TIME! NO MORE MAD, MR. LOVESCRUNCH!
HEY, LOVESCRUNCH--! THAT'S PRETTY GOOD! HE LOVES TO CRUNCH. YOU KNOW CRUNCH, LIKE EATING? LOOK AT HIM. GET IT?
MRS. KAMINSKI..?
YOU KNOW WHAT YOU ARE, DEANIE? YOU'RE A BRAT. I'M SORRY I BROUGHT YOU WITH ME WHEN I RAN AWAY. I'M GOING TO TAKE YOU BACK IN THE MORNING.
POOR MR. SCR--LOVEJOY. HE'S PROBABLY SORRY HE RAN INTO US. BECAUSE OF YOU.

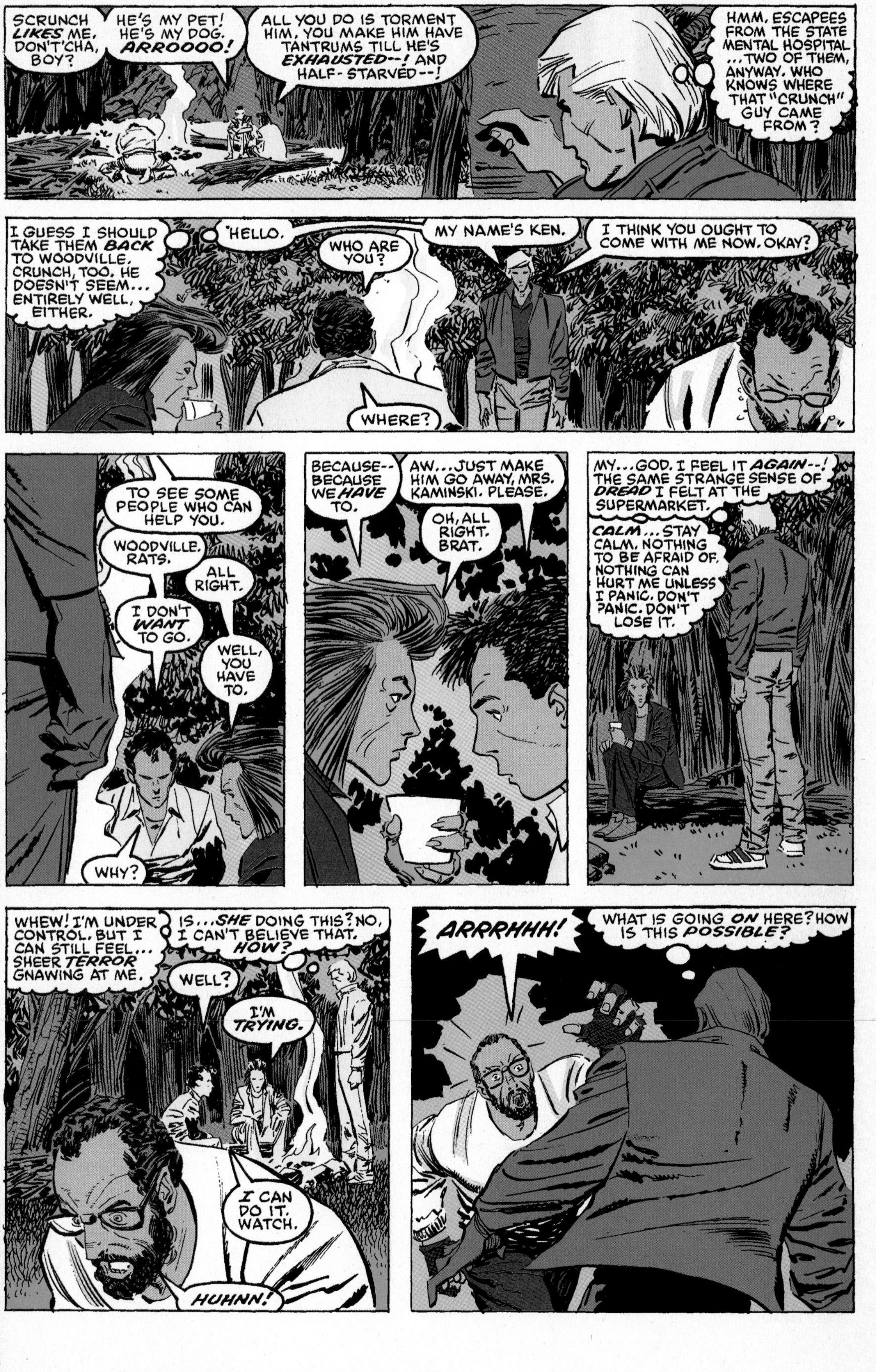
SCRUNCH LIKES ME, DON'T'CHA, BOY?
HE'S MY PET! HE'S MY DOG. ARROOOO!
ALL YOU DO IS TORMENT HIM. YOU MAKE HIM HAVE TANTRUMS TILL HE'S EXHAUSTED--! AND HALF-STARVED--!
HMM. ESCAPEES FROM THE STATE MENTAL HOSPITAL ...TWO OF THEM, ANYWAY. WHO KNOWS WHERE THAT "CRUNCH" GUY CAME FROM?
I GUESS I SHOULD TAKE THEM BACK TO WOODVILLE. CRUNCH, TOO. HE DOESN'T SEEM... ENTIRELY WELL, EITHER.
"HELLO.
WHO ARE YOU?
MY NAME'S KEN.
I THINK YOU OUGHT TO COME WITH ME NOW, OKAY?
WHERE?
TO SEE SOME PEOPLE WHO CAN HELP YOU.
WOODVILLE. RATS.
ALL RIGHT.
I DON'T WANT TO GO.
WELL, YOU HAVE TO.
WHY?
BECAUSE-- BECAUSE WE HAVE TO.
AW...JUST MAKE HIM GO AWAY, MRS. KAMINSKI. PLEASE.
OH, ALL RIGHT. BRAT.
MY...GOD. I FEEL IT AGAIN--! THE SAME STRANGE SENSE OF DREAD I FELT AT THE SUPERMARKET.
CALM...STAY CALM. NOTHING TO BE AFRAID OF. NOTHING CAN HURT ME UNLESS I PANIC. DON'T PANIC. DON'T LOSE IT.
WHEW! I'M UNDER CONTROL. BUT I CAN STILL FEEL... SHEER TERROR GNAWING AT ME.
IS...SHE DOING THIS? NO, I CAN'T BELIEVE THAT. HOW?
WELL?
I'M TRYING.
I CAN DO IT. WATCH.
HUHNN!
ARRRHHH!
WHAT IS GOING ON HERE? HOW IS THIS POSSIBLE?

FUFFF!

AMAZING! HE'S A *LOT* STRONGER THAN A GUY HIS SIZE-- OR EVEN *MY* SIZE-- SHOULD BE.

SHE MAKES PEOPLE AFRAID... THE KID GIVES THEM FITS OF RAGE... AND THIS LITTLE GUY IS A REGULAR MIGHTY MOUSE!

THERE MUST BE A RATIONAL EXPLANATION.

HA! SURE. JUST LIKE THERE IS FOR WHAT *I* CAN DO...

SHE'S STILL AT IT. STILL CLAWING AT MY SELF-CONTROL.

HOW DO YOU *DO* THAT?

I DON'T KNOW.

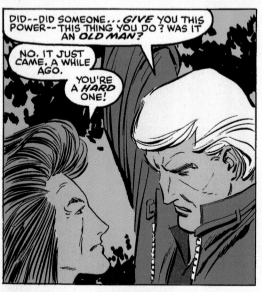

DID--DID SOMEONE... *GIVE* YOU THIS POWER-- THIS THING YOU DO? WAS IT AN *OLD MAN?*

NO. IT JUST CAME, A WHILE AGO.

YOU'RE A *HARD* ONE!

YES. SO LET'S JUST ALL GET IN THE CAR, NOW, OKAY.

NO MATTER HOW HARD I TRY, YOU WON'T *BUDGE--!* THAT'S VERY UNUSUAL.

SCRUNCH, BOY, YOU'RE LETTING ME DOWN!

I'M GIVING YOU *ALL...I...CAN--!*

NOW, GET BACK *OVER* THERE--!

100

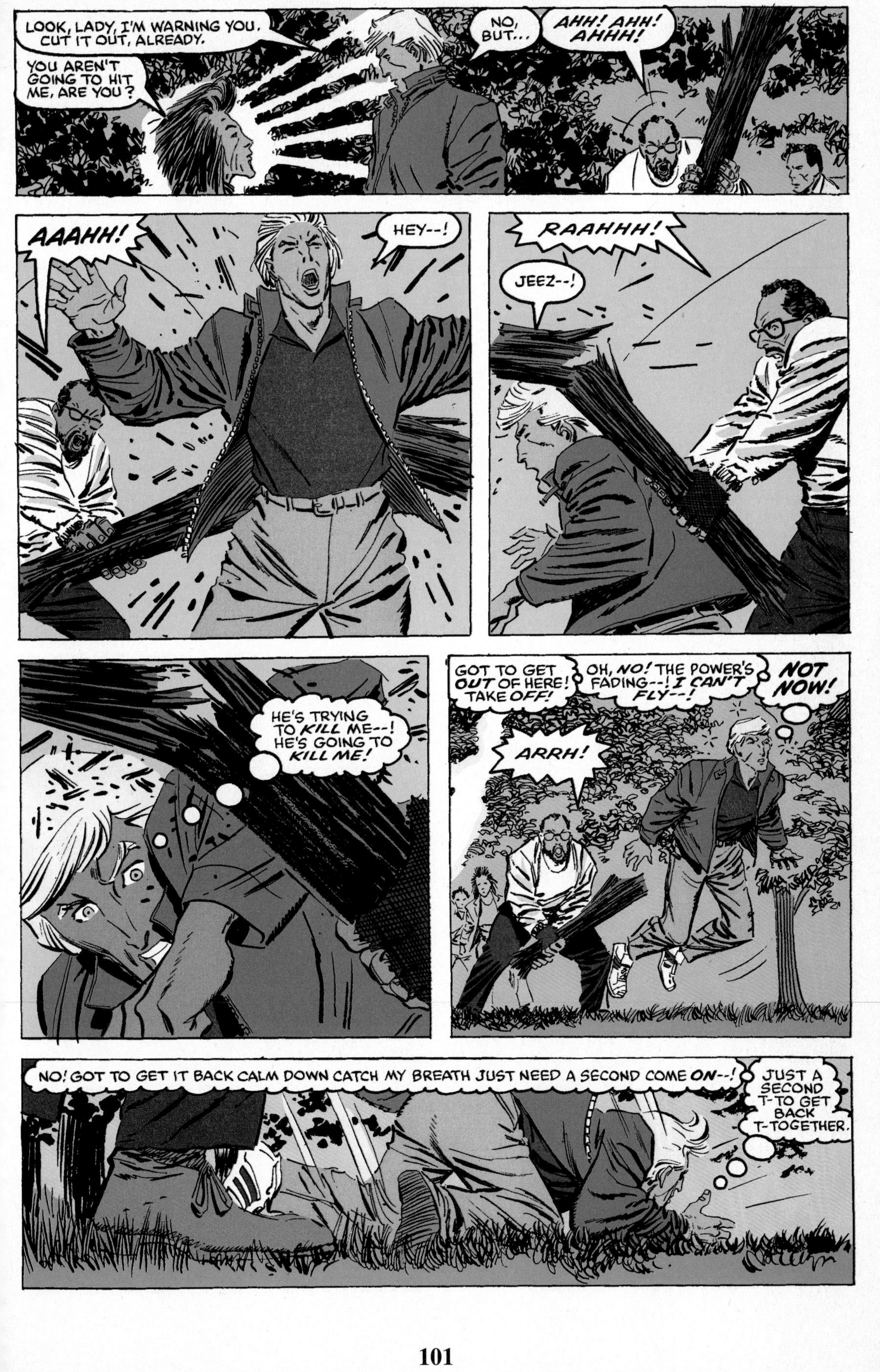
LOOK, LADY, I'M WARNING YOU. CUT IT OUT, ALREADY.
YOU AREN'T GOING TO HIT ME, ARE YOU?
NO, BUT...
AHH! AHH! AHHH!
AAAHH!
HEY--!
RAAHHH!
JEEZ--!
HE'S TRYING TO KILL ME--! HE'S GOING TO KILL ME!
GOT TO GET OUT OF HERE! TAKE OFF!
OH, NO! THE POWER'S FADING--! I CAN'T FLY--!
NOT NOW!
ARRH!
NO! GOT TO GET IT BACK CALM DOWN CATCH MY BREATH JUST NEED A SECOND COME ON--!
JUST A SECOND T-TO GET BACK T-TOGETHER.

RAHH! AHH!

HE'S ON *TOP* OF ME--!

CAN'T LET HIM HIT ME--! MOVE! MOVE! ROLL-- *OW!*

YAHHH!

HUHHH...

GONE, THEY'RE GONE.

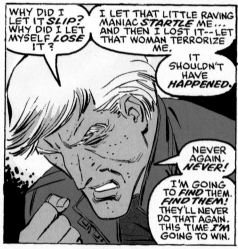

WHY DID I LET IT *SLIP?* WHY DID I LET MYSELF *LOSE* IT?

I LET THAT LITTLE RAVING MANIAC *STARTLE* ME... AND THEN I LOST IT--LET THAT WOMAN TERRORIZE ME.

IT SHOULDN'T HAVE *HAPPENED.*

NEVER AGAIN, *NEVER!*

I'M GOING TO *FIND* THEM, *FIND THEM!* THEY'LL NEVER DO THAT AGAIN. THIS TIME *I'M* GOING TO WIN.

BUT MINUTES LATER...

NOT A *TRACE!* CAN'T FIND THEM *ANY-WHERE*--!

I COULD-- COULD *KILL*...

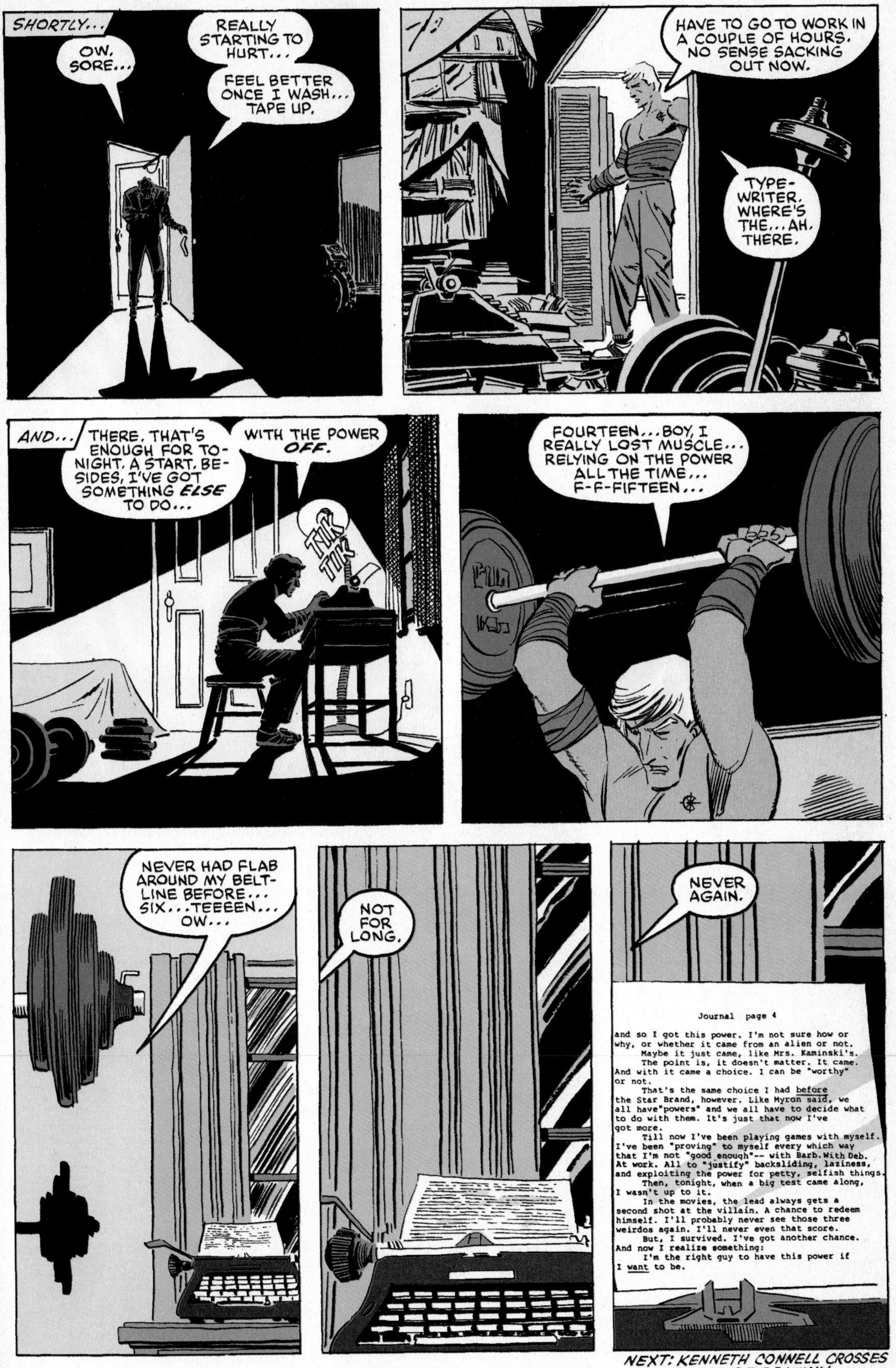
SHORTLY...
OW. SORE...
REALLY STARTING TO HURT...
FEEL BETTER ONCE I WASH... TAPE UP.
HAVE TO GO TO WORK IN A COUPLE OF HOURS. NO SENSE SACKING OUT NOW.
TYPE-WRITER. WHERE'S THE... AH. THERE.
AND...
THERE. THAT'S ENOUGH FOR TO-NIGHT. A START. BE-SIDES, I'VE GOT SOMETHING ELSE TO DO...
WITH THE POWER OFF.
TIK TIK
FOURTEEN... BOY, I REALLY LOST MUSCLE... RELYING ON THE POWER ALL THE TIME... F-F-FIFTEEN...
NEVER HAD FLAB AROUND MY BELT-LINE BEFORE... SIX...TEEEEN... OW...
NOT FOR LONG.
NEVER AGAIN.
Journal page 4
and so I got this power. I'm not sure how or why, or whether it came from an alien or not.
Maybe it just came, like Mrs. Kaminski's.
The point is, it doesn't matter. It came. And with it came a choice. I can be "worthy" or not.
That's the same choice I had before the Star Brand, however. Like Myron said, we all have"powers" and we all have to decide what to do with them. It's just that now I've got more.
Till now I've been playing games with myself. I've been "proving" to myself every which way that I'm not "good enough"-- with Barb. With Deb. At work. All to "justify" backsliding, laziness, and exploiting the power for petty, selfish things.
Then, tonight, when a big test came along, I wasn't up to it.
In the movies, the lead always gets a second shot at the villain. A chance to redeem himself. I'll probably never see those three weirdos again. I'll never even that score.
But, I survived. I've got another chance. And now I realize something:
I'm the right guy to have this power if I want to be.
NEXT: KENNETH CONNELL CROSSES THE "LINE OF DEATH"!

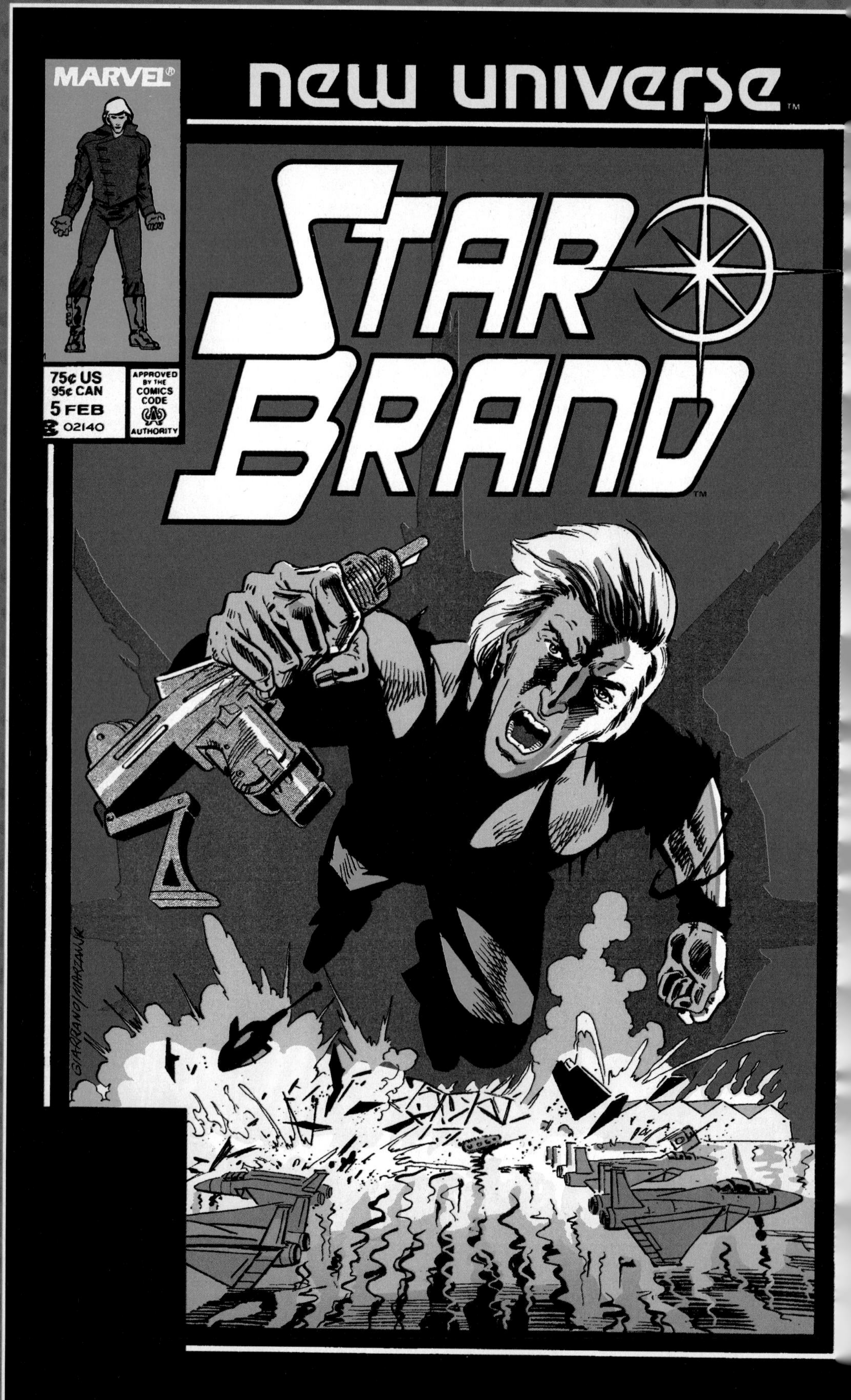

MARVEL®
NEW UNIVERSE™
STAR BRAND™
75¢ US
95¢ CAN
5 FEB
02140
APPROVED BY THE COMICS CODE AUTHORITY
GIARRANO/MARZAN JR

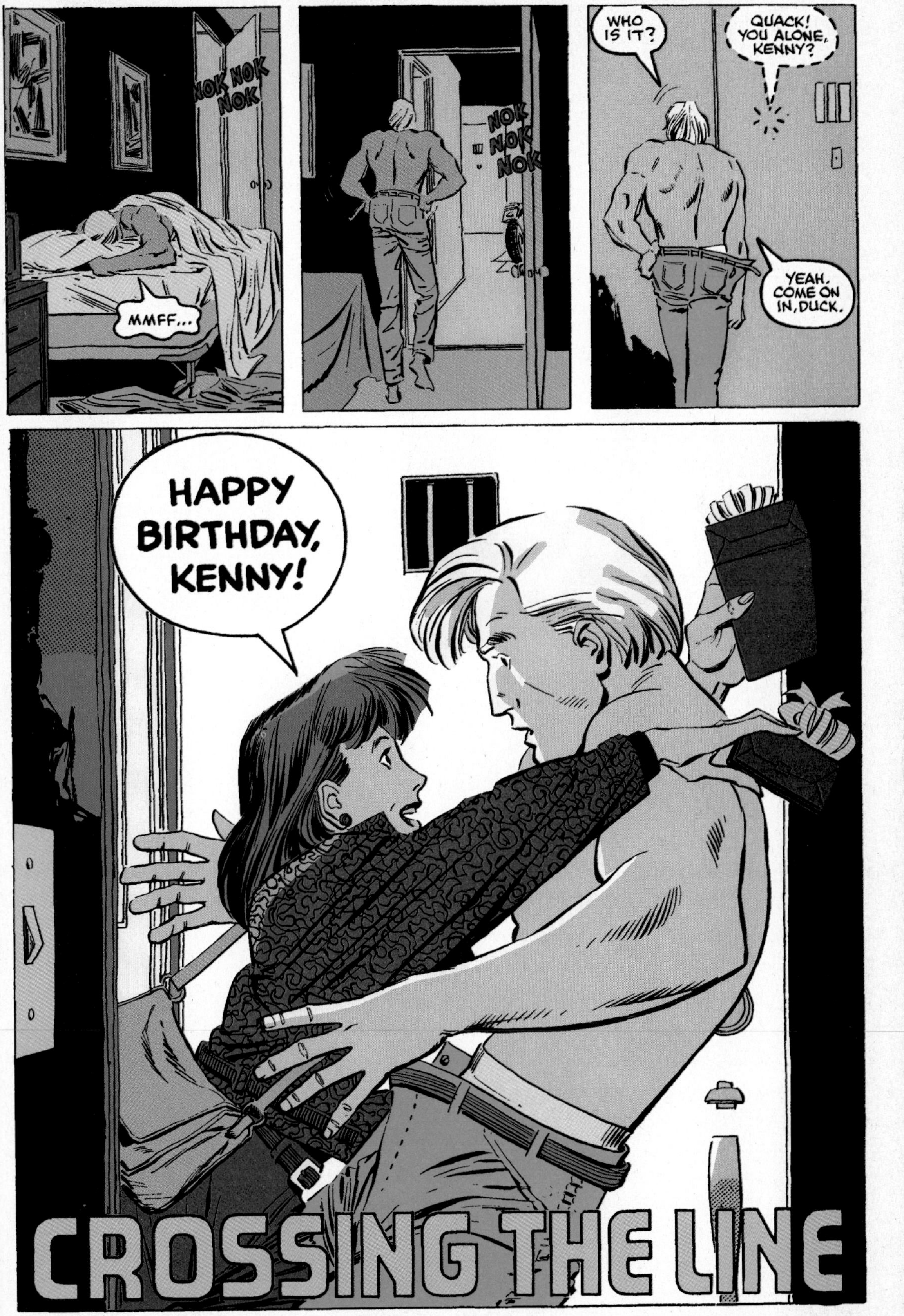
NOK NOK NOK
MMFF...
NOK NOK NOK
WHO IS IT?
QUACK! YOU ALONE, KENNY?
YEAH. COME ON IN, DUCK.
HAPPY BIRTHDAY, KENNY!
CROSSING THE LINE

JIM SHOOTER SCRIPT · JOHN ROMITA, JR. PENCILS · AL WILLIAMSON INKS · JOE ROSEN LETTERS · JANET JACKSON COLORS · MICHAEL HIGGINS EDITING

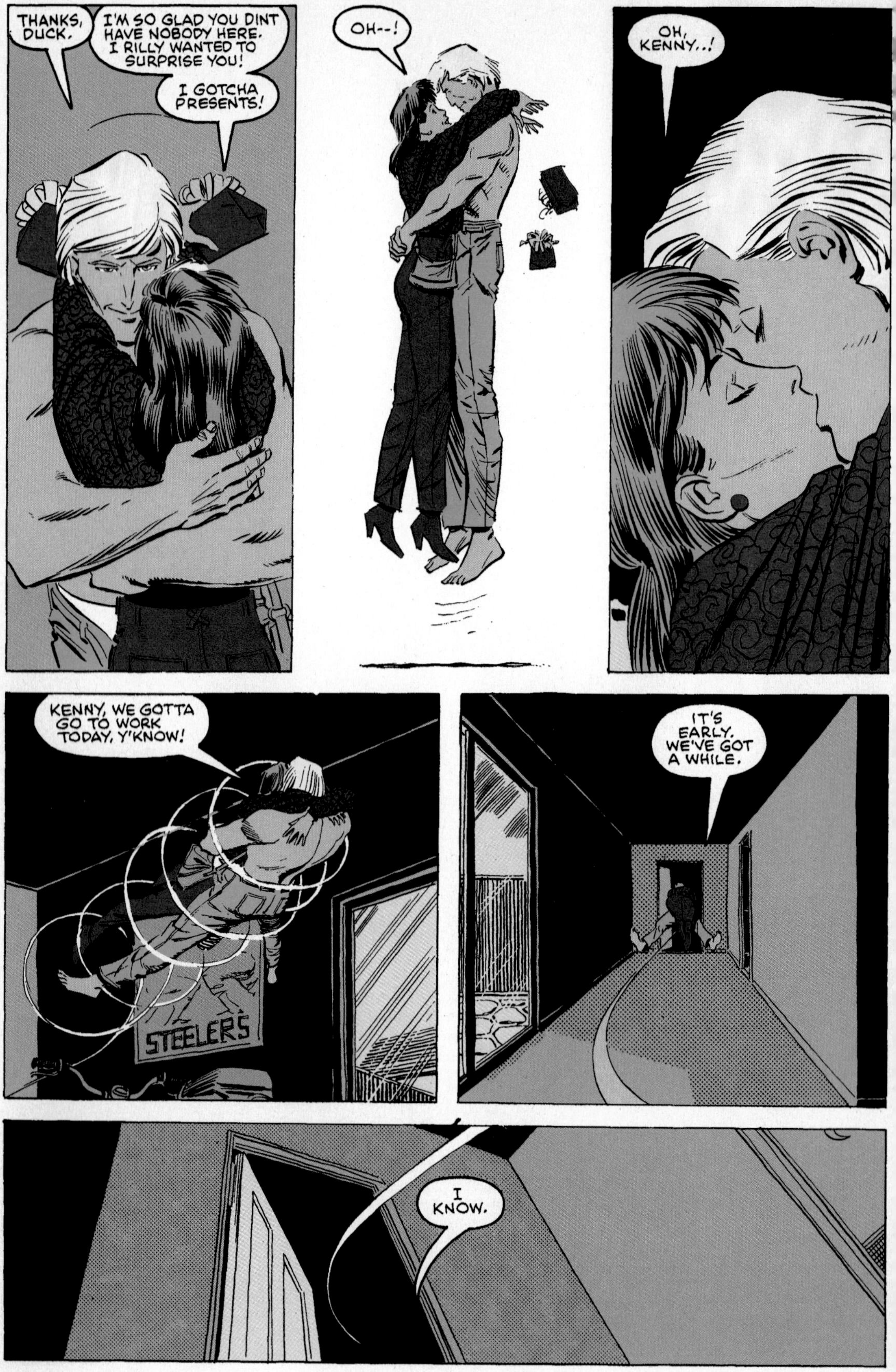
THANKS, DUCK.
I'M SO GLAD YOU DINT HAVE NOBODY HERE. I RILLY WANTED TO SURPRISE YOU!
I GOTCHA PRESENTS!
OH--!
OH, KENNY..!
KENNY, WE GOTTA GO TO WORK TODAY, Y'KNOW!
STEELER'S
IT'S EARLY. WE'VE GOT A WHILE.
I KNOW.

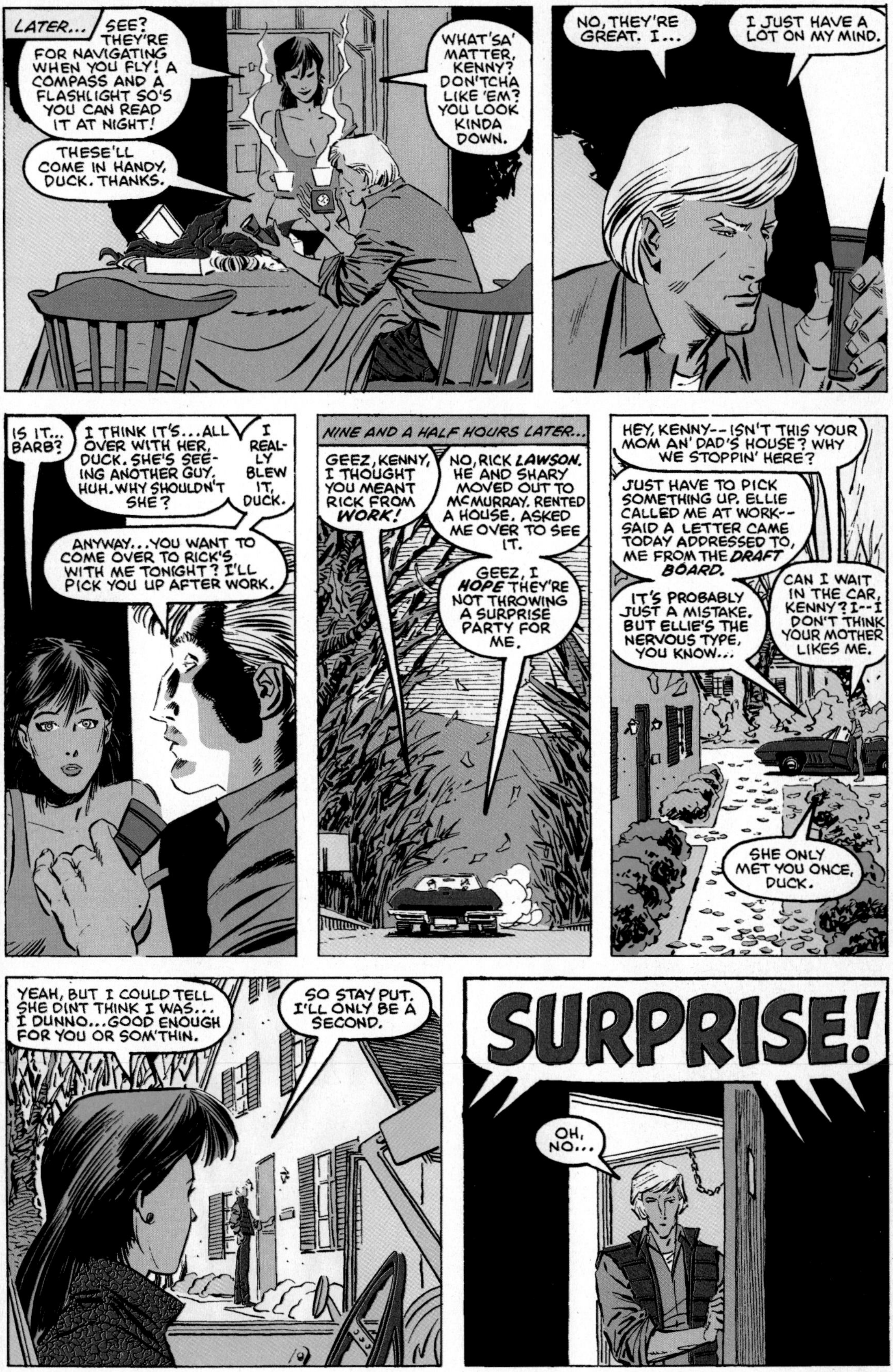
LATER...
SEE? THEY'RE FOR NAVIGATING WHEN YOU FLY! A COMPASS AND A FLASHLIGHT SO'S YOU CAN READ IT AT NIGHT!
THESE'LL COME IN HANDY, DUCK. THANKS.
WHAT'SA' MATTER, KENNY? DON'TCHA LIKE 'EM? YOU LOOK KINDA DOWN.
NO, THEY'RE GREAT. I...
I JUST HAVE A LOT ON MY MIND.
IS IT... BARB?
I THINK IT'S...ALL OVER WITH HER, DUCK. SHE'S SEEING ANOTHER GUY. HUH. WHY SHOULDN'T SHE?
I REALLY BLEW IT, DUCK.
ANYWAY...YOU WANT TO COME OVER TO RICK'S WITH ME TONIGHT? I'LL PICK YOU UP AFTER WORK.
NINE AND A HALF HOURS LATER...
GEEZ, KENNY, I THOUGHT YOU MEANT RICK FROM WORK!
NO, RICK LAWSON. HE AND SHARY MOVED OUT TO McMURRAY. RENTED A HOUSE. ASKED ME OVER TO SEE IT.
GEEZ, I HOPE THEY'RE NOT THROWING A SURPRISE PARTY FOR ME.
HEY, KENNY--ISN'T THIS YOUR MOM AN' DAD'S HOUSE? WHY WE STOPPIN' HERE?
JUST HAVE TO PICK SOMETHING UP. ELLIE CALLED ME AT WORK--SAID A LETTER CAME TODAY ADDRESSED TO, ME FROM THE DRAFT BOARD.
IT'S PROBABLY JUST A MISTAKE. BUT ELLIE'S THE NERVOUS TYPE, YOU KNOW...
CAN I WAIT IN THE CAR, KENNY? I--I DON'T THINK YOUR MOTHER LIKES ME.
SHE ONLY MET YOU ONCE, DUCK.
YEAH, BUT I COULD TELL SHE DINT THINK I WAS... I DUNNO...GOOD ENOUGH FOR YOU OR SOM'THIN.
SO STAY PUT. I'LL ONLY BE A SECOND.
SURPRISE!
OH, NO...

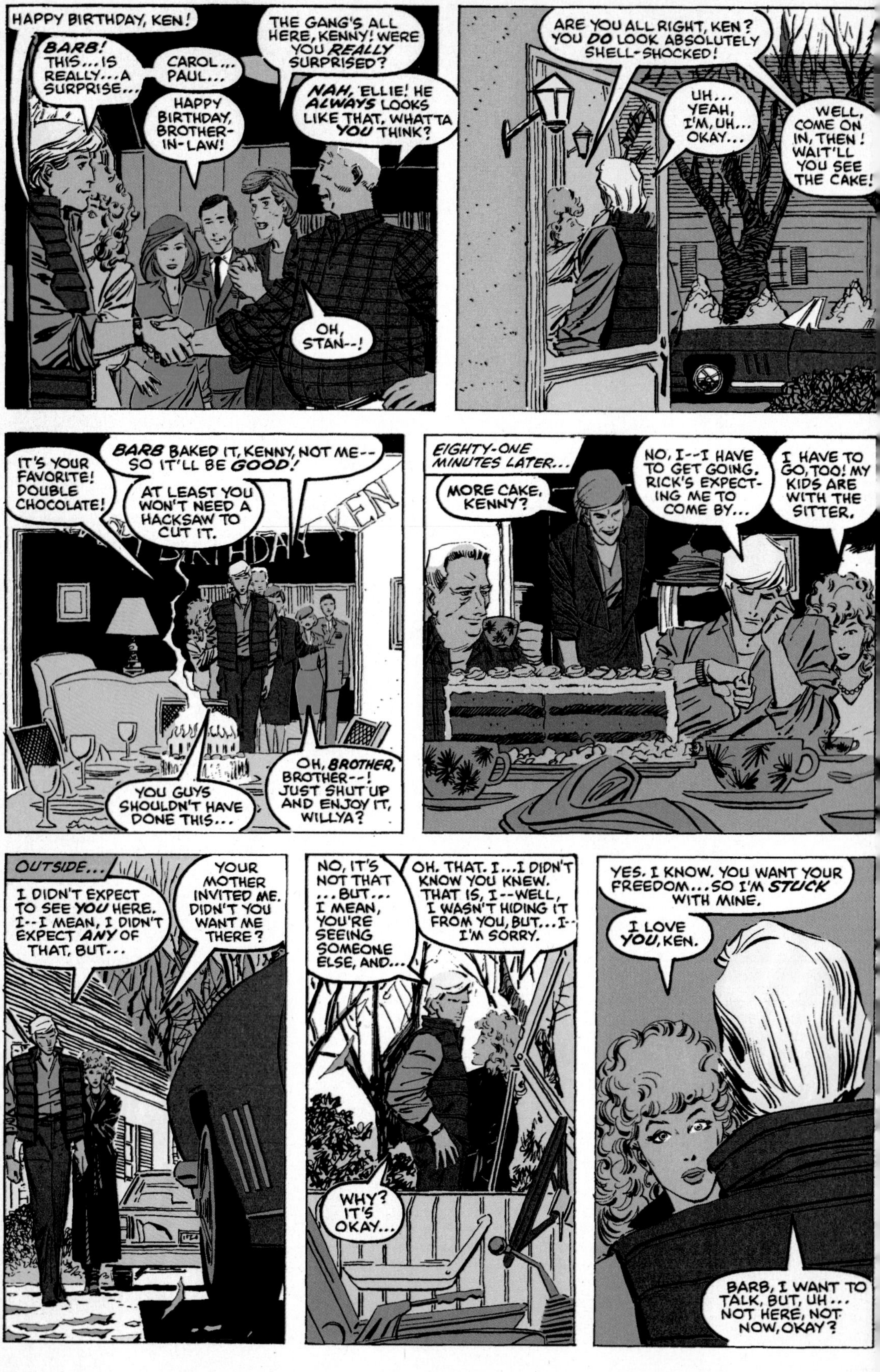

HAPPY BIRTHDAY, KEN!
BARB! THIS...IS REALLY...A SURPRISE...
CAROL... PAUL...
HAPPY BIRTHDAY, BROTHER-IN-LAW!
THE GANG'S ALL HERE, KENNY! WERE YOU REALLY SURPRISED?
NAH, ELLIE! HE ALWAYS LOOKS LIKE THAT. WHATTA YOU THINK?
OH, STAN--!
ARE YOU ALL RIGHT, KEN? YOU DO LOOK ABSOLUTELY SHELL-SHOCKED!
UH... YEAH, I'M, UH... OKAY...
WELL, COME ON IN, THEN! WAIT'LL YOU SEE THE CAKE!
IT'S YOUR FAVORITE! DOUBLE CHOCOLATE!
BARB BAKED IT, KENNY, NOT ME-- SO IT'LL BE GOOD!
AT LEAST YOU WON'T NEED A HACKSAW TO CUT IT.
YOU GUYS SHOULDN'T HAVE DONE THIS...
OH, BROTHER, BROTHER--! JUST SHUT UP AND ENJOY IT, WILLYA?
EIGHTY-ONE MINUTES LATER...
MORE CAKE, KENNY?
NO, I--I HAVE TO GET GOING. RICK'S EXPECTING ME TO COME BY...
I HAVE TO GO, TOO! MY KIDS ARE WITH THE SITTER.
OUTSIDE...
I DIDN'T EXPECT TO SEE YOU HERE. I--I MEAN, I DIDN'T EXPECT ANY OF THAT, BUT...
YOUR MOTHER INVITED ME. DIDN'T YOU WANT ME THERE?
NO, IT'S NOT THAT ...BUT... I MEAN, YOU'RE SEEING SOMEONE ELSE, AND...
OH. THAT. I...I DIDN'T KNOW YOU KNEW. THAT IS, I--WELL, I WASN'T HIDING IT FROM YOU, BUT...I-- I'M SORRY.
WHY? IT'S OKAY...
YES. I KNOW. YOU WANT YOUR FREEDOM...SO I'M STUCK WITH MINE.
I LOVE YOU, KEN.
BARB, I WANT TO TALK, BUT, UH... NOT HERE, NOT NOW, OKAY?

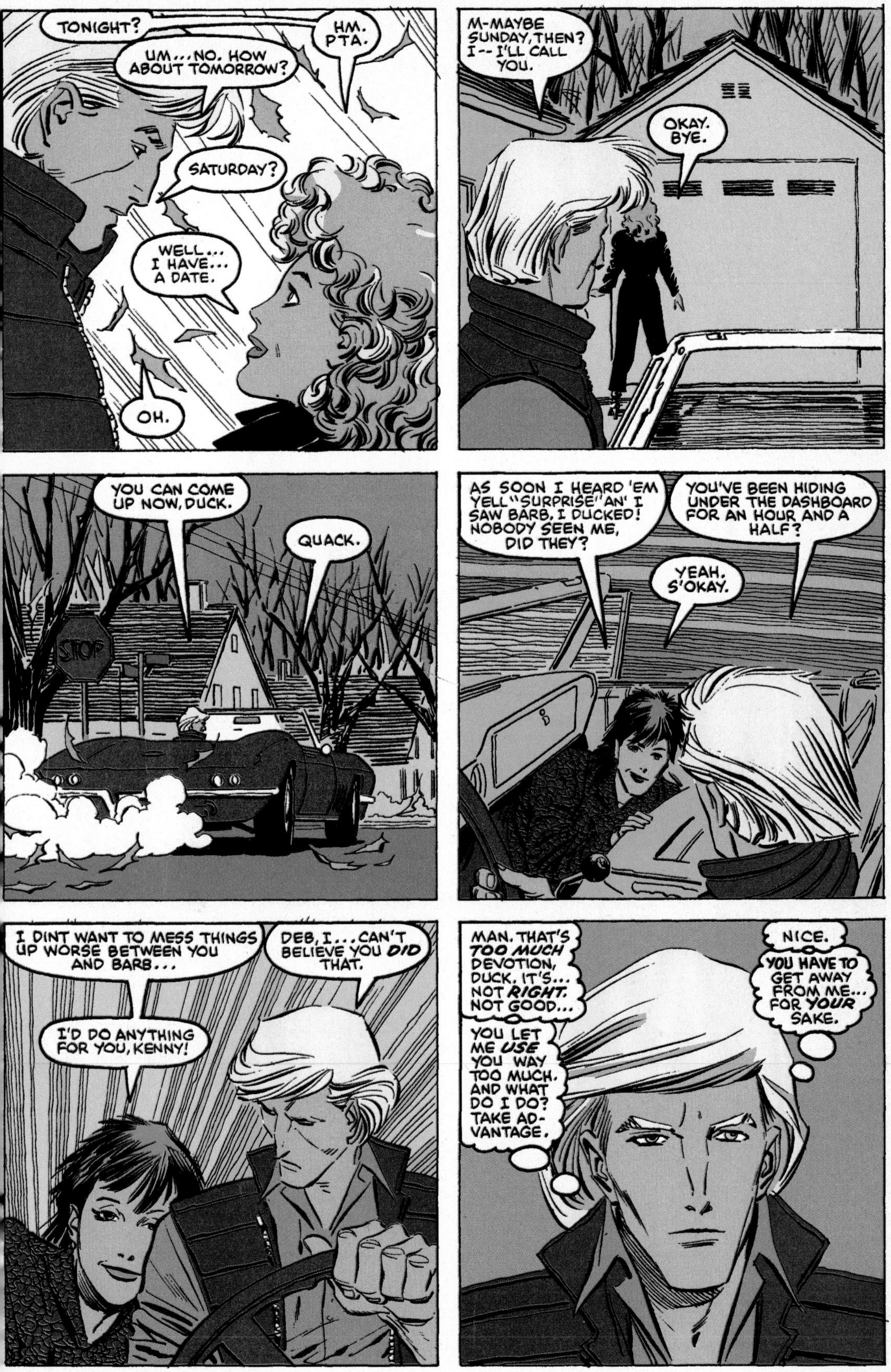
TONIGHT?
UM... NO. HOW ABOUT TOMORROW?
HM. PTA.
SATURDAY?
WELL... I HAVE... A DATE.
OH.
M-MAYBE SUNDAY, THEN? I-- I'LL CALL YOU.
OKAY. BYE.
YOU CAN COME UP NOW, DUCK.
QUACK.
STOP
AS SOON I HEARD 'EM YELL "SURPRISE" AN' I SAW BARB, I DUCKED! NOBODY SEEN ME, DID THEY?
YOU'VE BEEN HIDING UNDER THE DASHBOARD FOR AN HOUR AND A HALF?
YEAH, S'OKAY.
I DINT WANT TO MESS THINGS UP WORSE BETWEEN YOU AND BARB...
DEB, I...CAN'T BELIEVE YOU DID THAT.
I'D DO ANYTHING FOR YOU, KENNY!
MAN. THAT'S TOO MUCH DEVOTION, DUCK. IT'S... NOT RIGHT. NOT GOOD...
YOU LET ME USE YOU WAY TOO MUCH. AND WHAT DO I DO? TAKE AD-VANTAGE.
NICE.
YOU HAVE TO GET AWAY FROM ME... FOR YOUR SAKE.

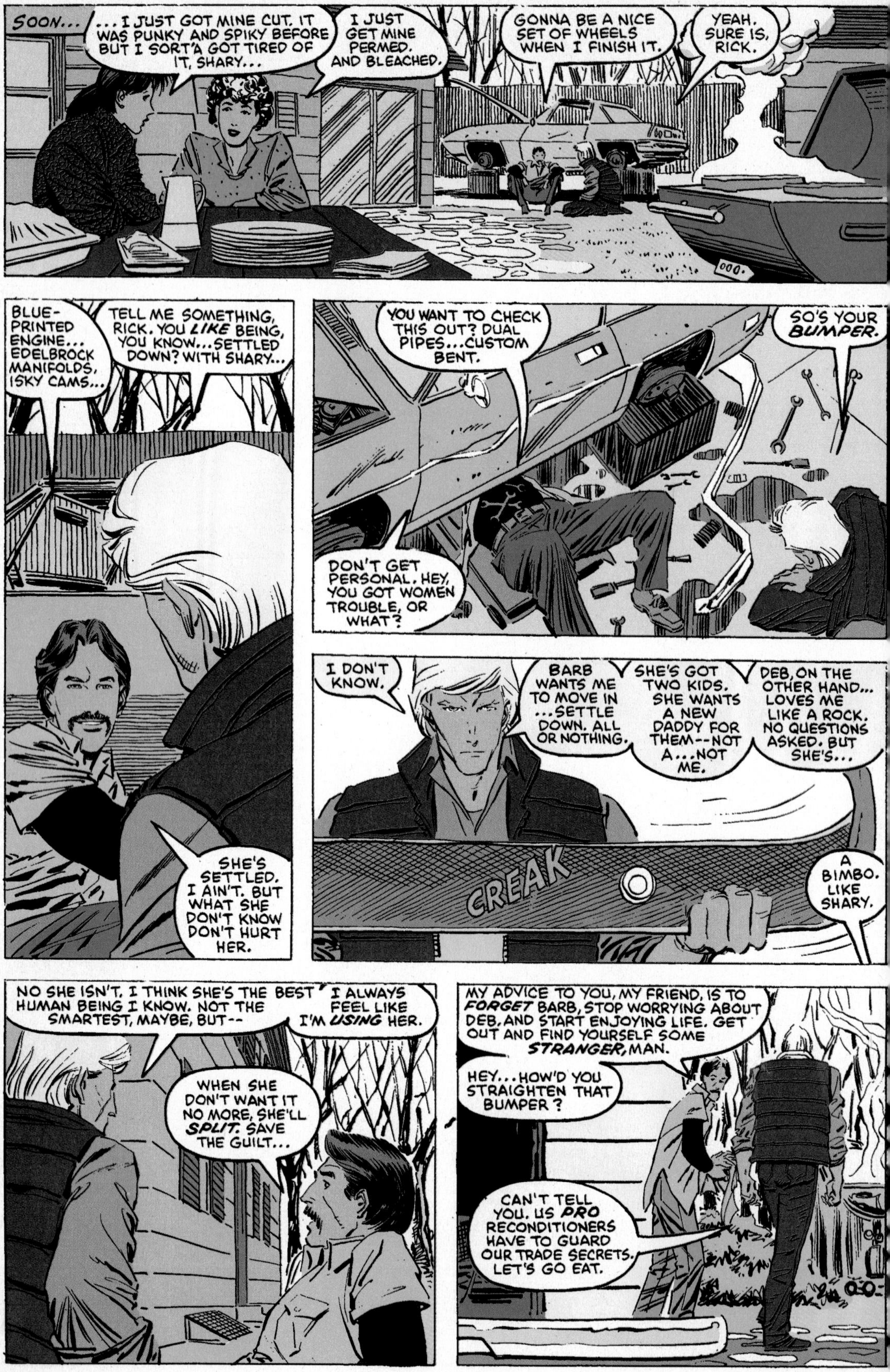
SOON...
...I JUST GOT MINE CUT. IT WAS PUNKY AND SPIKY BEFORE BUT I SORT'A GOT TIRED OF IT, SHARY...
I JUST GET MINE PERMED. AND BLEACHED.
GONNA BE A NICE SET OF WHEELS WHEN I FINISH IT.
YEAH. SURE IS, RICK.
BLUE-PRINTED ENGINE... EDELBROCK MANIFOLDS, ISKY CAMS...
TELL ME SOMETHING, RICK. YOU LIKE BEING, YOU KNOW...SETTLED DOWN? WITH SHARY...
SHE'S SETTLED. I AIN'T. BUT WHAT SHE DON'T KNOW DON'T HURT HER.
YOU WANT TO CHECK THIS OUT? DUAL PIPES...CUSTOM BENT.
SO'S YOUR BUMPER.
DON'T GET PERSONAL. HEY, YOU GOT WOMEN TROUBLE, OR WHAT?
I DON'T KNOW.
BARB WANTS ME TO MOVE IN ...SETTLE DOWN. ALL OR NOTHING.
SHE'S GOT TWO KIDS. SHE WANTS A NEW DADDY FOR THEM--NOT A...NOT ME.
DEB, ON THE OTHER HAND... LOVES ME LIKE A ROCK. NO QUESTIONS ASKED. BUT SHE'S...
CREAK
A BIMBO. LIKE SHARY.
NO SHE ISN'T. I THINK SHE'S THE BEST HUMAN BEING I KNOW. NOT THE SMARTEST, MAYBE, BUT--
I ALWAYS FEEL LIKE I'M USING HER.
WHEN SHE DON'T WANT IT NO MORE, SHE'LL SPLIT. SAVE THE GUILT...
MY ADVICE TO YOU, MY FRIEND, IS TO FORGET BARB, STOP WORRYING ABOUT DEB, AND START ENJOYING LIFE. GET OUT AND FIND YOURSELF SOME STRANGER, MAN.
HEY...HOW'D YOU STRAIGHTEN THAT BUMPER?
CAN'T TELL YOU. US PRO RECONDITIONERS HAVE TO GUARD OUR TRADE SECRETS. LET'S GO EAT.

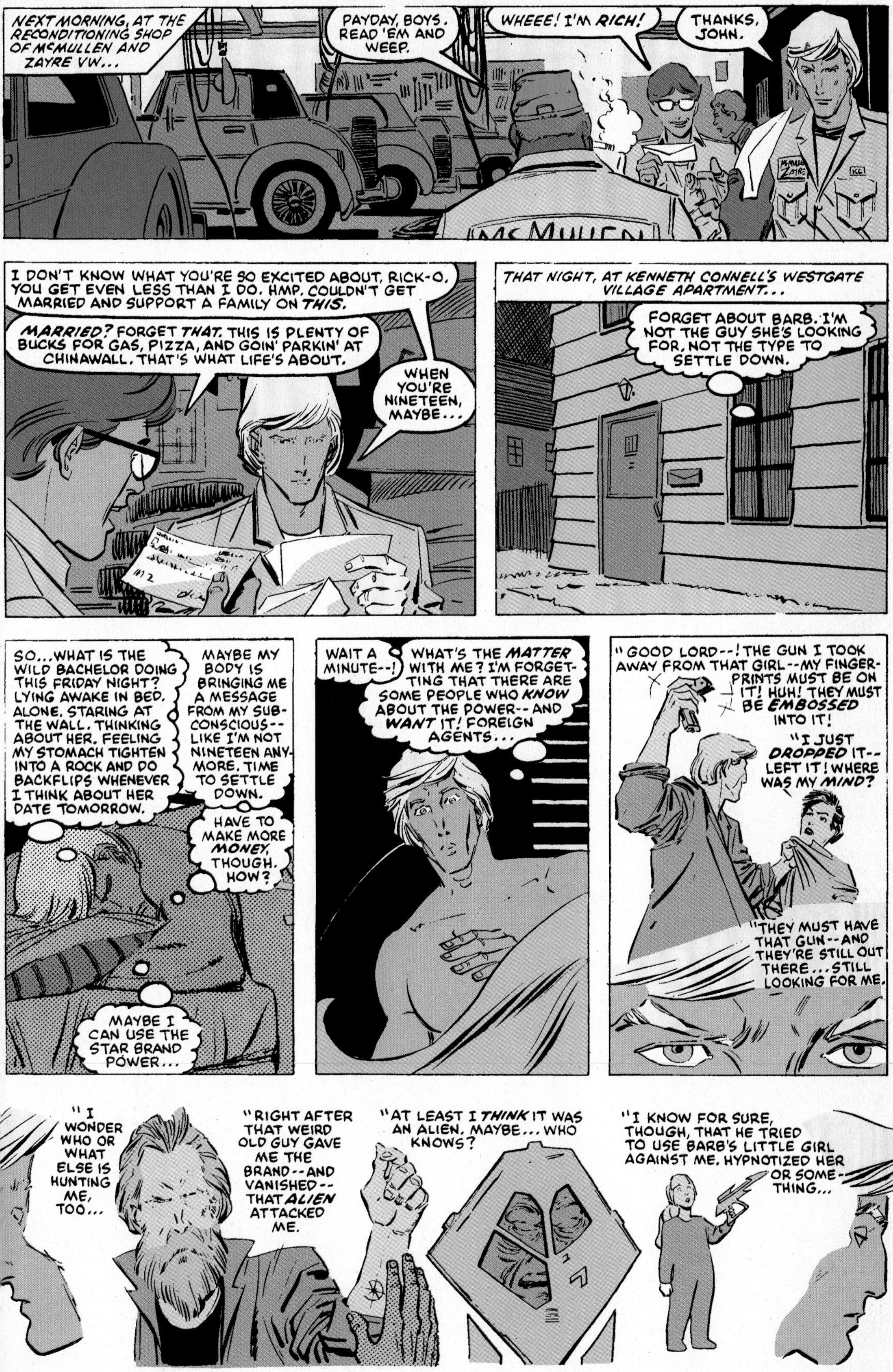

NEXT MORNING, AT THE RECONDITIONING SHOP OF McMULLEN AND ZAYRE VW...
PAYDAY, BOYS. READ 'EM AND WEEP.
WHEEE! I'M RICH!
THANKS, JOHN.
I DON'T KNOW WHAT YOU'RE SO EXCITED ABOUT, RICK-O. YOU GET EVEN LESS THAN I DO. HMP. COULDN'T GET MARRIED AND SUPPORT A FAMILY ON THIS.
MARRIED? FORGET THAT. THIS IS PLENTY OF BUCKS FOR GAS, PIZZA, AND GOIN' PARKIN' AT CHINAWALL. THAT'S WHAT LIFE'S ABOUT.
WHEN YOU'RE NINETEEN, MAYBE...
THAT NIGHT, AT KENNETH CONNELL'S WESTGATE VILLAGE APARTMENT...
FORGET ABOUT BARB. I'M NOT THE GUY SHE'S LOOKING FOR, NOT THE TYPE TO SETTLE DOWN.
SO...WHAT IS THE WILD BACHELOR DOING THIS FRIDAY NIGHT? LYING AWAKE IN BED. ALONE. STARING AT THE WALL. THINKING ABOUT HER. FEELING MY STOMACH TIGHTEN INTO A ROCK AND DO BACKFLIPS WHENEVER I THINK ABOUT HER DATE TOMORROW.
MAYBE MY BODY IS BRINGING ME A MESSAGE FROM MY SUB-CONSCIOUS--LIKE I'M NOT NINETEEN ANYMORE. TIME TO SETTLE DOWN.
HAVE TO MAKE MORE MONEY, THOUGH. HOW?
MAYBE I CAN USE THE STAR BRAND POWER...
WAIT A MINUTE--!
WHAT'S THE MATTER WITH ME? I'M FORGETTING THAT THERE ARE SOME PEOPLE WHO KNOW ABOUT THE POWER--AND WANT IT! FOREIGN AGENTS...
"GOOD LORD--! THE GUN I TOOK AWAY FROM THAT GIRL--MY FINGERPRINTS MUST BE ON IT! HUH! THEY MUST BE EMBOSSED INTO IT!
"I JUST DROPPED IT--LEFT IT! WHERE WAS MY MIND?
"THEY MUST HAVE THAT GUN--AND THEY'RE STILL OUT THERE...STILL LOOKING FOR ME.
"I WONDER WHO OR WHAT ELSE IS HUNTING ME, TOO...
"RIGHT AFTER THAT WEIRD OLD GUY GAVE ME THE BRAND--AND VANISHED--THAT ALIEN ATTACKED ME.
"AT LEAST I THINK IT WAS AN ALIEN. MAYBE... WHO KNOWS?
"I KNOW FOR SURE, THOUGH, THAT HE TRIED TO USE BARB'S LITTLE GIRL AGAINST ME. HYPNOTIZED HER OR SOMETHING...

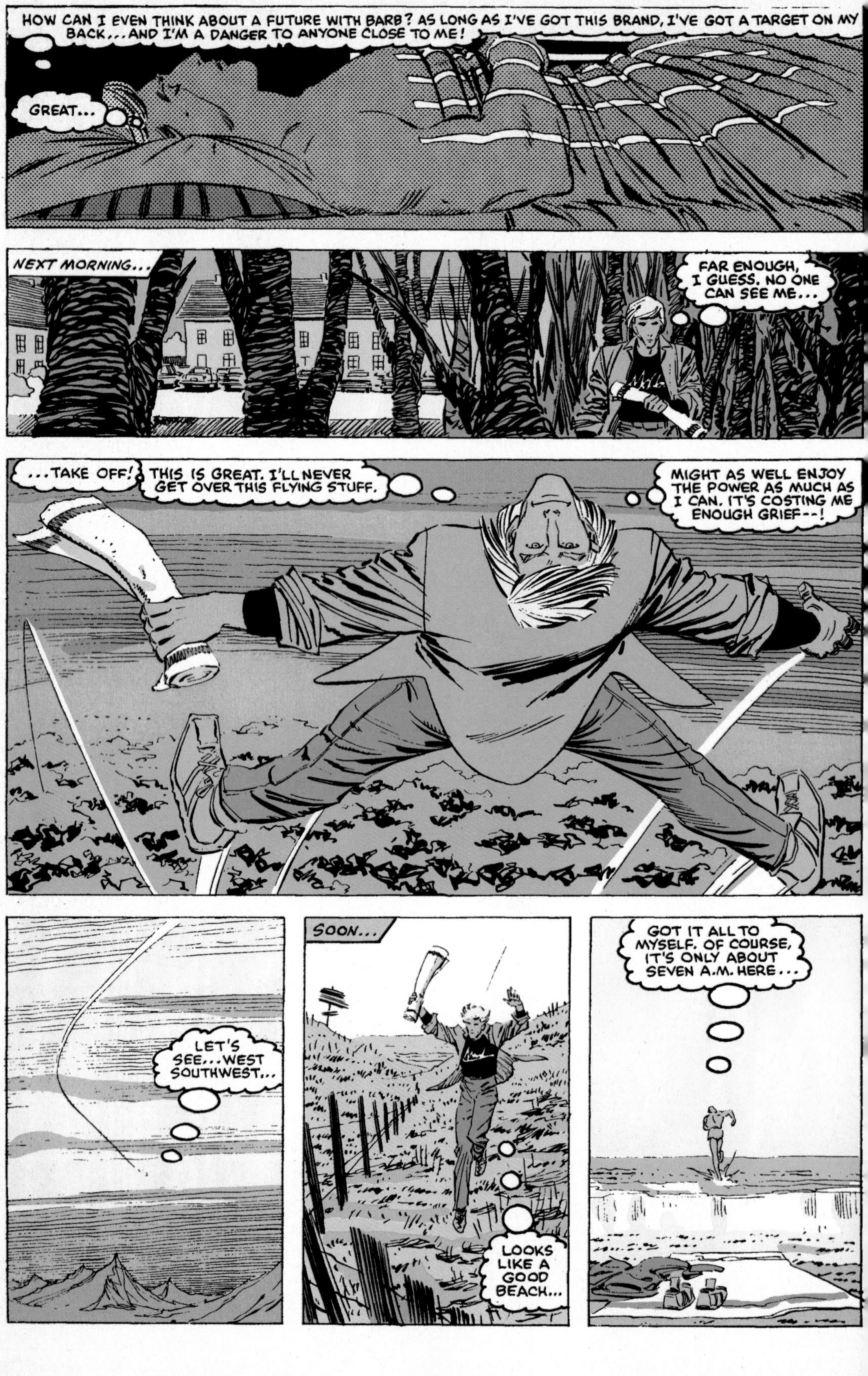
HOW CAN I EVEN THINK ABOUT A FUTURE WITH BARB? AS LONG AS I'VE GOT THIS BRAND, I'VE GOT A TARGET ON MY BACK... AND I'M A DANGER TO ANYONE CLOSE TO ME!
GREAT...
NEXT MORNING...
FAR ENOUGH, I GUESS. NO ONE CAN SEE ME...
...TAKE OFF!
THIS IS GREAT. I'LL NEVER GET OVER THIS FLYING STUFF.
MIGHT AS WELL ENJOY THE POWER AS MUCH AS I CAN. IT'S COSTING ME ENOUGH GRIEF--!
LET'S SEE... WEST SOUTHWEST...
SOON...
LOOKS LIKE A GOOD BEACH...
GOT IT ALL TO MYSELF. OF COURSE, IT'S ONLY ABOUT SEVEN A.M. HERE...

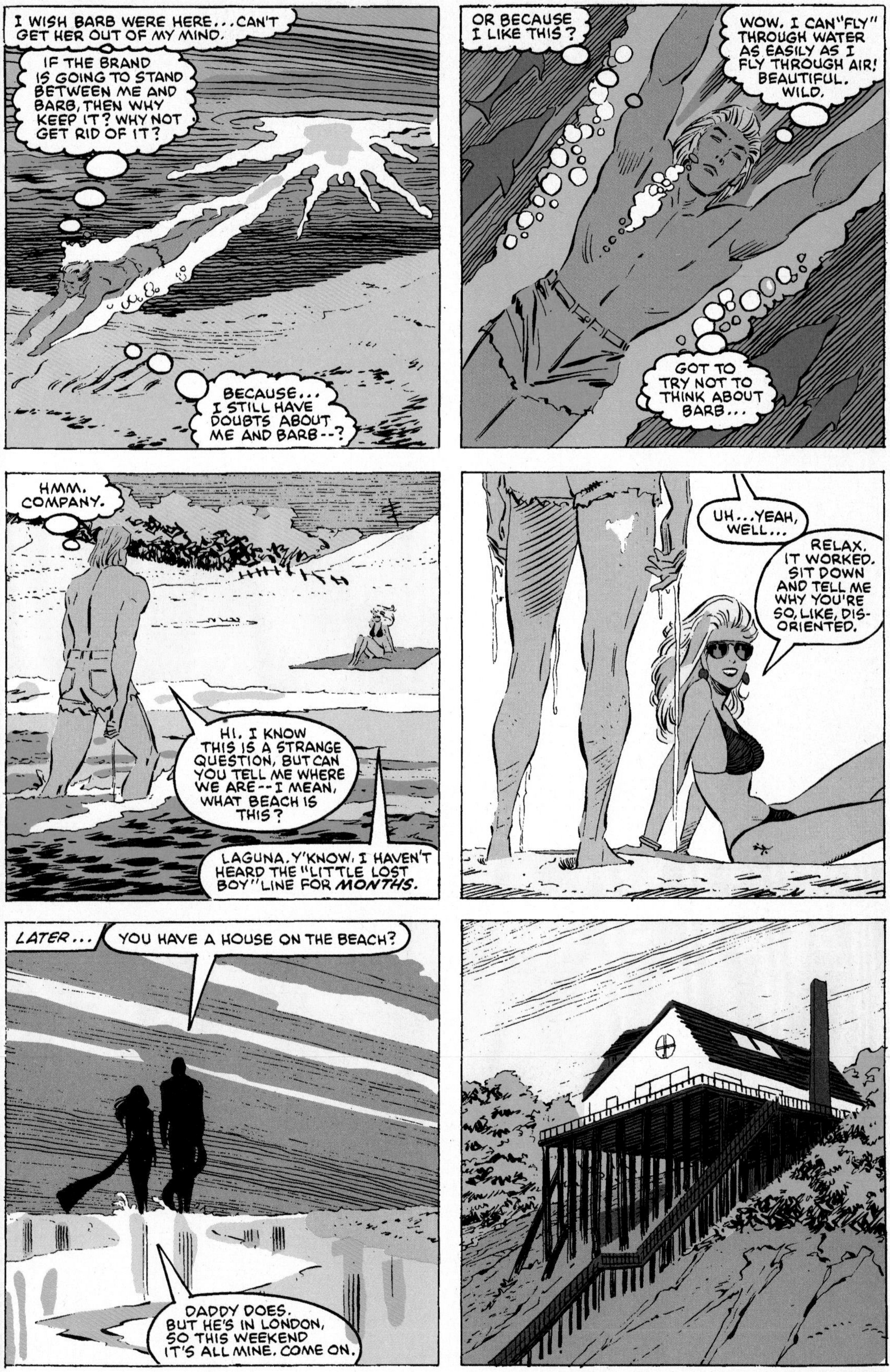

I WISH BARB WERE HERE... CAN'T GET HER OUT OF MY MIND.
IF THE BRAND IS GOING TO STAND BETWEEN ME AND BARB, THEN WHY KEEP IT? WHY NOT GET RID OF IT?
BECAUSE... I STILL HAVE DOUBTS ABOUT ME AND BARB--?
OR BECAUSE I LIKE THIS?
WOW. I CAN "FLY" THROUGH WATER AS EASILY AS I FLY THROUGH AIR! BEAUTIFUL. WILD.
GOT TO TRY NOT TO THINK ABOUT BARB...
HMM. COMPANY.
HI. I KNOW THIS IS A STRANGE QUESTION, BUT CAN YOU TELL ME WHERE WE ARE--I MEAN, WHAT BEACH IS THIS?
LAGUNA. Y'KNOW, I HAVEN'T HEARD THE "LITTLE LOST BOY" LINE FOR *MONTHS.*
UH...YEAH, WELL...
RELAX. IT WORKED. SIT DOWN AND TELL ME WHY YOU'RE SO, LIKE, DIS-ORIENTED.
LATER...
YOU HAVE A HOUSE ON THE BEACH?
DADDY DOES. BUT HE'S IN LONDON, SO THIS WEEKEND IT'S ALL MINE. COME ON.

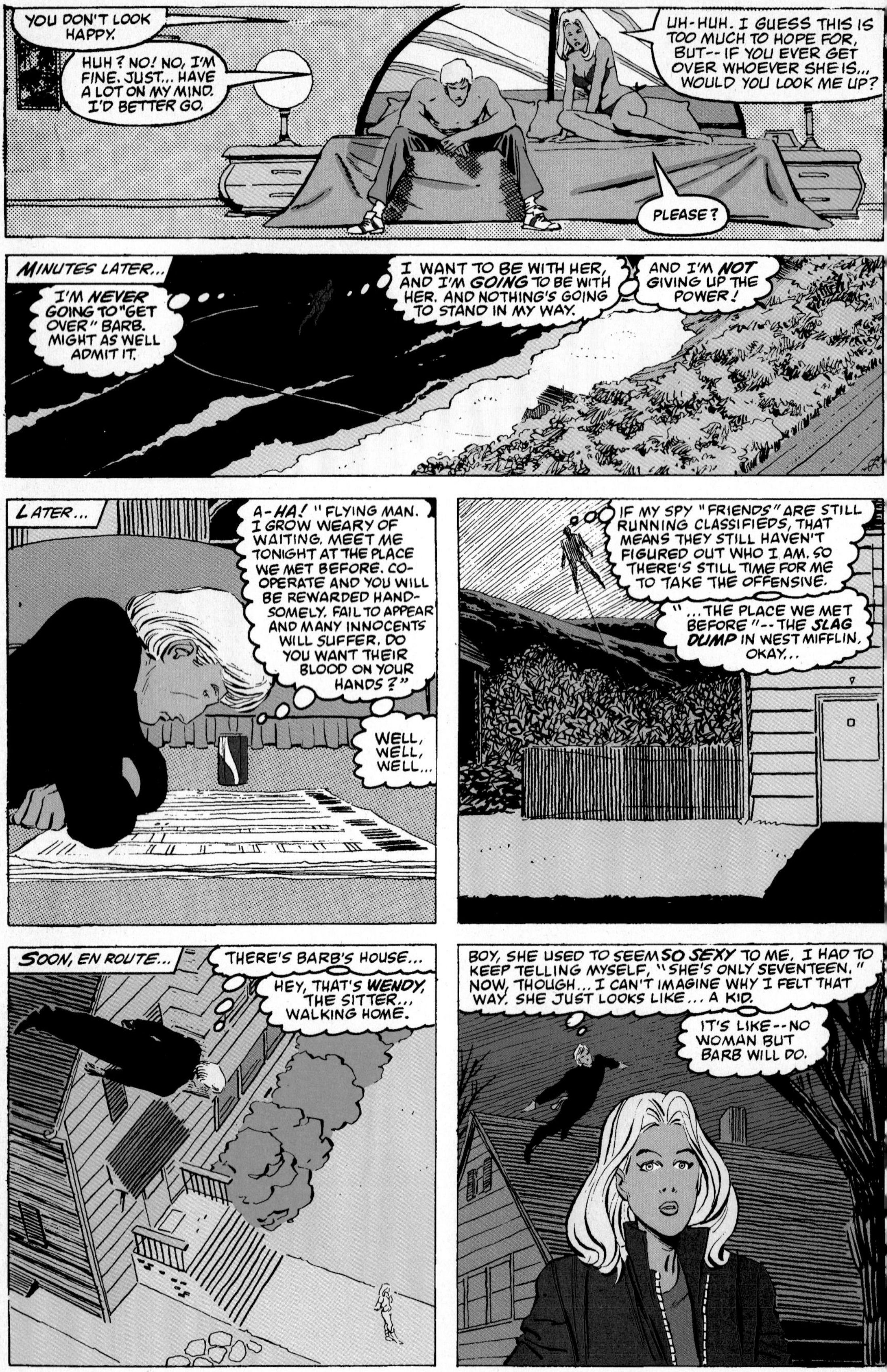

YOU DON'T LOOK HAPPY.
HUH? NO! NO, I'M FINE. JUST... HAVE A LOT ON MY MIND. I'D BETTER GO.
UH-HUH. I GUESS THIS IS TOO MUCH TO HOPE FOR, BUT-- IF YOU EVER GET OVER WHOEVER SHE IS... WOULD YOU LOOK ME UP?
PLEASE?
MINUTES LATER...
I'M NEVER GOING TO "GET OVER" BARB. MIGHT AS WELL ADMIT IT.
I WANT TO BE WITH HER, AND I'M GOING TO BE WITH HER. AND NOTHING'S GOING TO STAND IN MY WAY.
AND I'M NOT GIVING UP THE POWER!
LATER...
A-HA! "FLYING MAN. I GROW WEARY OF WAITING. MEET ME TONIGHT AT THE PLACE WE MET BEFORE. CO-OPERATE AND YOU WILL BE REWARDED HANDSOMELY. FAIL TO APPEAR AND MANY INNOCENTS WILL SUFFER. DO YOU WANT THEIR BLOOD ON YOUR HANDS?"
WELL, WELL, WELL...
IF MY SPY "FRIENDS" ARE STILL RUNNING CLASSIFIEDS, THAT MEANS THEY STILL HAVEN'T FIGURED OUT WHO I AM. SO THERE'S STILL TIME FOR ME TO TAKE THE OFFENSIVE.
"...THE PLACE WE MET BEFORE"-- THE SLAG DUMP IN WEST MIFFLIN. OKAY...
SOON, EN ROUTE...
THERE'S BARB'S HOUSE...
HEY, THAT'S WENDY, THE SITTER... WALKING HOME.
BOY, SHE USED TO SEEM SO SEXY TO ME. I HAD TO KEEP TELLING MYSELF, "SHE'S ONLY SEVENTEEN." NOW, THOUGH... I CAN'T IMAGINE WHY I FELT THAT WAY. SHE JUST LOOKS LIKE... A KID.
IT'S LIKE--NO WOMAN BUT BARB WILL DO.

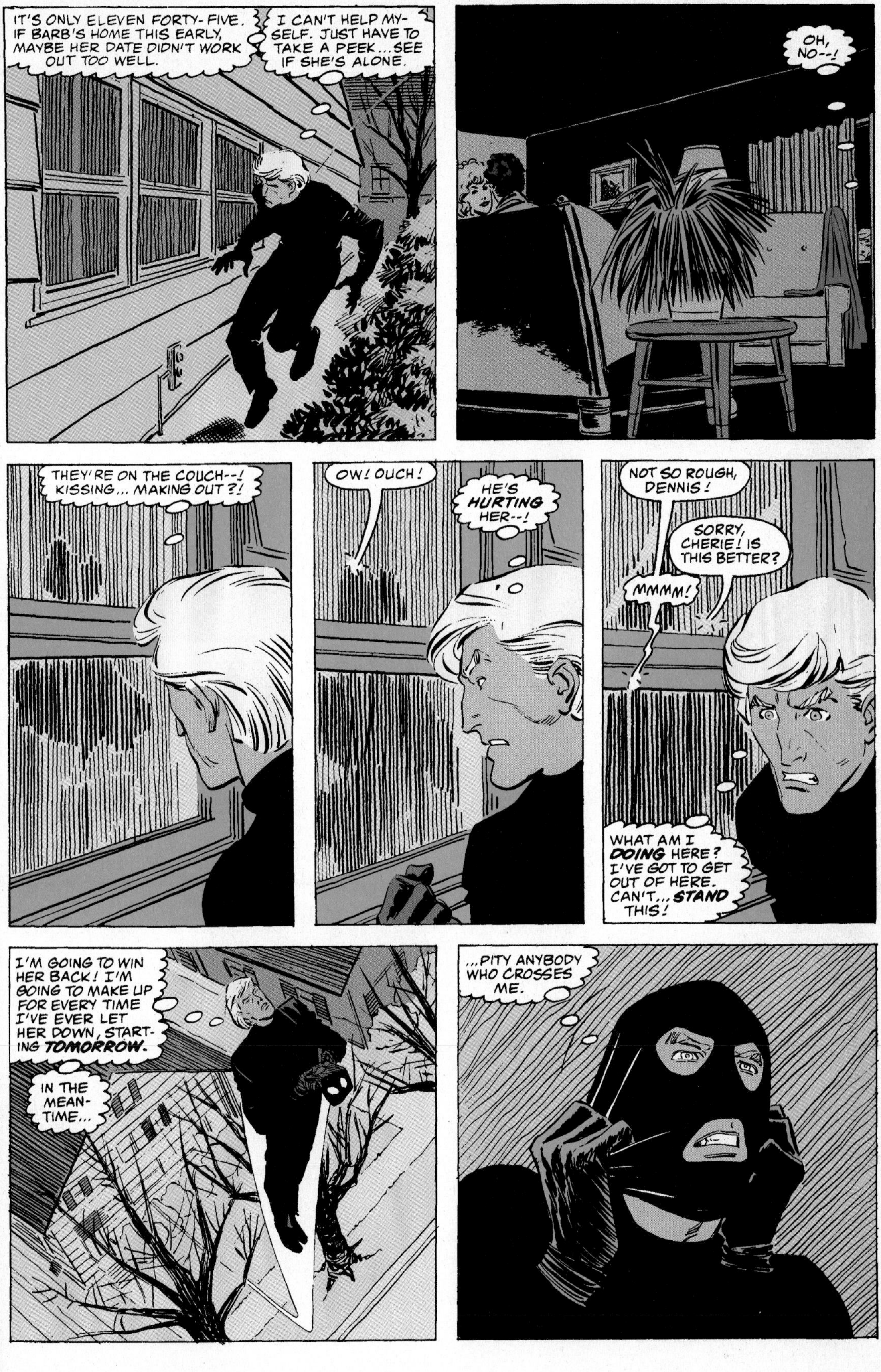
IT'S ONLY ELEVEN FORTY-FIVE. IF BARB'S HOME THIS EARLY, MAYBE HER DATE DIDN'T WORK OUT TOO WELL.
I CAN'T HELP MY-SELF. JUST HAVE TO TAKE A PEEK...SEE IF SHE'S ALONE.
OH, NO--!
THEY'RE ON THE COUCH--! KISSING... MAKING OUT?!
OW! OUCH!
HE'S HURTING HER--!
NOT SO ROUGH, DENNIS!
SORRY, CHERIE! IS THIS BETTER?
MMMM!
WHAT AM I DOING HERE? I'VE GOT TO GET OUT OF HERE. CAN'T... STAND THIS!
I'M GOING TO WIN HER BACK! I'M GOING TO MAKE UP FOR EVERY TIME I'VE EVER LET HER DOWN, STARTING TOMORROW.
IN THE MEAN-TIME...
...PITY ANYBODY WHO CROSSES ME.

SOON, AT THE SLAG DUMP...

AH... *THERE!* BOY, FOR SPIES, THESE GUYS HAVE NO IMAGINATION. SAME SET UP AS LAST TIME-- THE CAR PARKED UNDER THE STREETLIGHT... BACK-UP PEOPLE HIDING NEARBY.

LAST TIME, I WAS CURIOUS TO FIND OUT HOW THEY FOUND OUT ABOUT ME AND HOW MUCH THEY KNEW-- SO I *TALKED* TO THEM ...AND STUPIDLY LET THAT GIRL GET A LOOK AT ME. NOT TO MENTION MY FINGERPRINTS ON HER GUN.

THIS TIME I'LL STAY OUT OF SIGHT...

"...AND WAIT...UNTIL *THEY* GET TIRED OF WAITING..."

...AND FOLLOW THEM TO THEIR LAIR.

AND, IN OAKLAND...

A STUDENT RESIDENCE...

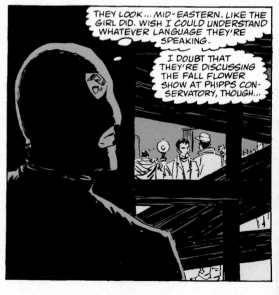

THEY LOOK... MID-EASTERN. LIKE THE GIRL DID. WISH I COULD UNDERSTAND WHATEVER LANGUAGE THEY'RE SPEAKING.

I DOUBT THAT THEY'RE DISCUSSING THE FALL FLOWER SHOW AT PHIPPS CON-SERVATORY, THOUGH...

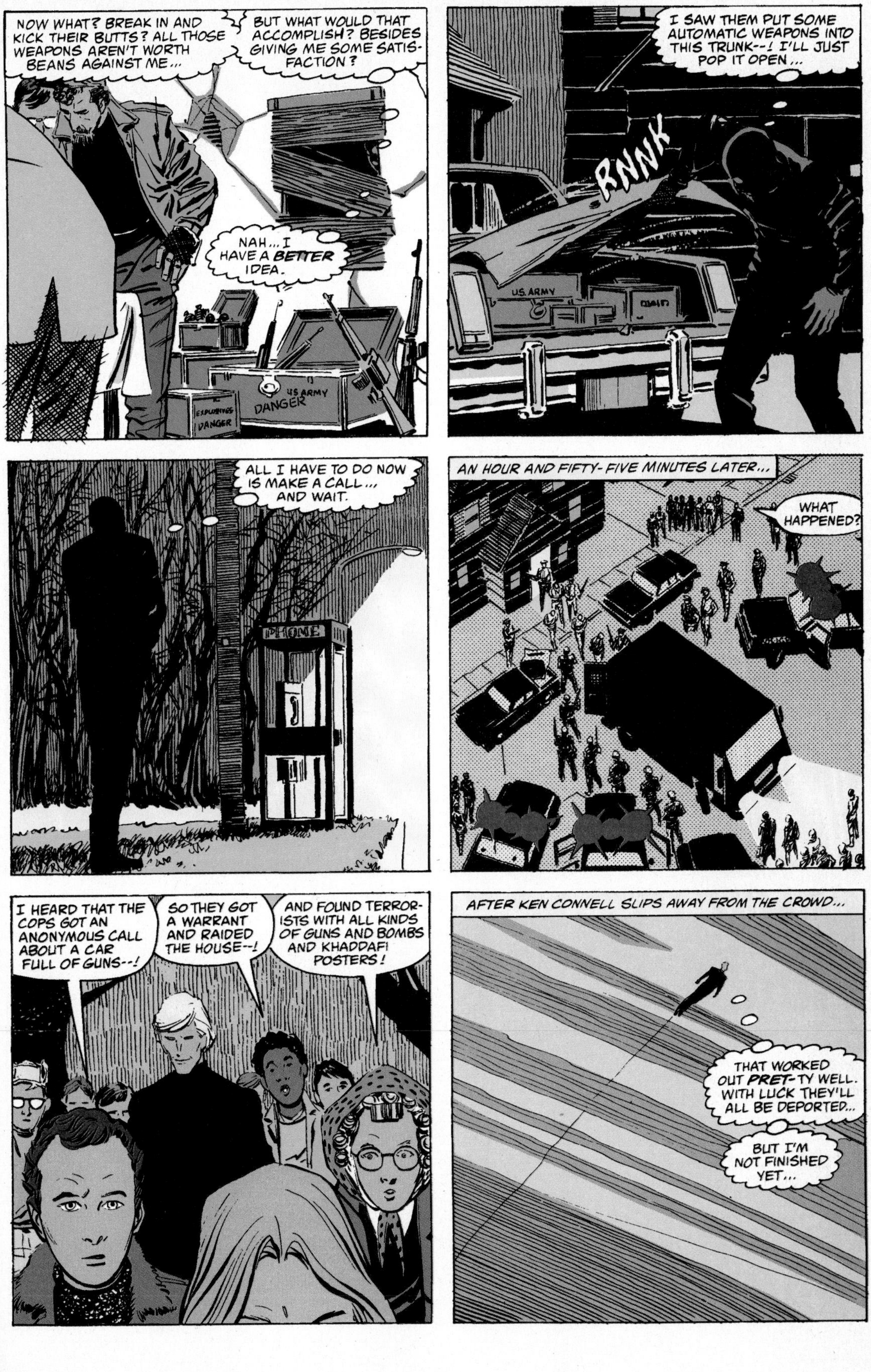
NOW WHAT? BREAK IN AND KICK THEIR BUTTS? ALL THOSE WEAPONS AREN'T WORTH BEANS AGAINST ME...
BUT WHAT WOULD THAT ACCOMPLISH? BESIDES GIVING ME SOME SATIS-FACTION?
NAH... I HAVE A BETTER IDEA.
U.S. ARMY
DANGER
EXPLOSIVES
DANGER
I SAW THEM PUT SOME AUTOMATIC WEAPONS INTO THIS TRUNK--! I'LL JUST POP IT OPEN...
RNNK
U.S. ARMY
ALL I HAVE TO DO NOW IS MAKE A CALL..., AND WAIT.
PHONE
AN HOUR AND FIFTY-FIVE MINUTES LATER...
WHAT HAPPENED?
I HEARD THAT THE COPS GOT AN ANONYMOUS CALL ABOUT A CAR FULL OF GUNS--!
SO THEY GOT A WARRANT AND RAIDED THE HOUSE--!
AND FOUND TERROR-ISTS WITH ALL KINDS OF GUNS AND BOMBS AND KHADDAFI POSTERS!
AFTER KEN CONNELL SLIPS AWAY FROM THE CROWD...
THAT WORKED OUT PRET-TY WELL. WITH LUCK THEY'LL ALL BE DEPORTED...
BUT I'M NOT FINISHED YET...

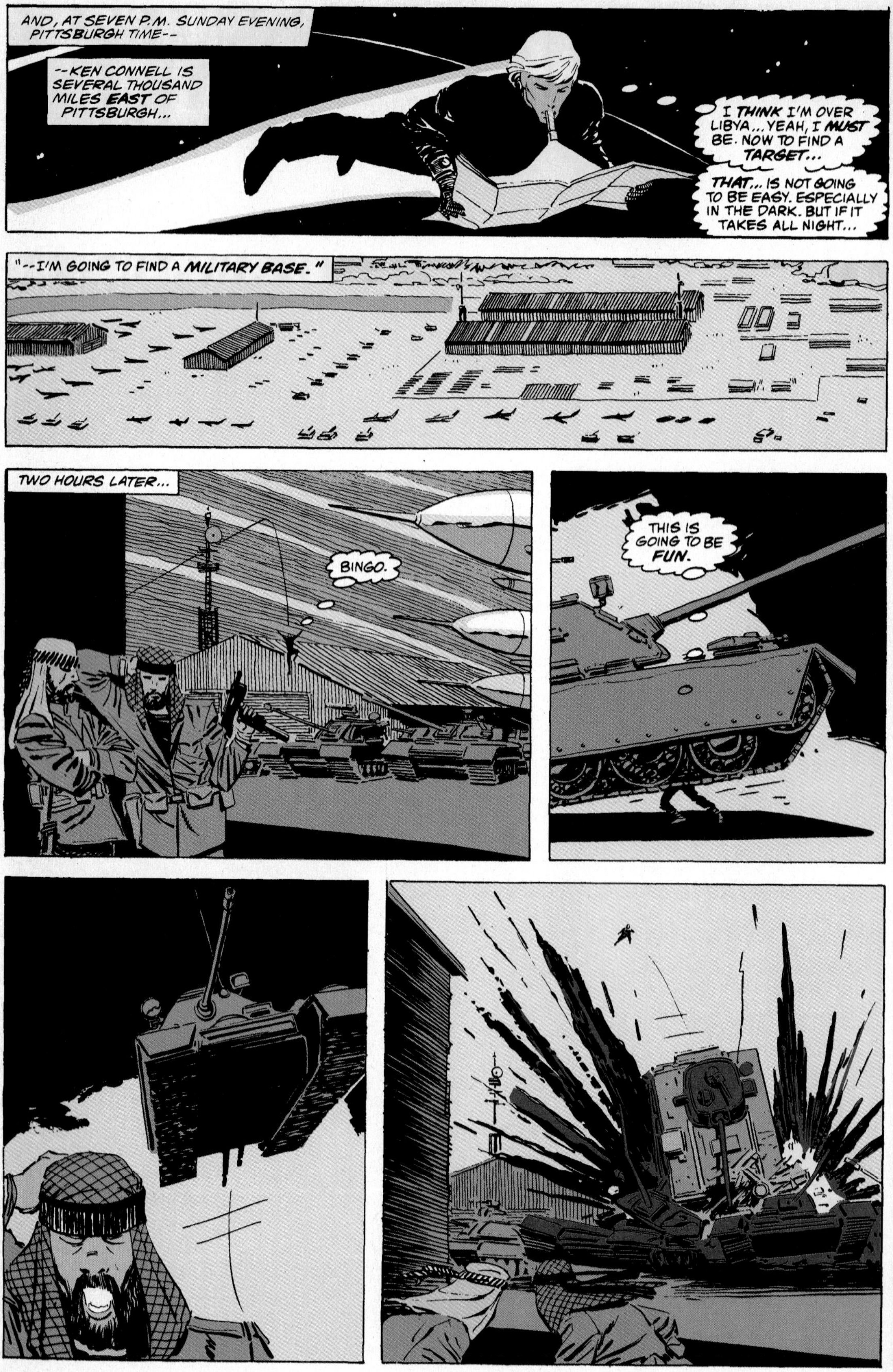
AND, AT SEVEN P.M. SUNDAY EVENING, PITTSBURGH TIME--
--KEN CONNELL IS SEVERAL THOUSAND MILES EAST OF PITTSBURGH...
I THINK I'M OVER LIBYA... YEAH, I MUST BE. NOW TO FIND A TARGET...
THAT... IS NOT GOING TO BE EASY. ESPECIALLY IN THE DARK. BUT IF IT TAKES ALL NIGHT...
"--I'M GOING TO FIND A MILITARY BASE."
TWO HOURS LATER...
BINGO.
THIS IS GOING TO BE FUN.

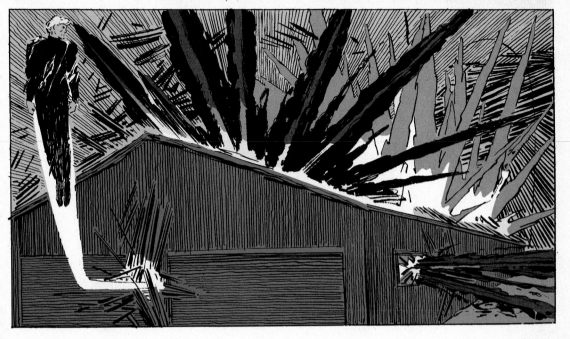

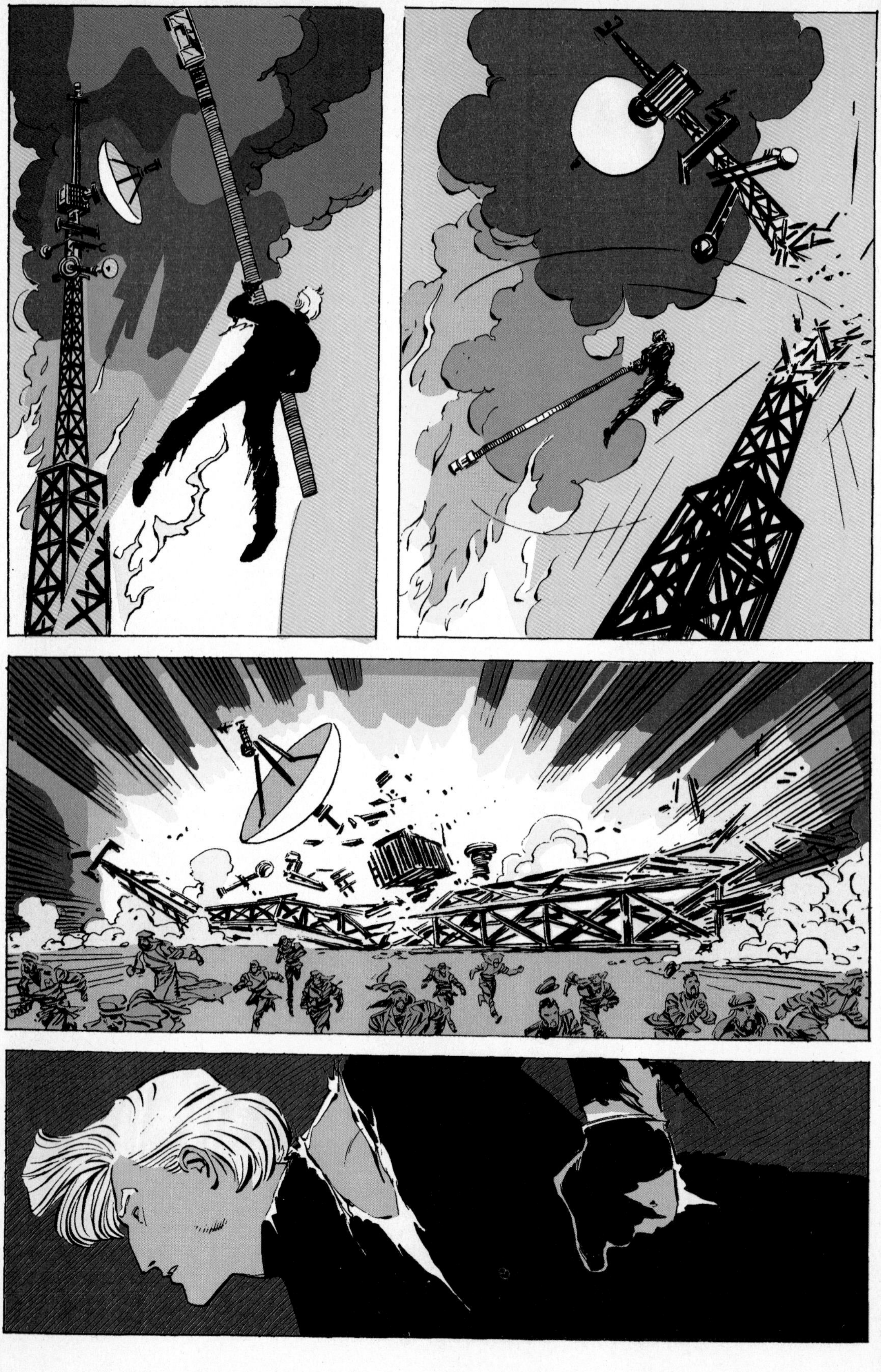

YOU! YOU'RE AN OFFICER! YOU'LL DO!

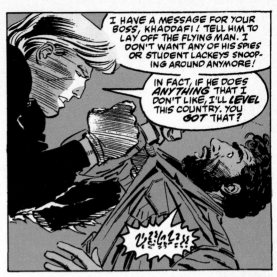

I HAVE A MESSAGE FOR YOUR BOSS, KHADDAFI! TELL HIM TO LAY OFF THE FLYING MAN. I DON'T WANT ANY OF HIS SPIES OR STUDENT LACKEYS SNOOPING AROUND ANYMORE!

IN FACT, IF HE DOES ANYTHING THAT I DON'T LIKE, I'LL LEVEL THIS COUNTRY. YOU GOT THAT?

SOME TIME LATER, IN WESTGATE VILLAGE...

I DON'T THINK THAT GUY UNDERSTOOD A WORD I SAID...

...BUT IF KHADDAFI DOESN'T GET THE DRIFT, NEXT TIME I'LL MAKE IT A POINT TO SPEAK TO HIM IN PERSON.

ELEVEN P.M.! WONDER WHAT OL' RAY TANNEHILL HAS TO SAY FOR HIMSELF TONIGHT...

CLICK

...KDKA NEWS HAS LEARNED THAT THE PITT STUDENTS ARRESTED EARLY THIS MORNING AT THEIR RESIDENCE IN OAKLAND ARE MEMBERS OF THE MOST EXTREME FACTION OF A RADICAL TERRORIST ORGANIZATION LOYAL TO LIBYAN LEADER MUAMMAR-AL-QADDAFI.

POLICE SAY THAT AN ANONYMOUS CALLER GAVE THEM THE TIP THAT LED THEM TO THE LARGEST CACHE OF ILLEGAL WEAPONS EVER FOUND IN PENNSYLVANIA...

ARM SAL

I LOVE IT.

THE NEXT DAY...

MEMORIAL SCHOOL

THERE'S BARB--!

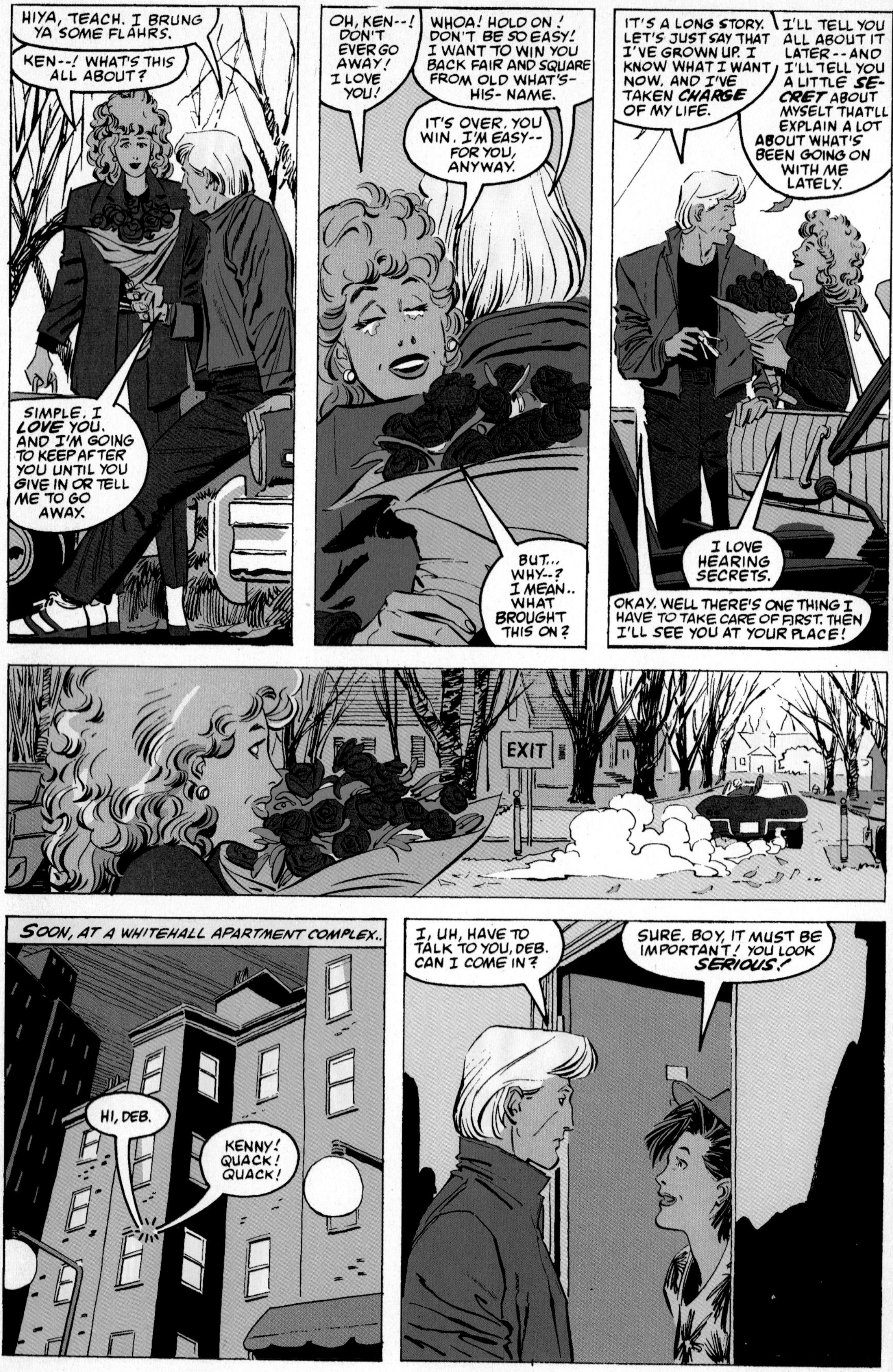
HIYA, TEACH. I BRUNG YA SOME FLAHRS.
KEN--! WHAT'S THIS ALL ABOUT?
SIMPLE. I LOVE YOU. AND I'M GOING TO KEEP AFTER YOU UNTIL YOU GIVE IN OR TELL ME TO GO AWAY.
OH, KEN--! DON'T EVER GO AWAY! I LOVE YOU!
WHOA! HOLD ON! DON'T BE SO EASY! I WANT TO WIN YOU BACK FAIR AND SQUARE FROM OLD WHAT'S-HIS-NAME.
IT'S OVER. YOU WIN. I'M EASY--FOR YOU, ANYWAY.
BUT... WHY--? I MEAN.. WHAT BROUGHT THIS ON?
IT'S A LONG STORY. LET'S JUST SAY THAT I'VE GROWN UP. I KNOW WHAT I WANT NOW. AND I'VE TAKEN CHARGE OF MY LIFE.
I'LL TELL YOU ALL ABOUT IT LATER--AND I'LL TELL YOU A LITTLE SECRET ABOUT MYSELT THAT'LL EXPLAIN A LOT ABOUT WHAT'S BEEN GOING ON WITH ME LATELY.
I LOVE HEARING SECRETS.
OKAY. WELL THERE'S ONE THING I HAVE TO TAKE CARE OF FIRST. THEN I'LL SEE YOU AT YOUR PLACE!
EXIT
SOON, AT A WHITEHALL APARTMENT COMPLEX..
HI, DEB.
KENNY! QUACK! QUACK!
I, UH, HAVE TO TALK TO YOU, DEB. CAN I COME IN?
SURE. BOY, IT MUST BE IMPORTANT! YOU LOOK SERIOUS!

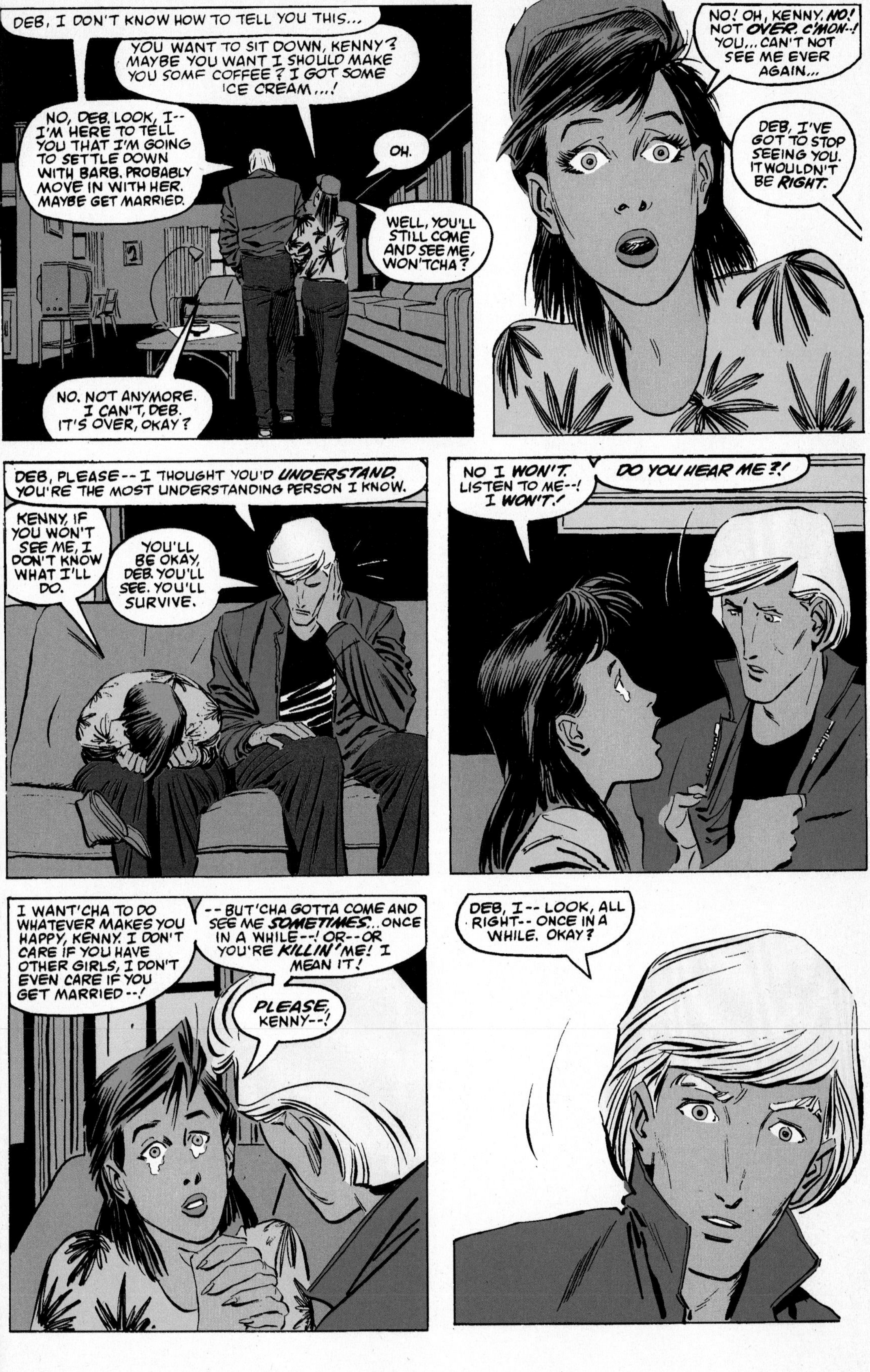
DEB, I DON'T KNOW HOW TO TELL YOU THIS...
YOU WANT TO SIT DOWN, KENNY? MAYBE YOU WANT I SHOULD MAKE YOU SOME COFFEE? I GOT SOME ICE CREAM....!
NO, DEB, LOOK, I-- I'M HERE TO TELL YOU THAT I'M GOING TO SETTLE DOWN WITH BARB. PROBABLY MOVE IN WITH HER. MAYBE GET MARRIED.
OH.
WELL, YOU'LL STILL COME AND SEE ME, WON'TCHA?
NO. NOT ANYMORE. I CAN'T, DEB. IT'S OVER, OKAY?
NO! OH, KENNY, NO! NOT OVER. C'MON--! YOU... CAN'T NOT SEE ME EVER AGAIN...
DEB, I'VE GOT TO STOP SEEING YOU. IT WOULDN'T BE RIGHT.
DEB, PLEASE-- I THOUGHT YOU'D UNDERSTAND. YOU'RE THE MOST UNDERSTANDING PERSON I KNOW.
KENNY, IF YOU WON'T SEE ME, I DON'T KNOW WHAT I'LL DO.
YOU'LL BE OKAY, DEB. YOU'LL SEE. YOU'LL SURVIVE.
NO I WON'T. LISTEN TO ME--! I WON'T.!
DO YOU HEAR ME?!
I WANT'CHA TO DO WHATEVER MAKES YOU HAPPY, KENNY. I DON'T CARE IF YOU HAVE OTHER GIRLS, I DON'T EVEN CARE IF YOU GET MARRIED--!
--BUT'CHA GOTTA COME AND SEE ME SOMETIMES!...ONCE IN A WHILE--! OR--OR YOU'RE KILLIN' ME! I MEAN IT!
PLEASE, KENNY--!
DEB, I-- LOOK, ALL RIGHT-- ONCE IN A WHILE. OKAY?

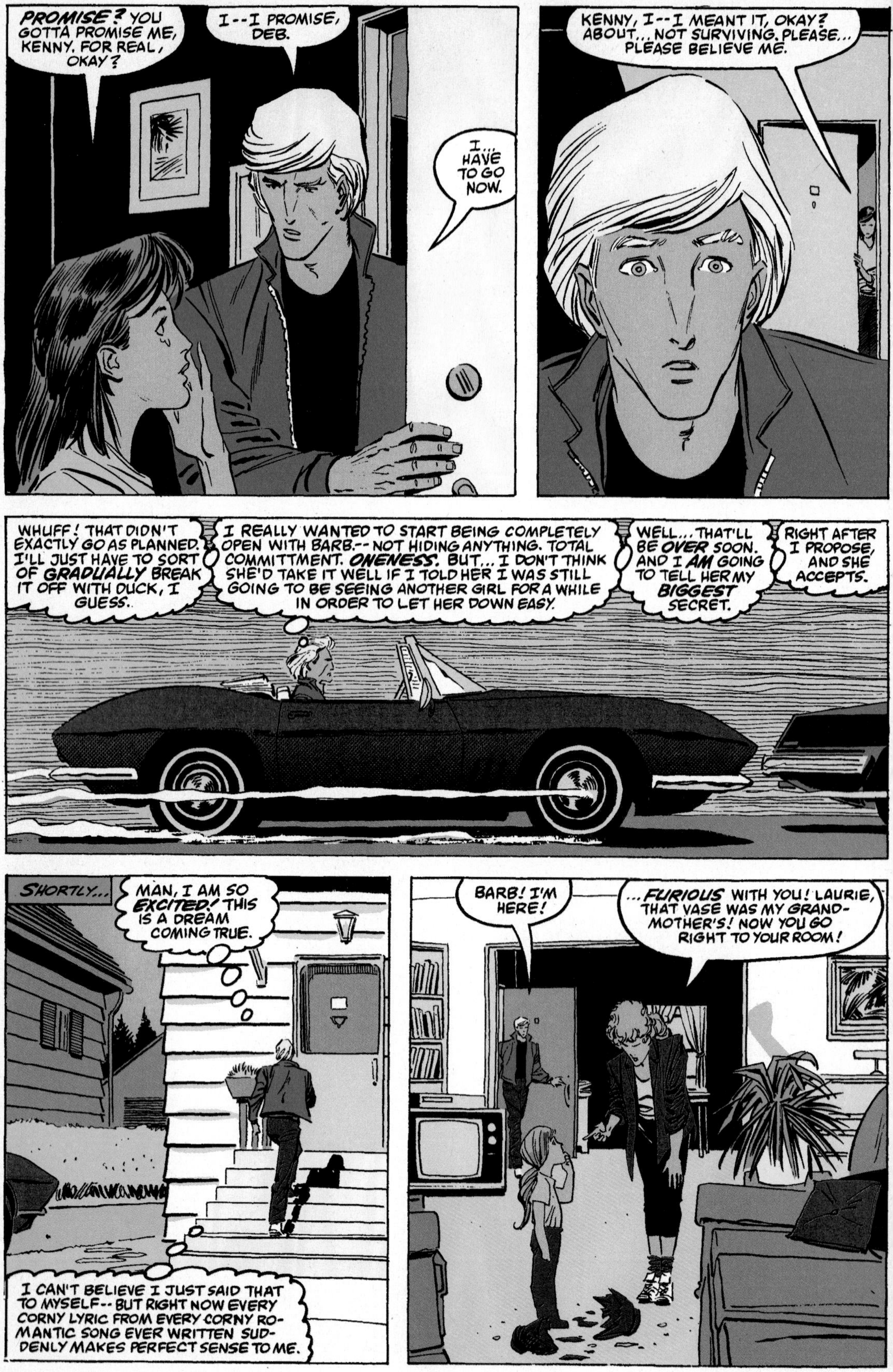
PROMISE? YOU GOTTA PROMISE ME, KENNY. FOR REAL, OKAY?
I--I PROMISE, DEB.
I... HAVE TO GO NOW.
KENNY, I--I MEANT IT, OKAY? ABOUT... NOT SURVIVING. PLEASE... PLEASE BELIEVE ME.
WHUFF! THAT DIDN'T EXACTLY GO AS PLANNED. I'LL JUST HAVE TO SORT OF GRADUALLY BREAK IT OFF WITH DUCK, I GUESS.
I REALLY WANTED TO START BEING COMPLETELY OPEN WITH BARB.-- NOT HIDING ANYTHING. TOTAL COMMITTMENT. ONENESS. BUT... I DON'T THINK SHE'D TAKE IT WELL IF I TOLD HER I WAS STILL GOING TO BE SEEING ANOTHER GIRL FOR A WHILE IN ORDER TO LET HER DOWN EASY.
WELL... THAT'LL BE OVER SOON. AND I AM GOING TO TELL HER MY BIGGEST SECRET.
RIGHT AFTER I PROPOSE, AND SHE ACCEPTS.
SHORTLY...
MAN, I AM SO EXCITED! THIS IS A DREAM COMING TRUE.
I CAN'T BELIEVE I JUST SAID THAT TO MYSELF-- BUT RIGHT NOW EVERY CORNY LYRIC FROM EVERY CORNY ROMANTIC SONG EVER WRITTEN SUDDENLY MAKES PERFECT SENSE TO ME.
BARB! I'M HERE!
...FURIOUS WITH YOU! LAURIE, THAT VASE WAS MY GRANDMOTHER'S! NOW YOU GO RIGHT TO YOUR ROOM!

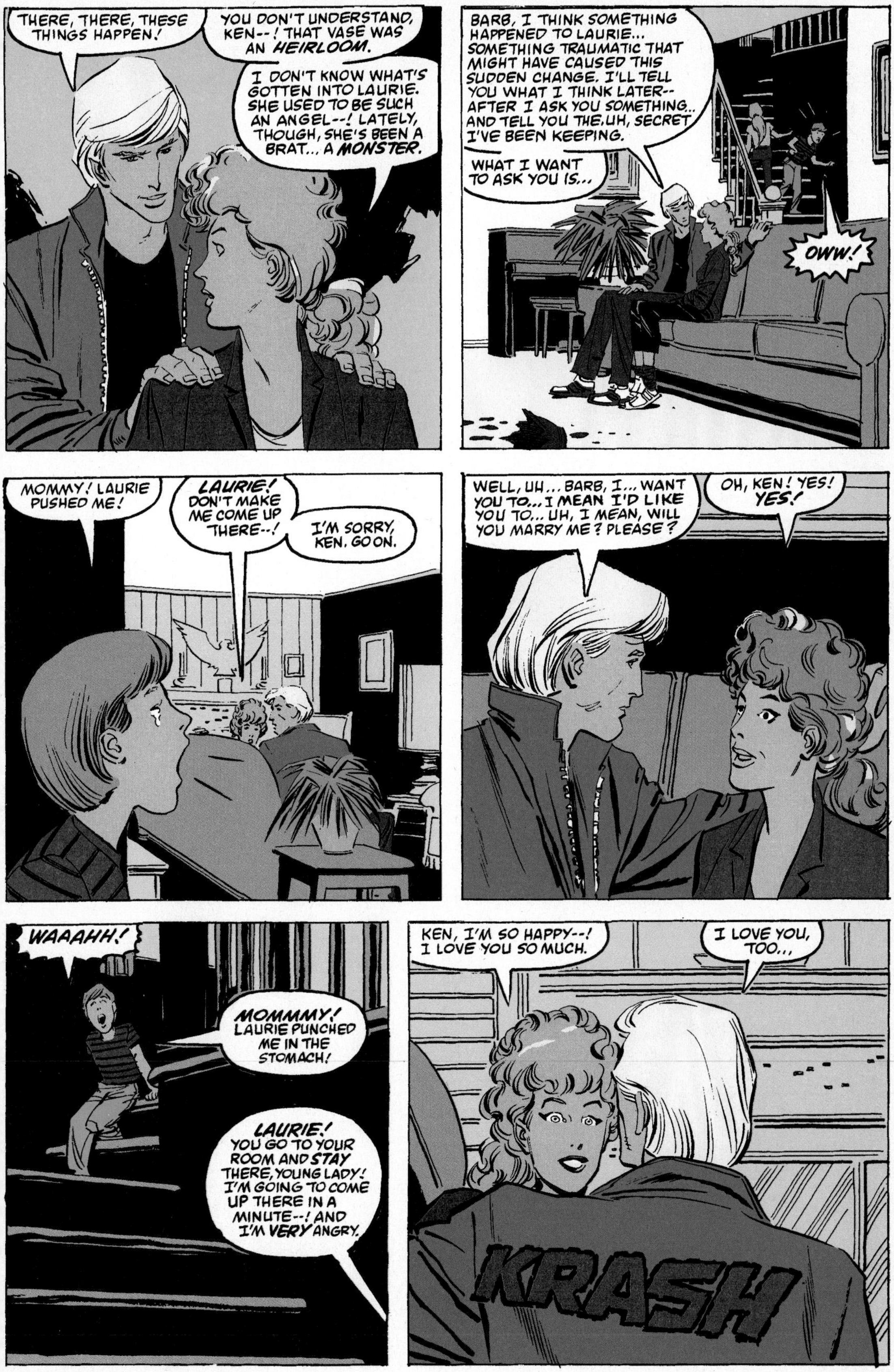
THERE, THERE, THESE THINGS HAPPEN!
YOU DON'T UNDERSTAND, KEN--! THAT VASE WAS AN HEIRLOOM.
I DON'T KNOW WHAT'S GOTTEN INTO LAURIE. SHE USED TO BE SUCH AN ANGEL--! LATELY, THOUGH, SHE'S BEEN A BRAT... A MONSTER.
BARB, I THINK SOMETHING HAPPENED TO LAURIE... SOMETHING TRAUMATIC THAT MIGHT HAVE CAUSED THIS SUDDEN CHANGE. I'LL TELL YOU WHAT I THINK LATER-- AFTER I ASK YOU SOMETHING.. AND TELL YOU THE, UH, SECRET I'VE BEEN KEEPING.
WHAT I WANT TO ASK YOU IS...
OWW!
MOMMY! LAURIE PUSHED ME!
LAURIE! DON'T MAKE ME COME UP THERE--!
I'M SORRY, KEN. GO ON.
WELL, UH... BARB, I... WANT YOU TO... I MEAN I'D LIKE YOU TO... UH, I MEAN, WILL YOU MARRY ME? PLEASE?
OH, KEN! YES! YES!
WAAAHH!
MOMMMY! LAURIE PUNCHED ME IN THE STOMACH!
LAURIE! YOU GO TO YOUR ROOM AND STAY THERE, YOUNG LADY! I'M GOING TO COME UP THERE IN A MINUTE--! AND I'M VERY ANGRY.
KEN, I'M SO HAPPY--! I LOVE YOU SO MUCH.
I LOVE YOU, TOO...
KRASH

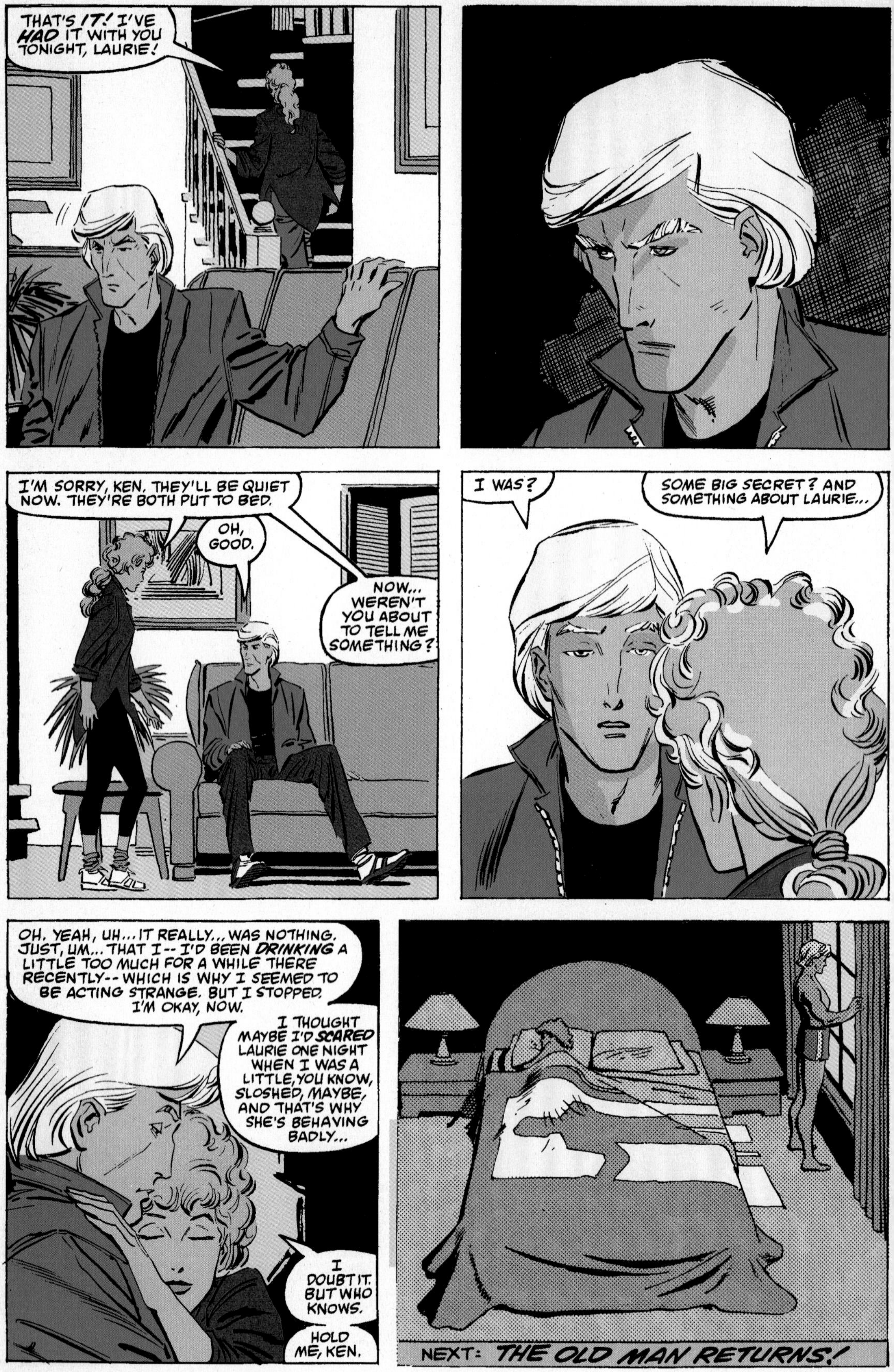
THAT'S *IT!* I'VE *HAD* IT WITH YOU TONIGHT, LAURIE!
I'M SORRY, KEN. THEY'LL BE QUIET NOW. THEY'RE BOTH PUT TO BED.
OH, GOOD.
NOW... WEREN'T YOU ABOUT TO TELL ME SOMETHING?
I WAS?
SOME BIG SECRET? AND SOMETHING ABOUT LAURIE...
OH. YEAH, UH... IT REALLY... WAS NOTHING. JUST, UM... THAT I-- I'D BEEN *DRINKING* A LITTLE TOO MUCH FOR A WHILE THERE RECENTLY-- WHICH IS WHY I SEEMED TO BE ACTING STRANGE. BUT I STOPPED. I'M OKAY, NOW.
I THOUGHT MAYBE I'D *SCARED* LAURIE ONE NIGHT WHEN I WAS A LITTLE, YOU KNOW, SLOSHED, MAYBE, AND THAT'S WHY SHE'S BEHAVING BADLY...
I DOUBT IT. BUT WHO KNOWS.
HOLD ME, KEN.
NEXT: *THE OLD MAN RETURNS!*

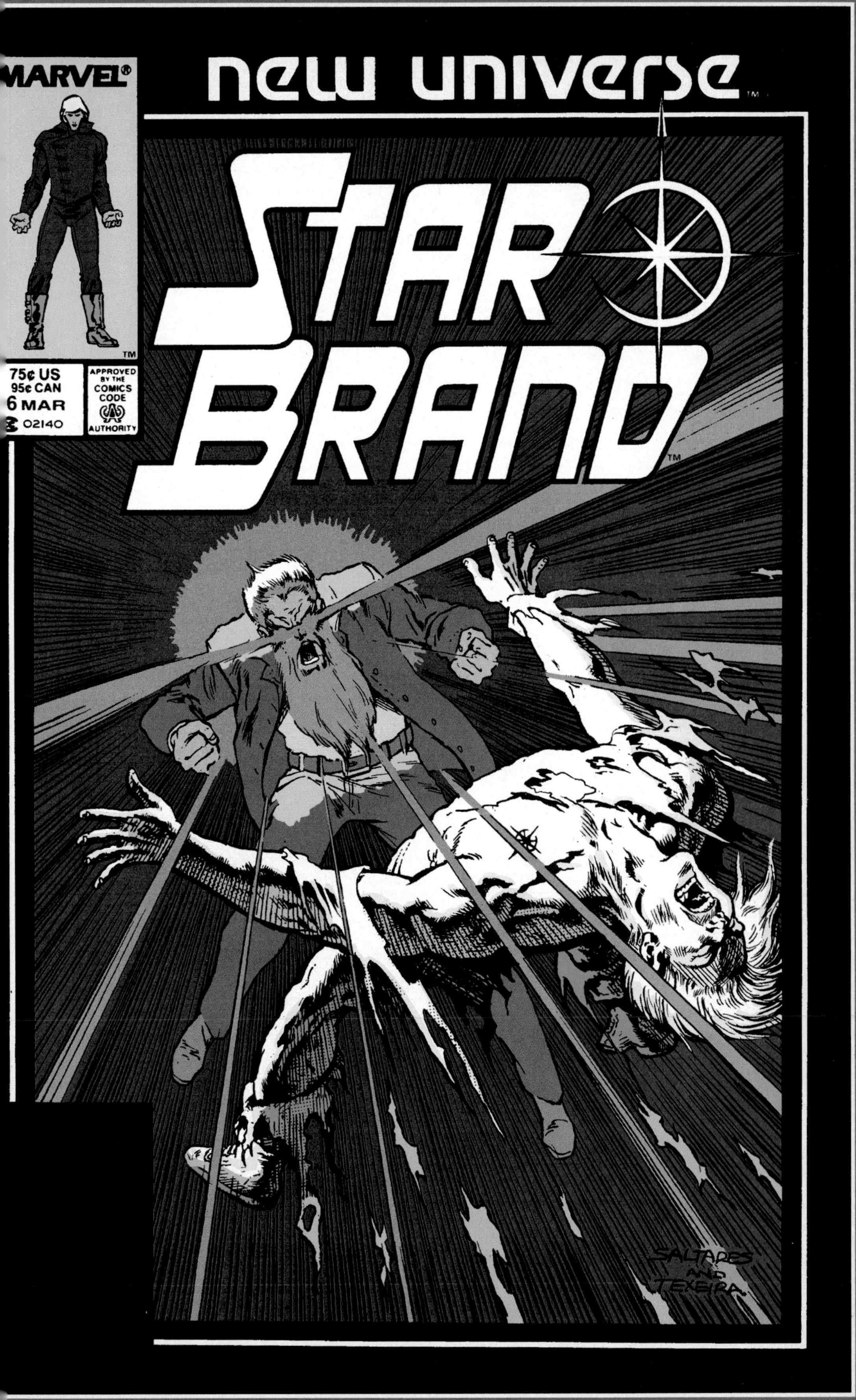
MARVEL®
NEW UNIVERSE™
STAR BRAND™
75¢ US
95¢ CAN
6 MAR
02140
APPROVED BY THE COMICS CODE AUTHORITY
SALTARES AND TEXEIRA

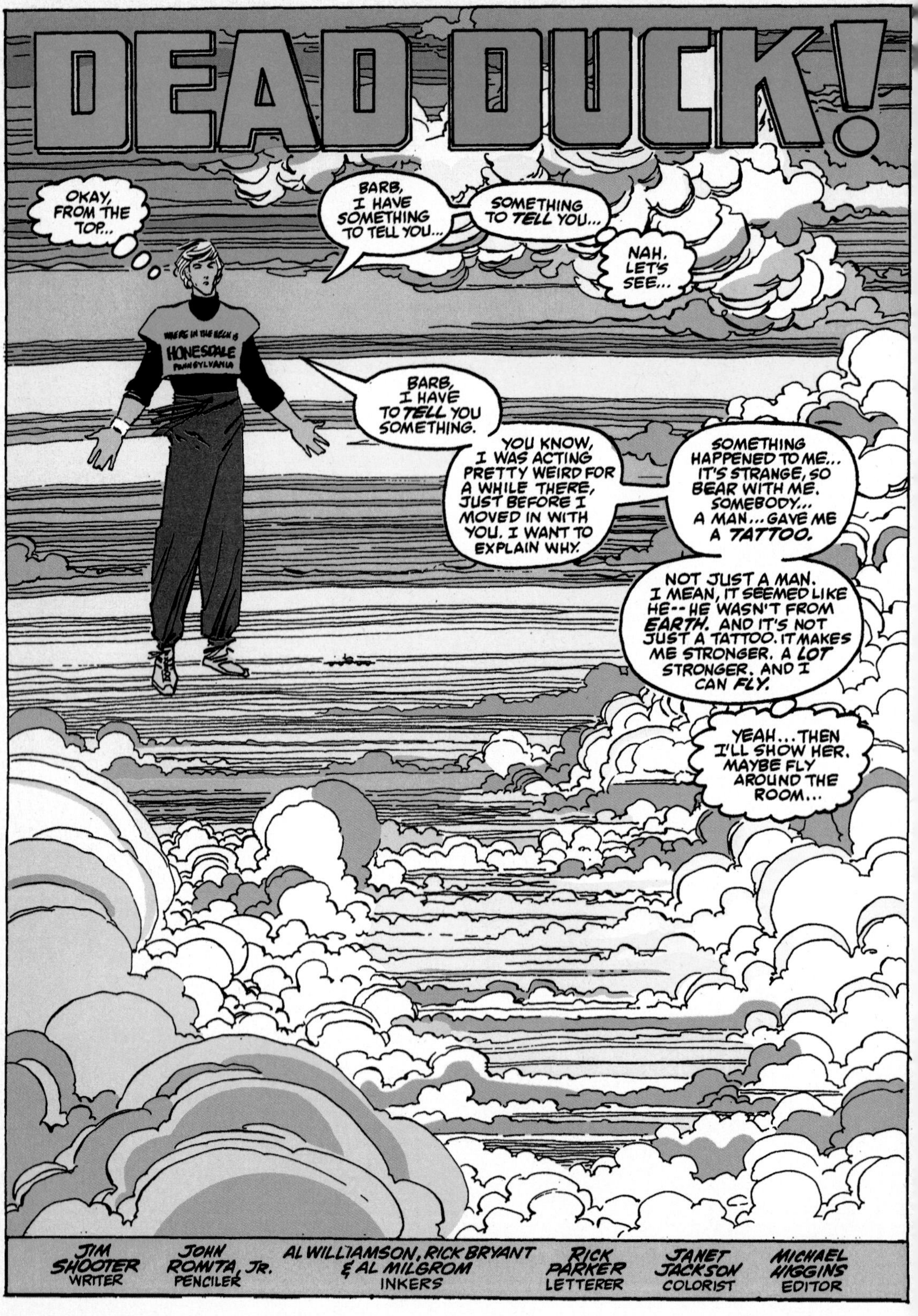
DEAD DUCK!
OKAY, FROM THE TOP...
BARB, I HAVE SOMETHING TO TELL YOU...
SOMETHING TO TELL YOU...
NAH. LET'S SEE...
WHERE IN THE HECK IS HONESDALE PENNSYLVANIA
BARB, I HAVE TO TELL YOU SOMETHING.
YOU KNOW, I WAS ACTING PRETTY WEIRD FOR A WHILE THERE, JUST BEFORE I MOVED IN WITH YOU. I WANT TO EXPLAIN WHY.
SOMETHING HAPPENED TO ME... IT'S STRANGE, SO BEAR WITH ME. SOMEBODY... A MAN... GAVE ME A TATTOO.
NOT JUST A MAN. I MEAN, IT SEEMED LIKE HE-- HE WASN'T FROM EARTH. AND IT'S NOT JUST A TATTOO. IT MAKES ME STRONGER. A LOT STRONGER. AND I CAN FLY.
YEAH... THEN I'LL SHOW HER. MAYBE FLY AROUND THE ROOM...
JIM SHOOTER WRITER
JOHN ROMITA, JR. PENCILER
AL WILLIAMSON, RICK BRYANT & AL MILGROM INKERS
RICK PARKER LETTERER
JANET JACKSON COLORIST
MICHAEL HIGGINS EDITOR

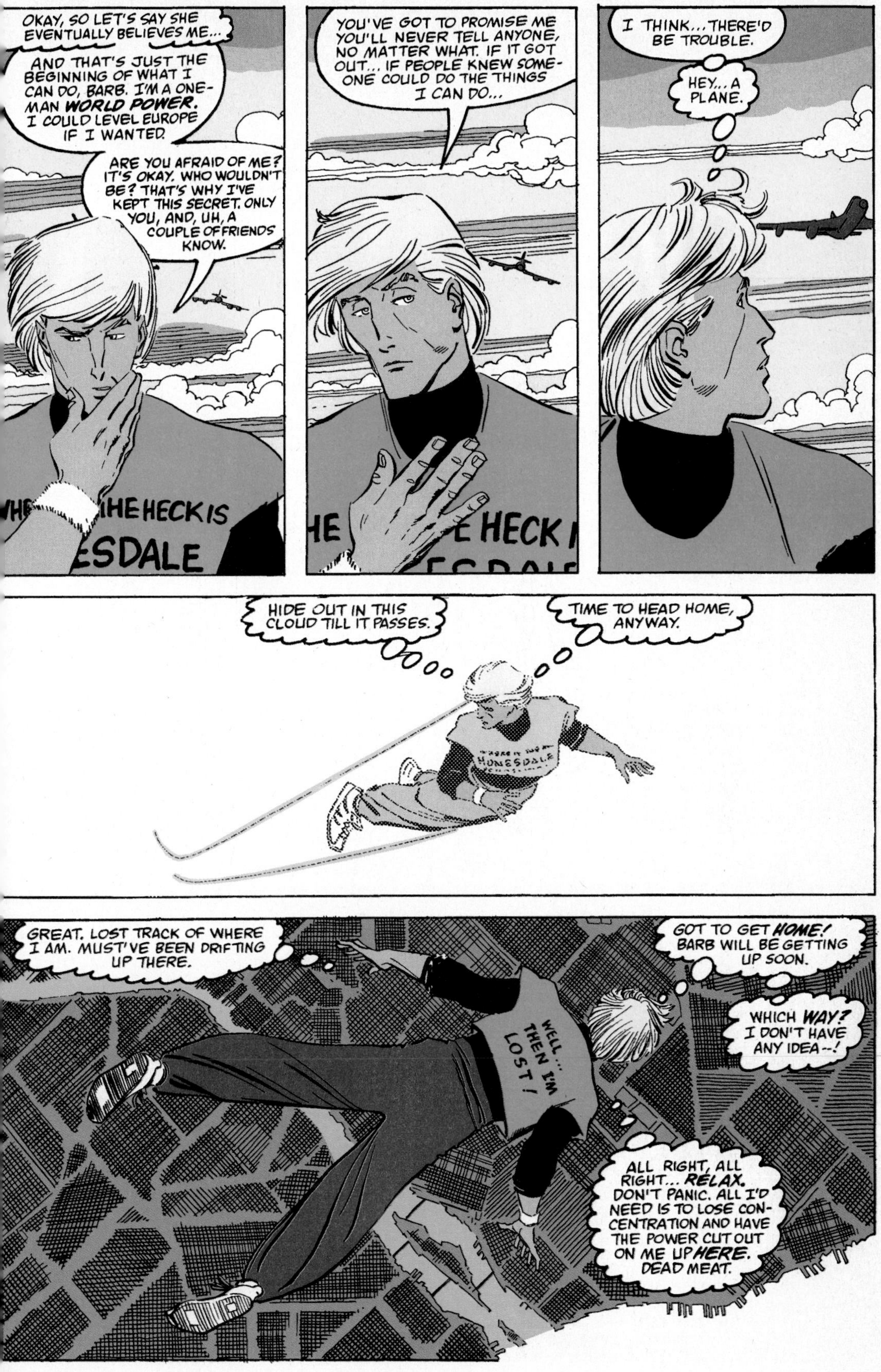

OKAY, SO LET'S SAY SHE EVENTUALLY BELIEVES ME...
AND THAT'S JUST THE BEGINNING OF WHAT I CAN DO, BARB. I'M A ONE-MAN WORLD POWER. I COULD LEVEL EUROPE IF I WANTED.
ARE YOU AFRAID OF ME? IT'S OKAY. WHO WOULDN'T BE? THAT'S WHY I'VE KEPT THIS SECRET. ONLY YOU, AND, UH, A COUPLE OF FRIENDS KNOW.
YOU'VE GOT TO PROMISE ME YOU'LL NEVER TELL ANYONE, NO MATTER WHAT. IF IT GOT OUT... IF PEOPLE KNEW SOMEONE COULD DO THE THINGS I CAN DO...
I THINK... THERE'D BE TROUBLE.
HEY... A PLANE.
HIDE OUT IN THIS CLOUD TILL IT PASSES.
TIME TO HEAD HOME, ANYWAY.
GREAT. LOST TRACK OF WHERE I AM. MUST'VE BEEN DRIFTING UP THERE.
GOT TO GET HOME! BARB WILL BE GETTING UP SOON.
WHICH WAY? I DON'T HAVE ANY IDEA--!
WELL... THEN I'M LOST!
ALL RIGHT, ALL RIGHT... RELAX. DON'T PANIC. ALL I'D NEED IS TO LOSE CONCENTRATION AND HAVE THE POWER CUT OUT ON ME UP HERE. DEAD MEAT.

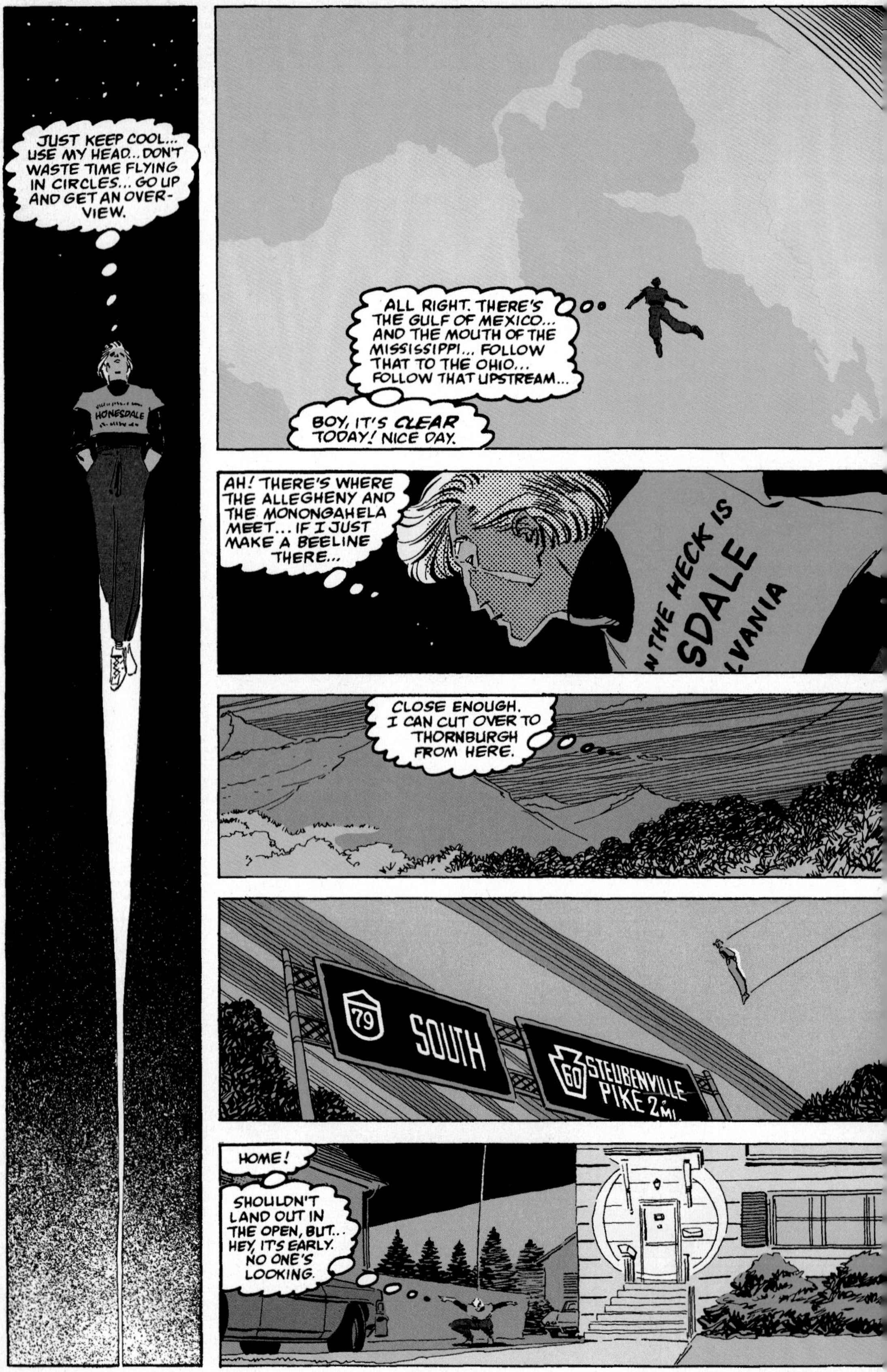

JUST KEEP COOL... USE MY HEAD... DON'T WASTE TIME FLYING IN CIRCLES... GO UP AND GET AN OVER-VIEW.
HONESDALE
ALL RIGHT. THERE'S THE GULF OF MEXICO... AND THE MOUTH OF THE MISSISSIPPI... FOLLOW THAT TO THE OHIO... FOLLOW THAT UPSTREAM...
BOY, IT'S CLEAR TODAY! NICE DAY.
AH! THERE'S WHERE THE ALLEGHENY AND THE MONONGAHELA MEET... IF I JUST MAKE A BEELINE THERE...
CLOSE ENOUGH. I CAN CUT OVER TO THORNBURGH FROM HERE.
79
SOUTH
60
STEUBENVILLE PIKE 2 MI
HOME!
SHOULDN'T LAND OUT IN THE OPEN, BUT... HEY, IT'S EARLY. NO ONE'S LOOKING.

INSIDE...

HM HM HUH-HM-HMM...! BUT YOU'RE GONNA FACE A MOMENT OF TRUTH..!

THREE SCOOPS... FOUR SCOOPS... FI-- OOPS! BARB DOESN'T LIKE IT THAT STRONG...

...THE HM HM-HM OF WHAT BEGAN WITH A PASSIONATE START... BUT THAT CAN'T HAPPEN TO US... 'CAUSE IT'S ALWAYS BEEN A MATTER OF TRUST..

MINUTES LATER...

'MORNING, LOVE. HOW MANY?

SOUNDS DIFFICULT.

FIFTY-SIX GOOD ONES... AND A COUPLE OF CHEATS...

IT IS...

...WITH THE POWER OFF, THAT IS.

I SMELL COFFEE! YOU'RE... GREAT!

UH-HUH. SO LET'S FOOL AROUND. WHAT DO YOU SAY?

OH, KEN--! WE CAN'T NOW. IT'S ALMOST TIME TO GET THE KIDS READY FOR SCHOOL.

SOON...

'BYE, MOMMY! 'BYE, KEN!

WATASH ELEMENTARY

HAVE A GOOD DAY, TROOPS!

AND...

KEN... MAY I ASK YOU SOMETHING? ARE YOU SECRETLY A SATANIST?

WHAT?

WHEN YOU WERE EXERCISING I NOTICED THAT STRANGE TATTOO, OR WHATEVER IT IS ON YOUR FOOT. JUST LIKE THE ONE THAT USED TO BE ON YOUR PALM.

I KNOW, THEY WASH OFF WITH A SPECIAL SOAP, RIGHT? BUT WHAT IS IT WITH THOSE THINGS? WHY DO YOU KEEP PUTTING THEM ON?

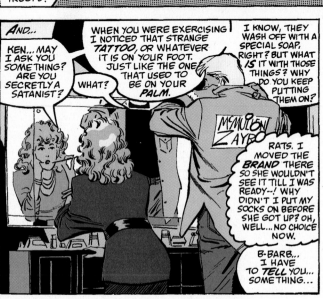

McMULÓN ZAYRO

RATS. I MOVED THE BRAND THERE SO SHE WOULDN'T SEE IT TILL I WAS READY--! WHY DIDN'T I PUT MY SOCKS ON BEFORE SHE GOT UP? OH, WELL... NO CHOICE NOW.

B-BARB... I HAVE TO TELL YOU... SOMETHING...

YES?

I, UH... FORGOT ALL ABOUT THAT DUMB FAKE TATTOO ON MY HEEL. I, UH... GOT IT AT A PARTY A WHILE BACK. I'LL, UH... GET IT OFF AT WORK TODAY. LACQUER THINNER OUGHTTA DO IT...

131

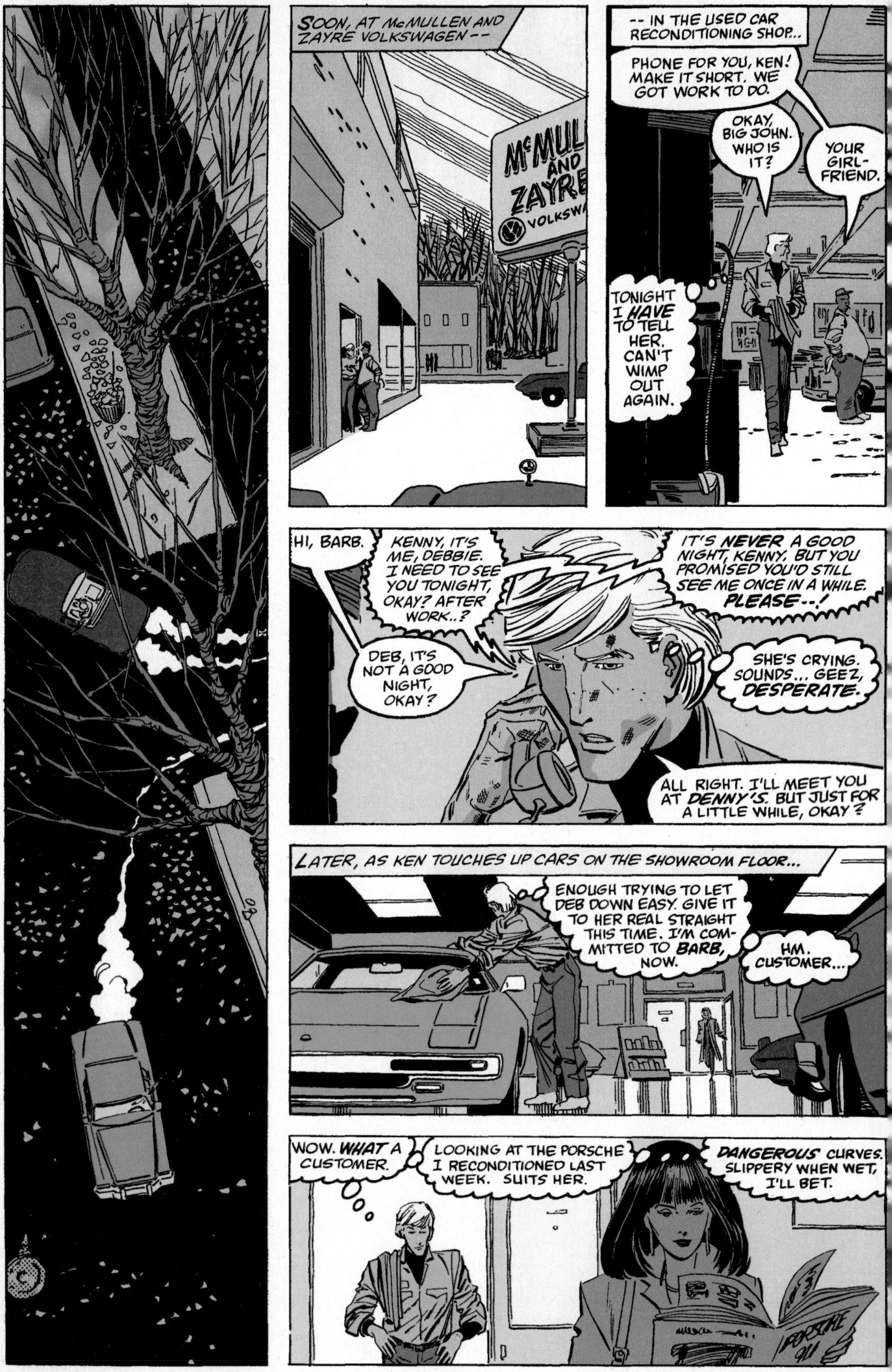

SOON, AT McMULLEN AND ZAYRE VOLKSWAGEN --
McMULL AND ZAYRE VOLKSWA
-- IN THE USED CAR RECONDITIONING SHOP...
PHONE FOR YOU, KEN! MAKE IT SHORT. WE GOT WORK TO DO.
OKAY, BIG JOHN. WHO IS IT?
YOUR GIRL-FRIEND.
TONIGHT I HAVE TO TELL HER. CAN'T WIMP OUT AGAIN.
HI, BARB.
KENNY, IT'S ME, DEBBIE. I NEED TO SEE YOU TONIGHT, OKAY? AFTER WORK..?
DEB, IT'S NOT A GOOD NIGHT, OKAY?
IT'S NEVER A GOOD NIGHT, KENNY. BUT YOU PROMISED YOU'D STILL SEE ME ONCE IN A WHILE. PLEASE--!
SHE'S CRYING. SOUNDS... GEEZ, DESPERATE.
ALL RIGHT. I'LL MEET YOU AT DENNY'S. BUT JUST FOR A LITTLE WHILE, OKAY?
LATER, AS KEN TOUCHES UP CARS ON THE SHOWROOM FLOOR...
ENOUGH TRYING TO LET DEB DOWN EASY. GIVE IT TO HER REAL STRAIGHT THIS TIME. I'M COMMITTED TO BARB, NOW.
HM. CUSTOMER...
WOW. WHAT A CUSTOMER.
LOOKING AT THE PORSCHE I RECONDITIONED LAST WEEK. SUITS HER.
DANGEROUS CURVES. SLIPPERY WHEN WET, I'LL BET.
PORSCHE 911

KENNETH! VAHT IS YOU ARE DOING?

VIPING DOWN CARS VAS IS DUSTY, EMIL.

WIPING DOWN DUSTY CARS, MR. VAJDAK.

ZO! ZIS CAN VAIT. MR. ZAYRE VOULD LIKE THAT YOU COME TO HIS OFFICE. IN-*MEDIATELY!*

AND...

HELLO, MR. ZAYRE. YOU WANTED TO SEE ME?

RIGHT. COME ON IN.

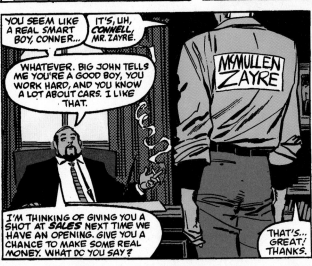

YOU SEEM LIKE A REAL SMART BOY, CONNER...

IT'S, UH, *CONNELL*, MR. ZAYRE.

WHATEVER. BIG JOHN TELLS ME YOU'RE A GOOD BOY, YOU WORK HARD, AND YOU KNOW A LOT ABOUT CARS. I LIKE THAT.

I'M THINKING OF GIVING YOU A SHOT AT *SALES* NEXT TIME WE HAVE AN OPENING. GIVE YOU A CHANCE TO MAKE SOME REAL MONEY. WHAT DO YOU SAY?

McMULLEN ZAYRE

THAT'S... GREAT! THANKS.

YEAH. OKAY, KID, BACK TO WORK. OH, AND WHEN YOU GO BACK DOWN TO THE BASEMENT, TAKE MY CADDY AND GIVE IT A WASH, WILLYA? IT'S IN THE MAIN SHOP GETTING GREASED.

SHORTLY...

"SMART BOY." HUH. THAT LARDBUTT MAKES MY SKIN CRAWL. MORE THAN EMIL DOES.

BUT, WOW, A SALES-MAN JOB--! I *KNOW* I CAN SELL CARS... AND START BRINGING HOME SOME DECENT MONEY... MAKE LIFE A LITTLE EASIER AND BETTER FOR BARB... AND HER KIDS.

OUR KIDS, NOW...SORT OF, I GUESS. PACKAGE DEAL. THEY COME WITH BARB. IF I'M GOING TO BE IN THE FAMILY, I'VE *GOT* TO CONTRIBUTE MORE.

ELEVATOR

I *NEED* THAT JOB.

HMPH. I *DON'T* NEED TO SEE MORE OF LARDBUTT AND EMIL, THOUGH. AND THEY'RE ALWAYS RIDING THE SALES GUYS.

PACKAGE DEAL.

OH, WELL.

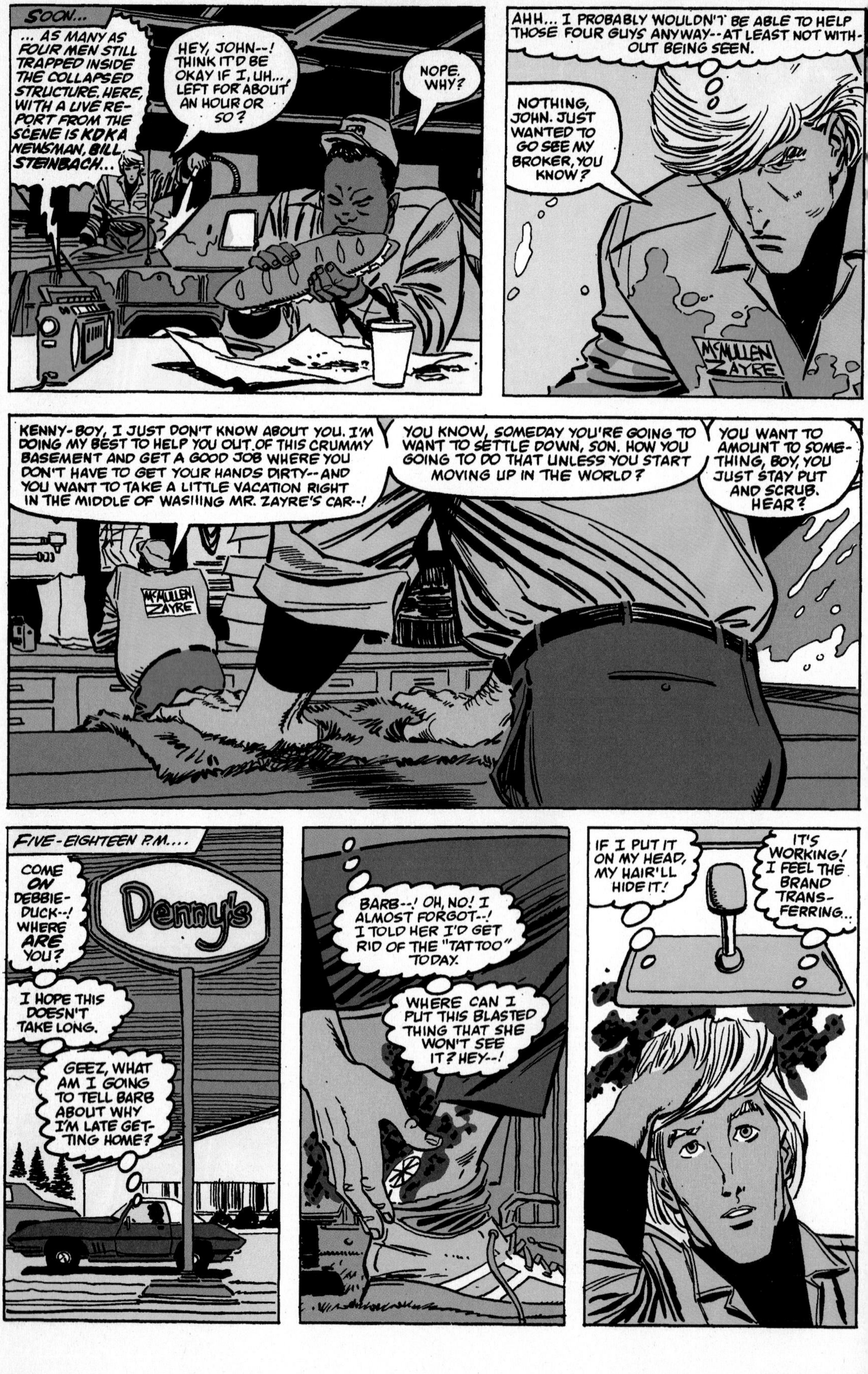
SOON...
... AS MANY AS FOUR MEN STILL TRAPPED INSIDE THE COLLAPSED STRUCTURE. HERE, WITH A LIVE REPORT FROM THE SCENE IS KDKA NEWSMAN, BILL STEINBACH...
HEY, JOHN--! THINK IT'D BE OKAY IF I, UH... LEFT FOR ABOUT AN HOUR OR SO?
NOPE. WHY?
AHH... I PROBABLY WOULDN'T BE ABLE TO HELP THOSE FOUR GUYS ANYWAY--AT LEAST NOT WITHOUT BEING SEEN.
NOTHING, JOHN. JUST WANTED TO GO SEE MY BROKER, YOU KNOW?
McMULLEN ZAYRE
KENNY-BOY, I JUST DON'T KNOW ABOUT YOU. I'M DOING MY BEST TO HELP YOU OUT OF THIS CRUMMY BASEMENT AND GET A GOOD JOB WHERE YOU DON'T HAVE TO GET YOUR HANDS DIRTY--AND YOU WANT TO TAKE A LITTLE VACATION RIGHT IN THE MIDDLE OF WASHING MR. ZAYRE'S CAR--!
YOU KNOW, SOMEDAY YOU'RE GOING TO WANT TO SETTLE DOWN, SON. HOW YOU GOING TO DO THAT UNLESS YOU START MOVING UP IN THE WORLD?
YOU WANT TO AMOUNT TO SOMETHING, BOY, YOU JUST STAY PUT AND SCRUB. HEAR?
McMULLEN ZAYRE
FIVE-EIGHTEEN P.M....
COME ON DEBBIE-DUCK--! WHERE ARE YOU?
Denny's
I HOPE THIS DOESN'T TAKE LONG.
GEEZ, WHAT AM I GOING TO TELL BARB ABOUT WHY I'M LATE GETTING HOME?
BARB--! OH, NO! I ALMOST FORGOT--! I TOLD HER I'D GET RID OF THE "TATTOO" TODAY.
WHERE CAN I PUT THIS BLASTED THING THAT SHE WON'T SEE IT? HEY--!
IF I PUT IT ON MY HEAD, MY HAIR'LL HIDE IT!
IT'S WORKING! I FEEL THE BRAND TRANSFERRING...

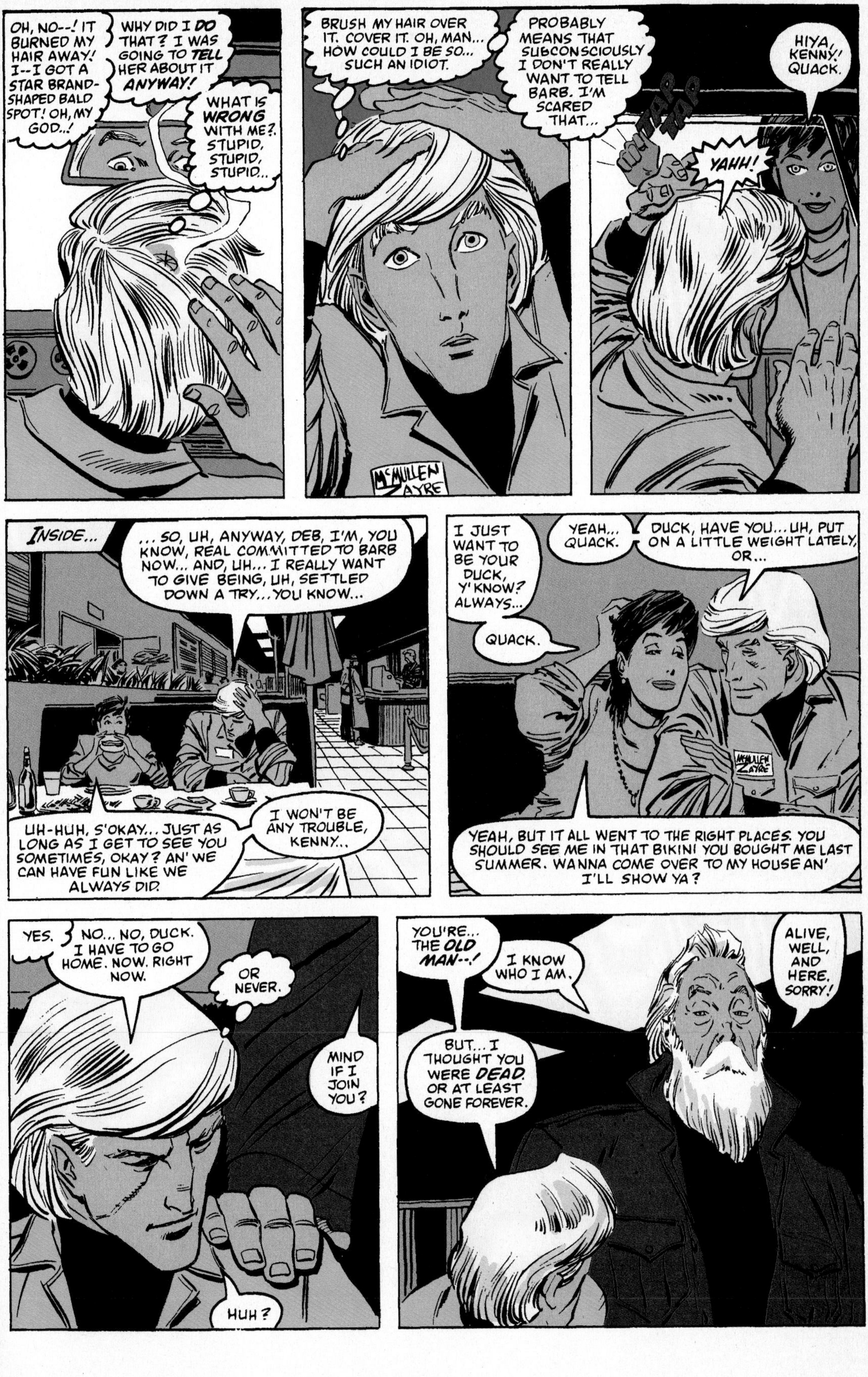
OH, NO--! IT BURNED MY HAIR AWAY! I--I GOT A STAR BRAND-SHAPED BALD SPOT! OH, MY GOD..!
WHY DID I DO THAT? I WAS GOING TO TELL HER ABOUT IT ANYWAY!
WHAT IS WRONG WITH ME?. STUPID, STUPID, STUPID...
BRUSH MY HAIR OVER IT. COVER IT. OH, MAN... HOW COULD I BE SO... SUCH AN IDIOT.
PROBABLY MEANS THAT SUBCONSCIOUSLY I DON'T REALLY WANT TO TELL BARB. I'M SCARED THAT...
McMULLEN ZAYRE
HIYA, KENNY! QUACK.
TAP TAP
YAHH!
INSIDE...
...SO, UH, ANYWAY, DEB, I'M, YOU KNOW, REAL COMMITTED TO BARB NOW... AND, UH... I REALLY WANT TO GIVE BEING, UH, SETTLED DOWN A TRY... YOU KNOW...
UH-HUH, S'OKAY... JUST AS LONG AS I GET TO SEE YOU SOMETIMES, OKAY? AN' WE CAN HAVE FUN LIKE WE ALWAYS DID.
I WON'T BE ANY TROUBLE, KENNY...
I JUST WANT TO BE YOUR DUCK, Y'KNOW? ALWAYS...
QUACK.
YEAH... QUACK.
DUCK, HAVE YOU... UH, PUT ON A LITTLE WEIGHT LATELY, OR...
McMULLEN ZAYRE
YEAH, BUT IT ALL WENT TO THE RIGHT PLACES. YOU SHOULD SEE ME IN THAT BIKINI YOU BOUGHT ME LAST SUMMER. WANNA COME OVER TO MY HOUSE AN' I'LL SHOW YA?
YES.
NO... NO, DUCK. I HAVE TO GO HOME. NOW. RIGHT NOW.
OR NEVER.
MIND IF I JOIN YOU?
HUH?
YOU'RE... THE OLD MAN--!
I KNOW WHO I AM.
ALIVE, WELL, AND HERE. SORRY!
BUT... I THOUGHT YOU WERE DEAD. OR AT LEAST GONE FOREVER.

MISS, DO YOU HAVE ANY BIRD'S EGGS?

JUST, UH... REGULAR CHICKEN EGGS.

GIVE ME SIX. RAW.

O-KAY...

KENNY, WHO IS THIS?

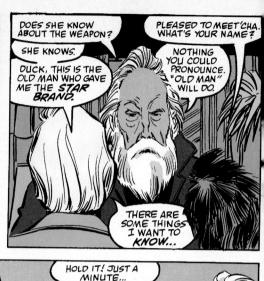

DOES SHE KNOW ABOUT THE WEAPON?

SHE KNOWS.

DUCK, THIS IS THE OLD MAN WHO GAVE ME THE STAR BRAND.

PLEASED TO MEET'CHA. WHAT'S YOUR NAME?

NOTHING YOU COULD PRONOUNCE. "OLD MAN" WILL DO.

THERE ARE SOME THINGS I WANT TO KNOW...

...LIKE, WHERE ARE YOU FROM? WHY DID YOU GIVE ME THIS "WEAPON"... THEN FAKE YOUR OWN DEATH AND VANISH?

THAT ALIEN, SPACEMAN, WHATEVER, WHO ATTACKED ME--DID YOU HAVE SOMETHING TO DO WITH THAT? WAS IT YOU WHO LEFT ME THOSE INDESTRUCTIBLE CLOTHES? WHY DID...

HOLD IT! JUST A MINUTE...

YOU ASK TOO MANY QUESTIONS.

I GAVE YOU THE WEAPON FOR THE SAME REASON ATLAS GAVE HERCULES THE SKY TO HOLD. THE BURDEN HAD BECOME WEARISOME.

I GATHER THAT IT HAS CAUSED SOME INCONVENIENCE, TOO... OR ELSE YOU WOULDN'T HAVE PLACED IT IN ITS PRESENT... PECULIAR LOCATION.

ARE YOU HERE TO... TAKE IT BACK?

TAKE? NO, NO...IT'S YOURS, NOW. NOT MINE TO TAKE...EVEN IF SUCH A THING WERE POSSIBLE.

I CAME BACK BECAUSE HONOR DEMANDS THAT I INFORM YOU OF SOME THINGS THAT YOU, AS THE BEARER OF THE WEAPON, SHOULD ATTEND TO.

LIKE WHAT?

THIS ISN'T THE PLACE TO DISCUSS IT. WE'LL TALK LATER. I'LL CALL YOU.

OH, AND JUST A WORD OF ADVICE-- IF YOU MOVE IT AGAIN -- SAY, WHEN YOU GO TO YOUR BARBER -- KEEP IT ON THE OUTSIDE OF YOUR BODY. IT WASN'T DESIGNED FOR MUCOUS MEMBRANES. UNDERSTAND?

WOW. I-- I DON'T KNOW WHAT TO MAKE OF THIS. I NEVER EXPECTED TO SEE HIM AGAIN.

DON'T WORRY, KENNY! EVERYTHING'LL BE ALL RIGHT!

YEAH... I GUESS. I'D BETTER GO, DUCK.

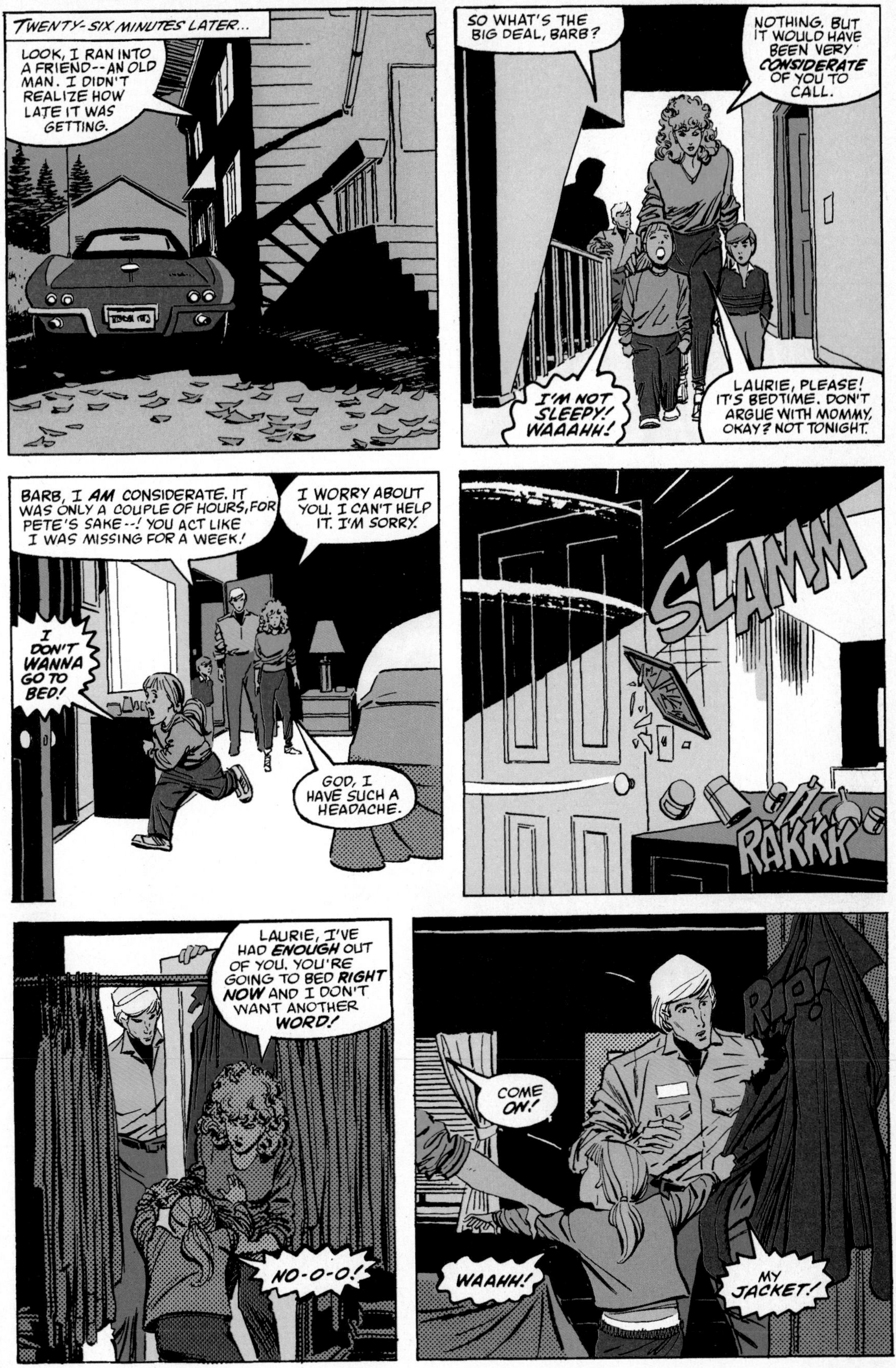

TWENTY-SIX MINUTES LATER...
LOOK, I RAN INTO A FRIEND--AN OLD MAN. I DIDN'T REALIZE HOW LATE IT WAS GETTING.
SO WHAT'S THE BIG DEAL, BARB?
NOTHING. BUT IT WOULD HAVE BEEN VERY CONSIDERATE OF YOU TO CALL.
I'M NOT SLEEPY! WAAAHH!
LAURIE, PLEASE! IT'S BEDTIME. DON'T ARGUE WITH MOMMY, OKAY? NOT TONIGHT.
BARB, I AM CONSIDERATE. IT WAS ONLY A COUPLE OF HOURS, FOR PETE'S SAKE--! YOU ACT LIKE I WAS MISSING FOR A WEEK!
I WORRY ABOUT YOU. I CAN'T HELP IT. I'M SORRY.
I DON'T WANNA GO TO BED!
GOD, I HAVE SUCH A HEADACHE.
SLAMM
RAKKK
LAURIE, I'VE HAD ENOUGH OUT OF YOU. YOU'RE GOING TO BED RIGHT NOW AND I DON'T WANT ANOTHER WORD!
NO-O-O!
RIP!
COME ON!
WAAHH!
MY JACKET!

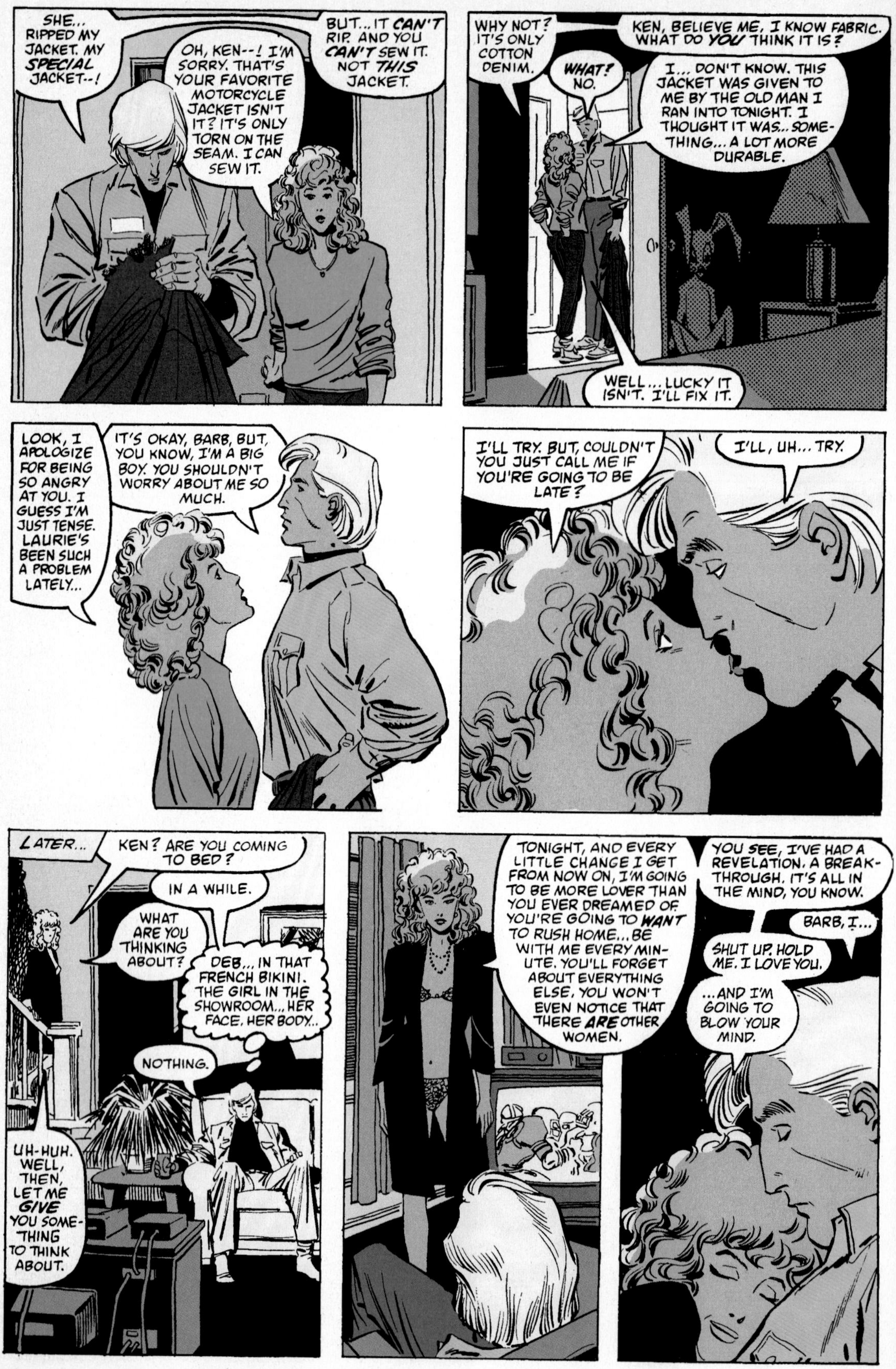
SHE... RIPPED MY JACKET. MY SPECIAL JACKET--!
OH, KEN--! I'M SORRY. THAT'S YOUR FAVORITE MOTORCYCLE JACKET ISN'T IT? IT'S ONLY TORN ON THE SEAM. I CAN SEW IT.
BUT... IT CAN'T RIP. AND YOU CAN'T SEW IT. NOT THIS JACKET.
WHY NOT? IT'S ONLY COTTON DENIM.
KEN, BELIEVE ME, I KNOW FABRIC. WHAT DO YOU THINK IT IS?
WHAT! NO.
I... DON'T KNOW. THIS JACKET WAS GIVEN TO ME BY THE OLD MAN I RAN INTO TONIGHT. I THOUGHT IT WAS... SOMETHING... A LOT MORE DURABLE.
WELL... LUCKY IT ISN'T. I'LL FIX IT.
LOOK, I APOLOGIZE FOR BEING SO ANGRY AT YOU. I GUESS I'M JUST TENSE. LAURIE'S BEEN SUCH A PROBLEM LATELY...
IT'S OKAY, BARB, BUT, YOU KNOW, I'M A BIG BOY. YOU SHOULDN'T WORRY ABOUT ME SO MUCH.
I'LL TRY. BUT, COULDN'T YOU JUST CALL ME IF YOU'RE GOING TO BE LATE?
I'LL, UH... TRY.
LATER...
KEN? ARE YOU COMING TO BED?
IN A WHILE.
WHAT ARE YOU THINKING ABOUT?
DEB... IN THAT FRENCH BIKINI. THE GIRL IN THE SHOWROOM... HER FACE. HER BODY...
NOTHING.
UH-HUH. WELL, THEN, LET ME GIVE YOU SOMETHING TO THINK ABOUT.
TONIGHT, AND EVERY LITTLE CHANCE I GET FROM NOW ON, I'M GOING TO BE MORE LOVER THAN YOU EVER DREAMED OF. YOU'RE GOING TO WANT TO RUSH HOME... BE WITH ME EVERY MINUTE. YOU'LL FORGET ABOUT EVERYTHING ELSE. YOU WON'T EVEN NOTICE THAT THERE ARE OTHER WOMEN.
YOU SEE, I'VE HAD A REVELATION. A BREAKTHROUGH. IT'S ALL IN THE MIND, YOU KNOW.
BARB, I...
SHUT UP. HOLD ME. I LOVE YOU.
...AND I'M GOING TO BLOW YOUR MIND.

I'LL BE WAITING.

NOT FOR LONG.

WOW.

MAN, I CAN'T... I JUST DON'T *UNDERSTAND*..! EVERY TIME I THINK I KNOW *ANYTHING*, SOMETHING HAPPENS. EVERYTHING *CHANGES*.

LIKE...THAT JACKET--! IT *CAN'T* BE JUST DENIM! IT SURVIVED A *NUCLEAR BLAST*! BUT...

BORROW BOBBY'S MICROSCOPE...

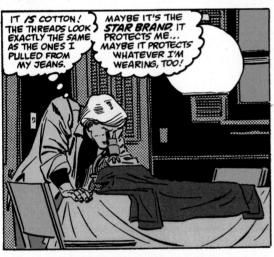

IT *IS* COTTON! THE THREADS LOOK EXACTLY THE SAME AS THE ONES I PULLED FROM MY JEANS.

MAYBE IT'S THE *STAR BRAND*, IT PROTECTS ME... MAYBE IT PROTECTS WHATEVER I'M WEARING, TOO!

NAH. THAT CAN'T BE IT. WHEN I'VE GOTTEN INTO TROUBLE WEARING JUST REGULAR CLOTHES THEY'VE GOTTEN TRASHED.

THINK I'LL TAKE A CLOSE LOOK AT THIS THING...

THERE GOES SOME MORE HAIR...

NOK NOK NOK

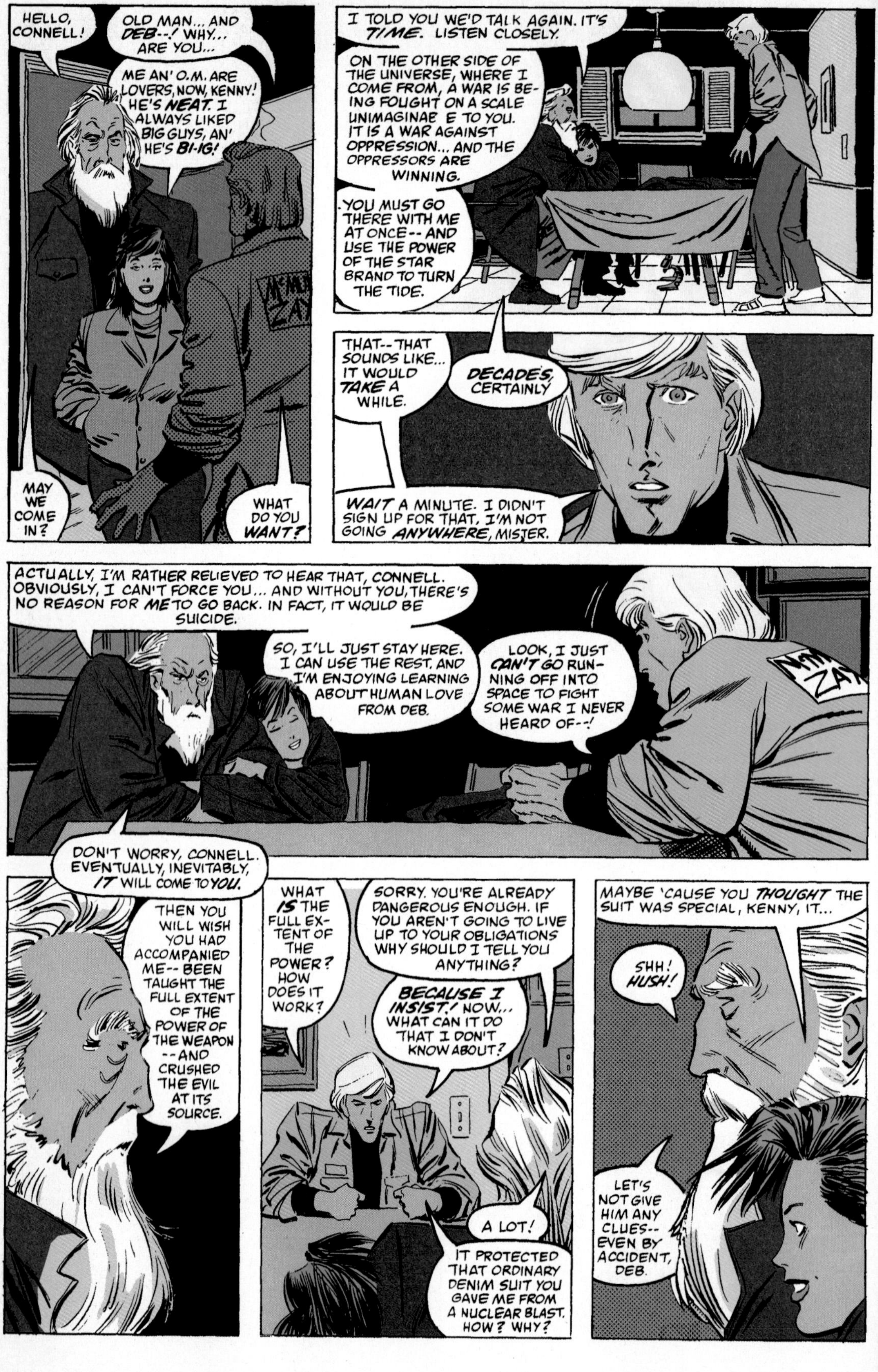
HELLO, CONNELL!
OLD MAN... AND DEB--! WHY... ARE YOU...
ME AN' O.M. ARE LOVERS, NOW, KENNY! HE'S NEAT. I ALWAYS LIKED BIG GUYS, AN' HE'S BI-IG!
MAY WE COME IN?
WHAT DO YOU WANT?
I TOLD YOU WE'D TALK AGAIN. IT'S TIME. LISTEN CLOSELY.
ON THE OTHER SIDE OF THE UNIVERSE, WHERE I COME FROM, A WAR IS BEING FOUGHT ON A SCALE UNIMAGINAE E TO YOU. IT IS A WAR AGAINST OPPRESSION... AND THE OPPRESSORS ARE WINNING.
YOU MUST GO THERE WITH ME AT ONCE-- AND USE THE POWER OF THE STAR BRAND TO TURN THE TIDE.
THAT-- THAT SOUNDS LIKE... IT WOULD TAKE A WHILE.
DECADES, CERTAINLY
WAIT A MINUTE. I DIDN'T SIGN UP FOR THAT. I'M NOT GOING ANYWHERE, MISTER.
ACTUALLY, I'M RATHER RELIEVED TO HEAR THAT, CONNELL. OBVIOUSLY, I CAN'T FORCE YOU... AND WITHOUT YOU, THERE'S NO REASON FOR ME TO GO BACK. IN FACT, IT WOULD BE SUICIDE.
SO, I'LL JUST STAY HERE. I CAN USE THE REST. AND I'M ENJOYING LEARNING ABOUT HUMAN LOVE FROM DEB.
LOOK, I JUST CAN'T GO RUNNING OFF INTO SPACE TO FIGHT SOME WAR I NEVER HEARD OF--!
DON'T WORRY, CONNELL. EVENTUALLY, INEVITABLY, IT WILL COME TO YOU.
THEN YOU WILL WISH YOU HAD ACCOMPANIED ME-- BEEN TAUGHT THE FULL EXTENT OF THE POWER OF THE WEAPON --AND CRUSHED THE EVIL AT ITS SOURCE.
WHAT IS THE FULL EXTENT OF THE POWER? HOW DOES IT WORK?
SORRY. YOU'RE ALREADY DANGEROUS ENOUGH. IF YOU AREN'T GOING TO LIVE UP TO YOUR OBLIGATIONS WHY SHOULD I TELL YOU ANYTHING?
BECAUSE I INSIST! NOW... WHAT CAN IT DO THAT I DON'T KNOW ABOUT?
A LOT!
IT PROTECTED THAT ORDINARY DENIM SUIT YOU GAVE ME FROM A NUCLEAR BLAST. HOW? WHY?
MAYBE 'CAUSE YOU THOUGHT THE SUIT WAS SPECIAL, KENNY, IT...
SHH! HUSH!
LET'S NOT GIVE HIM ANY CLUES-- EVEN BY ACCIDENT, DEB.

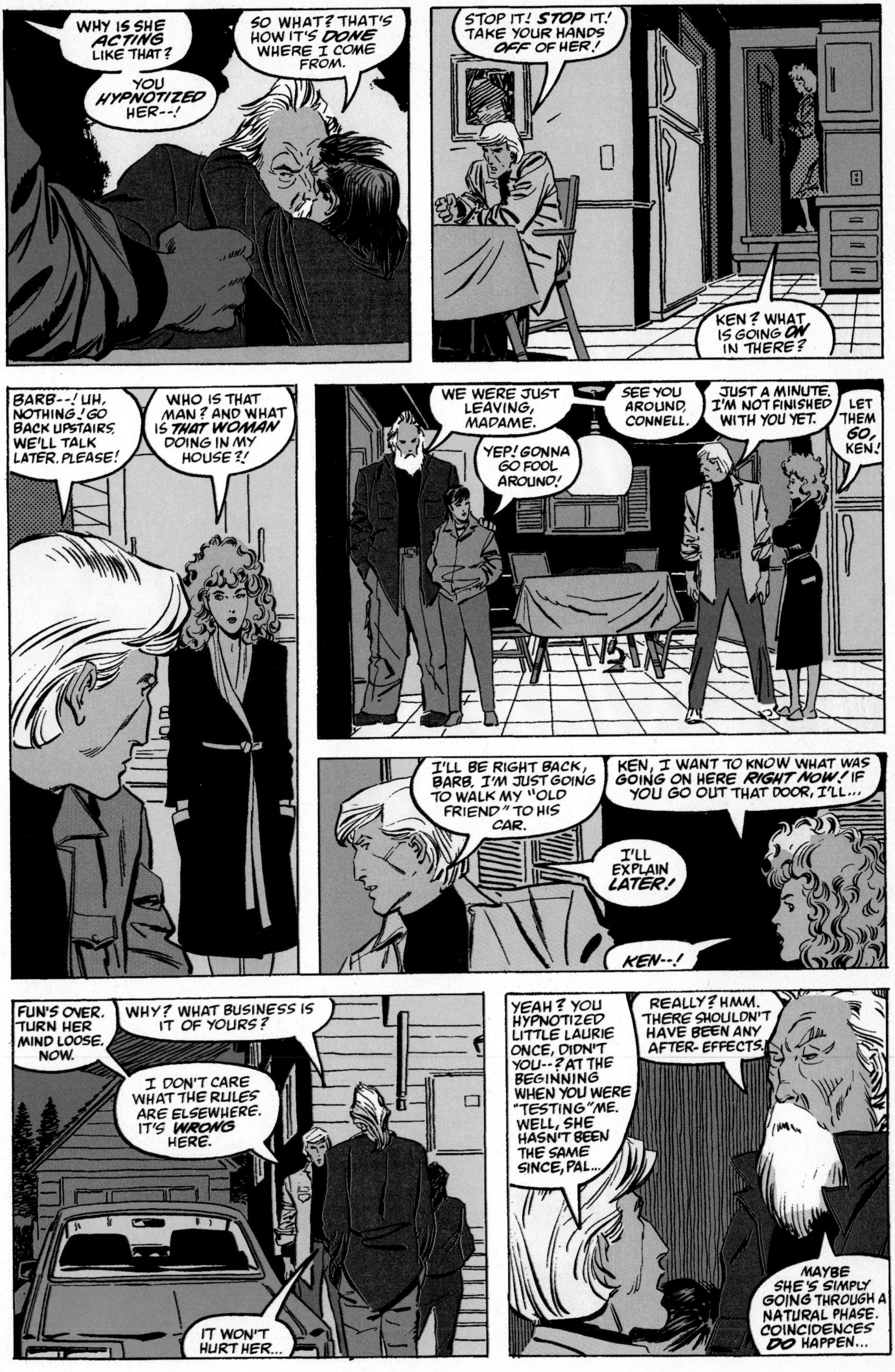
WHY IS SHE ACTING LIKE THAT?
YOU HYPNOTIZED HER--!
SO WHAT? THAT'S HOW IT'S DONE WHERE I COME FROM.
STOP IT! STOP IT! TAKE YOUR HANDS OFF OF HER!
KEN? WHAT IS GOING ON IN THERE?
BARB--! UH, NOTHING! GO BACK UPSTAIRS, WE'LL TALK LATER. PLEASE!
WHO IS THAT MAN? AND WHAT IS THAT WOMAN DOING IN MY HOUSE?!
WE WERE JUST LEAVING, MADAME.
YEP! GONNA GO FOOL AROUND!
SEE YOU AROUND, CONNELL.
JUST A MINUTE. I'M NOT FINISHED WITH YOU YET.
LET THEM GO, KEN!
I'LL BE RIGHT BACK, BARB. I'M JUST GOING TO WALK MY "OLD FRIEND" TO HIS CAR.
KEN, I WANT TO KNOW WHAT WAS GOING ON HERE RIGHT NOW! IF YOU GO OUT THAT DOOR, I'LL...
I'LL EXPLAIN LATER!
KEN--!
FUN'S OVER. TURN HER MIND LOOSE. NOW.
WHY? WHAT BUSINESS IS IT OF YOURS?
I DON'T CARE WHAT THE RULES ARE ELSEWHERE. IT'S WRONG HERE.
IT WON'T HURT HER...
YEAH? YOU HYPNOTIZED LITTLE LAURIE ONCE, DIDN'T YOU--? AT THE BEGINNING WHEN YOU WERE "TESTING" ME. WELL, SHE HASN'T BEEN THE SAME SINCE, PAL...
REALLY? HMM. THERE SHOULDN'T HAVE BEEN ANY AFTER-EFFECTS.
MAYBE SHE'S SIMPLY GOING THROUGH A NATURAL PHASE. COINCIDENCES DO HAPPEN...

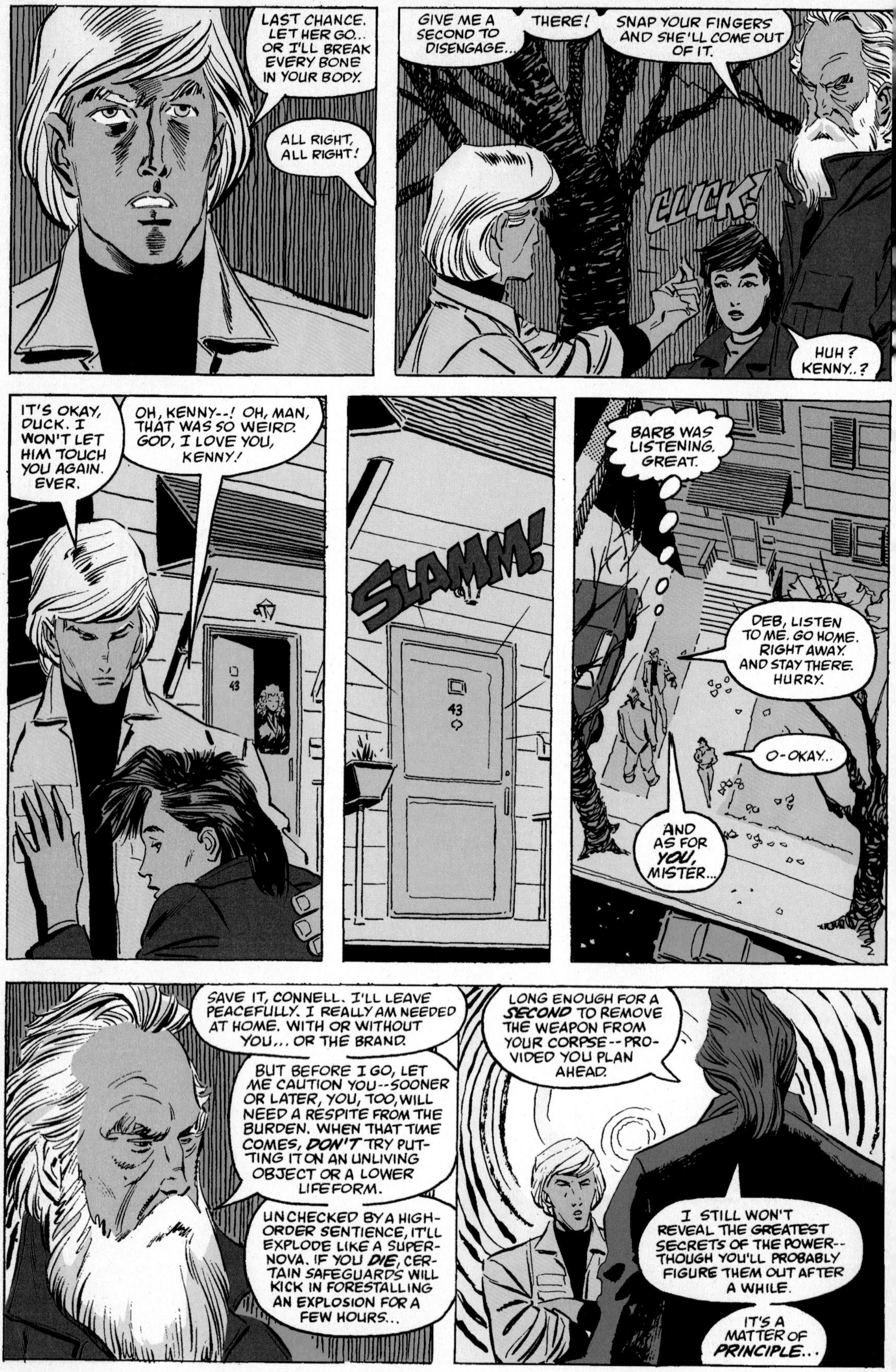
LAST CHANCE. LET HER GO... OR I'LL BREAK EVERY BONE IN YOUR BODY.
ALL RIGHT, ALL RIGHT!
GIVE ME A SECOND TO DISENGAGE...
THERE!
SNAP YOUR FINGERS AND SHE'LL COME OUT OF IT.
CLICK!
HUH? KENNY..?
IT'S OKAY, DUCK. I WON'T LET HIM TOUCH YOU AGAIN. EVER.
OH, KENNY--! OH, MAN, THAT WAS SO WEIRD. GOD, I LOVE YOU, KENNY!
SLAMM!
BARB WAS LISTENING. GREAT.
DEB, LISTEN TO ME. GO HOME. RIGHT AWAY. AND STAY THERE. HURRY.
O-OKAY...
AND AS FOR YOU, MISTER...
SAVE IT, CONNELL. I'LL LEAVE PEACEFULLY. I REALLY AM NEEDED AT HOME. WITH OR WITHOUT YOU... OR THE BRAND.
BUT BEFORE I GO, LET ME CAUTION YOU--SOONER OR LATER, YOU, TOO, WILL NEED A RESPITE FROM THE BURDEN. WHEN THAT TIME COMES, DON'T TRY PUTTING IT ON AN UNLIVING OBJECT OR A LOWER LIFEFORM.
UNCHECKED BY A HIGH-ORDER SENTIENCE, IT'LL EXPLODE LIKE A SUPERNOVA. IF YOU DIE, CERTAIN SAFEGUARDS WILL KICK IN FORESTALLING AN EXPLOSION FOR A FEW HOURS...
LONG ENOUGH FOR A SECOND TO REMOVE THE WEAPON FROM YOUR CORPSE--PROVIDED YOU PLAN AHEAD.
I STILL WON'T REVEAL THE GREATEST SECRETS OF THE POWER--THOUGH YOU'LL PROBABLY FIGURE THEM OUT AFTER A WHILE.
IT'S A MATTER OF PRINCIPLE...

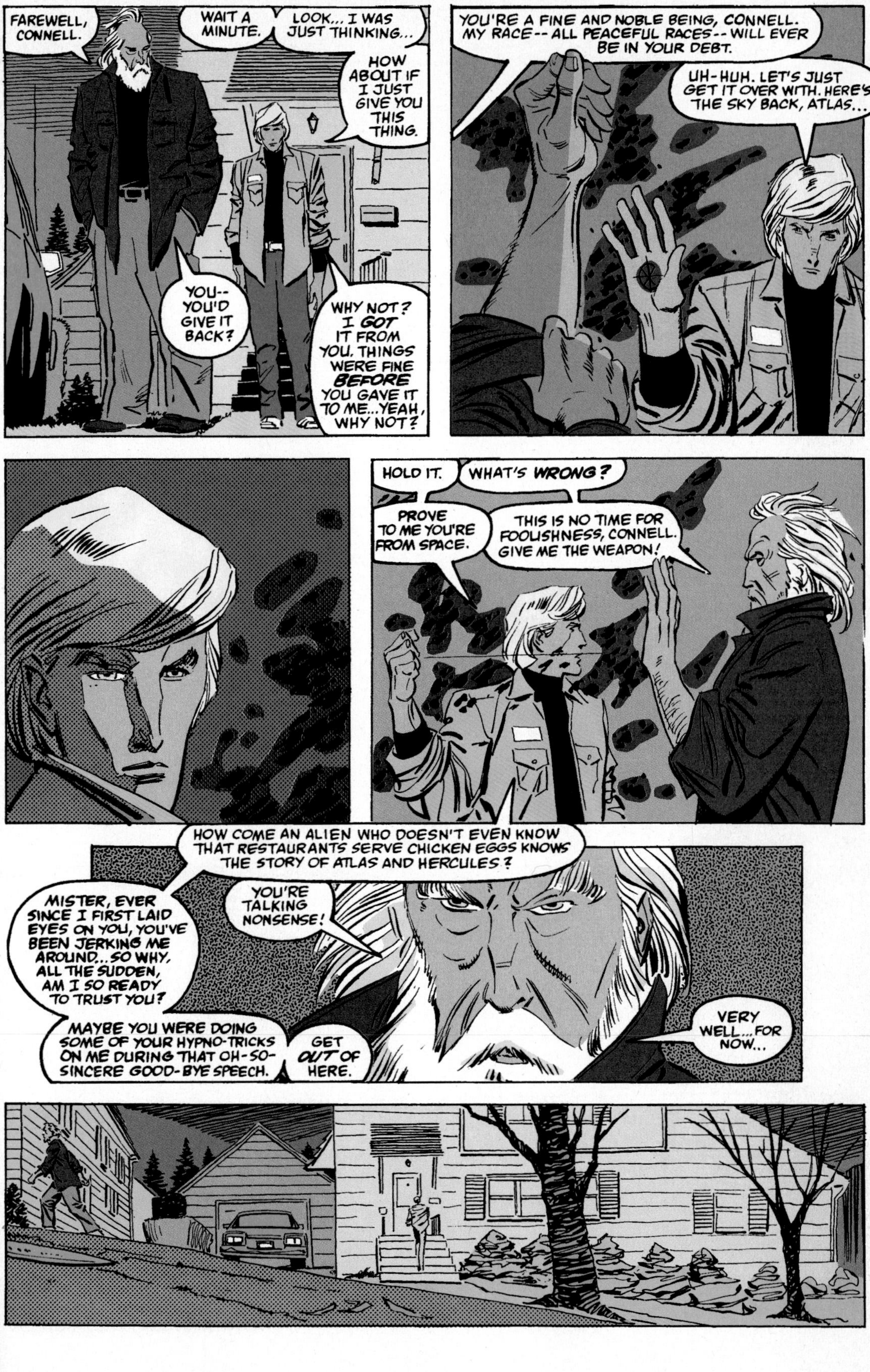
FAREWELL, CONNELL.
WAIT A MINUTE.
LOOK... I WAS JUST THINKING...
HOW ABOUT IF I JUST GIVE YOU THIS THING.
YOU-- YOU'D GIVE IT BACK?
WHY NOT? I GOT IT FROM YOU. THINGS WERE FINE BEFORE YOU GAVE IT TO ME...YEAH, WHY NOT?
YOU'RE A FINE AND NOBLE BEING, CONNELL. MY RACE-- ALL PEACEFUL RACES-- WILL EVER BE IN YOUR DEBT.
UH-HUH. LET'S JUST GET IT OVER WITH. HERE'S THE SKY BACK, ATLAS...
HOLD IT.
WHAT'S WRONG?
PROVE TO ME YOU'RE FROM SPACE.
THIS IS NO TIME FOR FOOLISHNESS, CONNELL. GIVE ME THE WEAPON!
HOW COME AN ALIEN WHO DOESN'T EVEN KNOW THAT RESTAURANTS SERVE CHICKEN EGGS KNOWS THE STORY OF ATLAS AND HERCULES?
MISTER, EVER SINCE I FIRST LAID EYES ON YOU, YOU'VE BEEN JERKING ME AROUND...SO WHY, ALL THE SUDDEN, AM I SO READY TO TRUST YOU?
YOU'RE TALKING NONSENSE!
MAYBE YOU WERE DOING SOME OF YOUR HYPNO-TRICKS ON ME DURING THAT OH-SO-SINCERE GOOD-BYE SPEECH.
GET OUT OF HERE.
VERY WELL...FOR NOW...

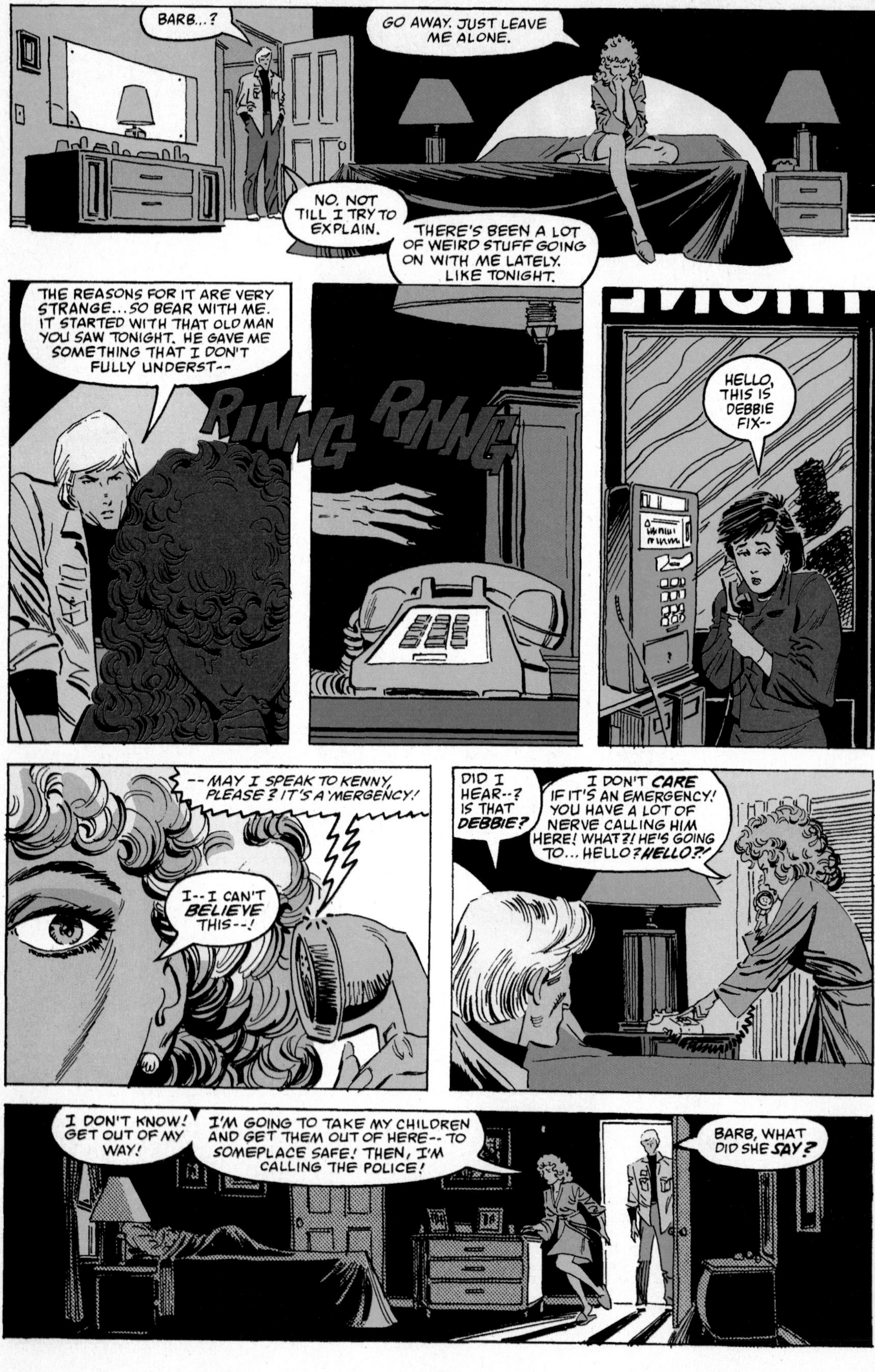

BARB...?
GO AWAY. JUST LEAVE ME ALONE.
NO. NOT TILL I TRY TO EXPLAIN.
THERE'S BEEN A LOT OF WEIRD STUFF GOING ON WITH ME LATELY. LIKE TONIGHT.
THE REASONS FOR IT ARE VERY STRANGE... SO BEAR WITH ME. IT STARTED WITH THAT OLD MAN YOU SAW TONIGHT. HE GAVE ME SOMETHING THAT I DON'T FULLY UNDERST--
RINNG RINNG
HELLO, THIS IS DEBBIE FIX--
--MAY I SPEAK TO KENNY, PLEASE? IT'S A 'MERGENCY!
I--I CAN'T BELIEVE THIS--!
DID I HEAR--? IS THAT DEBBIE?
I DON'T CARE IF IT'S AN EMERGENCY! YOU HAVE A LOT OF NERVE CALLING HIM HERE! WHAT?! HE'S GOING TO... HELLO? HELLO?!
I DON'T KNOW! GET OUT OF MY WAY!
I'M GOING TO TAKE MY CHILDREN AND GET THEM OUT OF HERE-- TO SOMEPLACE SAFE! THEN, I'M CALLING THE POLICE!
BARB, WHAT DID SHE SAY?

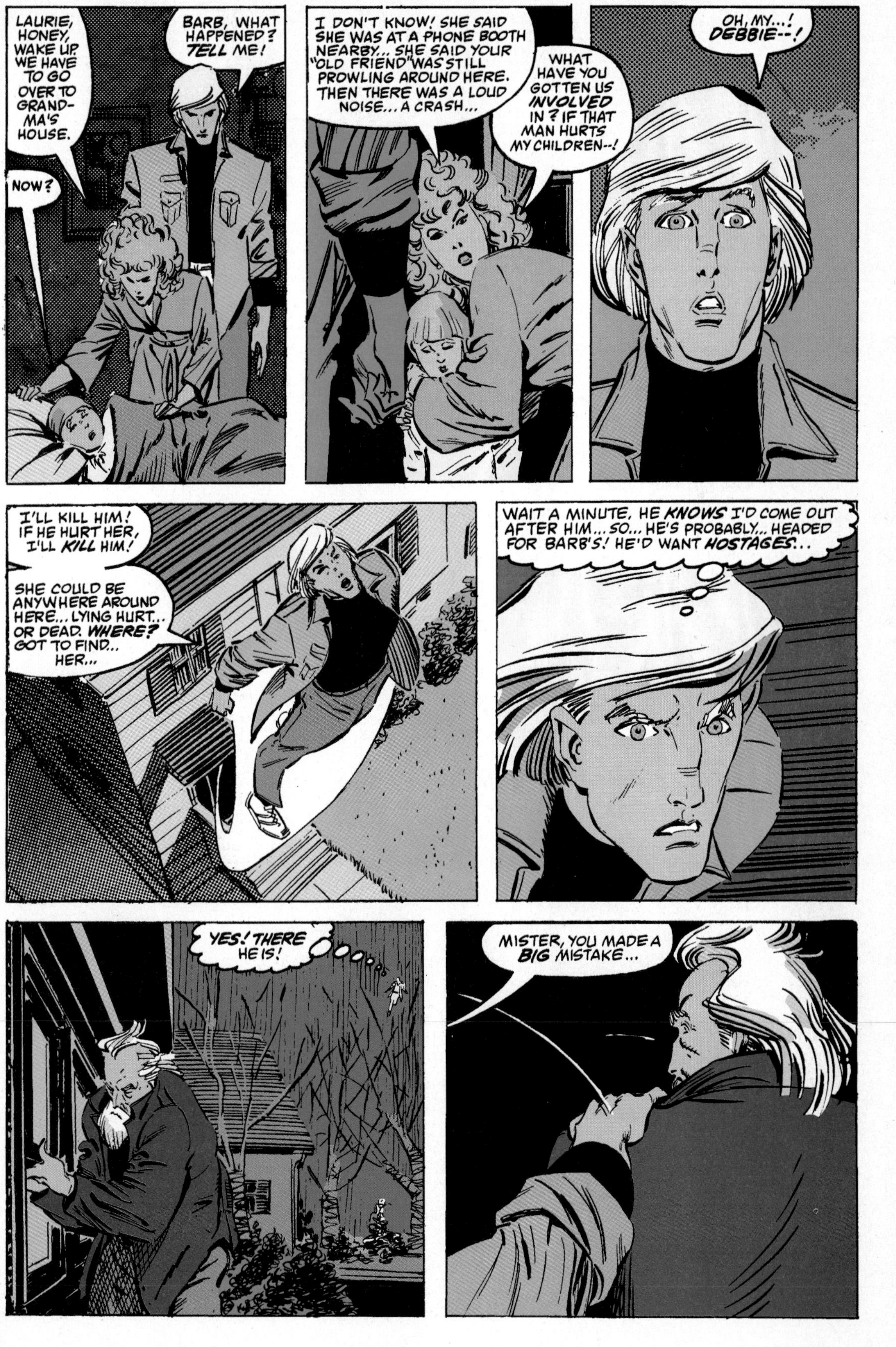
LAURIE, HONEY, WAKE UP. WE HAVE TO GO OVER TO GRAND-MA'S HOUSE.
BARB, WHAT HAPPENED? TELL ME!
NOW?
I DON'T KNOW! SHE SAID SHE WAS AT A PHONE BOOTH NEARBY... SHE SAID YOUR "OLD FRIEND" WAS STILL PROWLING AROUND HERE. THEN THERE WAS A LOUD NOISE... A CRASH...
WHAT HAVE YOU GOTTEN US INVOLVED IN? IF THAT MAN HURTS MY CHILDREN--!
OH, MY...! DEBBIE--!
I'LL KILL HIM! IF HE HURT HER, I'LL KILL HIM!
SHE COULD BE ANYWHERE AROUND HERE... LYING HURT... OR DEAD. WHERE? GOT TO FIND... HER...
WAIT A MINUTE. HE KNOWS I'D COME OUT AFTER HIM... SO... HE'S PROBABLY... HEADED FOR BARB'S! HE'D WANT HOSTAGES...
YES! THERE HE IS!
MISTER, YOU MADE A BIG MISTAKE...

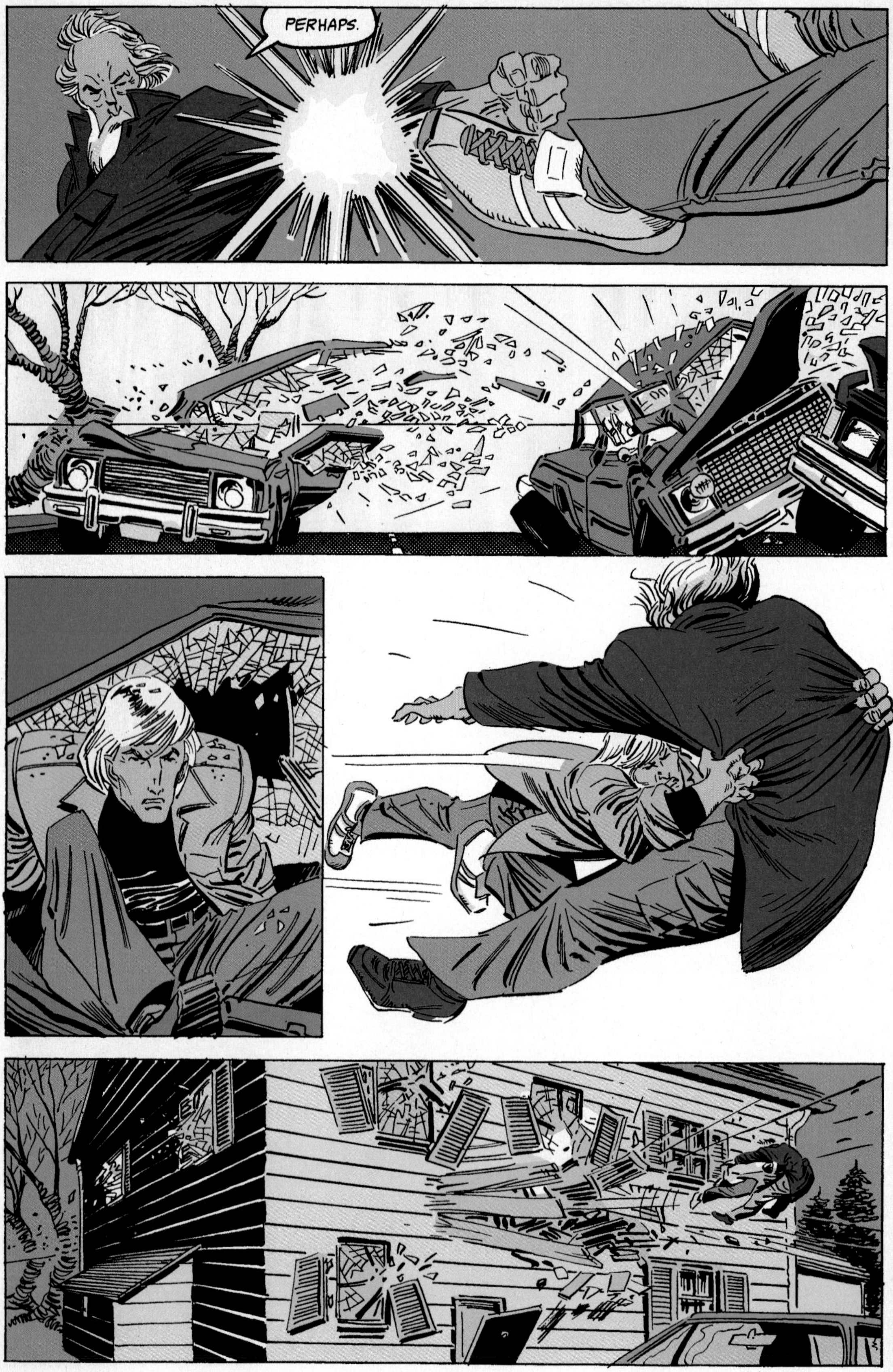
PERHAPS.

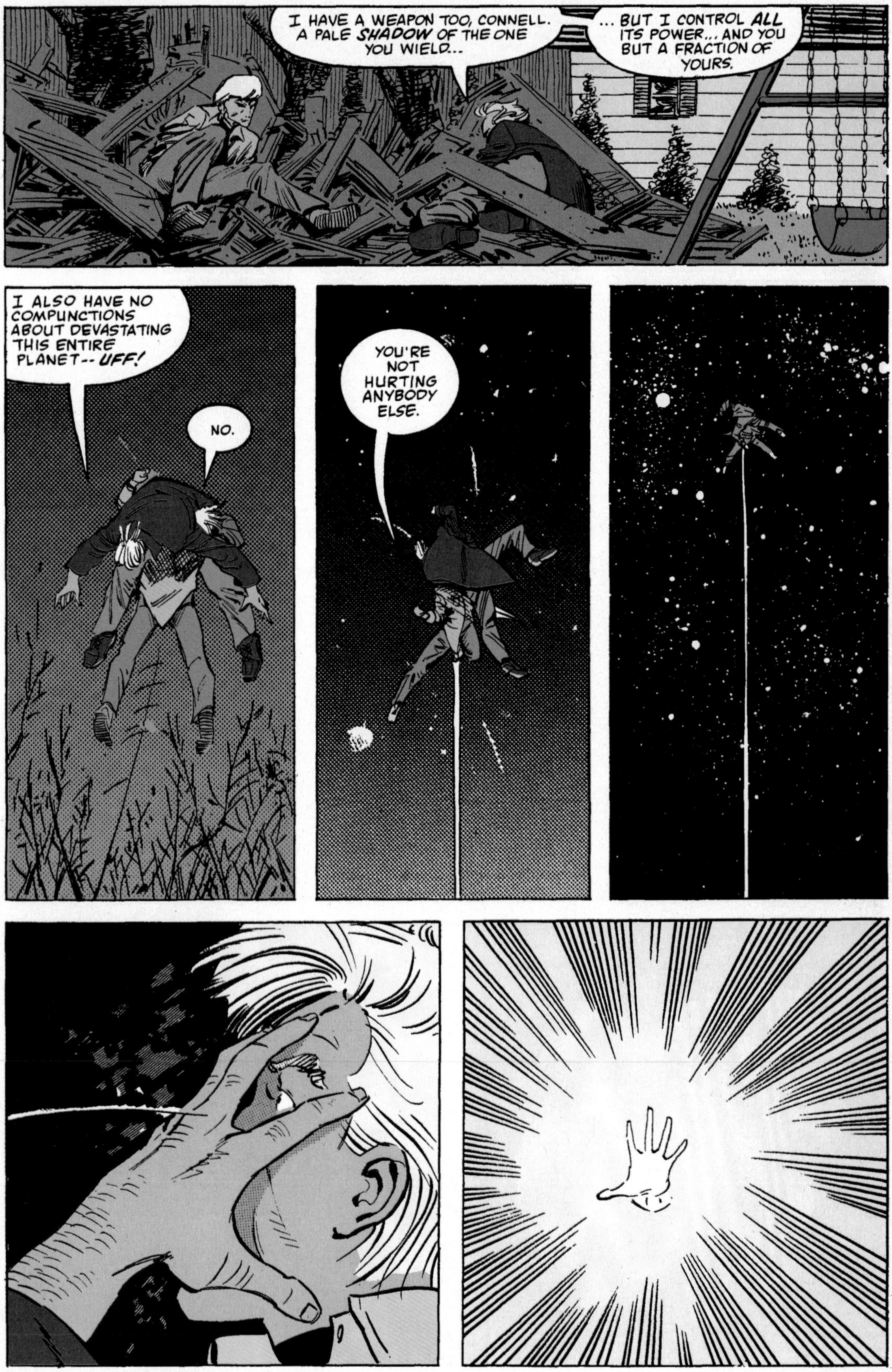
I HAVE A WEAPON TOO, CONNELL. A PALE SHADOW OF THE ONE YOU WIELD...
... BUT I CONTROL ALL ITS POWER... AND YOU BUT A FRACTION OF YOURS.
I ALSO HAVE NO COMPUNCTIONS ABOUT DEVASTATING THIS ENTIRE PLANET-- UFF!
NO.
YOU'RE NOT HURTING ANYBODY ELSE.

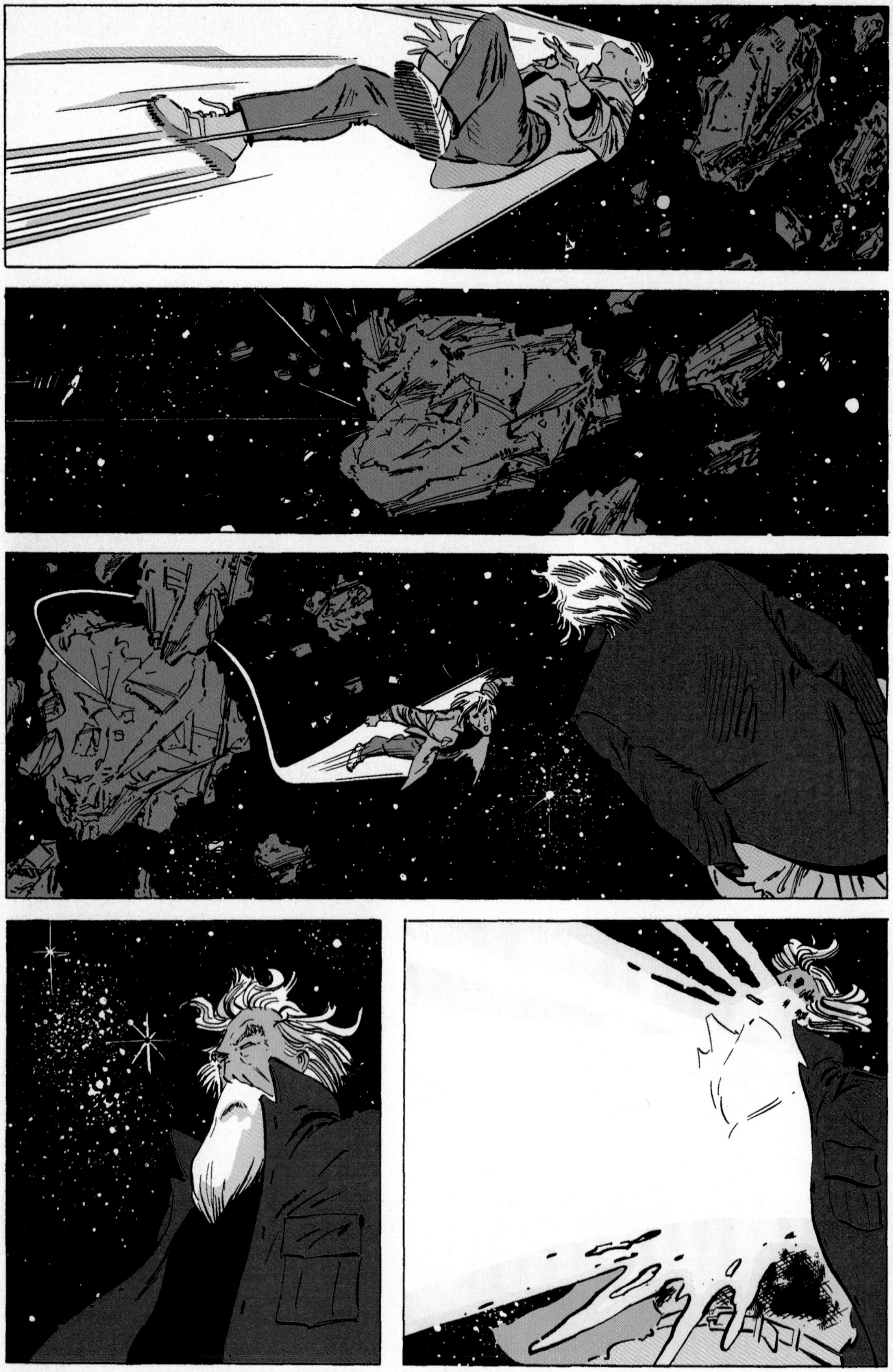

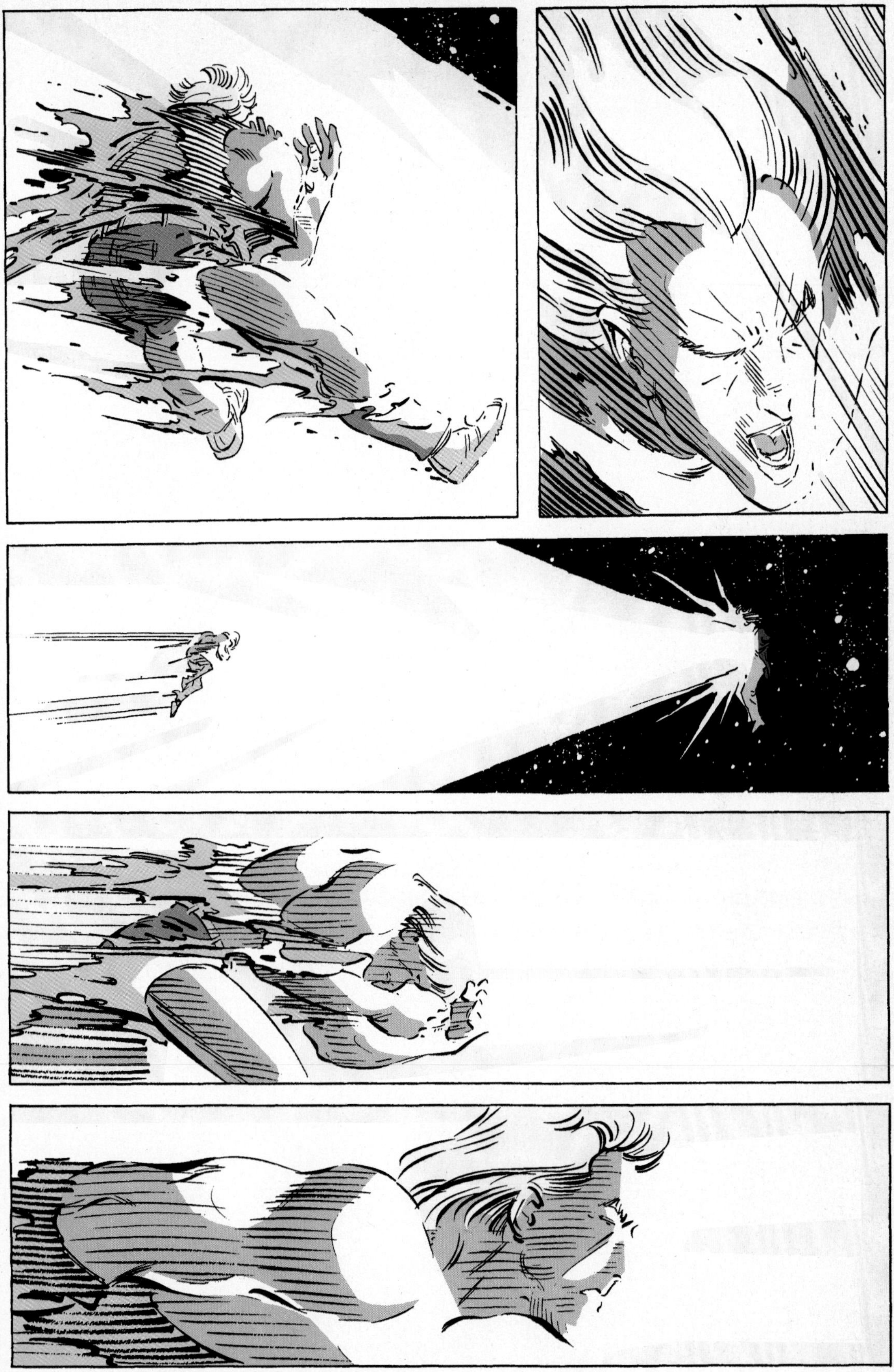

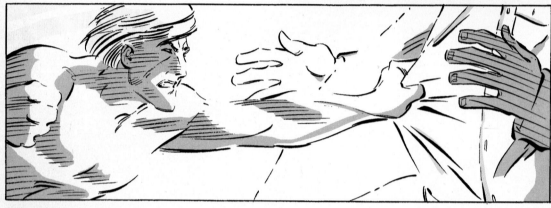

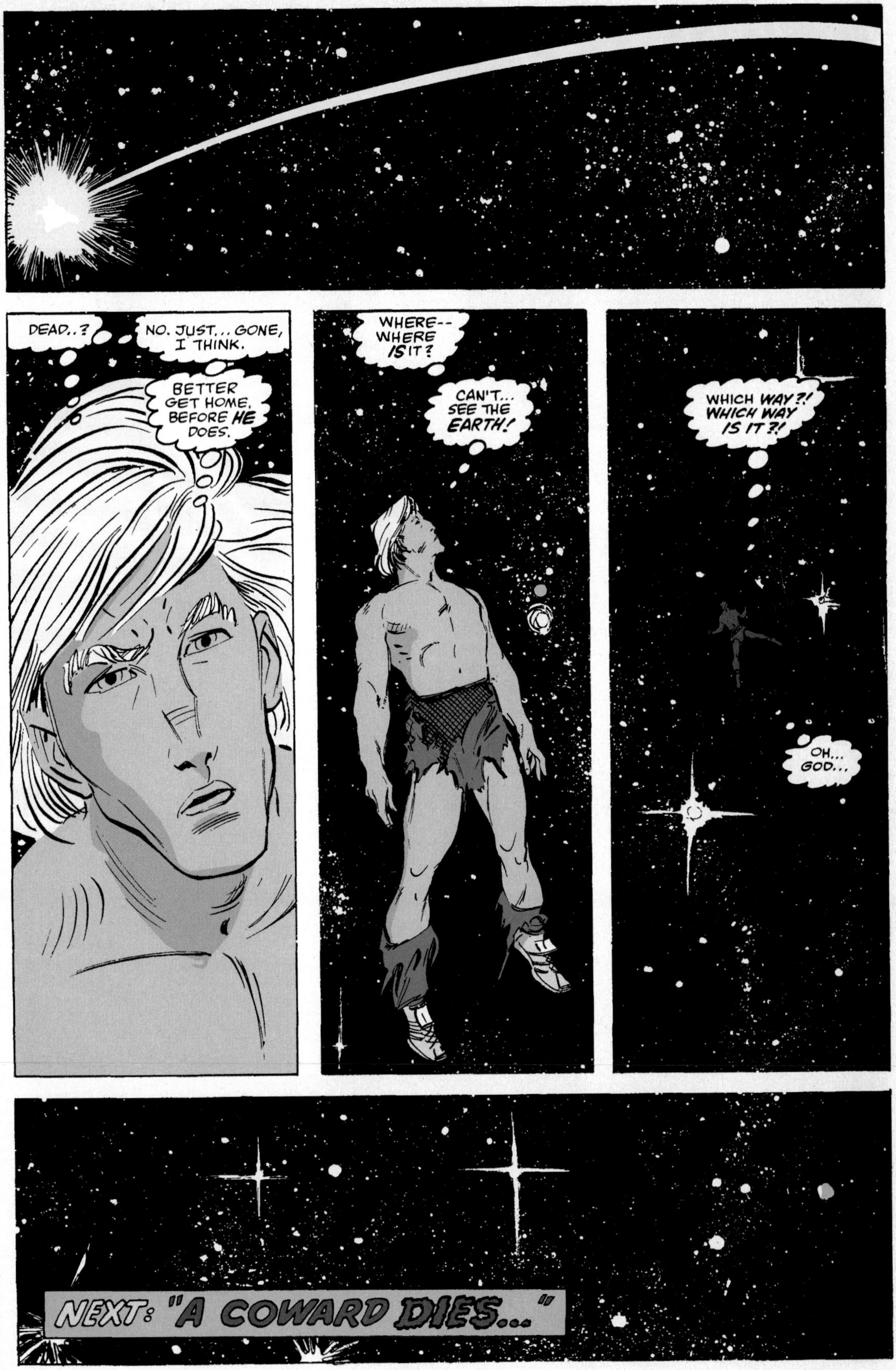
DEAD..?
NO. JUST... GONE, I THINK.
BETTER GET HOME, BEFORE HE DOES.
WHERE-- WHERE IS IT?
CAN'T... SEE THE EARTH!
WHICH WAY?! WHICH WAY IS IT?!
OH... GOD...
NEXT: "A COWARD DIES..."

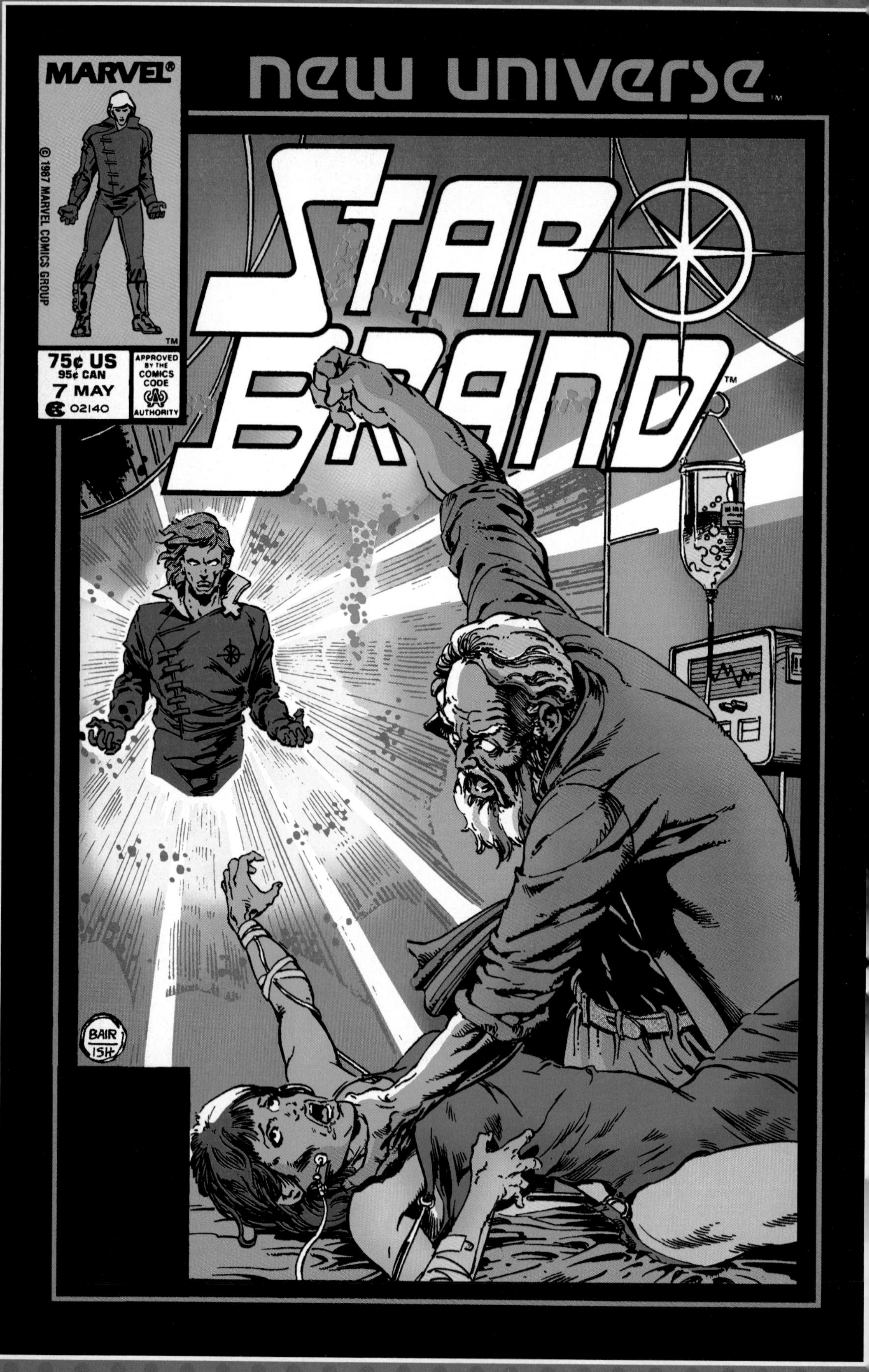
MARVEL®
NEW UNIVERSE ™
STAR BRAND ™
© 1987 MARVEL COMICS GROUP
75¢ US
95¢ CAN
7 MAY
02140
APPROVED BY THE COMICS CODE AUTHORITY
BAIR ISH

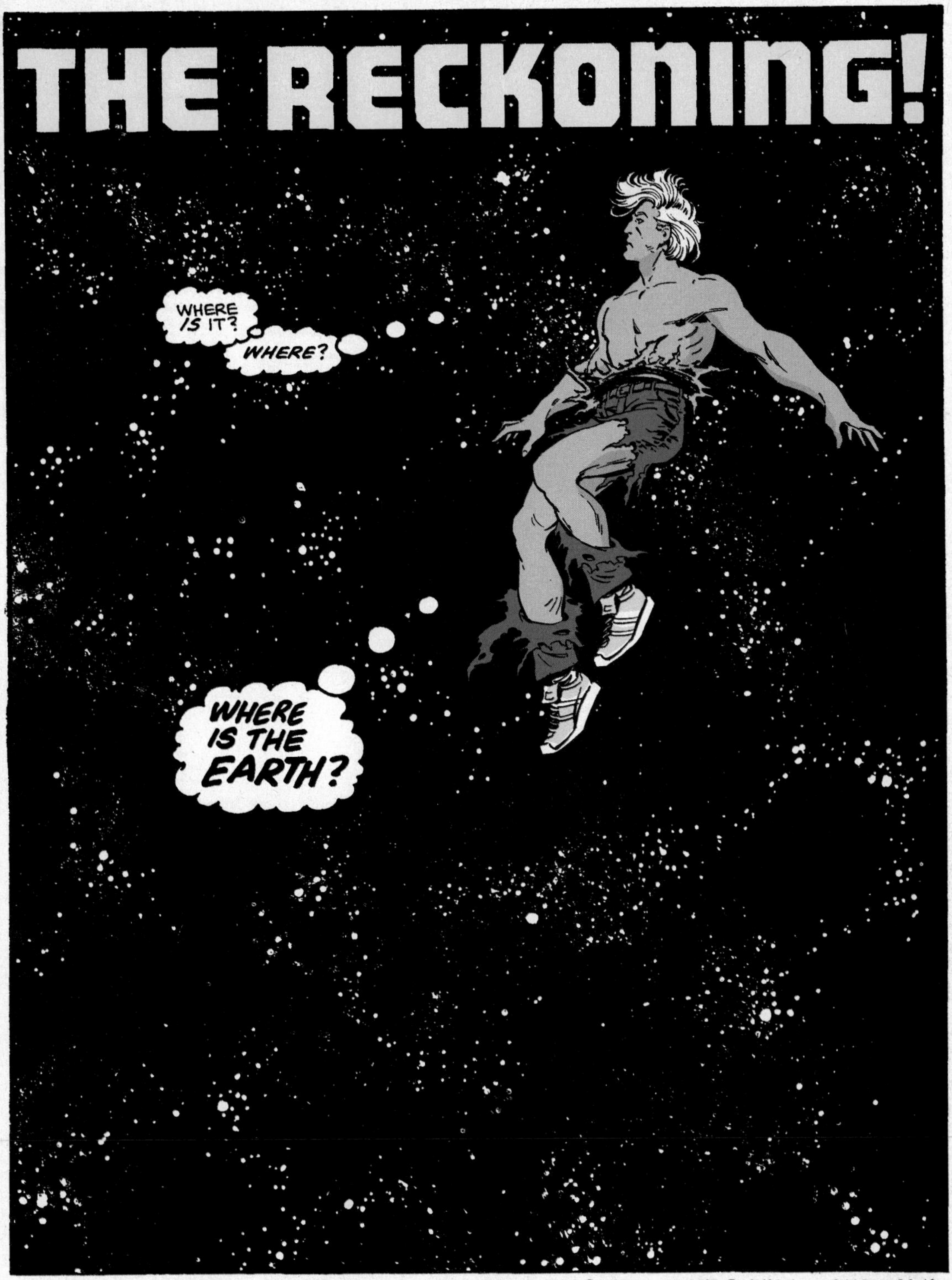
THE RECKONING!
WHERE IS IT?
WHERE?
WHERE IS THE EARTH?

JIM SHOOTER *PLOT/EDITOR IN CHIEF* ROY THOMAS *SCRIPT* JOHN ROMITA, JR. *PENCILER* ART NICHOLS *INKER* JOE ROSEN *LETTERER* JANET JACKSON *COLORIST* MICHAEL HIGGINS *EDITOR*

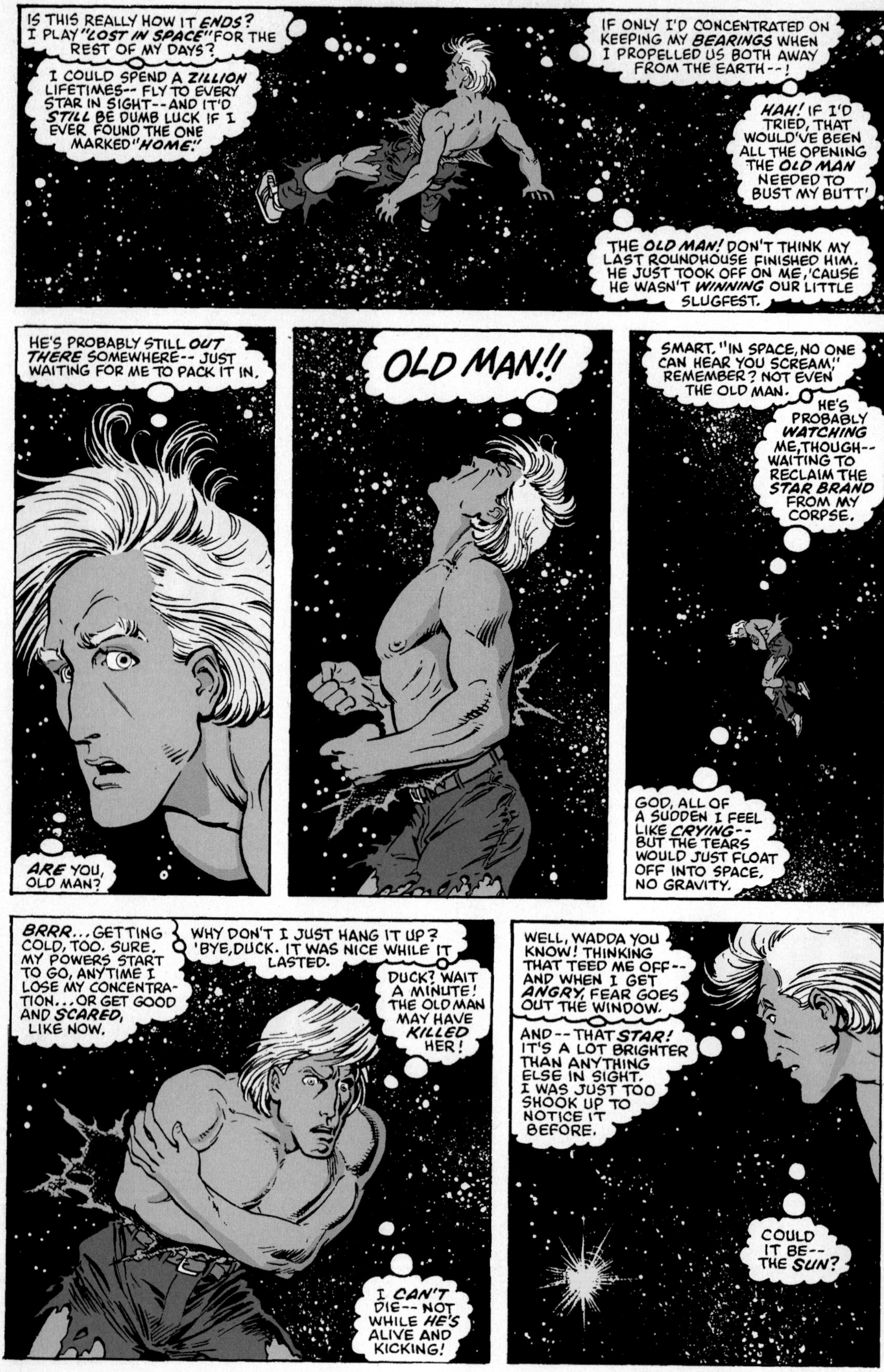
IS THIS REALLY HOW IT ENDS? I PLAY "LOST IN SPACE" FOR THE REST OF MY DAYS?
I COULD SPEND A ZILLION LIFETIMES-- FLY TO EVERY STAR IN SIGHT--AND IT'D STILL BE DUMB LUCK IF I EVER FOUND THE ONE MARKED "HOME."
IF ONLY I'D CONCENTRATED ON KEEPING MY BEARINGS WHEN I PROPELLED US BOTH AWAY FROM THE EARTH--!
HAH! IF I'D TRIED, THAT WOULD'VE BEEN ALL THE OPENING THE OLD MAN NEEDED TO BUST MY BUTT!
THE OLD MAN! DON'T THINK MY LAST ROUNDHOUSE FINISHED HIM. HE JUST TOOK OFF ON ME, 'CAUSE HE WASN'T WINNING OUR LITTLE SLUGFEST.
HE'S PROBABLY STILL OUT THERE SOMEWHERE-- JUST WAITING FOR ME TO PACK IT IN.
ARE YOU, OLD MAN?
OLD MAN!!
SMART. "IN SPACE, NO ONE CAN HEAR YOU SCREAM," REMEMBER? NOT EVEN THE OLD MAN.
HE'S PROBABLY WATCHING ME, THOUGH-- WAITING TO RECLAIM THE STAR BRAND FROM MY CORPSE.
GOD, ALL OF A SUDDEN I FEEL LIKE CRYING-- BUT THE TEARS WOULD JUST FLOAT OFF INTO SPACE, NO GRAVITY.
BRRR... GETTING COLD, TOO. SURE. MY POWERS START TO GO, ANYTIME I LOSE MY CONCENTRATION... OR GET GOOD AND SCARED, LIKE NOW.
WHY DON'T I JUST HANG IT UP? 'BYE, DUCK. IT WAS NICE WHILE IT LASTED.
DUCK? WAIT A MINUTE! THE OLD MAN MAY HAVE KILLED HER!
I CAN'T DIE-- NOT WHILE HE'S ALIVE AND KICKING!
WELL, WADDA YOU KNOW! THINKING THAT TEED ME OFF-- AND WHEN I GET ANGRY, FEAR GOES OUT THE WINDOW.
AND--THAT STAR! IT'S A LOT BRIGHTER THAN ANYTHING ELSE IN SIGHT. I WAS JUST TOO SHOOK UP TO NOTICE IT BEFORE.
COULD IT BE-- THE SUN?

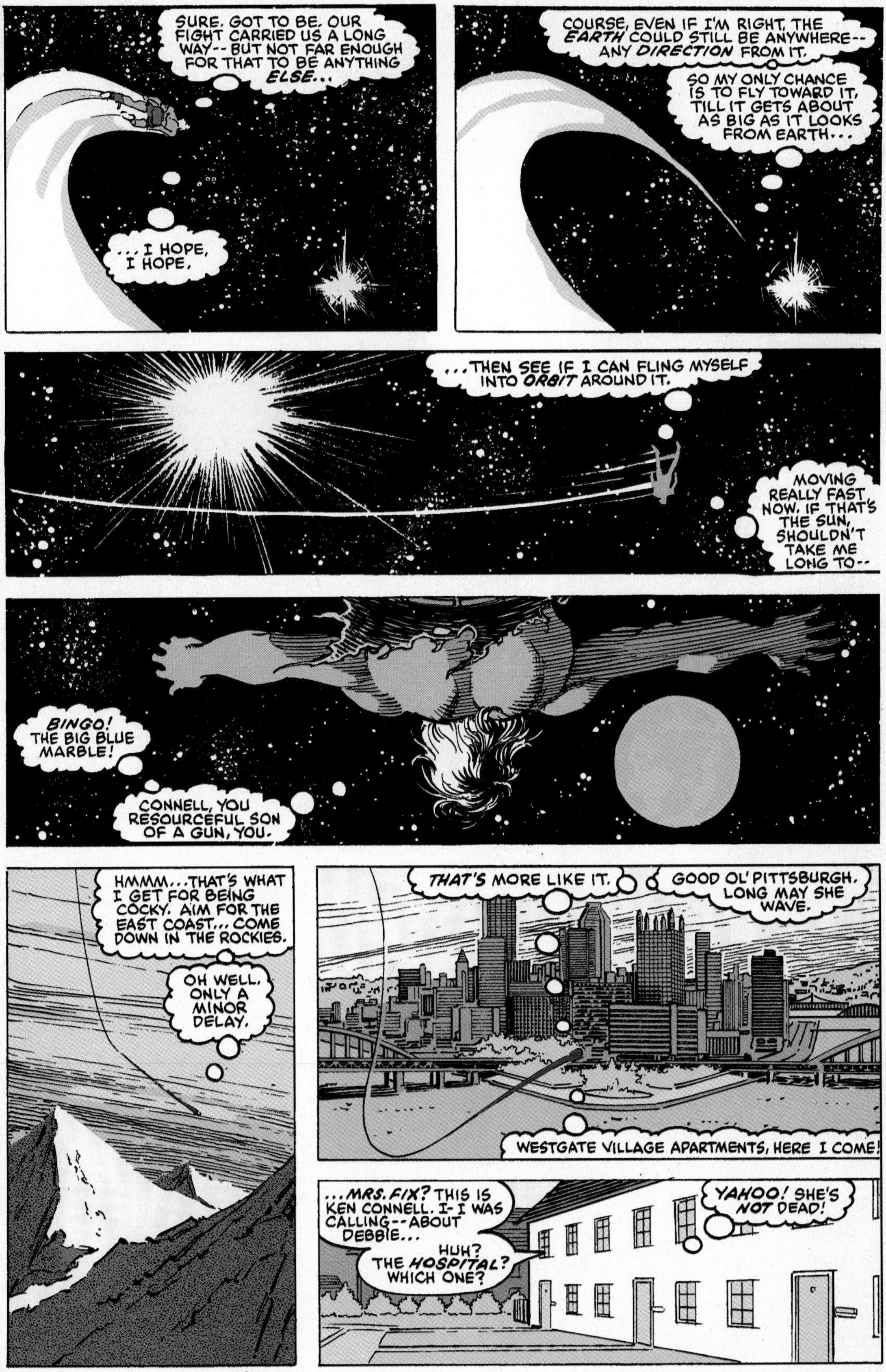

SURE. GOT TO BE. OUR FIGHT CARRIED US A LONG WAY-- BUT NOT FAR ENOUGH FOR THAT TO BE ANYTHING ELSE...
...I HOPE, I HOPE.
COURSE, EVEN IF I'M RIGHT, THE EARTH COULD STILL BE ANYWHERE-- ANY DIRECTION FROM IT.
SO MY ONLY CHANCE IS TO FLY TOWARD IT, TILL IT GETS ABOUT AS BIG AS IT LOOKS FROM EARTH...
...THEN SEE IF I CAN FLING MYSELF INTO ORBIT AROUND IT.
MOVING REALLY FAST NOW. IF THAT'S THE SUN, SHOULDN'T TAKE ME LONG TO--
BINGO! THE BIG BLUE MARBLE!
CONNELL, YOU RESOURCEFUL SON OF A GUN, YOU.
HMMM...THAT'S WHAT I GET FOR BEING COCKY. AIM FOR THE EAST COAST... COME DOWN IN THE ROCKIES.
OH WELL, ONLY A MINOR DELAY.
THAT'S MORE LIKE IT.
GOOD OL' PITTSBURGH. LONG MAY SHE WAVE.
WESTGATE VILLAGE APARTMENTS, HERE I COME!
...MRS. FIX? THIS IS KEN CONNELL. I- I WAS CALLING-- ABOUT DEBBIE...
HUH? THE HOSPITAL? WHICH ONE?
YAHOO! SHE'S NOT DEAD!

I'LL LOOK IN ON HER RIGHT AWAY, MRS. FIX.

G'BYE.

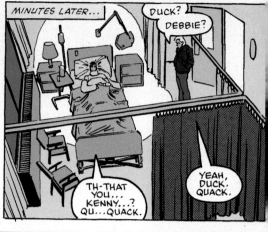

MINUTES LATER...

DUCK? DEBBIE?

TH-THAT YOU... KENNY...? QU...QUACK.

YEAH, DUCK, QUACK.

KENNY... HE JUST ...TOUCHED ME... AND IT WAS LIKE I WAS ON FIRE...

I KNOW, DUCK. TAKE IT EASY. DON'T TRY TO TALK NOW.

IF ONLY I'D NEVER SEEN THIS BRAND--I'VE BEEN SO AFRAID FOR YOU...

YOU SHOONT BE...SHOONT BE 'FRAID...

I'M THE ONE... SHOULD BE AFRAID. WAS AFRAID. 'FRAID OF THE OLD MAN...SO I CALLED BARB'S.

LOVE YOU...SO I GOTTA FACE ANYTHING...ANY-BODY...TRIES TO HURT YOU...EVEN HIM.

BUT Y'KNOW SOMETHIN'? I DON'T THINK...HE'S RILLY AN OLD MAN...AT ALL.

KENNY? YOU STILL HERE?

YES.

WELL, YOU SHOONT BE. YOU GOT OTHER PEOPLE TO CHECK ON ...'SIDES A HALF-DEAD DUCK. QUACK.

QU-QUACK.

SOON...

HI, BARB. YOU OKAY?

YEAH.

SO. DECIDED NOT TO TAKE IT ON THE LAM WITH THE KIDS, AFTER ALL, HUH?

DOESN'T LOOK LIKE IT.

CAN I COME IN?

SURE.

LOOK, BARB, I KNOW I--

THERE'S NOTHING TO TALK ABOUT, KEN. I SHOULD'VE READ THE HANDWRITING ON THE WALL WHEN I FOUND THOSE PHOTOS OF DEBBIE FIX AT YOUR PLACE.

INSTEAD, I ASKED YOU TO MOVE IN... SO I GUESS I GOT WHAT I DESERVED.

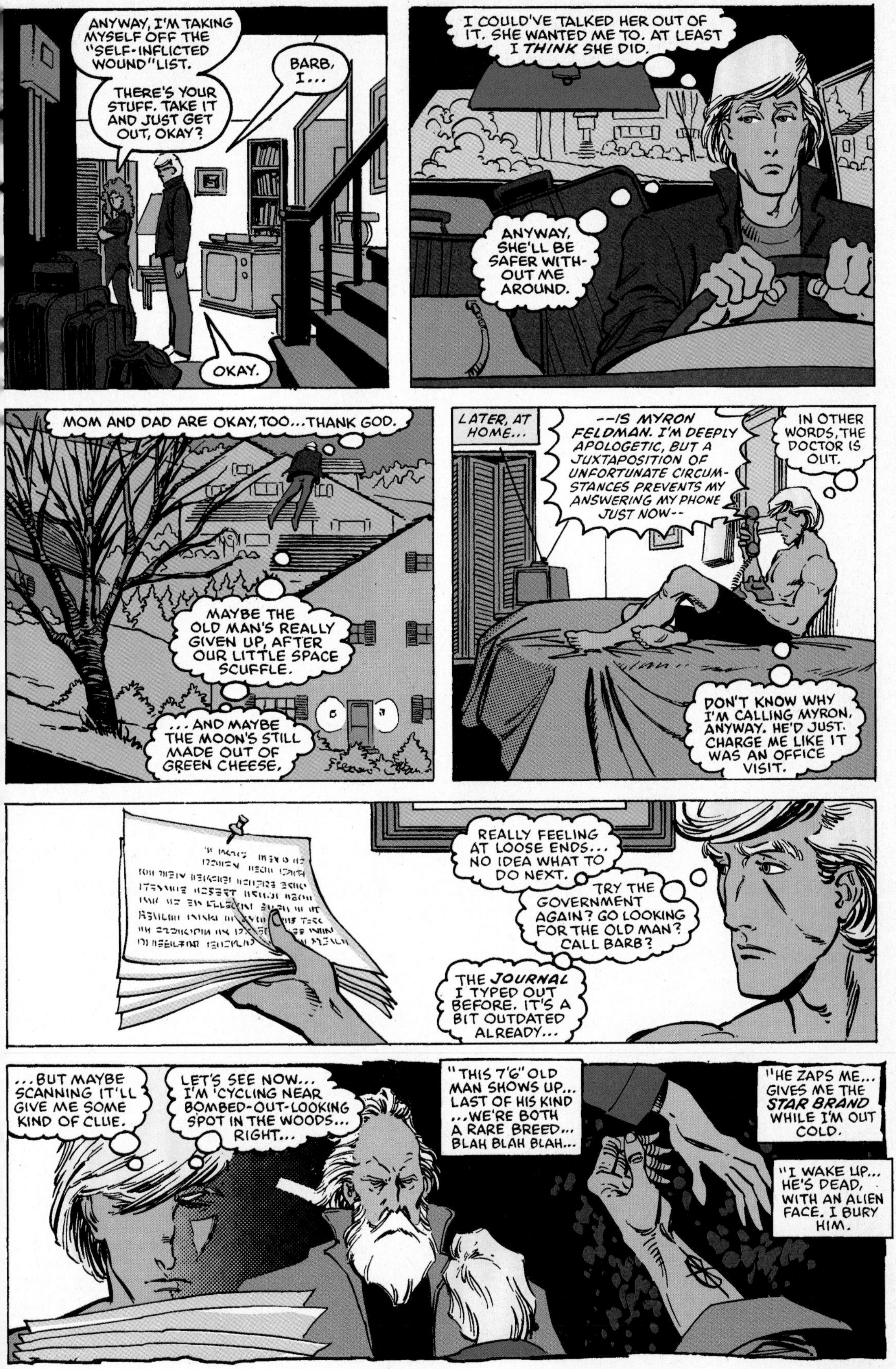
ANYWAY, I'M TAKING MYSELF OFF THE "SELF-INFLICTED WOUND" LIST.
THERE'S YOUR STUFF. TAKE IT AND JUST GET OUT, OKAY?
BARB, I...
OKAY.
I COULD'VE TALKED HER OUT OF IT. SHE WANTED ME TO. AT LEAST I THINK SHE DID.
ANYWAY, SHE'LL BE SAFER WITHOUT ME AROUND.
MOM AND DAD ARE OKAY, TOO... THANK GOD.
MAYBE THE OLD MAN'S REALLY GIVEN UP, AFTER OUR LITTLE SPACE SCUFFLE.
...AND MAYBE THE MOON'S STILL MADE OUT OF GREEN CHEESE.
LATER, AT HOME...
--IS MYRON FELDMAN. I'M DEEPLY APOLOGETIC, BUT A JUXTAPOSITION OF UNFORTUNATE CIRCUMSTANCES PREVENTS MY ANSWERING MY PHONE JUST NOW--
IN OTHER WORDS, THE DOCTOR IS OUT.
DON'T KNOW WHY I'M CALLING MYRON, ANYWAY. HE'D JUST CHARGE ME LIKE IT WAS AN OFFICE VISIT.
REALLY FEELING AT LOOSE ENDS... NO IDEA WHAT TO DO NEXT.
TRY THE GOVERNMENT AGAIN? GO LOOKING FOR THE OLD MAN? CALL BARB?
THE JOURNAL I TYPED OUT BEFORE. IT'S A BIT OUTDATED ALREADY...
...BUT MAYBE SCANNING IT'LL GIVE ME SOME KIND OF CLUE.
LET'S SEE NOW... I'M 'CYCLING NEAR BOMBED-OUT-LOOKING SPOT IN THE WOODS... RIGHT...
"THIS 7'6" OLD MAN SHOWS UP... LAST OF HIS KIND ...WE'RE BOTH A RARE BREED... BLAH BLAH BLAH...
"HE ZAPS ME... GIVES ME THE STAR BRAND WHILE I'M OUT COLD.
"I WAKE UP... HE'S DEAD, WITH AN ALIEN FACE. I BURY HIM.

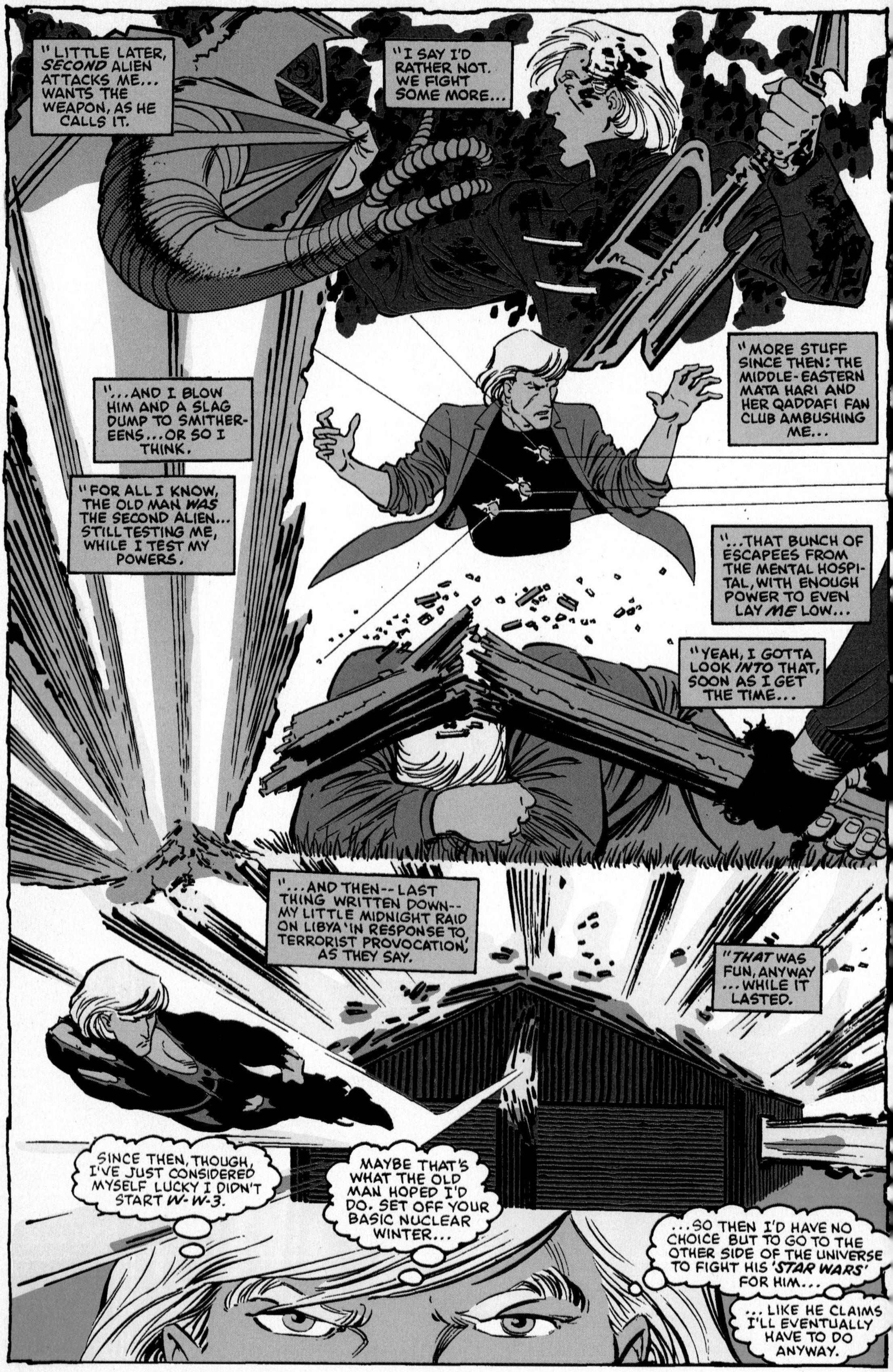
"LITTLE LATER, SECOND ALIEN ATTACKS ME... WANTS THE WEAPON, AS HE CALLS IT.
"I SAY I'D RATHER NOT. WE FIGHT SOME MORE...
"...AND I BLOW HIM AND A SLAG DUMP TO SMITHEREENS...OR SO I THINK.
"FOR ALL I KNOW, THE OLD MAN WAS THE SECOND ALIEN... STILL TESTING ME, WHILE I TEST MY POWERS.
"MORE STUFF SINCE THEN: THE MIDDLE-EASTERN MATA HARI AND HER QADDAFI FAN CLUB AMBUSHING ME...
"...THAT BUNCH OF ESCAPEES FROM THE MENTAL HOSPITAL, WITH ENOUGH POWER TO EVEN LAY ME LOW...
"YEAH, I GOTTA LOOK INTO THAT, SOON AS I GET THE TIME...
"...AND THEN--LAST THING WRITTEN DOWN--MY LITTLE MIDNIGHT RAID ON LIBYA 'IN RESPONSE TO TERRORIST PROVOCATION,' AS THEY SAY.
"THAT WAS FUN, ANYWAY ...WHILE IT LASTED.
SINCE THEN, THOUGH, I'VE JUST CONSIDERED MYSELF LUCKY I DIDN'T START W-W-3.
MAYBE THAT'S WHAT THE OLD MAN HOPED I'D DO. SET OFF YOUR BASIC NUCLEAR WINTER...
...SO THEN I'D HAVE NO CHOICE BUT TO GO TO THE OTHER SIDE OF THE UNIVERSE TO FIGHT HIS 'STAR WARS' FOR HIM...
...LIKE HE CLAIMS I'LL EVENTUALLY HAVE TO DO ANYWAY.

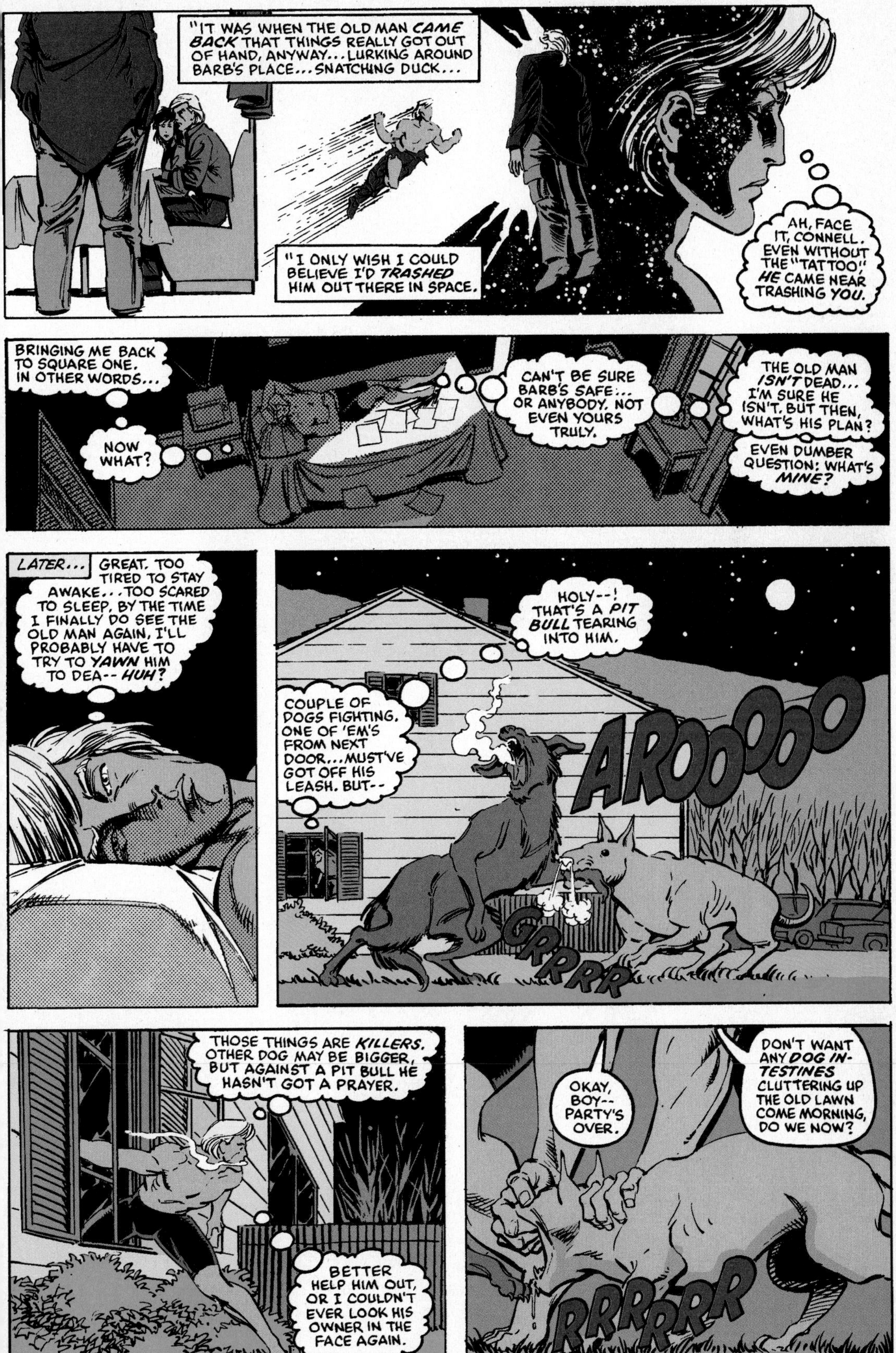
"IT WAS WHEN THE OLD MAN CAME BACK THAT THINGS REALLY GOT OUT OF HAND, ANYWAY... LURKING AROUND BARB'S PLACE... SNATCHING DUCK...
"I ONLY WISH I COULD BELIEVE I'D TRASHED HIM OUT THERE IN SPACE.
AH, FACE IT, CONNELL. EVEN WITHOUT THE "TATTOO" HE CAME NEAR TRASHING YOU.
BRINGING ME BACK TO SQUARE ONE. IN OTHER WORDS...
NOW WHAT?
CAN'T BE SURE BARB'S SAFE... OR ANYBODY. NOT EVEN YOURS TRULY.
THE OLD MAN ISN'T DEAD... I'M SURE HE ISN'T. BUT THEN, WHAT'S HIS PLAN?
EVEN DUMBER QUESTION: WHAT'S MINE?
LATER...
GREAT. TOO TIRED TO STAY AWAKE... TOO SCARED TO SLEEP. BY THE TIME I FINALLY DO SEE THE OLD MAN AGAIN, I'LL PROBABLY HAVE TO TRY TO YAWN HIM TO DEA-- HUH?
COUPLE OF DOGS FIGHTING. ONE OF 'EM'S FROM NEXT DOOR... MUST'VE GOT OFF HIS LEASH. BUT--
HOLY--! THAT'S A PIT BULL TEARING INTO HIM.
AROOOOOO
GRRRR
THOSE THINGS ARE KILLERS. OTHER DOG MAY BE BIGGER, BUT AGAINST A PIT BULL HE HASN'T GOT A PRAYER.
BETTER HELP HIM OUT, OR I COULDN'T EVER LOOK HIS OWNER IN THE FACE AGAIN.
OKAY, BOY-- PARTY'S OVER.
DON'T WANT ANY DOG INTESTINES CLUTTERING UP THE OLD LAWN COME MORNING, DO WE NOW?
RRRRRR

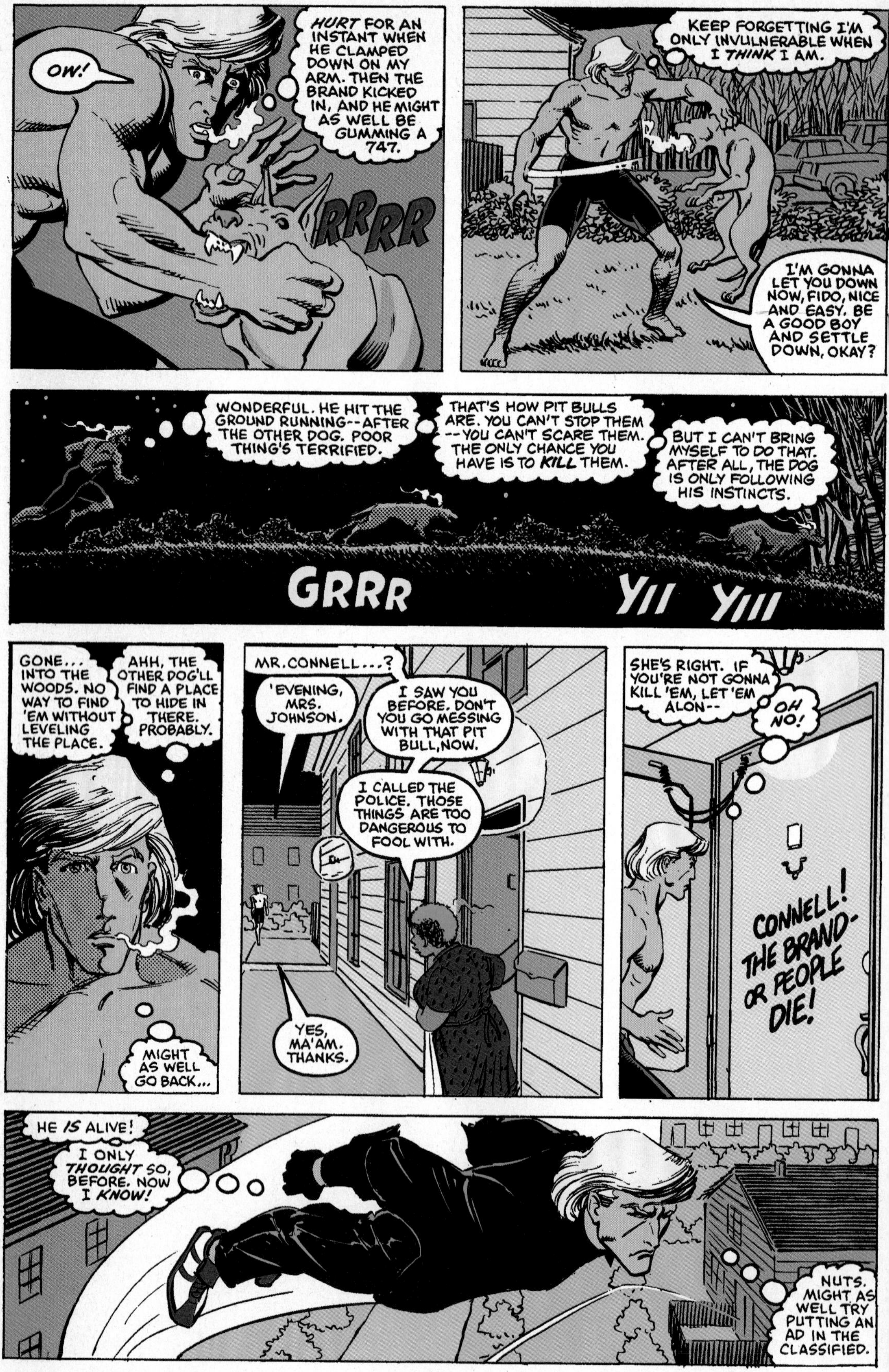
OW!
HURT FOR AN INSTANT WHEN HE CLAMPED DOWN ON MY ARM. THEN THE BRAND KICKED IN, AND HE MIGHT AS WELL BE GUMMING A 747.
RRRR
KEEP FORGETTING I'M ONLY INVULNERABLE WHEN I THINK I AM.
I'M GONNA LET YOU DOWN NOW, FIDO, NICE AND EASY. BE A GOOD BOY AND SETTLE DOWN, OKAY?
WONDERFUL. HE HIT THE GROUND RUNNING--AFTER THE OTHER DOG. POOR THING'S TERRIFIED.
THAT'S HOW PIT BULLS ARE. YOU CAN'T STOP THEM --YOU CAN'T SCARE THEM. THE ONLY CHANCE YOU HAVE IS TO KILL THEM.
BUT I CAN'T BRING MYSELF TO DO THAT. AFTER ALL, THE DOG IS ONLY FOLLOWING HIS INSTINCTS.
GRRR
YII YIII
GONE... INTO THE WOODS. NO WAY TO FIND 'EM WITHOUT LEVELING THE PLACE.
AHH, THE OTHER DOG'LL FIND A PLACE TO HIDE IN THERE. PROBABLY.
MIGHT AS WELL GO BACK...
MR. CONNELL...?
'EVENING, MRS. JOHNSON.
I SAW YOU BEFORE. DON'T YOU GO MESSING WITH THAT PIT BULL, NOW.
I CALLED THE POLICE. THOSE THINGS ARE TOO DANGEROUS TO FOOL WITH.
YES, MA'AM. THANKS.
SHE'S RIGHT. IF YOU'RE NOT GONNA KILL 'EM, LET 'EM ALON--
OH NO!
CONNELL! THE BRAND-- OR PEOPLE DIE!
HE IS ALIVE!
I ONLY THOUGHT SO, BEFORE. NOW I KNOW!
NUTS. MIGHT AS WELL TRY PUTTING AN AD IN THE CLASSIFIED.

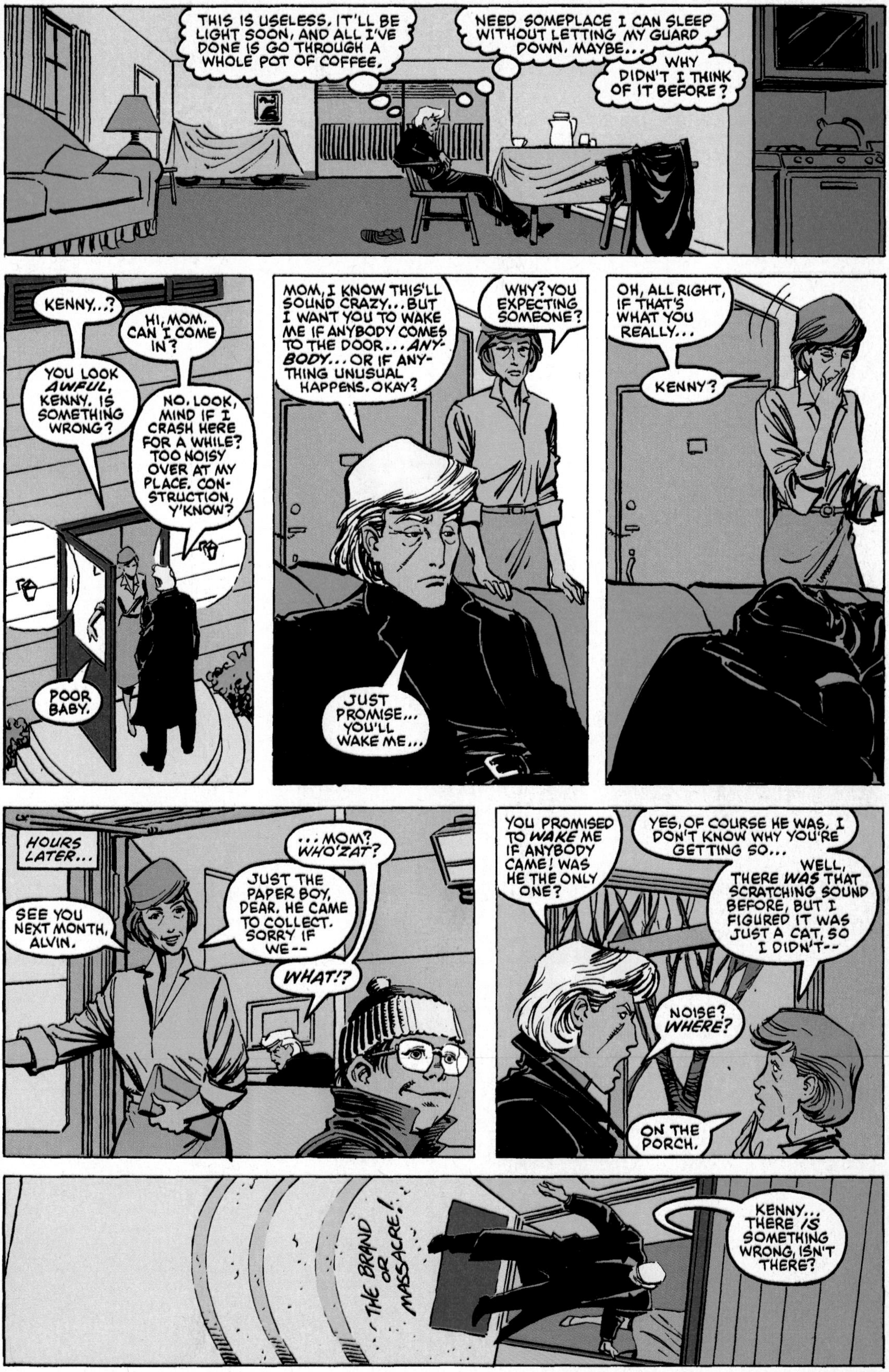
THIS IS USELESS. IT'LL BE LIGHT SOON, AND ALL I'VE DONE IS GO THROUGH A WHOLE POT OF COFFEE.
NEED SOMEPLACE I CAN SLEEP WITHOUT LETTING MY GUARD DOWN. MAYBE...
WHY DIDN'T I THINK OF IT BEFORE?
KENNY...?
HI, MOM. CAN I COME IN?
YOU LOOK AWFUL, KENNY. IS SOMETHING WRONG?
NO. LOOK, MIND IF I CRASH HERE FOR A WHILE? TOO NOISY OVER AT MY PLACE. CONSTRUCTION, Y'KNOW?
POOR BABY.
MOM, I KNOW THIS'LL SOUND CRAZY... BUT I WANT YOU TO WAKE ME IF ANYBODY COMES TO THE DOOR... ANYBODY... OR IF ANYTHING UNUSUAL HAPPENS. OKAY?
WHY? YOU EXPECTING SOMEONE?
JUST PROMISE... YOU'LL WAKE ME...
OH, ALL RIGHT, IF THAT'S WHAT YOU REALLY...
KENNY?
HOURS LATER...
SEE YOU NEXT MONTH, ALVIN.
...MOM? WHO'ZAT?
JUST THE PAPER BOY, DEAR. HE CAME TO COLLECT. SORRY IF WE--
WHAT!?
YOU PROMISED TO WAKE ME IF ANYBODY CAME! WAS HE THE ONLY ONE?
YES, OF COURSE HE WAS. I DON'T KNOW WHY YOU'RE GETTING SO...
WELL, THERE WAS THAT SCRATCHING SOUND BEFORE, BUT I FIGURED IT WAS JUST A CAT, SO I DIDN'T--
NOISE? WHERE?
ON THE PORCH.
THE BRAND OF MASSACRE!
KENNY... THERE IS SOMETHING WRONG, ISN'T THERE?

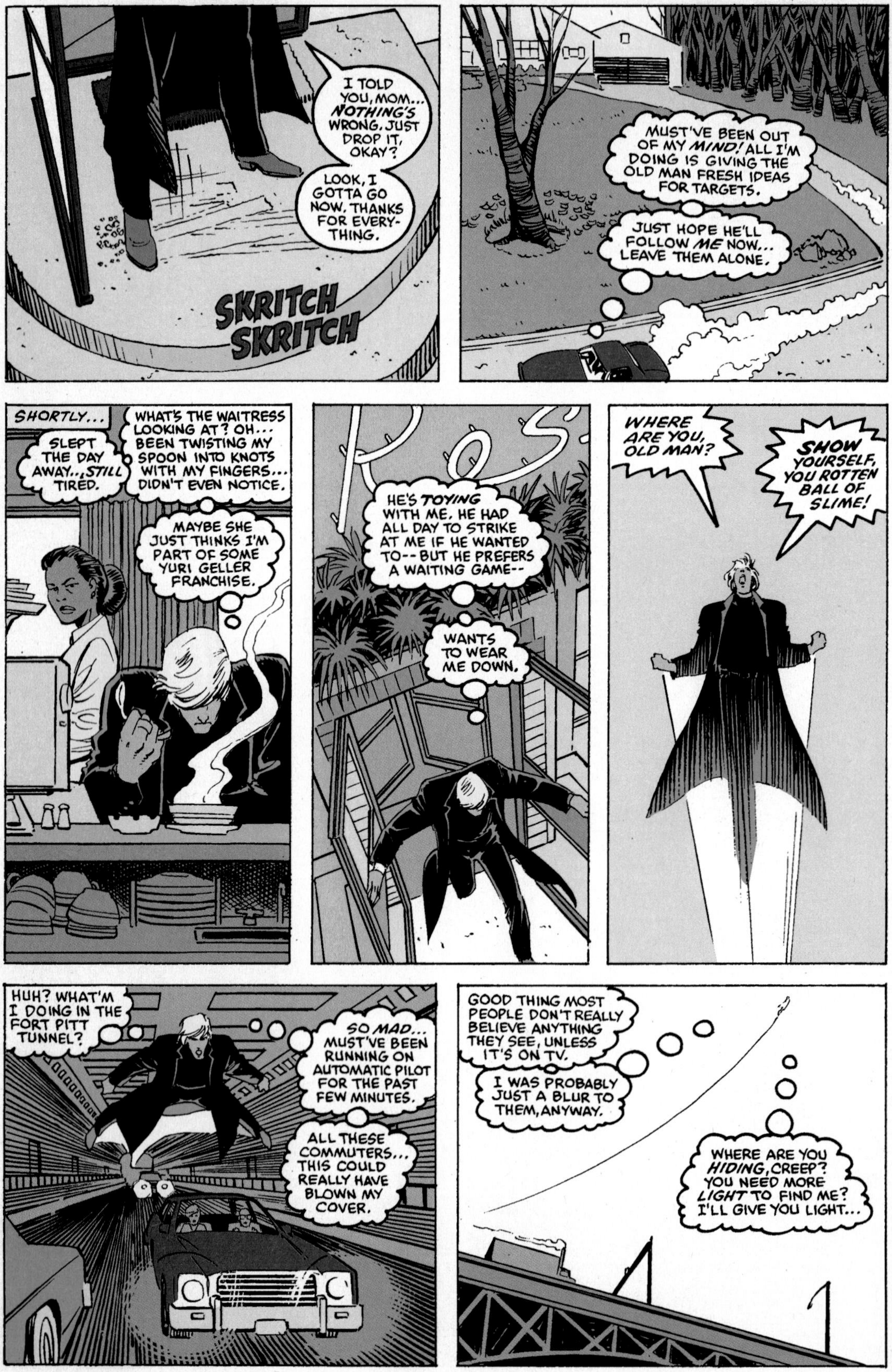
I TOLD YOU, MOM... NOTHING'S WRONG. JUST DROP IT, OKAY?
LOOK, I GOTTA GO NOW. THANKS FOR EVERYTHING.
SKRITCH SKRITCH
MUST'VE BEEN OUT OF MY MIND! ALL I'M DOING IS GIVING THE OLD MAN FRESH IDEAS FOR TARGETS.
JUST HOPE HE'LL FOLLOW ME NOW... LEAVE THEM ALONE.
SHORTLY...
SLEPT THE DAY AWAY... STILL TIRED.
WHAT'S THE WAITRESS LOOKING AT? OH... BEEN TWISTING MY SPOON INTO KNOTS WITH MY FINGERS... DIDN'T EVEN NOTICE.
MAYBE SHE JUST THINKS I'M PART OF SOME YURI GELLER FRANCHISE.
HE'S TOYING WITH ME. HE HAD ALL DAY TO STRIKE AT ME IF HE WANTED TO-- BUT HE PREFERS A WAITING GAME--
WANTS TO WEAR ME DOWN.
WHERE ARE YOU, OLD MAN?
SHOW YOURSELF, YOU ROTTEN BALL OF SLIME!
HUH? WHAT'M I DOING IN THE FORT PITT TUNNEL?
SO MAD... MUST'VE BEEN RUNNING ON AUTOMATIC PILOT FOR THE PAST FEW MINUTES.
ALL THESE COMMUTERS... THIS COULD REALLY HAVE BLOWN MY COVER.
GOOD THING MOST PEOPLE DON'T REALLY BELIEVE ANYTHING THEY SEE, UNLESS IT'S ON TV.
I WAS PROBABLY JUST A BLUR TO THEM, ANYWAY.
WHERE ARE YOU HIDING, CREEP? YOU NEED MORE LIGHT TO FIND ME? I'LL GIVE YOU LIGHT...

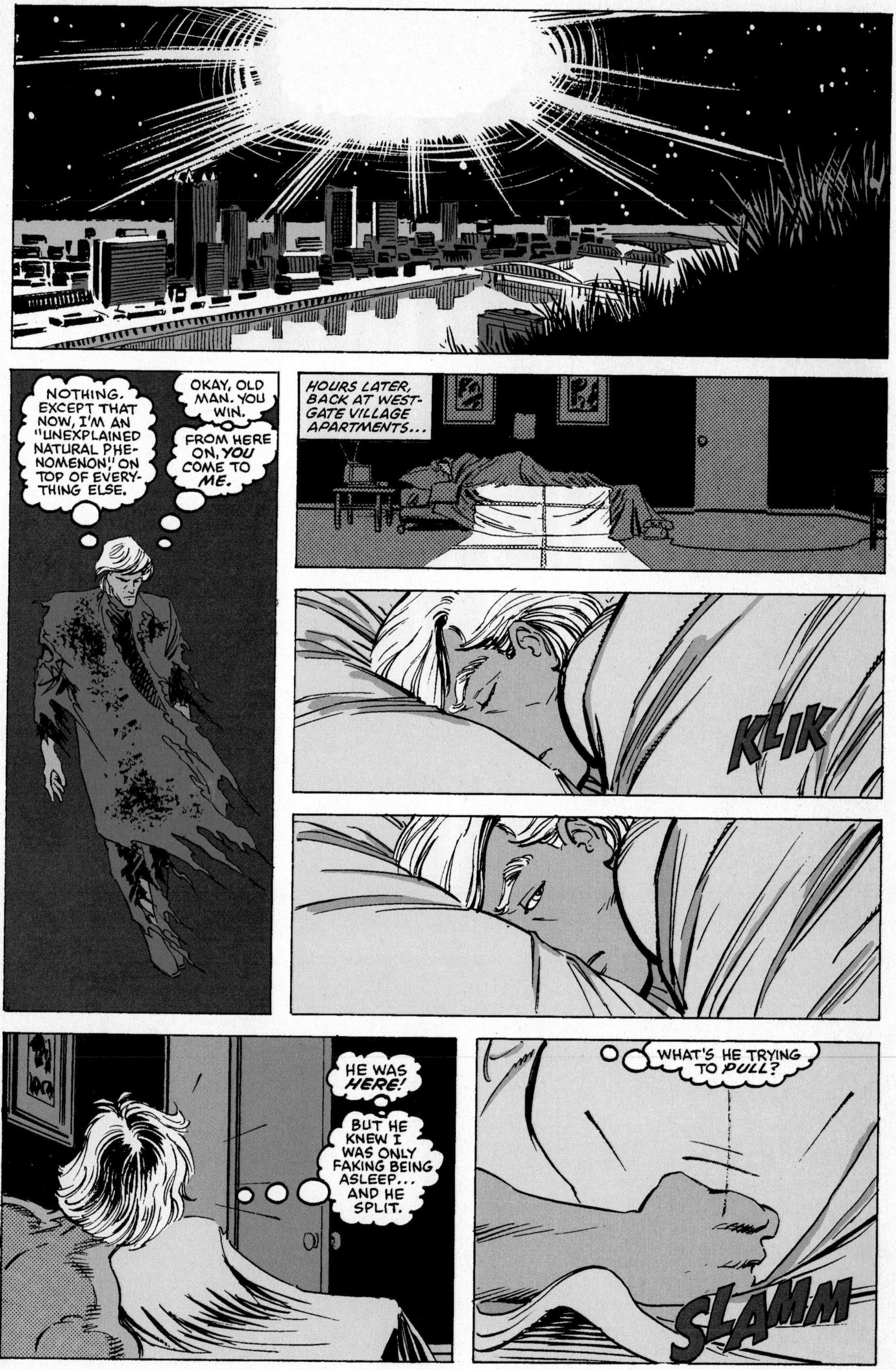

NOTHING. EXCEPT THAT NOW, I'M AN "UNEXPLAINED NATURAL PHENOMENON," ON TOP OF EVERYTHING ELSE.
OKAY, OLD MAN. YOU WIN.
FROM HERE ON, YOU COME TO ME.
HOURS LATER, BACK AT WESTGATE VILLAGE APARTMENTS...
KLIK
HE WAS HERE!
BUT HE KNEW I WAS ONLY FAKING BEING ASLEEP... AND HE SPLIT.
WHAT'S HE TRYING TO PULL?
SLAMM

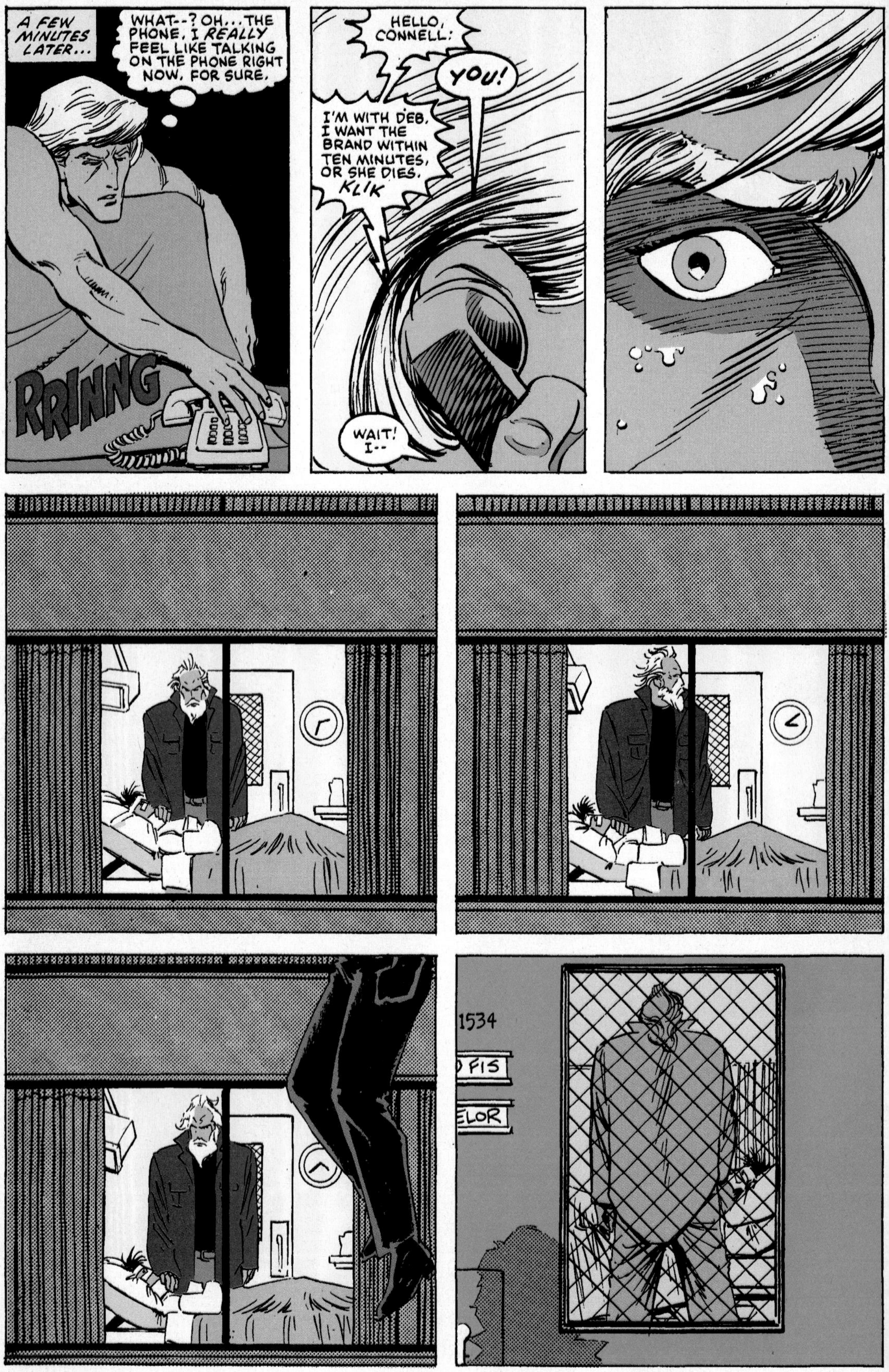
A FEW MINUTES LATER...
WHAT--? OH... THE PHONE. I REALLY FEEL LIKE TALKING ON THE PHONE RIGHT NOW, FOR SURE.
RRINNG
HELLO, CONNELL.
YOU!
I'M WITH DEB. I WANT THE BRAND WITHIN TEN MINUTES, OR SHE DIES.
KLIK
WAIT! I--
1534
FIS
ELOR

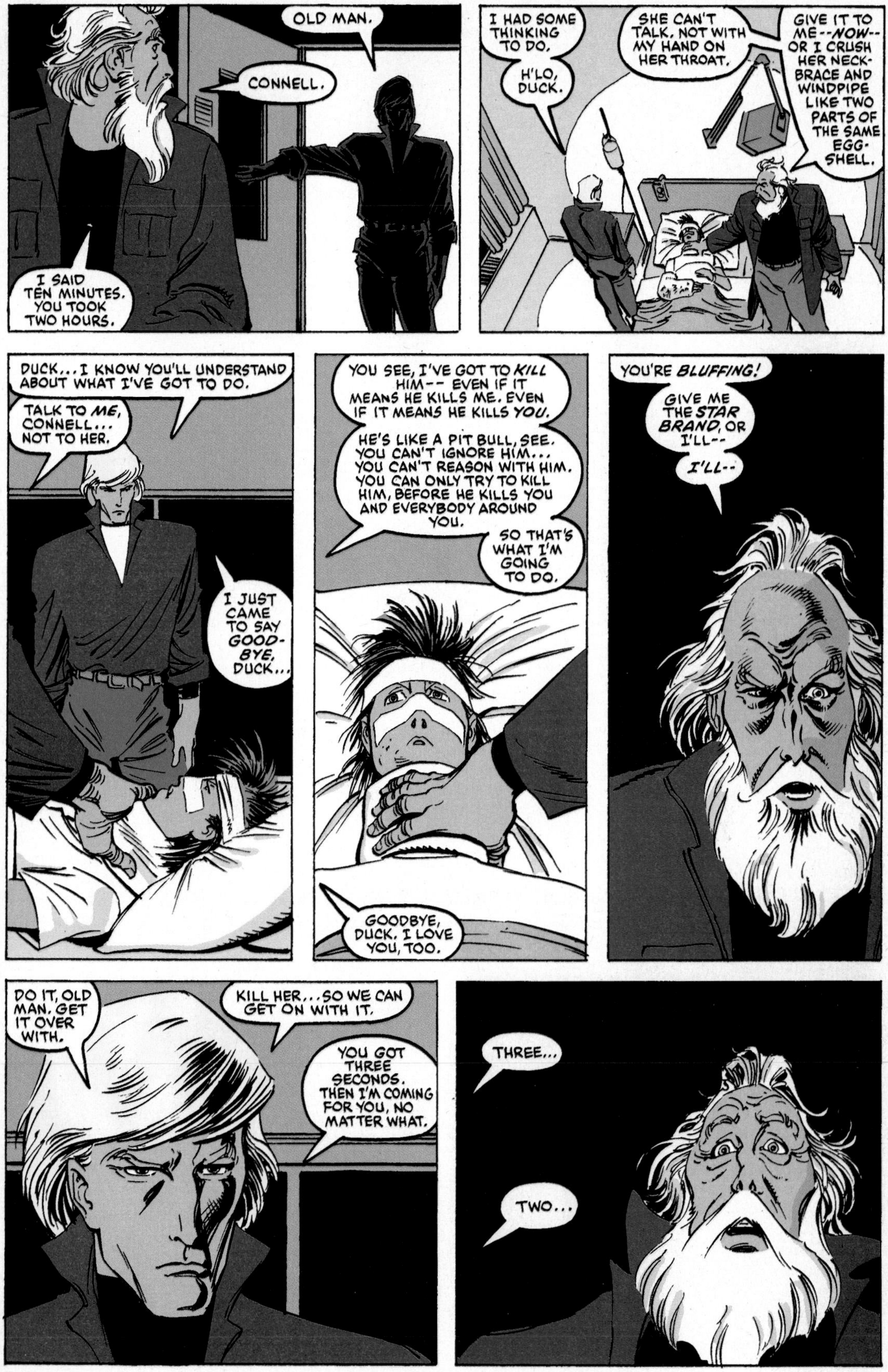
OLD MAN.
CONNELL.
I SAID TEN MINUTES. YOU TOOK TWO HOURS.
I HAD SOME THINKING TO DO.
H'LO, DUCK.
SHE CAN'T TALK, NOT WITH MY HAND ON HER THROAT.
GIVE IT TO ME--NOW--OR I CRUSH HER NECK-BRACE AND WINDPIPE LIKE TWO PARTS OF THE SAME EGG-SHELL.
DUCK... I KNOW YOU'LL UNDERSTAND ABOUT WHAT I'VE GOT TO DO.
TALK TO ME, CONNELL... NOT TO HER.
I JUST CAME TO SAY GOOD-BYE, DUCK...
YOU SEE, I'VE GOT TO KILL HIM-- EVEN IF IT MEANS HE KILLS ME. EVEN IF IT MEANS HE KILLS YOU.
HE'S LIKE A PIT BULL, SEE. YOU CAN'T IGNORE HIM... YOU CAN'T REASON WITH HIM. YOU CAN ONLY TRY TO KILL HIM, BEFORE HE KILLS YOU AND EVERYBODY AROUND YOU.
SO THAT'S WHAT I'M GOING TO DO.
GOODBYE, DUCK. I LOVE YOU, TOO.
YOU'RE BLUFFING!
GIVE ME THE STAR BRAND, OR I'LL--
I'LL--
DO IT, OLD MAN. GET IT OVER WITH.
KILL HER... SO WE CAN GET ON WITH IT.
YOU GOT THREE SECONDS. THEN I'M COMING FOR YOU, NO MATTER WHAT.
THREE...
TWO...

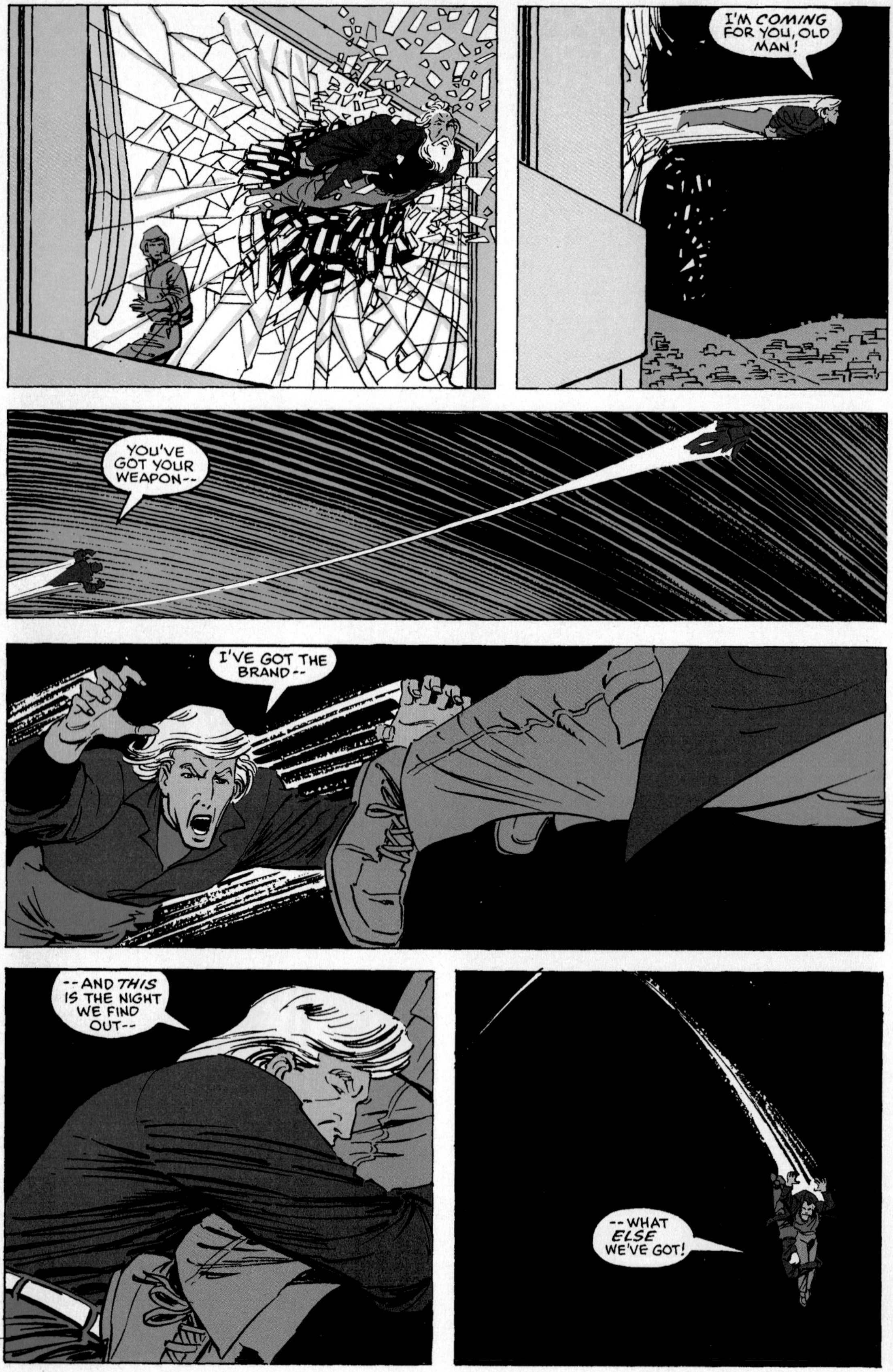
I'M COMING FOR YOU, OLD MAN!
YOU'VE GOT YOUR WEAPON--
I'VE GOT THE BRAND--
--AND THIS IS THE NIGHT WE FIND OUT--
--WHAT ELSE WE'VE GOT!

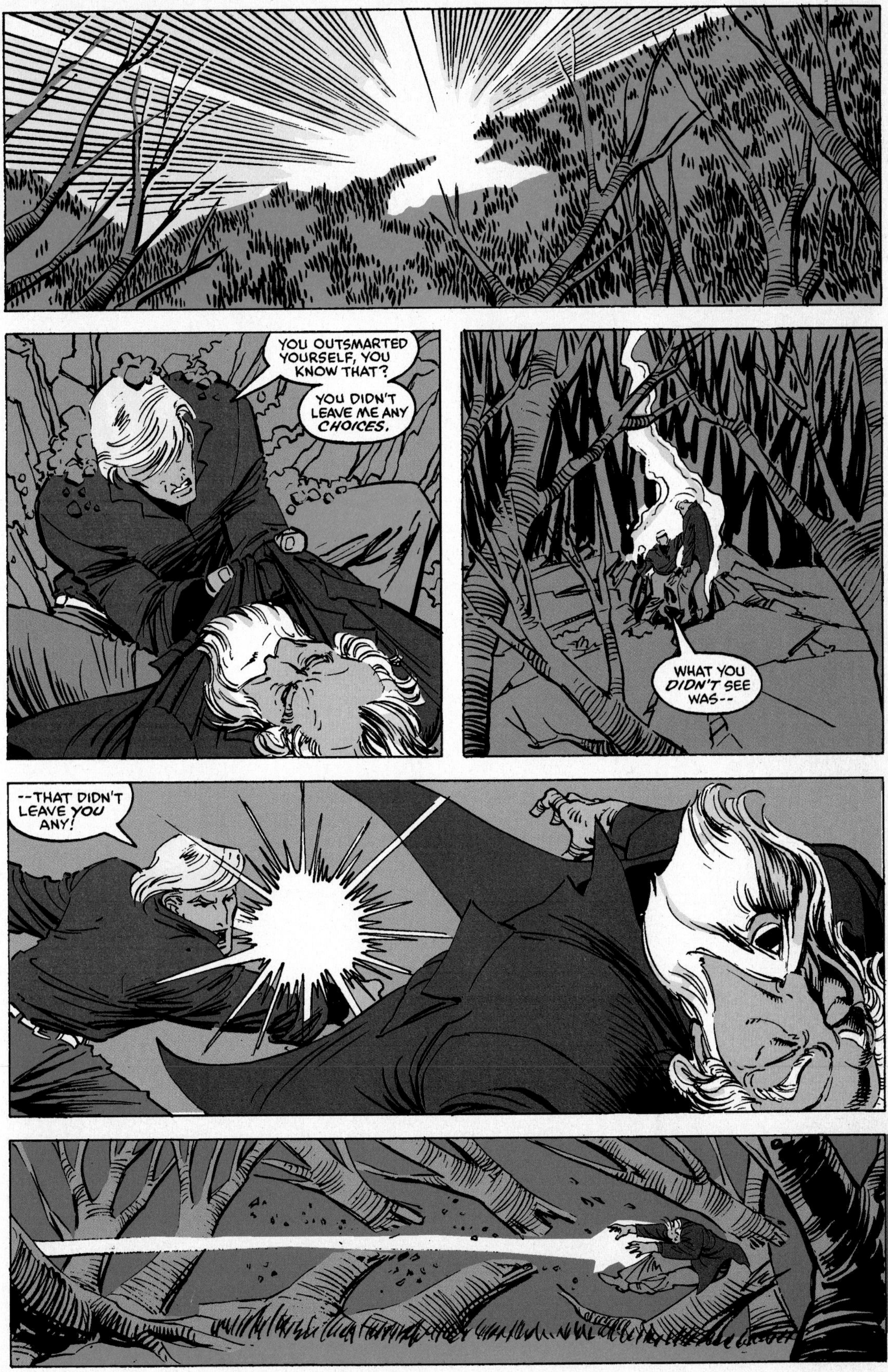
YOU OUTSMARTED YOURSELF, YOU KNOW THAT?
YOU DIDN'T LEAVE ME ANY *CHOICES.*
WHAT YOU *DIDN'T* SEE WAS--
--THAT DIDN'T LEAVE *YOU* ANY!

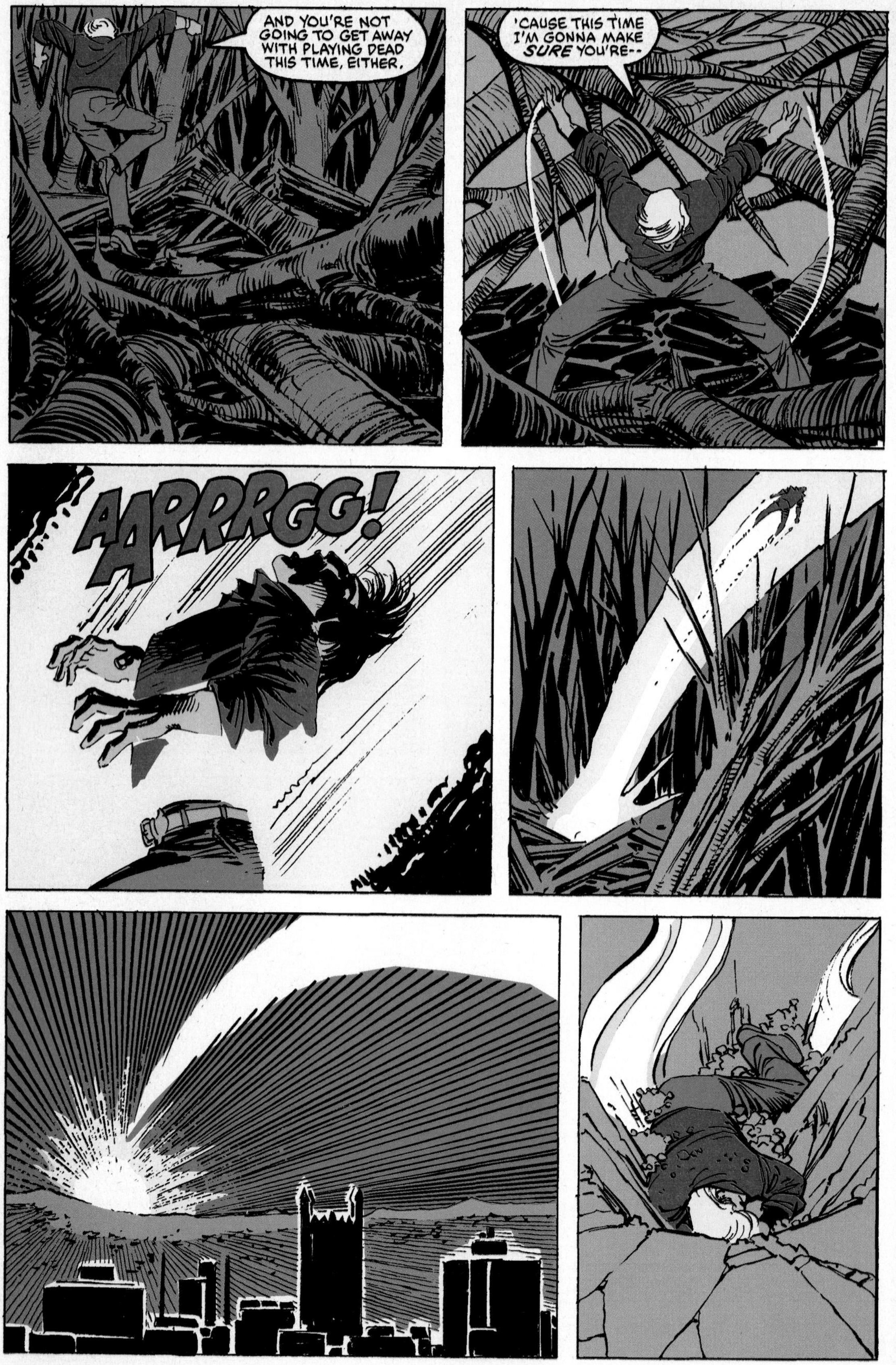
AND YOU'RE NOT GOING TO GET AWAY WITH PLAYING DEAD THIS TIME, EITHER.
'CAUSE THIS TIME I'M GONNA MAKE SURE YOU'RE--
AARRRGG!

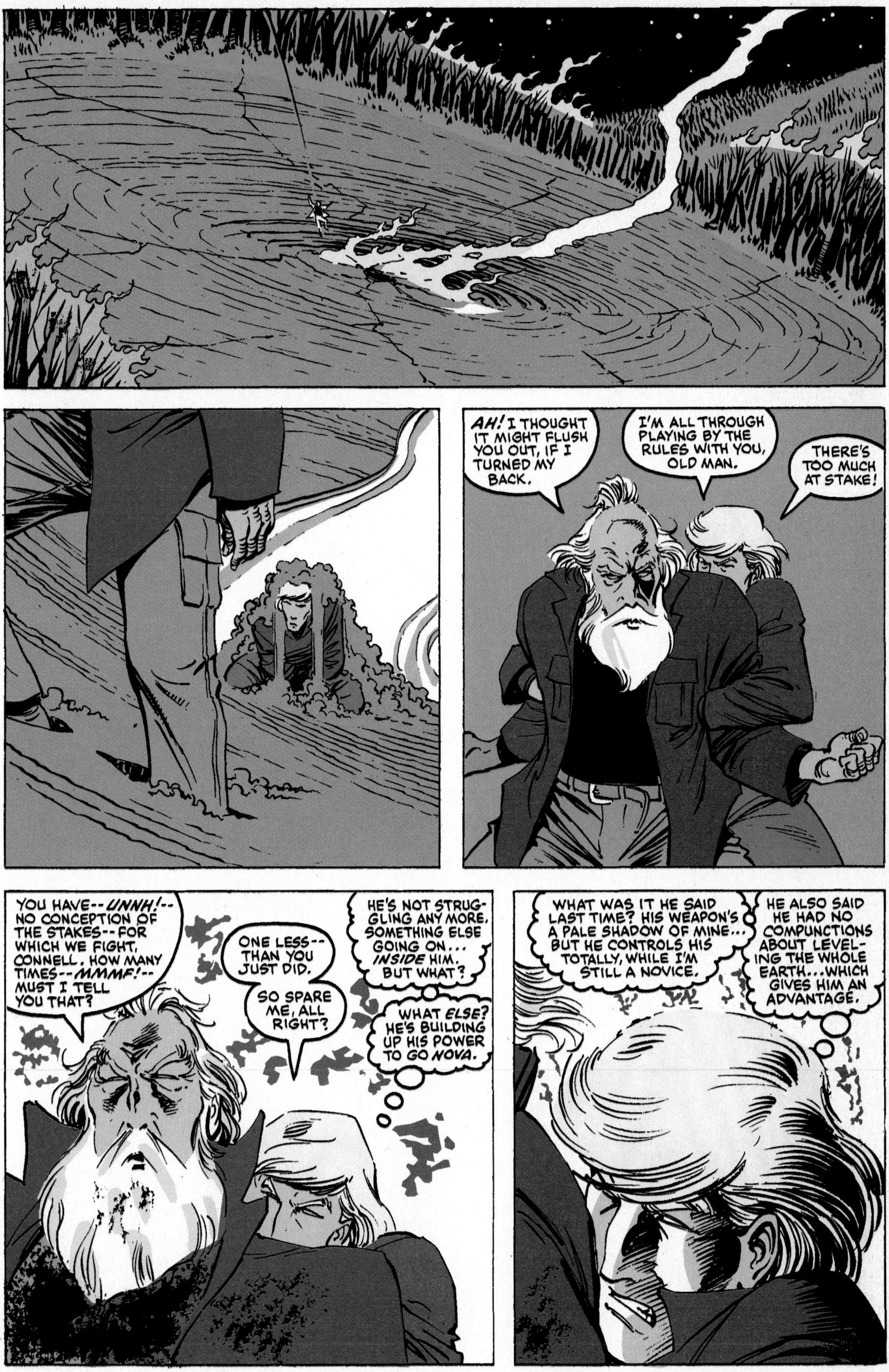
AH! I THOUGHT IT MIGHT FLUSH YOU OUT, IF I TURNED MY BACK.
I'M ALL THROUGH PLAYING BY THE RULES WITH YOU, OLD MAN.
THERE'S TOO MUCH AT STAKE!
YOU HAVE--UNNH!--NO CONCEPTION OF THE STAKES--FOR WHICH WE FIGHT, CONNELL. HOW MANY TIMES--MMMF!--MUST I TELL YOU THAT?
ONE LESS--THAN YOU JUST DID.
SO SPARE ME, ALL RIGHT?
HE'S NOT STRUGGLING ANY MORE. SOMETHING ELSE GOING ON... INSIDE HIM. BUT WHAT?
WHAT ELSE? HE'S BUILDING UP HIS POWER TO GO NOVA.
WHAT WAS IT HE SAID LAST TIME? HIS WEAPON'S A PALE SHADOW OF MINE... BUT HE CONTROLS HIS TOTALLY, WHILE I'M STILL A NOVICE.
HE ALSO SAID HE HAD NO COMPUNCTIONS ABOUT LEVELING THE WHOLE EARTH... WHICH GIVES HIM AN ADVANTAGE.

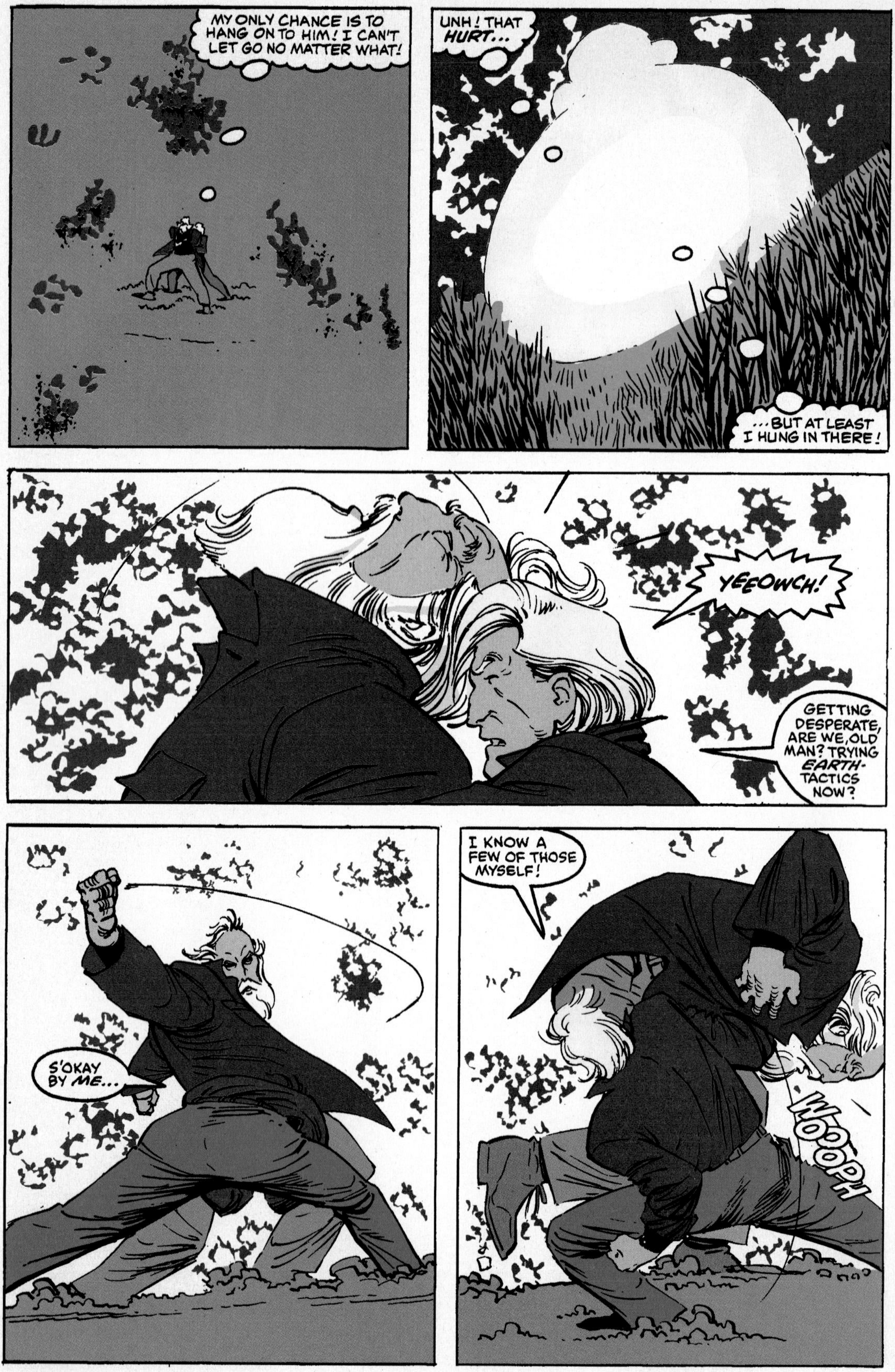
MY ONLY CHANCE IS TO HANG ON TO HIM! I CAN'T LET GO NO MATTER WHAT!
UNH! THAT *HURT*...
...BUT AT LEAST I HUNG IN THERE!
YEEOWCH!
GETTING DESPERATE, ARE WE, OLD MAN? TRYING *EARTH*-TACTICS NOW?
S'OKAY BY *ME*...
I KNOW A FEW OF THOSE MYSELF!
WOOPH

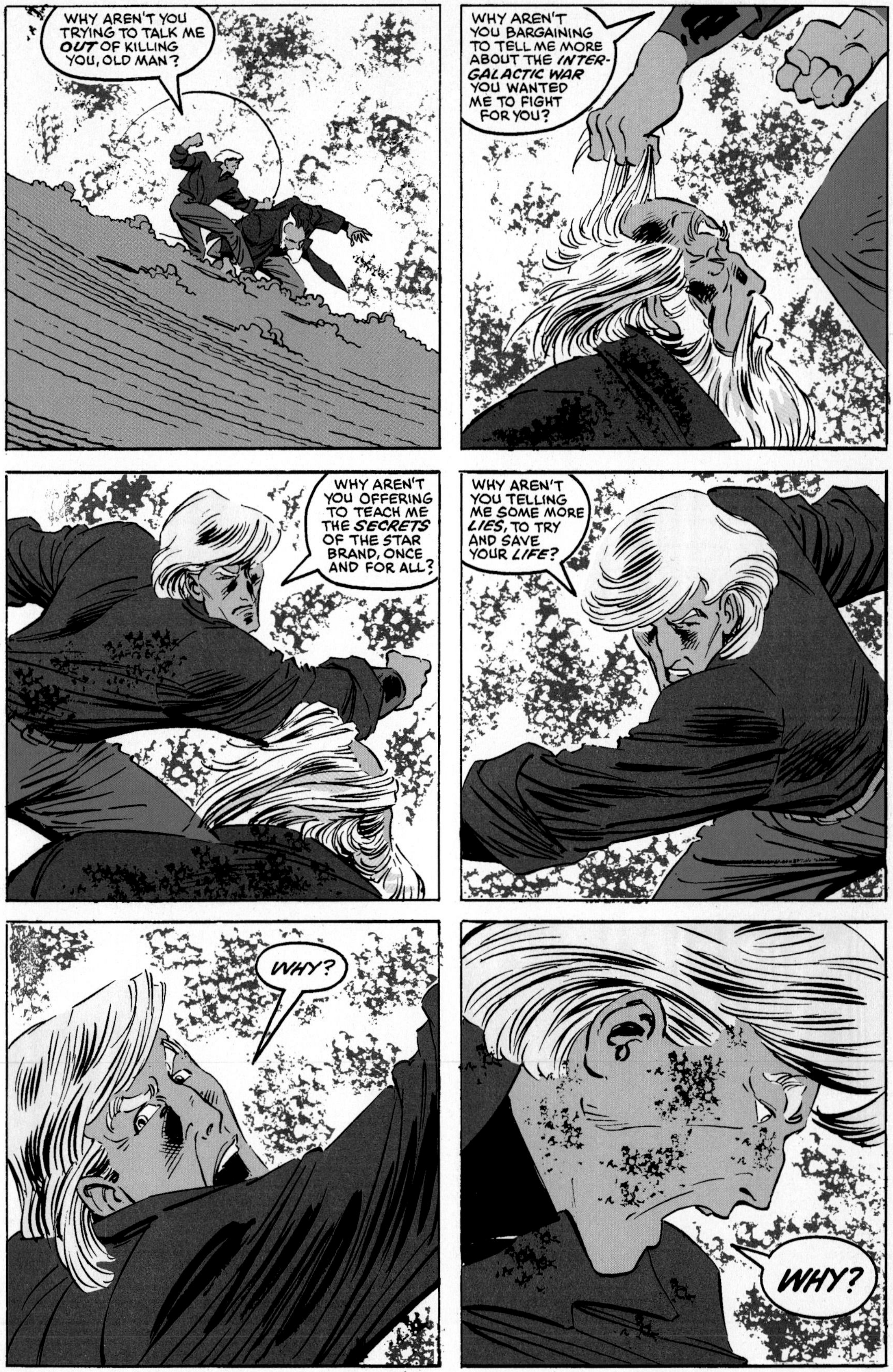
WHY AREN'T YOU TRYING TO TALK ME OUT OF KILLING YOU, OLD MAN?
WHY AREN'T YOU BARGAINING TO TELL ME MORE ABOUT THE INTER-GALACTIC WAR YOU WANTED ME TO FIGHT FOR YOU?
WHY AREN'T YOU OFFERING TO TEACH ME THE SECRETS OF THE STAR BRAND, ONCE AND FOR ALL?
WHY AREN'T YOU TELLING ME SOME MORE LIES, TO TRY AND SAVE YOUR LIFE?
WHY?
WHY?

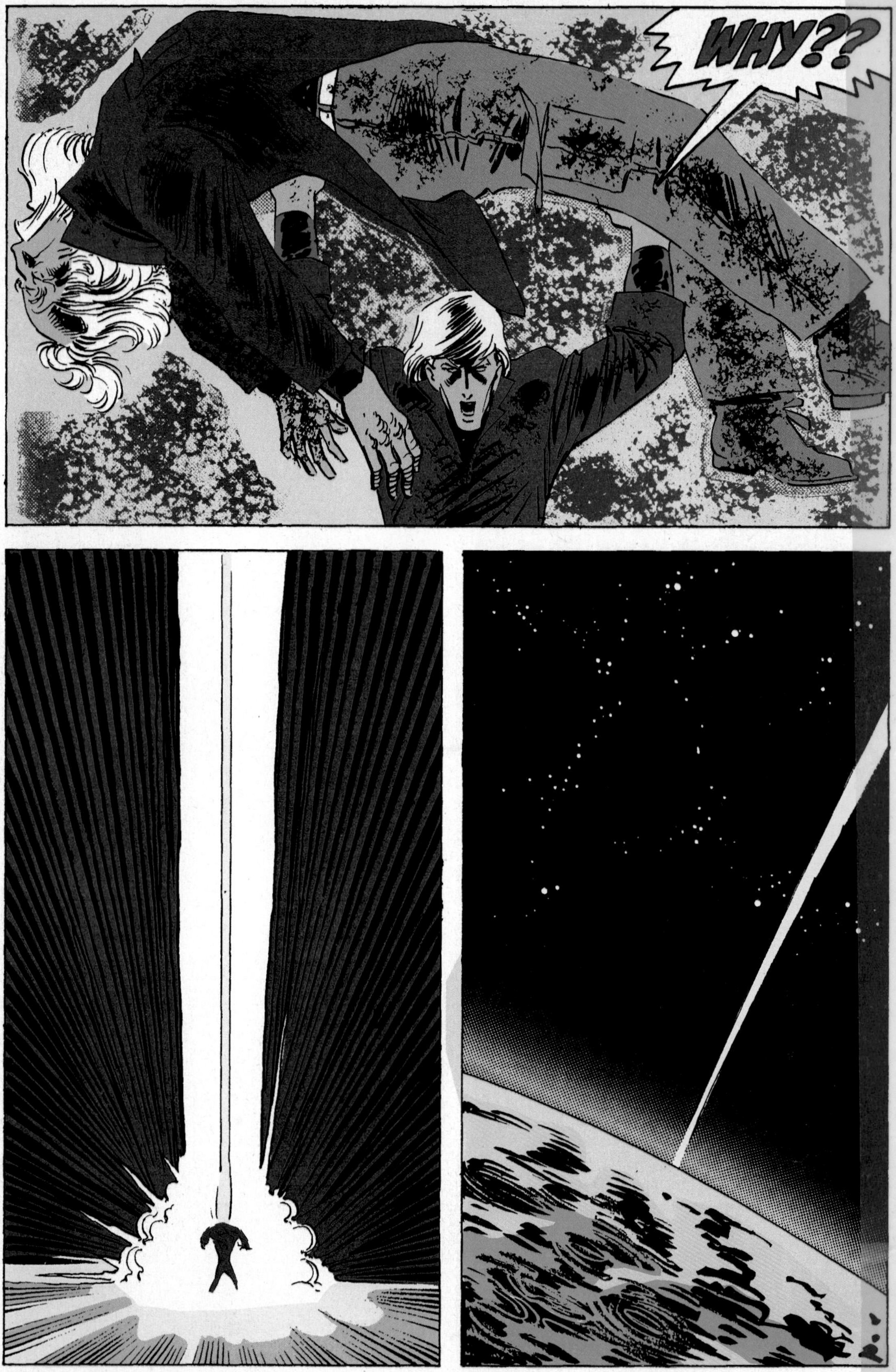
WHY??

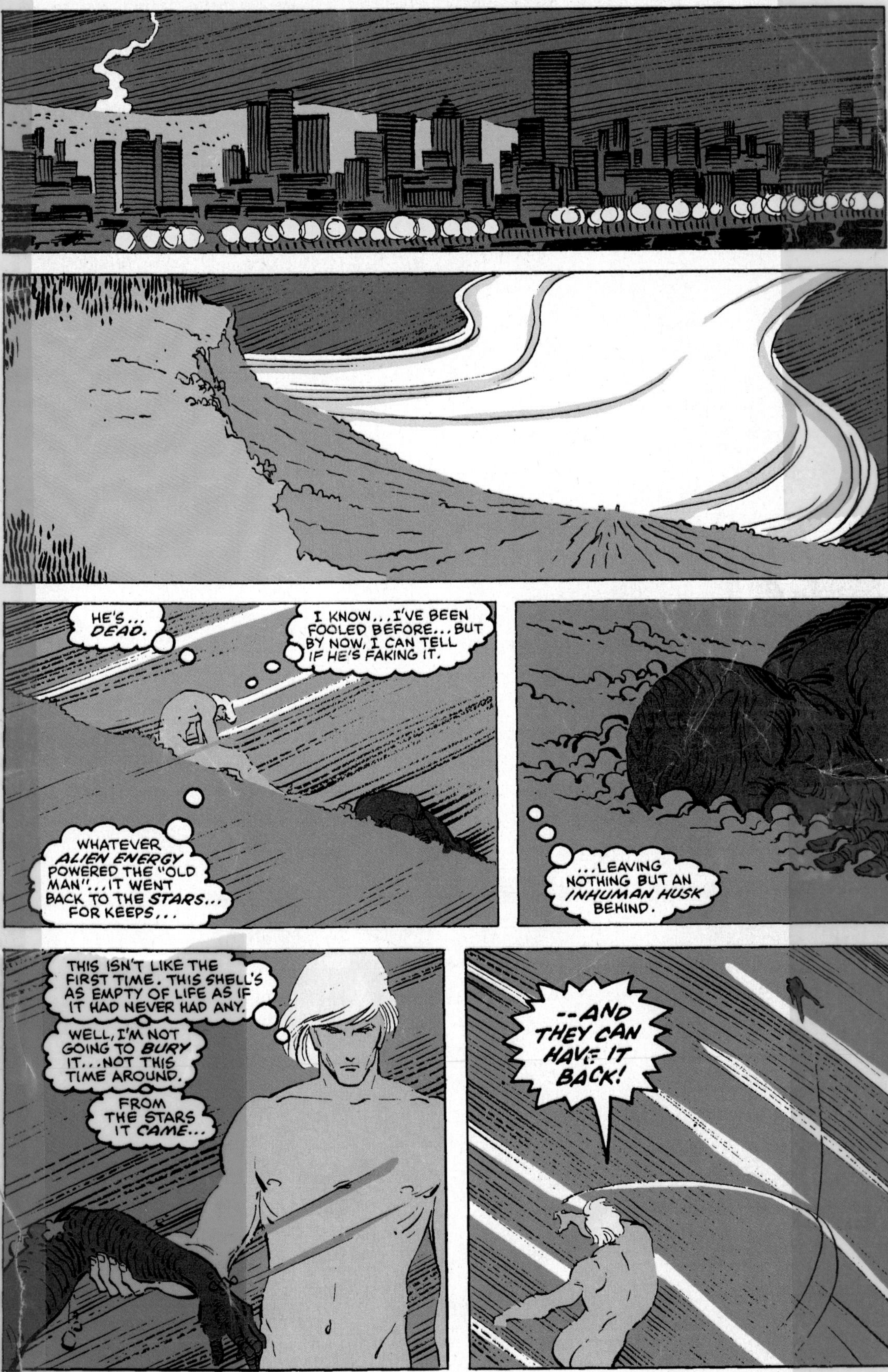
HE'S... DEAD.
I KNOW...I'VE BEEN FOOLED BEFORE...BUT BY NOW, I CAN TELL IF HE'S FAKING IT.
WHATEVER ALIEN ENERGY POWERED THE "OLD MAN"...IT WENT BACK TO THE STARS... FOR KEEPS,...
...LEAVING NOTHING BUT AN INHUMAN HUSK BEHIND.
THIS ISN'T LIKE THE FIRST TIME. THIS SHELL'S AS EMPTY OF LIFE AS IF IT HAD NEVER HAD ANY.
WELL, I'M NOT GOING TO BURY IT...NOT THIS TIME AROUND.
FROM THE STARS IT CAME...
--AND THEY CAN HAVE IT BACK!

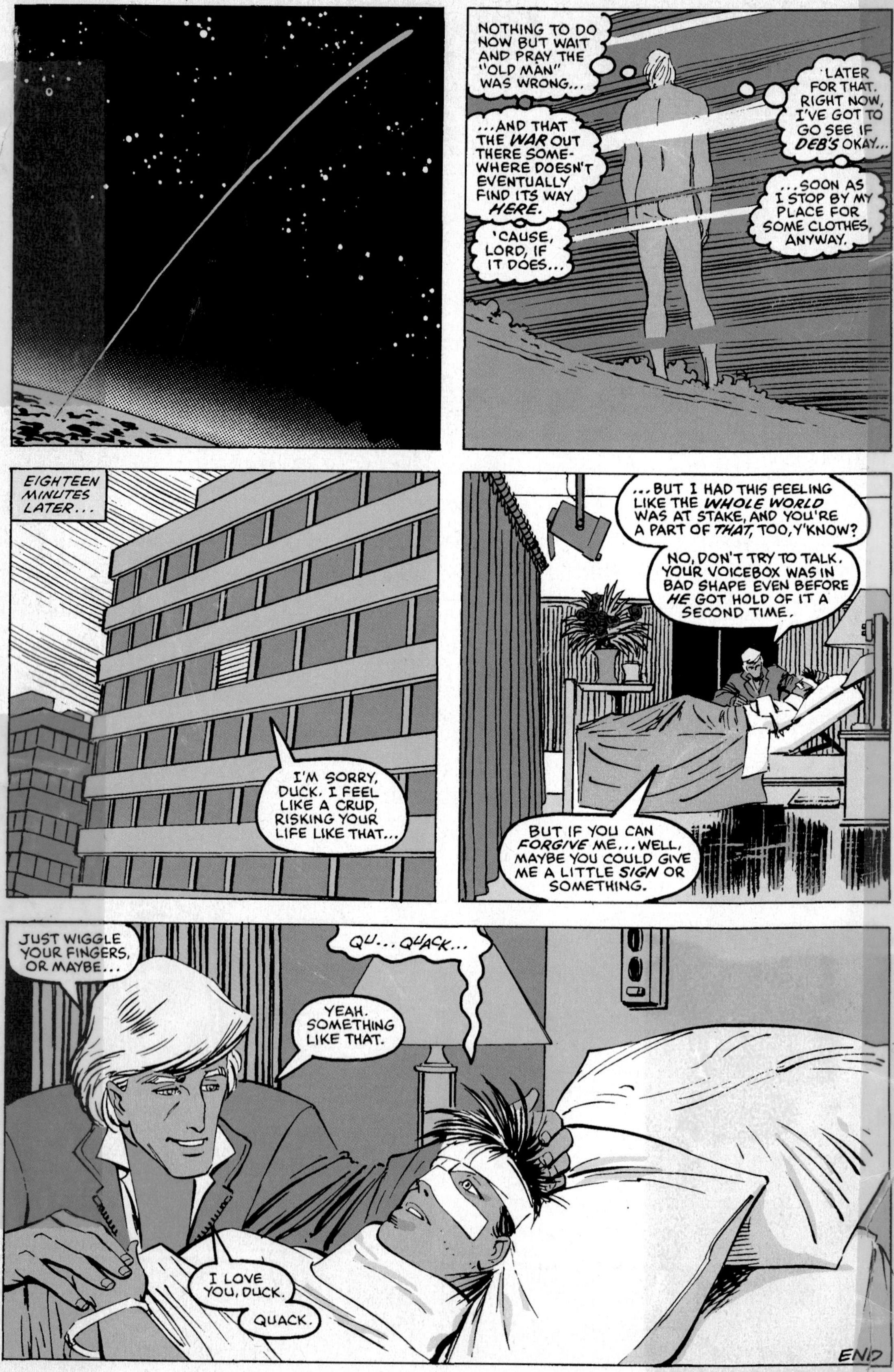
NOTHING TO DO NOW BUT WAIT AND PRAY THE "OLD MAN" WAS WRONG...
...AND THAT THE WAR OUT THERE SOMEWHERE DOESN'T EVENTUALLY FIND ITS WAY HERE.
'CAUSE, LORD, IF IT DOES...
LATER FOR THAT. RIGHT NOW, I'VE GOT TO GO SEE IF DEB'S OKAY...
...SOON AS I STOP BY MY PLACE FOR SOME CLOTHES, ANYWAY.
EIGHTEEN MINUTES LATER...
I'M SORRY, DUCK. I FEEL LIKE A CRUD, RISKING YOUR LIFE LIKE THAT...
...BUT I HAD THIS FEELING LIKE THE WHOLE WORLD WAS AT STAKE, AND YOU'RE A PART OF THAT, TOO, Y'KNOW?
NO, DON'T TRY TO TALK. YOUR VOICEBOX WAS IN BAD SHAPE EVEN BEFORE HE GOT HOLD OF IT A SECOND TIME.
BUT IF YOU CAN FORGIVE ME... WELL, MAYBE YOU COULD GIVE ME A LITTLE SIGN OR SOMETHING.
JUST WIGGLE YOUR FINGERS, OR MAYBE...
QU... QUACK...
YEAH. SOMETHING LIKE THAT.
I LOVE YOU, DUCK.
QUACK.
END